LOST IN ACTION

This story is dedicated
to the thousands of American and Filipino
servicemen who died during the Second World War
on Bataan and Corregidor
or in the prison camps in that part of the world
—especially those who will forever
be listed as "lost in action."
They are the heroes.
To we who survived ruthless captors,
whose only desire was the annihilation of those captors,
"there are no heroes, only survivors."
This book is especially dedicated to the families
of those who will always remain
"lost in action,"
who have suffered for years not knowing
what happened to their loved ones.
It is hoped that this graphic, detailed story
will, in some way, help.

LOST IN ACTION

A World War II Soldier's
Account of Capture on Bataan
and Imprisonment by the Japanese

by

Dick Bilyeu

McFarland & Company, Inc., Publishers
Jefferson, North Carolina, and London

Acknowledgments: It is impossible to give proper credit to all those responsible for helping me to complete this project. I do wish them all to know they have my heartfelt thanks for their assistance. Individually, I want to thank first my wife for having whatever it is she has that allowed her to put up with me and my nightmares of World War II. Without her, this book would never have been written. Her counsel and criticisms were invaluable. Second, I want to thank Joan Colby for her speedy typing and willingness to do things more than once. I am indebted to Bob Gillespie, an old family friend, who did what he could to make an old soldier's words readable. And finally, to Bob and Sheila, I thank you for your help, patience, and abilities in transcribing from tape to paper.

92

Bilyeu

British Library Cataloguing-in-Publication data are available

Library of Congress Cataloguing-in-Publication Data

Bilyeu, Dick, 1921–
    Lost in action : a World War II soldier's account of capture on
Bataan and imprisonment by the Japanese / by Dick Bilyeu.
    p.   cm.
    ISBN 0-89950-605-4 (lib. bdg. : 50# alk. paper) ∞
    1. Bilyeu, Dick, 1921–   .   2. World War, 1939–1945 — Prisoners and
prisons, Japanese.   3. World War, 1939–1945 — Personal narratives,
American.   4. Prisoners of war — Philippines — Biography.
5. Prisoners of war — United States — Biography.   I. Title.
D805.P6B55   1991
940.54'7252'095991 — dc20   90-53606
                                                                              CIP

Manufactured in the United States of America

McFarland & Company, Inc., Publishers
Box 611, Jefferson, North Carolina 28640

Table of Contents

Foreword

I began to work on this book in 1973. It took a full ten years to complete. In a larger sense, however, the work on this project began on December 7, 1941, and will not end until my last breath. It has not been easy to put down on paper the events of World War II that took place in the First Battle of the Philippine Islands and the horrors of three and one-half years in prisoner of war camps. But it has, in my opinion, been necessary. Many of the happenings of that war have been forgotten. The events of this engagement in the Philippines, and the suffering of the men who lost their dignity as well as their freedom during that war cannot be forgotten. Moreover, many things happened during that war that have never been told. In this book I have tried to relate as graphically as I know how some of those events of which little has been written.

The events described in this book are true and represent the story of World War II as I saw it at the time. Although historians with greater knowledge of the wider aspects of the war and those who benefit from hindsight may at times disagree with observations I make, the reader should keep in mind that throughout the book I am relating events as they took place then, as I saw them. In order to protect the privacy, and in some cases the integrity of those involved, the names I use throughout are fictitious with the exception of my own and that of Joe Blair, a close and personal friend.

Chapter 1

The long, lonely hours of guard duty at the field switchboard at Fort Hughes dragged along slowly until 0330 on the morning of December 8, 1941 (December 7, U.S.), when suddenly all hell broke loose. Communications lines to Corregidor and the other islands in Manila Bay lit up at the same time.

I lifted the receiver to answer, but all I got was a recording that kept repeating over and over, "Oahu has been bombed! Oahu has been bombed!" Unable to get any clarification on this message from Corregidor, I began cranking the EE8 field telephone used for communications within the battery command. I needed the corporal of the guard.

Corporal John Bell answered. I requested his presence at the command post as soon as possible. Within minutes he was at the switchboard, and I handed him the headset. He listened for some time, and then asked, "How long has this been coming over?" When I answered it had been more than half an hour since the line first lit up, he suggested that this was more than likely the beginning of a large-scale maneuver. He then ordered me to stay at my station and monitor the telephone continuously, keeping him informed of any messages I might receive from the regiment on Corregidor.

Most of the men in this anti-aircraft artillery unit assumed something big was in the making, as we had been in this field position for the past three weeks. So it was easy for me to accept Bell's explanation that this was probably the start of a planned maneuver. Certainly, I could not have realized that this was the beginning of World War II.

The message continued to come over the line, never changing; nor was I able to cut in and ask anything. There was a separate communications line between our unit and G Battery of the 59th Coast Artillery, which was also stationed on Fort Hughes. I rang their command post, asking if they had any information about what was happening. Their operator knew nothing and informed me he was getting the same message. I hung up the phone and waited for whatever was to come.

It was near 0600 when our commander came into the area. When I saw him walking toward me, somehow I knew this was not just another maneuver. His shell helmet was pulled low over his brow, and the chin strap was pulled so tight it cut into his face. As he neared the command post I could see the stern lines in his face, and his step seemed to quicken as he neared the switchboard. He was in full battle gear. Seldom had I seen an officer with all his field gear. This in itself caused me to believe that there was something much bigger going on than just another training exercise.

Lieutenant Wilson had only recently assumed command of the unit, but he had established himself in the minds of the men as an extremely tough but very fair commander. He weighed just under two hundred pounds and stood nearly six feet tall. He had broad shoulders and hair as black as coal. His eyes were ice blue. They seemed to see completely through you whenever he looked your way.

Very shortly all doubts were dispelled when Wilson issued his first order.

"Get all our men in full battle dress and man your battle stations. The Japanese have bombed Pearl Harbor, and there is every reason to believe we will be under attack before this day is over. I want all personnel to stand by their guns, unpack live ammunition, and be ready for action on my order."

I had heard the order to stand by for action hundreds of times. In the past it had been issued only in training exercises, but there was now an ominous connotation. The order for us to unpack live ammunition excited me more than anything else since coming to the islands. I had not yet seen live ammunition for the guns. This was a new experience for me. I could see the excitement on the faces of the men around me.

As we worked a thick quiet descended over the entire area. The only thing that could be heard was the sound of men scurrying from place to place. There was little talking, just running, with an occasional order from the noncommissioned officers to get this or get that. Within half an hour we assumed our battle stations and stood by for an order from the commander, whatever that order might be.

Suddenly the stillness was broken by the ringing of the telephone. Normally that ring would have gone entirely unnoticed, but that morning was far from being normal. Every person inside the gun position heard that ring and we waited quietly while Bell listened. He put the ear piece down and turned to face the crew. His face was chalk-white. He said, "The Japanese have bombed Pearl Harbor, and even though the United States has not officially declared war, we must consider that we have been in a state of war with Japan since that bombing." It was near 0830, December 8, 1941.

The excitement running through me at the time was almost beyond description. I was only nineteen years old and had absolutely no concept of what was going on, nor what was in store for me.

At the west end of the Rock 2 14-inch coast artillery guns faced the China Sea. These guns were for defense against an attack from the sea. They had a range of more than 20 miles. Each projectile weighed more than a ton. Two more of these long-range guns were positioned near the central and south side of the island, and could be brought to bear on any gun ships the Japanese might try to slip through the south channel of Manila Bay. The two guns could cover parts of the southern tip of the island of Luzon and could hit any targets attempting to come through the straits of Mendora.

Directly in the center of the island were 8 12-inch mortar-type guns, each with a 360-degree traverse radius. These guns had a range of 16 miles, and their shells ranged in weight from 600 to 1,200 pounds. They were "23-inch mortar model 1896," breech-loading, with separate powder charge. At the eastern part of the island was an anti-aircraft battery of 4 guns—3-inch 50s, capable of firing 20 rounds per minute with a good crew. Their maximum altitude range was 20,000 to 22,000 feet. We never realized that the Japanese could fly at 25,000 feet and bomb the hell out of us. We were convinced these guns could hit them regardless of how high they flew. We figured all we had to do was wait until they came in, then simply blow them out of the sky and that would be that. As it turned out, all we did was make a lot of noise while the bastards pounded us with bombs. My assignment on the first day of World War II was with this anti-aircraft battery.

No infantry soldiers were assigned to the island. We knew that if a ground attack should occur we would have to abandon our artillery weapons and become infantry soldiers. Every soldier on the island had been trained in this dual role, and each of us knew what would be required if and when this occurred.

Wilson established his command post at the north side of the gun positions and settled down to the task of establishing communications with his operations officer. We spent the next two hours hauling live ammunition to the gun positions and uncrating it for use when ordered. This ammunition had to be carried from the supply tunnel some two hundred yards away. The shells were stored in boxes of four rounds each. Each box weighed approximately eighty pounds and had to be transported on the backs of the crew members. There were no shot-carts for the new anti-aircraft weapons such as we used with the larger coast artillery batteries.

To make sure we were ready, Bell, our gun chief, suggested we go through some drills using the dummy ammunition we had practiced with for the past two weeks. This type of training had been the routine each morning since we had arrived in the field. But things were different with live ammunition right in the gun pit with us. The practice continued until Bell was satisfied we were ready. We were then given the command to cease fire and to take the dummy ammunition from the gun pit. It would never be used again.

The pit was cleared and the live ammunition was arranged near the gun; then we were told to rest. Talking was limited to the job at hand. Each man looked over his personal gear: helmet, ammo belt, and canteen (was it full and hooked onto the belt far enough back so as not to be in the way when the firing started?).

Everything seemed to be in order as far as I was concerned. I found myself wondering how I would react to battle. I remembered some of the World War I veterans back in Missouri. Their stories of trench warfare, the gas attacks, and the bayonet fighting scared the hell out of me. I wondered if anyone was watching my face. If so, could they see my fears? Damn, I sure as hell hoped not!

When this war got hot, I wondered if I would be able to stand up and do what I had been trained to do. Would I run? Could I fight to the death? Hell, I didn't know! I had no idea what I would do.

I couldn't sit there. I decided to move the live ammunition. Anything to cover the fears that had to be showing all over me. If the expended rounds came back from the breech and hit the live rounds, it could cause serious damage to the shell casings and the live rounds might not go into the breech. When we were ordered to start firing there wouldn't be time to inspect each round. If a round should jam in the breech after the fuse was cut, we could have serious problems. The damn thing might explode in the breech of the gun. We sure as hell didn't need that. The Japs would do enough damage without us killing ourselves. I saw Private Rogers sitting nearby. I said, "Rogers, give me a hand moving this live ammo back farther from the weapons; the shell casings can be thrown from the back of the weapon into the live ammo and cause us hell." Bell heard and nodded his approval. This finished, I sat back again and waited.

I could feel the tension in the air and see it on the faces of the men, most of whom were in their late teens or early twenties. We had come from all walks of life, from the hills and farms of America as well as the cities. Some had been hobos, others had survived the Depression years and had joined the army as I did in order to eat. Some were well educated and others, like me, had little or no skills or formal education of any extent. I was there because there was nothing where I came from that offered any future. The army seemed like an interesting place to be.

When I enlisted, I sure as hell didn't plan on having to fight a war. That was the last thing on my mind. Nonetheless here I was, scared as hell, not so much of the Japs as I was about whether I would stand and fight or run when the fighting started, afraid I wouldn't be able to do my part. Good God! None of us had any combat experience. I sure as hell hoped I could do as well as the other men. They were probably feeling the same as I. A glance at their faces confirmed what I thought. I had to stop thinking about what might happen. Hell, the Japs might not hit us. If they were close enough for that, we would have heard something before now. I would take things by the hour and not worry about what I couldn't see.

Some of our noncommissioned officers had combat experience, like Staff Sergeant Thompson, First Sergeant Kelsey, and one of our platoon sergeants, Sergeant Selso. All of them had seen combat service in World War I. This knowledge gave me some consolation. At least we had leaders who knew what was in store.

As I was pondering these things, Thompson and Kelso entered the parapet. I watched them survey the faces of the men. They seemed to be able to read our fears and confusion. Thompson said, "Look, things will be all right. I can assure you the Japs are not going to land on this island for some time. You men have been trained well, and I don't doubt that all of you will do your job well when the time comes. There is a strong possibility we will be attacked from the air, but look at this place. You have a good barricade around your gun, and if a bomb should hit outside this parapet it would only shake the hell out of you. You would not be hit. Just take things easy, do your job, as I am sure you will, and it will be all right." As he was leaving the parapet, he turned and said, "I will be damned proud to serve with each of you."

4

Thompson usually wasn't this talkative, especially with the enlisted personnel. But he was respected by all as a true leader with quality to back up his words. After he had gone I felt much better. Somehow, I no longer felt so scared and alone.

The fact that I was in the middle of Manila Bay, some eight thousand miles from home, on an island no larger than one mile long and four hundred yards wide no longer bothered me. Our officers and noncommissioned officers knew what to do; they would make sure we performed well. Goddamn! If I could only relax, lie back and wait. But wait for what? There I went again, letting my mind run wild. Hell, I didn't know what I was waiting for. That was the hardest of all. Waiting for the unknown. I had to take it easy. Things would work out all right; that's what Thompson said.

I wondered what time it was. Had I eaten anything that morning? I couldn't remember. It had been some morning. I asked no one in particular, "Has anyone got the time?" I thought it was time for chow. Someone answered my question. "It's eleven o'clock." Hell, an hour before dinner time. I'd just lie back and wait.

The little field phone started ringing; it sounded like it could be heard a mile away. Bell picked up the receiver, turned toward the crew, and shouted, "Man your guns. There are dive bombers east of us, toward Manila."

Each man charged for his position in a single movement. First we heard the low drone of aircraft engines. Then they came into view. There were two of them. They seemed to be flying very slowly, as if aware of what might be waiting for them. They were moving from north to south, then turned to the west, then slowly turned back north toward us. They were still out of range of Fort Drum, some four miles south of the island. Suddenly they increased their speed and headed directly for us. The drone of the engines became very loud, and it was obvious we would be their target.

"Stand by for action" I heard Bell shout as he held the receiver to his ear. His right hand was held high in the air, ready to give the signal to commence firing. I could feel the tension mount inside me and could see it in every face around the gun. I stood at the breach of the weapon with the lanyard gripped in my right hand and the gunner's glove on my left, waiting for the shell to be laid into the breach of the piece.

I glanced in the direction of the sound of the engines and as I did I saw them start their long dive toward us. Then I heard it: the loud sharp command, "Commence firing!" Simultaneously all four guns in the battery belched fire, and for the next few minutes were firing as fast as possible. A shell was laid in the breach of the weapon. I would then slam it forward as hard as I could. I could feel the shell seat itself inside the barrel. Then the breach block would knock my gloved hand free, and with my right hand snapping the lanyard, I could see fire spewing from the muzzle of the gun barrel. The sharp explosions rang inside my head as another shell was placed in front of my gun for the next round. On and on we fired, my mind so occupied with the gun I didn't hear or see anything. Only the round as it was placed in front of me meant anything at all.

5

After a few rounds were fired, I didn't even look at the shell; I knew it was in place and, almost automatically, another round was on the way. I glanced up and saw black puffs of smoke from the exploding rounds near the planes. Suddenly the two planes veered off to their left, in the direction of Corregidor, out of range of our guns, and I heard the order, "Cease fire."

My ears were ringing from the explosions of the shells. As I looked around the gun pit, I saw brass casings strewn all around the parapet. It suddenly occurred to me that our crew had just fired our first shots of the war. Even though the planes survived without a scratch, they certainly had been made aware of our presence. I was convinced the reason they veered away from us was because our deadly fire was more than they could take.

With this thought in mind and the blast of the exploding shells still ringing in my ears, I began to sponge out the bore of the weapon in preparation for the next assault. The other members of the crew were busy picking up the spent brass and removing it from the parapet to make room for more ammunition. Everyone was trying to talk at the same time. We talked about nothing in particular, just laughing, slapping each other on the back, and shaking each other's hands. We congratulated each other on how well we had performed. I knew that we were congratulating ourselves because we didn't fail or falter when the action started, as I had feared I might. At this point I was sure we could take anything the bastards could hand out. Hell, they couldn't even get through our field of fire to bomb us! They would think long and hard before sending those planes back over *this* position!

The next time they flew over this island we would have the fifty-caliber "ack ack" guns in position; and if they got under those artillery pieces, we would rip their underbellies wide open with our machine guns. That would show the little bastards we meant business! Bell wanted the fifties mounted that morning, so why in hell didn't we put them in position? We might have gotten one of those planes. Damn! Wouldn't that have been something?

Chapter 2

The first action of the war was over, and each of us on Fort Hughes was feeling more confident. We spent the next two days digging foxholes. We also dug out a very large hole for an ammunition dump. The experience of having to drag those heavy boxes all the way from the tunnel showed us the benefit of a storage dump closer to the guns. We selected a spot near the center of the four-gun emplacement. We dug the hole deep enough so the ammo would be below the surface of the ground, and then placed large timbers across the hole that we covered with dirt and sand. We left a small entrance at one side that could be negotiated by a man. We hoped this cover would protect the ammo from the bombs. Our next move was to dig trenches from the gun positions to the new ammo dump. This would enable us to keep our heads below the surface while hauling the ammo to our guns. These trenches would offer good protection against flying shrapnel in case we were bombed.

During the evenings we spent all our extra time digging our foxholes, making them as comfortable as possible. There were several radios in the area, and when there were news broadcasts, each radio had a group of men around it. We were hungry for news of the war. The sneak attack on Pearl Harbor seemed to be getting all the attention, but interestingly enough, we in the islands were also being mentioned in the news reports. The Japanese had bombed the navy yard across the bay from us at Cavite. This was news for us; we had seen smoke in that direction and heard aircraft, but assumed Manila was getting hit. On December 10, the day started off with the announcement of breakfast at four in the morning. The commander wanted everyone finished before daylight. He ordered that the guns be manned at all times and that only two men were to be allowed away from the gun at any given time. We were also told not to bunch into groups, especially in the mess area. We were to get our food and return to the gun position to eat.

The mess area was two hundred yards from the guns near the supply tunnel entrance. Our battery supply, our extra ammo for the artillery pieces, and the small arms ammo were in the tunnel.

When I arrived for breakfast, the only light that could be seen was from the gas burners on the field ranges. The food was served in complete darkness. It was like a three-ring circus trying to manuever our way back to the gun position through the maze of trenches and foxholes that had been dug over the past two days. The little pathways were barely traceable in the darkness; rather than taking a chance of spilling hot coffee on someone in his trench or foxhole, I sat and drank my coffee before proceeding back to my area. I then went on to the gun emplacement and finished my breakfast. All the men on the crew were finished eating before daylight and likely no one had any serious burns from spilled coffee. But this eating experience was certainly the subject of conversation for the next hour or so.

Walking due east for a short distance to a slit-trench, I could see the sun rising over the bay. Even at this early hour the heat was becoming unbearable. Today would be a hot one! There was no breeze, and the tropical flies were buzzing about my head. Over on Corregidor I saw a mist rising from the ground area near what was known as "bottom side." One would never imagine from this peaceful setting that we were at war with anyone. It was easy to get carried away with the beauty of the place. Far off to the southeast the mainland could be seen clearly. As I looked out toward the China Sea, it seemed to go on forever.

Fort Drum, the concrete battleship, was only four miles away. There seemed to be no activity in the area at all; still I knew their gun crews, like ours were busy getting things in order. To the south of us, toward Mendora, I saw fishing boats, their sails glittering in the morning sun. I supposed they were out for the day's catch. I'd seen them a thousand times before, but that morning I saw them in a much different light. They seemed almost unreal. Yet, the peaceful scene before me made me hope the events over the past two days had been only a bad dream. But I knew better. Turning away from the picturesque scene, I returned to my gun position and waited.

I was in my position for only a short while when the little field phone started ringing. This ringing sound had become synonymous with fear. It rang once more before Bell picked up the receiver. As he held the receiver to his ear, I got the feeling we would be told a to man our gun position again.

When he turned facing the crew that was standing in anticipation, I heard his order loud and clear: "Stand by your gun and prepare for action!" He held the headset and watched the men scurry about. All I heard was the rattle of mess gear or other personal items hanging on our web belts. Again I heard that commanding voice yelling, "There are high-flying bombers approaching us from the south." Straining my ears, I could hear the low drone of their engines. I wondered if our fighter planes were in the air. I sure as hell couldn't hear them. Bell didn't say how many there were, nor did he say if they were dive bombers or heavy ones. I remembered him saying they were high-flying bombers. What did he mean? The droning sound of the engines was becoming clearer, and I kept staring into the sky in the direction they were supposed to be coming from. There was nothing, just the droning sound.

Turning back to the task at hand, I heard Bell sound off: "Nine heavy Japanese bombers approaching from the south. Stand by for action." His voice was loud and clear, calm and confident. His seemingly confident manner was reassuring to me. I felt at that moment that we could handle anything the Japs could throw our way, and I welcomed the opportunity to test our will and nerve against what had now become the enemy.

8

Looking across the gun that was now tracking the bombers, Rogers was holding the round of ammunition ready to drop into the fuse cutter. He seemed anxious to start. The knuckles on his hands were white as he gripped the projectile end of the shell. Private Gene Honeycutt, the loader, was opening and closing his hands, then drying them on the legs of his pants, making sure he wouldn't drop a round when it came across to him. Bell had the headset to his ear with one hand raised, ready to drop it when the signal came to commence firing. My hand was gripping the small handle of the lanyard. The perspiration inside my gloved hand was worse now and I wished I had time to remove it and dry my hand before the firing started. It was too late for that now. Bell dropped his hand and at the same time issued the command: "Commence firing." The round dropped into the fuse cutter and was in the breach almost in a single movement. I slammed the shell forward and heard all four guns belch fire at the same time.

The bombers were making their run directly at us from the south and the gun was depressed very low in that direction. Since they were coming straight at us, our gun pointer continued to elevate the gun as they came closer. We continued to fire until the gun was at its maximum elevation; then we stopped firing, traversed the weapon 180 degrees, and then picked up the target as they flew away from us. They were flying toward Corregidor and at that moment nothing had fallen in our area. Then, all hell broke loose!

Bombs were falling everywhere! The earth shook like an earthquake. I couldn't tell where they were hitting, but they were so close my eardrums felt as though they were being blown out of my head. I could feel the pressure behind my eyes as one bomb exploded on the edge of the barricade. My breath was forced out of me and I couldn't get any oxygen; it seemed to have all been sucked out of the air. I found myself gasping, clutching at my clothing and my throat. I was in complete panic. I had been blown away from my gun. In my panic I rose up as another bomb exploded. This one blew the shell helmet from my head, snapping the chin strap. The force was so great I thought my head had been torn from my body as I went sailing through the air, landing face down in the sand some eight feet from the entrance to the gun pit. It seemed to me the entire Japanese air force had been sent to this very spot, and were bent on destroying this single gun position.

As suddenly as it had started, it stopped. Except for the ringing inside my head and the spangles that were flashing in front of my eyes, there was complete silence. I couldn't hear anyone moving. What the hell happened? Were we all dead? I was afraid to open my eyes, scared of what I might see.

At last I regained enough courage to open my eyes to see where I was. People were lying everywhere. I wondered if they were just staying down, were injured, or worse yet, were dead.

The left side of my chest was burning horribly. My clothing was stripped and torn away, and what I still had was on fire. I worked at getting the fire out, and looked to see if any limbs were missing. My right shoulder was

9

injured, and I discovered burns over a large portion of my left shoulder and arm. Realizing my legs were okay, I stood up and started walking around the gun pit. Some of the others were getting to their feet as well. They, too, were looking to see if anything was missing. Some were groaning, others were lying motionless around the gun outriggers. It wasn't possible yet to know if there were any fatalities. From what I could see, some were injured seriously, others had only minor cuts and burns. After some time, the entire crew was moving about; it was apparent that nobody had been killed, but, by God, we sure as hell had been mauled by this group of bombers. What was worse, we didn't even hit one of them. All we did was make a lot of noise and get our asses blown off for our efforts.

Bell was moving among us, checking our injuries. He sent me outside the parapet and directed one of the less injured men to take me to the dispensary. There I was examined by an enlisted medic from the navy. He had only been with us for two days. I had several small slivers of shrapnel in my left shoulder, with burns over a large part of my neck and back. After removing several pieces of the metal, he bandaged the injured areas and returned me to duty status. There I was told I would be awarded the Purple Heart for wounds received in action on the second day of the war.

As I returned through the battery area and saw the aftermath of the bombing, I knew the Japs could hit us at will and that our guns would only force them higher. The fear I experienced at the moment caused me to wonder how I had managed thus far not to run. When I saw the massive destruction, for the first time in my life I knew the true meaning of fear. I had been given a firsthand glimpse of how fragile life is. Had I seen this before the bombers came, I doubt that I could have stood and fired my weapon.

Reports were coming in from the other units at the west end of the island. They were hit the hardest and suffered the heaviest casualties. Our unit suffered only injuries so far as anyone knew, so we were called in to bury the dead from those nearby units.

Our sister battery of the 59th Coast Artillery Regiment was hit hardest and suffered the most casualties. The rest of the day my outfit helped bury their dead and assist them in getting their wounded into the larger tunnel where the main medical facility for the fort was located.

The commander designated an area at the south-central part of the island near the beach as the cemetery for Fort Hughes.

That evening, when all the details were completed, I returned to my own unit. Even though I was dog-tired, I knew I must dig my foxhole deeper and get more sandbags for protection. There was no need for orders to do this and none were given. We had had a real lesson in survival.

In spite of the beating we had taken, the morale of the soldiers was high. But I could sense an anger within me that hadn't been there before, a realization that to survive this war my entire outlook on life would have to change. Hell, I hadn't seen very many people die from natural causes, much less slaughtered wholesale. Things like this only happened in stories I had read or heard from my father or other men who had fought in other wars. I knew now that I had become a part of those stories and those histories. The change would not be an easy one for me. I was just a farm boy from the Midwest. Nonetheless, change I must. How dare those Jap bastards try to kill me!

That night in the darkness of my foxhole, with only a candle for light, I wrote a letter home to my parents. I went through years of pure hell in this war before I learned they had received it. My mother gave it back to me and I have kept it ever since. As I look at it, it's easy to see how high the morale was during this dark point in my life: "Don't worry about me. We will have the Japanese army beat within two months and this war will be over." Most of us, at that time, really believed this would be the case.

Almost every day during the rest of December, the Japanese pounded us. Corregidor was the main target, but the other islands—Fort Hughes, Fort Drum, and Fort Frank—were also targets. Each day the Japs made their runs, and each day we blasted away with our anti-aircraft guns. However, the results were always the same. The Japs blasted the hell out of us, and we just made a lot of noise. We only made them fly higher.

Each time the bombers came over, whether I was on the gun or not, the feeling was always the same. I felt like the goddamned bombs were aimed directly between my shoulders and would hit any second, blowing me out of this world. This was the most helpless feeling I had ever known. If I could only have shot back knowing I was killing some of them, I wouldn't have felt so helpless. Hell, if I could have thrown something at the sons-of-bitches knowing I had hit them—anything—it would have helped. I knew it would be better than being here waiting for the goddamned bomb to drill me between the shoulders.

By the middle of December, word reached us that the Japanese had landed a large force north of Luzon, at Lingaye Gulf. At the same time they had established a beachhead south of us at Lagaspi, only eighty miles away.

As is always the case, rumors were running wild. There were rumors of our forces being outnumbered by as much as forty to one at each of these landing areas and that the Jap hordes were overrunning us everywhere. Since there was nothing we could do on this small island to help them, we listened and waited. During this period we were under constant alert as the bombings continued.

As the Japanese south of us marched toward manila, we started hearing the artillery bursts from the fighting. It didn't take any great genius to figure out how rapidly the Japs were moving in our direction. It would be only a matter of time until their artillery would be within range. When that happened, we would not only be at the mercy of their bombers, but also would come under their artillery fire. One thing was certain if they could hit us with their field artillery weapons, some of our coast artillery guns could get a crack at them. Their gunners wouldn't get off as easily as the bomber crews had.

During this time, the Japanese navy had kept out of range and out of

11

sight of our long-range guns. These weapons had been idle, but as the sound of artillery got nearer and nearer, it looked as if they would get in some licks. I hoped I had an opportunity to fire those guns when that time came.

On Christmas Day of 1941, the Japanese artillery opened fire from the southern force that had emplaced themselves along the southern shore of Manila Bay. From several spots they opened up on all the small forts inside the bay. It appeared they wanted to let us know how much artillery they had been able to bring up from their southern command. The first rounds fell on Fort Frank, the little island nearest the mainland at the southern end of the bay. Before we could locate where they were firing from, all of us came under attack. When the first rounds hit our fort, everybody took cover. We couldn't get our heads above the ground for fear of being hit. Their shells were exploding everywhere. I couldn't tell if any of our units were answering their fire. For the next forty-eight hours, those shells kept on falling. During the daylight hours we were hit by both the artillery shells and the bombers. Sometimes it seemed like the bombers filled in the space when the gunners were resting. Only when the bombers were around us did we get out of our foxholes. Still, it was extremely difficult to concentrate on what had to be done, knowing what those bombs could do or what would happen if a shell should hit the parapet. When the dive bombers were over us, I could hear their maching guns clattering; but when I heard them blasting away, I knew the bastards were searching for a target and were trying to plant one of their bombs on us. All our guns were shooting and I was aware of the smoke around each of the guns, making us an easy mark. Concentration was very tough. All we could do was stay as low as possible, keep on shooting, and hope our gun wasn't their target. As soon as the bombers left, it was back into the foxholes. There I listened to the bursting shells. Even when it was still, I could hear them exploding. Half the time, I couldn't tell if the sounds were actual shells or explosions in my mind. Only when a shell burst near me and I heard that awful whistling sound of flying shrapnel, could I tell.

At last! They had stopped! I waited, as there were more bursts inside my head. I closed my eyes and saw flashes in my mind. I waited some more, wanting to make sure. How long did I wait? I didn't know. Finally, I found enough courage to climb from the foxhole and start walking through our battery area. Every tree had been blown away! I walked away from the gun position, not even knowing why. It seemed every inch of the ground had been hit with something. There were large craters everywhere. The trenches we dug to the ammunition dump had large craters in several places, but portions of the trench were still intact. For the life of me, I couldn't see how anyone could have survived this bombardment.

On the evening of December 27, our detail with caring for the dead and wounded was over. The injured men had been evacuated and the dead buried, and I was back inside the battery area. The stillness was eerie. One felt something just had to happen. I was alone near my foxhole where it would be easy to get down quickly. I felt very alone as the darkness closed around me. I eased myself into the foxhole and snuggled down out of sight.

There was a tremendous fear creeping over me that I couldn't explain. I lay for what seemed like an eternity before coming out. When I finally emerged, I saw the moon shinging brightly. I listened for sounds, but there was nothing. If I could have heard even some people talking, it would have been a welcome sound. But there was nothing; just total silence.

I walked from the foxhole to the gun position a short distance away. As I entered I saw Bell standing in the moonlight talking in hushed tones with two other men from the gun crew. I joined them, glad to have someone around. We talked for some time about the shelling and bombing, avoiding any hint of our losses. Then we started inspecting the anti-aircraft gun for damage. Only minor repair would be needed to have the weapon ready for further action. Bell said, "We must do the repair work now, while there isn't any incoming fire. We must be ready if there is a raid tonight." While we did the necessary repairs, Bell scouted the area for people to man the weapon. There was grave concern that the Japs might attempt a landing after such a heavy bombardment, so in addition to rounding up troops to man the gun, there was a need for men to take up positions as beach defense against such a possibility. Word was passed that even those on the guns must be prepared to leave their weapons and defend the beaches.

Watching the men being sent to different areas, I was surprised to see so many able to take up positions. Our losses were minimal. Within minutes after word was passed about the possibility of a landing, we were either on the gun or out on the beach waiting.

Some of our troops had not eaten since the night before, but they went into a defensive posture without a word. I hadn't heard one word of complaint from these soldiers. We all knew if the Japs wanted to, they could come ashore quite easily if we weren't out on the beach defense positions.

While the first sergeant was arranging for the men to be fed, our other noncommissioned officers were out on the beach making sure all the men there were supplied with ammunition and were in the right positions. It was after midnight before the beaches were covered by riflemen and machine gunners, and the anti-aircraft guns were manned with minimal crews. I was given permission to leave the area for coffee. When I arrived at the mess area, I was served some coffee and also was given some salmon and crackers. Taking this, I returned to my area and crawled into my foxhole. After I ate, I went to sleep for the first time in forty-eight hours.

Early on the morning of December 28, I was awakened by Bell. Together we went to the command post for orders of the day. We were met by First Sergeant Kelsey, who asked, "How many of our men were killed during the bombardment since it started?" He was looking right at me when he asked and I replied, "Hell, Top, I haven't counted the living yet; perhaps when I get that number you can just subtract that number from what you had before the raid and come up with an answer." My sarcasm was not appreciated, and I knew before I closed my mouth I was in trouble. He chewed me out, then issued orders to organize a search of every inch of the battery area for any dead or wounded who couldn't get to the dispensary, and to report back to him.

I moved quickly, glad to get away from him and the command post area. I went to the mess area for coffee first, and to try and get something to eat. Remembering how long I was in the foxhole during the last raid without food, I wanted to be sure I got something before anything broke loose. I believed this was only a lull for the Japs; I had no doubt they would return with the bombers and the artillery. When they did, I'd have all I could do just keeping alive. I wanted to eat whatever I could get while I had the opportunity.

I was served hot tea along with a ration of cream of wheat, and informed that the only food left in the battery area was this and some corned beef and flour. I ate the stuff quickly and went directly to the dispensary, where I checked the casualty list for the past two days. Half of our battery had been treated during this period. Eight men had been killed. Most of the wounded had been returned to duty status. Only a few were evacuated to the main medical facility.

Making a list of the men killed and the wounded who had been taken into the main tunnel, I returned to the command post and gave this information to the first sergeant as ordered.

Returning to the gun position, I saw men coming back from the mess area, taking their cream of wheat and tea with them. For the most part they seemed relieved by the lull in the bombing and shelling. There were some smiles, even though some were bandaged and others had their arms in slings. There were some, however, who appeared to be in a daze, just walking and looking at the ground or far off into space.

Making my way through the maze of shell holes and bomb craters, I passed through the area where our barber shop had been. Our barber, a Filipino, had refused to leave us when the war started, and had set up his shop inside the battery area under a tree. He had dug himself a foxhole near the tree. Although he had been told he could leave the unit and go home anytime, he elected to remain with us. Remembering him as I walked by, I started looking for him. I soon saw what had happened. There had been a direct hit, blowing everything to hell! His barber chair was some thirty feet away from where it would normally have been. He had been blown to bits; his remains could have been placed in a shoe box. His equipment was scattered everywhere—in the tree limbs, on the grass, in the dirt, all over. Nothing was left. I could even see parts of his body sticking out of the dirt where his foxhole used to be.

This scene made me more angry than anything up to that point. I was angry at him for staying when he could have gone home; angry at the Japs for bombing this place, just plain angry at everything. I remembered the times I had gone to the barber's home on Mendora before the war started. I remembered his two sons and daughter and his wife. How would she be notified? There were millions of thoughts running through my mind at the moment. Christ, what a waste!

14

Chapter 3

By the end of December, it became apparent that the Japanese forces (especially those charging down from the north) could not be stopped by our forces on Luzon. Therefore, a last ditch stand would have to be made soon. A decision was made to transfer every man that could be spared from the units on the island fortresses into the infantry units as replacements. The reasoning behind this was simple: if the Japanese took Manila before the southern forces could withdraw around Manila Bay into Bataan, our command would be split in half, making that last ditch stand less effective. We were going to be used to slow their advance.

From what I could gather, it was a sure bet that the last stand would be in the area of the Bataan peninsula. The feeling seemed to be that Manila and Subic bays could be best defended by moving as many men from the artillery units into the defensive infantry units on Bataan; then, if worse came to worst, these men could be brought back at a later time. At any rate, more men were needed as infantrymen at the moment. They must slow the charging enemy long enough to allow our ground troops south of Manila to link up with the forces on Bataan.

On December 31, several hundred soldiers from the forts in the bay were assembled on the north mine dock on Corregidor for movement across the north channel into Bataan, about three and half miles away.

On Bataan, we were placed under the command of several noncommissioned officers from infantry units, who were awaiting our arrival. These NCOs held us in the port area until darkness before starting the march northward.

The people in charge made sure we had eaten before we moved out. All night long we trudged through thick brush alongside a narrow road until we were so worn-out we couldn't go any farther. When daylight came, the NCOs ordered us off the road and into the heavy jungle. We were told we would be there all day. Some time during the day, we were joined by some food service people who had field rations with them. These rations were "iron rations," corned beef hash and hardtack. I was told these were the same rations used by the United States during World War I. "Iron rations" had to be broken by hand before they could be eaten.

It was January 1, 1942, and soon after sundown we were rousted for another march. We marched for two hours, took a break for a short period, then returned to the road. When the sun started to rise, the NCOs ordered us back into the jungle to avoid detection by Jap spotters that might be on the lookout.

I was sound asleep when I heard the rumblings of artillery. I had heard this sound so many times before, I needed no explanation as to what it was. The fact that there was Japanese artillery in the area brought me out of a sound sleep. I estimated that the Japs were about ten miles northeast of where we were. Either we had covered more ground during our march, or the Japs had closed the distance to us. Later that afternoon a number of military units passed us on their way south. Because they were going away from the direction of the artillery fire, I began to wonder what was in store for me. Their noise, plus the sound of the artillery, prevented me from sleeping. It soon became apparent that these units were in retreat, and the infantry front line would be established right here. Hell! Our march was over. The thought of me being in the front line sent chills down my spine. I remembered how I had wished that I could shoot back. By God! The time was near. I felt sure I would be able to stand and fight. I had been beaten into the ground by Japanese bombs and shells. Right here, on this spot, it would stop! The memory of the torn body of our barber flashed through my mind. I could feel the anger rise at the thought of getting revenge. Instinctively I checked the pouch on my belt containing ammunition. I had done this a thousand times before, especially during the past two days.

It was well before dark when one of the NCOs came around and called off the names of about forty men to be assigned to a Filipino infantry unit. He was in charge of this group and directed us toward the west side of the main road. We were barely off the road when we were met by a first sergeant. He told us to remain in the area and rest until he returned; then he disappeared into the undergrowth. When he returned he called me over, telling the others to wait. He took me two hundred yards back in the brush and introduced me to Captain Williams, the company commander. The men who were singled out were to be assigned with this company.

"Do you know anything about what type of personnel are with you?" Williams asked.

I replied, "I believe most of them are artillerymen, but I know there were some cooks who joined us earlier, though I don't know if any of them are in this group."

"Do you know if any of them have been trained in the infantry?" he asked.

When I told him all of us were required to defend the beaches as infantrymen and that all of us had been under heavy artillery attack and bombing since the start of the war, he consulted with the first sergeant. I was promoted on the spot to staff sergeant and given one of the platoons. Sergeant Daughtry, the top sergeant, escorted me out of the command post and introduced me to the other NCOs. He then left me with my platoon.

I learned that most of them, like myself, had been newly assigned to this unit. Some had joined the unit near Clark Field only a few days before. Some had come in a day or so earlier, as I had, from Marvelious. The ranking man, as far as the American soldiers were concerned, was Corporal Hood. He had been with the unit when there were only three Americans: himself, First Sergeant Daughtry, and Captain Williams.

16

My next task was to learn as much as possible about the Filipinos in the platoon. Hood told me that the ranking NCO in that group, Sergeant Marcos, had been with the company since he came to it. He also told me Marcos had the respect of his men. He felt I should talk with him before talking with the other Filipinos in the platoon.

Hood and I searched the area until we found Marcos. He was with a small group of his men near the edge of the company perimeter. Seeing us in the half-light, he left the group and came forward. Hood introduced me, and I told him of my assignment. I let him know that I would need his help. After only a short conversation, I knew I wanted him as my assistant platoon sergeant. Specifically, he would be in charge of the Filipinos, but I also needed him to help run this infantry platoon.

Williams was still assigning men. Until this was completed, there was no way of getting an accurate count of the men in the platoon. I continued taking names as they came into the area.

Before I had finished talking with Marcos and inspecting our platoon, a runner found me and handed me a note from the commander. When I read it, I turned to Marcos and told him "The captain wants us now!" He turned to one of his men and said something in Tagalog, then the two of us ran to the command post.

When we entered the small tent, I saw a map displayed on a large board leaning against the side of the tent pole. Williams had a pointer in one hand and as soon as he was sure all NCOs were present, he explained that we were in a sort of staging area and pointed to the map where we were located. "Some of the units north of us have withdrawn, and we will be taking up a position in this area," he said. He pointed to a spot on the map. "I have received orders to move to another position, some three miles from here."

Motioning us closer to the map, he said, "We will be here at this bridge crossing. Most of our regiment will be east of this point, but the regimental command post is somewhere back here." Again he was pointing in a general area on the map. "I want you platoon leaders to return to your area and get the men ready to move out in fifteen minutes. Sergeant Daughtry, you will lead the company with me and the other headquarters staff, followed by the first platoon, then the second, and then the third, in that order. All right? Move out!"

By 1700 hours on January 2, 1942, we were on the move east toward Manila Bay. There were no vehicles in our company, so our movement was slow. We were in deep jungle with no roads, only animal trails to follow—and those only when they went in the direction we wanted to go. Otherwise, we had to cut through the thick undergrowth as best we could. The men up front had their work cut out for them. Those back in the column followed their trail. After some hours of trudging through the maze of vines and undergrowth, we came upon a dirt road running north to south. It appeared to have been traveled quite heavily, by both motor vehicles and animal-drawn vehicles. We hadn't walked but a short distance when the bridge we

17

had been shown on the map loomed in front of us. The word was passed for all to get off the road until a scouting party could cross the bridge, making sure the Japs hadn't beaten us there. Within minutes after they crossed, the company was on the bridge crossing to the south side of the small river.

Williams wasted no time in calling the platoon sergeants together. "The first platoon will deploy to the east of the bridge, taking up positions where they can cover the most likely approach in that sector. The first segeant and I will be along later. Move out! Sergeant Bilyeu, I want a machine gun placed at the north end of the bridge. Also, place one at the south end on the east side of the road. Make damn sure your riflemen know exactly where you position that machine gun on the north side of the river. I want the third platoon deployed farther west. There are some small branches leading in from that area and if the Japs know that, it could be a very hot spot. Be sure your men know of that possibility."

To all of us he said, "This road, especially the bridge, is extremely important. There are two of our armored units that will need the bridge. We are to defend it at all cost." He continued. "If the Japanese know of the two armored units retreating across the bridge, they will try to blow it. If they could do that, our final defense of the Bataan peninsula would surely be hurt."

My first night in the infantry passed without incident. I was even able to get some much-needed sleep. At first light I went to the command post to receive the orders of the day. I found that radio communications with other units had been established during the night. It appeared that all units of the 45th Infantry Division and the Philippine army were in place. Looking at the situation map, it appeared our division lines stretched from where we were to near the base of the mountain. Also, it wasn't far from where we were to the shoreline of Manila Bay. But in the thick jungle, one couldn't see anything farther than a few yards in any direction. The only open area I saw was the small river and the hole made by the road leading south.

I was told that two tank battalions would be coming through our lines and that my people must be prepared to assist them in any way possible. We hadn't waited long when the advance units began arriving at the bridge. I got back with my platoon and watched. I noticed that among the small military vehicles there were also some civilian automobiles being driven by soldiers. This bothered me. I feared this might be some Japanese trying to infiltrate our position.

When the first vehicle arrived on our side of the river, I asked the officer riding inside, "What the hell are those civilian vehicles doing back there? Are they with you?"

"Yes, we confiscated them along the way," was his reply. "We want to take them with us for military use when we have established our next line of defense. Some of our command cars were lost and we're going to use these in their place." With that, the column started moving, slowly at first, then picking up speed as it passed. Damn, they were a beat-looking bunch.

The clacking sound of the tanks could be heard over the other noises. I sure hoped we weren't trying to hide. The slapping of those tracks could be heard for miles. I could now hear the engines and it was apparent the tanks would be crossing the bridge. Across the bridge dust was rising and the air was filled with dust from the wheeled vehicles, making it difficult to breathe. I could imagine what it would be like when those tracking vehicles plowed into the dirt road on this side of the bridge. Looking across the bridge I could see dust rising high into the air and the thought crossed my mind that this would be easy for Japanese observers to see. What better marker could they ask for? The first tank on the bridge came slowly. It accelerated upon crossing and soon was traveling at maximum speed. There was nothing I could do but close my mouth and eyes and wait. When I opened my eyes again, I was being told by someone that this was the last of the tanks, that only a small engineering unit was left on the other side of the bridge, and that we should remain on alert for them.

With the arrival of the engineer team, my outpost at the northern end of the bridge was ordered across and put in position on the southern end of the crossing with the rest of the platoon. When questioned, they reported no signs of the Japanese chasing the engineers.

All day the engineers busied themselves wiring the bridge with explosives. Only when darkness came did they quit.

Early in the morning they were back on the job, climbing around the structure like monkeys. I could hear artillery fire west of us some five or six miles away, toward the base of the mountain. But here it was quiet. I listened to the orders being issued around the bridge and even though I knew nothing of this type of work, I felt that they were nearing completion of their task.

Suddenly, without warning, an automobile appeared at the north end of the bridge. It was Japanese! I couldn't believe it! The damn thing seemed to come from nowhere and was right at the end of the bridge! As is stopped, the dust rose up from around the vehicle and Japanese soldiers were standing up in it and looking in our direction. I dove into the machine gun pit and opened fire all in one single movement. As I did, I saw some of the engineers drop from where they were on the bridge into the water below. When I swept the vehicle with the machine gun, two of the Japs fell backwards. As the driver tried to turn the car around I swept it once more and it went off the steep embankment. Other machine guns were firing as it fell into the river. A cloud of smoke rose from where it went in and all firing stopped.

Each of us knew it was only a matter of time before this area would be occupied by the Japs—at least on the north side of the river. With all the men off the bridge, it was time to wire the charges on the structure. At last I saw the engineer officer signal that all was in readiness. Far back from the southern end, I watched one of his men attach the lead wire to the detonator. The engineer officer reported to Williams that since everything was ready to blow, he would leave one man behind to set off the charges, but the rest of his unit was pulling out. I watched as he drove away with his unit. They were going south, following the road the tanker took. As the last of

19

them disappeared, there was sort of a sinking feeling inside me. I suddenly realized that there were no other American forces between this unit and the Japs. I also realized that when the Japs came, this very spot would become a battleground. I had already been introduced with the arrival of that command car. I could still see in my mind's eye that son-of-a-bitch as he flew through the air, his rifle falling from his grip when he went over the back of the vehicle. I sure as hell didn't feel any remorse or guilt about that. That was the first time since the war started that I had taken revenge. One thing was certain. I knew that things would never be the same in my life; I was a different man.

Anticipating an attack, we placed two machine guns to cover the most likely lines of approach. Two more were on each end of the platoon. The company commander informed me that he had machine guns on the eastern flank of the company as well. I made sure all our men were aware of the storage areas and knew the best cover in the ammunition storage dump when bringing more ammo. If those bastards attempted a crossing at this point, I intended to make this the last charge some of them would ever make. We had an abundance of ammo at all machine gun positions and our riflemen were well supplied.

When I was satisfied that we were ready, I searched the area for Marcos. When I found him we discussed the problem of flying debris when the bridge was blown. We agreed that as soon as there was a sign of Japs in the area the engineer would blow the damn thing. With our platoon positioned at the river's edge, there was danger of getting injured by the blast. But if we moved away from the river we would reduce the effectiveness of the men. We didn't want that. We agreed to remain in position, but dig in deeper to protect against flying debris. We also agreed that he and I should stay as near one another as possible to avoid any confusion about what to do. I really believed this would become a hot spot soon. Within minutes of our talk I could hear the sounds of tools digging into the hot soil.

Daughtry came into our area to check the preparations. He cautioned that all of us should have a full canteen of water, and while filling them we should drink what we wanted. "I think when the Japs attack, there won't be time to fill your bottles," he stated. He called me aside and pointed toward a spot across the river.

"Sergeant, when the bridge goes, the Japs may try a crossing farther up there; it looks like the easiest approach route for them. The water is low and the shore area easy to travel on. They will approach the far end of the bridge, but after the blast there ain't no way they can cross there. I think they will cross farther up." He was pointing to the northern side. Then bringing his hand back farther upriver, he pointed to a low spot in the terrain running from a point near the road down to the river. "Tell your men in that area to watch that spot closely; get the area embedded in their minds so well they can see it in the dark. We don't know how long we will be asked to defend this spot." With that he left us to await what was to come.

The first sign of attack didn't come from the road as expected, but from

20

the eastern side of the bridge, downriver from us near the first platoon. I heard their machine guns open up, and everyone in my area snapped their heads in that direction. The firing was some three hundred yards from us and some of our rifles were sounding off. This fire was answered with explosions of mortar fire. The mortars were dropping all around our area, not just where the machine guns were. Most of them, however, were exploding in back of us, near the command post and our ammunition storage area. As one exploded in that area, I said a silent prayer that one didn't find the ammunition. It was too late to worry about that, but I was glad we drew extra ammunition that morning. All I could do at the moment was dig deeper and watch the approaches to the river on the other side.

The mortars exploding near me were painful to my ears, but weren't nearly as bad as the bombs I had been enduring for the past month. Still, they drove me crazy because they just kept coming and I couldn't tell where they were coming from. I sure as hell wished we had some mortars in our company. We could give them a taste of their own medicine. Then, as if my thoughts had been read, there were a number of explosions across the river. Our field artillery somewhere back near the base of the mountain was giving them hell. Because of this their mortars were stilled. We waited, knowing they could start again without warning.

We hugged the ground in our foxholes. Minutes passed and a number of artillery rounds exploded in their area. At last I regained enough courage to peek over the edge of the foxhole. There was movement in an opening in the trees about 150 yards from the end of the bridge. My eyes were glued to that spot. I was sure Japs were over there. I could feel my body tense up at the thought; I knew we would soon be under attack. The feeling was much the same as it was on that first day, only then it was airplanes. I didn't see the people we were shooting at. That movement out there were Japanese soldiers in the flesh, with nothing between them and me at the moment. Marcos' men could see them clearly. Without waiting for orders to fire, his squad opened up with everything they had. Then all along the river bank our company was firing machine guns and rifles. This was my first engagement in this kind of warfare, but I had been trained well and everything seemed easy. If we had been concealed from the enemy before, our position was now exposed and the fire fight started. Both sides of the river were alive with combatants.

I heard someone yell in back of me. Turning in that direction I saw someone signaling for us to get down. The firing on our side of the river ceased. Then it happened. The earth shook under me as the engineer blew the bridge. I took a chance and raised my head. The air was filled with rock and pieces of wood. When debris began hitting around me all I could do was get my head down and hope nothing fell into my foxhole. I waited for what seemed like an eternity before getting enough nerve to look over the edge of the hole. Where the bridge was only the abutments on each side were left. Everything else was in the river below. Across the river all was silent. We waited. Across the river there wasn't any movement. Apparently there was

21

only a small group in that first bunch, and when the bridge blew they retreated from the area. Fifteen minutes passed. Nothing. During this lull everyone resupplied their ammunition and refilled water bottles.

A check of my platoon indicated we were all okay; there were no injuries from the mortars or the falling debris. Morale seemed high and I felt good about the conflict. Returning to my foxhole I could see it was near six o'clock in the evening. I had a feeling that before the night was over, I would experience some of the cold truth of combat in an infantry company.

Darkness was around me now, and there was something scary about knowing we were the first line of defense against the enemy. I sat and waited. Suddenly the mortars from across the river opened up. Slowly at first, but increasing as they zeroed in on us. There wasn't anything we could do. They were out of sight at the moment and all we saw were the explosions from their rounds. All night long we watched through the darkness while they tossed the rounds from the mortars into our position. As far as I could tell, our company had not returned any fire at all. I watched that area that had been pointed out by the first sergeant until I imagined I saw every conceivable thing the Japanese had. I can't explain how I resisted shooting at those imagined objects.

At daybreak, another group of Japanese appeared at the bridge abutment across the river. They walked right out into the open as if they didn't know we were here. Hell, I knew they were aware of us. Still, there they were, standing right in the middle of that road. For a moment they stood and gazed across the river in our direction. Then the Filipinos in my platoon opened fire. At the same time both machine guns were sweeping the area. All along the company front I heard rifle and machine gun fire. My eyes were on the Japanese troops across the river.

Only seconds passed and there were human beings lying dead across the river. My platoon was responsible for their deaths. I could hear the screams from their wounded above the sound of rifle fire. I felt a knot in my stomach that nearly doubled me over. I turned and saw the grins on the faces of some of the other men. It was a look of complete satisfaction.

Later in the morning Williams passed the word that our lines west were not holding, that we would start withdrawing as quickly as possible. Already I could see our machine gunners breaking down their weapons in preparation for departure. The cooks were taking down their overhead canvas; pots and pans were clanging. Ammunition was loaded onto our ammo truck, which had been brought to us from command headquarters, and within minutes the company was ready to move.

The first and second platoons moved quickly, bayonets fixed and rifles held at ready. Each man checked to make sure he had adequate ammunition. Two of our automatic riflemen were sent forward as the company moved south. About one hundred yards from our position the mess sergeant set up a table. As the men marched by, each was issued some hardtack and salmon in a small can. Knowing the Japanese might cross the river at any point, the men needed no prodding to get them moving. Some of our artillery units

22

were firing over our heads. This was somewhat reassuring. I hoped there were no short rounds, but I was grateful for the cover.

Toward the mountain, I heard heavy fighting. Rifles and mortars as well as artillery could be heard firing at a very steady pace. It couldn't be more than four miles away. I sure hoped they could hold the Japs until our unit made it back to the next defense line.

All these thoughts were running through my mind when from my right I saw them. The Japs! They were charging from the jungle onto the road right into our ranks, screaming "Bonzi! Bonzi!" and firing and slashing with their bayonets. The only order I heard was, "Charge!" I didn't even know who yelled. We were taken by complete surprise. Most of us had slung our rifles over our shoulders. By the time we had them off and ready the Japs had completely wiped our company out. Those not killed fled in terror. When it was over and the Japs had melted back into the jungle, I found myself sitting several hundred yards from where it had started, alone and bewildered.

Looking back up the road, I could see several bodies—Japanese, Filipino, and American. How odd! I was sitting under a tree as if all were okay, with the sun shining brightly on the trees across the road. My shirt was torn across the front, and the right sleeve was gone. There was blood on my left forearm, but there wasn't any wound. Blood was on the front of my uniform and down the right leg of my trousers.

I could hear people talking noisily on the east side of the road. I wondered if they were Japs. I couldn't seem to get oriented as to where I was or what had happened. The sun was burning down on me now. Someone stepped from the brush on the other side of the road. It was a Filipino. Others came onto the road in full battle gear. I recognized them as a Filipino scout unit. Reality returned as my hand gripped the wooden stock of my rifle. I was fascinated by a popping sound coming from my right hand as I gripped my fingers around the stock, then opened them. There was blood on the stock that was starting to dry. The popping sound amused me. The Filipinos were all around me now, their company moving south. One of them came near me and hollered, "I got two of them, Sarge!" pointing at his bayonet. At that point I realized where I was and that it was imperative I find my unit, or what was left of it. I got to my feet and started walking south with the scout unit. This unit was part of the command that I was in, but at the time I joined up with them to march south I didn't know that.

When the scout unit arrived at the major command, I reported to the battalion commander. I learned that Williams and Daughtry were missing and probably dead. The others in the company? I didn't ask. It didn't seem to matter at the moment.

An intelligence officer called me to his area and took information from me about the bridge and asked several questions about the attack. I couldn't tell them everything about the attack, only that I had seen a number of bodies in the road and the estimated number of Japanese I had seen. I related the incident to the best of my ability and then was assigned to headquarters company with a reconnaissance platoon.

23

For the next ten days I did nothing but eat and sleep. There wasn't anything else to do here. We even had coffee, and although our rations had been reduced considerably, there were rice and cream of wheat to go with the iron rations. I felt fortunate to have this much food.

On January 11, the Japanese struck along the main highway leading into Bataan, but this time they were met with our artillery. For the first time since the war started, the bastards took a beating. They were stopped in their tracks. Each succeeding assault by them was repelled in spite of their increased shelling and bombing. Our lines held and fought back so fiercely the Japanese withdrew.

For the next several days the war consisted of probes by small units of the Japanese. Always they were thrown back. These victories, although minor, were a great source of morale for most of us. We had been beaten by them so many times that any win was a plus, no matter how small.

On January 13, I was promoted and given a platoon assigned to probe the Japanese lines. We were to gather as much information about their movements as possible. Our position, the Abucay line, was stable for the time being with the Japanese comparatively quite.

Each day we went out, sometimes probing as much as four to five miles. From what we could see, the Japanese activity had been west of us toward the mountain. As that part of the Battle for Bataan continued to warm up, there were reports filtering in that the defending lines near Mount Natib were falling apart. I heard someone say that General Wainright, who was commanding that sector, was in trouble. If he couldn't hold, we would have to withdraw farther into Bataan. After some time passed, we started our organized withdrawal. During this period we seemed to be playing a game of leap frog. One unit would stand and fight, while a sister unit would move south. This continued hour after hour, without rest and with very little food. After forty-eight hours of almost continual fighting and scrambling for safety, we reached a road running across Bataan from east to west. Here we were ordered to dig in. This would be the last stand for the "battling bastards of Bataan," as we had become known.

Our position along the cobblestone road had communications in place. It was obvious that a stand at this location had been planned for some time. I felt we could hold out indefinitely. Rumor had it that there would be thousands of troops and hundreds of planes. When they arrived, I suspected we would be relieved.

My unit drew up at the base of the mountain, west of the cane fields and under the cover of the jungle, some ten miles from the shoreline of Manila Bay. I learned that the army had a field hospital about four miles to the rear of this position. Even though we were bottled up about as close as any army could be, this was the best organization I had seen since the war began. By January 18, it was as if the war had stopped. My platoon ran probes as much as eight to ten miles without seeing one Jap. I felt the Japanese had learned of the troops and planes that were supposedly on the way and were pulling back before being destroyed.

During one of these probes we were ordered to skirt the jungle area along the eastern side of Bataan near the mountain. We were to keep off the main highway and observe any movement along that route. Specifically, we were to penetrate as far as possible, locate the Japanese military units, obtain as much information as we could, and avoid any contact with the enemy. It was standard procedure for more than one of us to collect and maintain intelligence information. This way, if one man were lost or killed, another man might get the information through to headquarters.

Our platoon now numbered fifty-six enlisted personnel and one officer. Of the fifty-six enlisted men, there were fourteen Americans. The rest were Filipino scouts, who were part of the American army. We moved out on February 5, 1942, heading north. All morning long we marched without a break, hewing, slicing, and cutting the brush in front of us while trying to keep as quiet as possible. We used the animal trails in order to make time, always keeping alert for signs of the Japs. During the afternoon I recognized that we were in the area of the old Abucay line. This was where the intelligence personnel cautioned us the Japanese were most likely to be found. We had seen nothing.

Our lieutenant was holding us in, tight against the mountain. We were high enough to observe the activities in the cane field and marsh land, and on the shoreline. During one of our stops for general observation, the point man signaled me forward. Grabbing my BAR man by the arm, I ran as quickly as possible to the front of the platoon. When I arrived at the point of the platoon, Private Johnston pointed off to the front and a little to the right at an old schoolhouse that he felt was suspicious.

Taking the field glasses from their case, I investigated the front of the building and the windows for anything out of the ordinary. I was looking for anything that would tell me this building was empty. There was a dirt road running off to the east, as well as a trail to the north. We didn't see any Japs in that area, but that didn't mean anything. It simply meant we didn't see them.

"Okay, Johnston, move back into the jungle a little, but keep that building in sight. Don't take your eyes off it. Here, take these glasses and watch for smoke, or anything that might indicate people are inside. I can't tell if there is any glass in those windows or not. I'll report back to Billingsley, then we'll be back."

Making a mental note of the surrounding area, I returned to make my report. "Lieutenant, I think we have something up forward. There is an old schoolhouse that has a road leading in from the east that looks traveled. There is another road that leads off to the southeast, just down below here some four to five hundred yards. The area between Private Johnston and the building is open, with little or no chance of getting to the building without being seen if there should be anyone inside. I think you should go up with me and take a look."

He nodded and started forward. I motioned to him to get down as we came closer. Finding Johnston, we crawled to the edge of the clearing.

"Lieutenant, if we could get inside the building and up in the bell tower we could map every inch of this area for six to seven miles north. You can see it's also a good observation point to the south. But I have a feeling there are Japs in there. With our orders to avoid contact, it might be better to bypass this area and go over toward the mountain, leaving two or three men here until we return. If by then they haven't seen any Japs, we could go in. This way is slow, but the delay would be worth it. When we get inside we can gather everything we need in an hour or so and still get back to our lines by tomorrow night."

"No," he answered. "We will go in now, and gather the information before dark, then we can move out before daylight in the morning. For Christ sake, Sergeant, we haven't seen anything resembling a Jap since we left. There isn't anyone there. Order the men to move forward at once."

"Lieutenant," I said, "may I suggest a squad of six to eight men go in first. The rest of us will move around to that timber near the building where we can cover them easily. The mission will have to be scrubbed if we engage a patrol."

"No, goddamn it!" he replied. "We go in as a unit and secure the building for the night." After some heated exchange, the order was issued to take the building.

As I explained the order to the ranking scout and told him the lieutenant didn't believe the school was held by the Japs, his only comment was, "I'm afraid, sir." This expression had become familiar to me as a signal of caution, rather than a statement of fear. I knew this Filipino sergeant to be without fear of anything. Marcos had served with me back at Abucay where I spent my first night in the infantry. I had learned that caution was appropriate.

By now the war had proven that in addition to the gear normally issued to foot soldiers, there was much to be said about some of the native weaponry. One of the most useful weapons was the "bolo," a large knife with a thick blade some twenty inches in length. The handle extended to thirty or more inches in length. It was good for clearing paths through the dense undergrowth in the jungle. Warring tribes throughout the islands found it an effective killing weapon. So did I.

When I had finished talking to Marcos, I drew my bolo from its sheath, clipped a small bamboo shoot, and watched it fall clean. Looking at Marcos, I had the feeling that the taking of this building wasn't going to be just another entry in my intelligence book.

Being only nineteen years of age, I was feeling somewhat insecure in issuing orders to older men in the platoon. Once again I confronted Billingsley, conveying my doubts and feelings about this order.

"Goddamn it, Sergeant," he said. "We have been fucking around here for at least half an hour while you are supposed to be getting the men on with this job. We haven't seen even a shadow of a Jap since we located that building. Now I aim to put this patrol inside that school, with or without you. If any Jap patrol comes through here I will destroy the bastards. Now if you can't order these men in, I will."

26

I gave the signal and the platoon started to move into the clearing. The lieutenant was at point with his BAR man. I was to his right, some eight to ten feet to his rear. Damn, I felt as naked as a jaybird. I couldn't have been more nervous if I was on Times Square stark-ass naked. As we went toward the building, not a sound or a movement was evident.

Damn, I was beginning to believe that I had been on the front too long. I signaled the platoon to move in fast. There wasn't anything around the front door that indicated anything but an empty building. I pushed the front door open and motioned the rest to follow, figuring to disperse after we had a good look from the bell tower. Entering, I could see an old piano up toward the blackboard to the right of a staircase leading to the bell tower and the attic. The floor was of rough lumber worn smooth from years of wear. Near the blackboard was an old desk. There were rows of seats on both sides of the aisle. I turned toward the lieutenant and as our eyes met I could read the satisfaction in his face.

The single room was beginning to fill up. Some of our men were still outside but most had entered. I was feeling a little foolish, when it suddenly seemed as if the whole floor and ceiling broke in. There were Japs coming from behind the piano, from under the floor, from out of the ceiling, and down the stairs. The "Bonzai! Bonzai!" yells were deafening as they came at us from everywhere.

An automatic weapon opened up from the staircase. The only thing to do was to charge into the mêlée of bayonets, knives, and gunfire, and slash at anything with a Jap uniform on. The wild bastards kept screaming and shooting so fast I couldn't think. I just ran toward them.

The lieutenant fell with the first burst from the automatic rifle. By now there were at least thirty of our men inside. The BAR man opened up not more than inches from my face. I could feel the heat from the muzzle of his gun. The machine gun on the staircase was silenced. Only rifles and bayonets were being used. The Japs were up front toward the blackboard, running forward. I unsheathed my bolo and was swinging at anything in front of me, when one son-of-a-bitch ran at me down the aisle with his bayonet. Stepping to one side I swung the bolo with all I had. His bayonet grazed my right hand as his head fell from his shoulder. The son-of-a-bitch continued to come forward. Then he fell, his bayonet sticking into the floor. As I turned another Jap was headed toward me from across the aisle. I was trying to get the bolo where I could swing on him, when Marcos pinned the bastard with his bayonet. Moving toward the front of the room, I stumbled over someone, landing flat on my stomach. The bolo flew from my hand as I went down. I rolled and started firing at the piano. I couldn't see anyone there. I just fired point blank at the damn thing. I suppose just because it was there. Then, as suddenly as it all began, it stopped. It was over, except for the strange smell of death. The powder smoke was so stifling I could hardly breathe. The silence in the building was deathly. Not a word was being spoken, no firing, no "Bonzi!" Just stillness. From the outside, the sight of this old school building in a peaceful little glen would make anyone warm in its simple beauty.

27

But inside thirty-one of our soldiers and fifteen Japanese were dead. I was too busy to think of this. I was more concerned with keeping the rest of us alive.

Getting up from the floor, I grabbed Marcos by the arm and along with the automatic rifleman, took the stairs to the attic as quickly as possible. To my relief, there weren't any more Japs in the attic, nor was anyone in the bell tower. Posting the BAR man to guard all approaches to the school, Marcos and I descended to the ground floor. We checked under everything for anyone who might still be alive. When I was sure there were no more Japanese, I posted guards at the front of the school and on the north side.

Moving among the dead, I began the grim task of removing their identification tags and putting them in my pocket. Marcos formed a detail to take the bodies from the school to an area at the edge of the jungle where we hoped we could hide them. A final count was made and the names of the dead were entered in the intelligence books—mine as well as the one we took from Billingsley. Marcos had that one. We compared notes, then went back once again to the school building, where we gathered what information we could from the dead Japanese. I removed the unit insignia from the uniform of the one I thought was their commander. I checked the remainder and found the same insignia on all of them. I took only the one and left.

Only after all of this was finished, did I realize what had happened. Twenty-three Filipinos and eight Americans were dead. The rest of us were injured.

In less than thirty minutes from the time of the last shot, our dead were buried. The intelligence information was recorded and what was left of our platoon melted back into the jungle. On our way back to our lines, we hoped against hope we wouldn't encounter another Jap patrol.

Shortly after midnight we were back at our unit. I reported the details of the ill-fated patrol that had been so "courageously" led by Billingsley, who had died with his men. Marcos and I agreed that to relate the disagreements we had with the lieutenant would serve no purpose and we would let it die where it was. The lieutenant would probably be awarded the Silver Star for gallantry, posthumously, and, depending on how useful the information was, maybe he deserved the award.

Our platoon was essentially destroyed on our mission and with morale at a very low ebb, the command determined we would be transferred to the rear with the service units for rest and recuperation.

In the rear guard area, three to four miles from the front line, at least I was out of the direct line of fire. I found these troops were, like myself, stragglers who had lost their unit or were otherwise unassigned. There were personnel from the navy, marine corps, medical personnel, quartermaster, and air corps. These men had either lost their ships or planes, or, like myself, their ranks had been so reduced through casualties they were rendered ineffective for combat. The commander of this service company was a lieutenant commander from one of the navy ships that had been sunk by the Japanese. In the jungle he looked like a marooned sailor totally out of his element.

We were here to rest and get our minds back to normal, and that was exactly what I intended to do. Just rest and eat. Forget school houses, jungle paths, snakes, and those goddamn monkeys that seemed to be able to survive regardless of how much shooting went on. They just screamed, and scared the hell out of me when I was trying my damnedest to be quiet.

During this time, word was passed around that the Japanese army had made a landing on the west side of Bataan, behind our lines, some fifteen miles away. It didn't take much intelligence to comprehend the seriousness of this. If they got into that area they could come over the mountain behind us and cause more problems. We needed the area on the tip of Bataan for storage of supplies for our front line units. If they occupied any of this area there would be no place for us to rest from the long hours of fighting up front.

Commander Broughton called me to his command post and informed me that I had been promoted to technical sergeant and would be reporting directly to him. The unassigned troops were to be organized into a provisional infantry battalion with the mission of dislodging the Japanese landing party on the west side of Bataan.

I had been there for the past five or six days and during that time had been issued new weapons and ammo. In general, I felt very good. I was told that the landing force, as far as anyone knew, was small. Even though the troops were not all infantry, they should be able to dislodge the Japanese in short order as we would outnumber them considerably.

On February 24, during the early morning hours, our unit moved out along the cobblestone road toward the west side of Bataan. We had adequate ammunition, water, and field rations for two days, which was the time thought needed to wipe out the landing party.

It was afternoon when the first elements reported contact with enemy forces. It was only a small force and from all indications the intelligence report was correct. Only a small force had apparently gotten ashore. I could hear small arms fire off to the south of the road, and all personnel were ordered off the road to the south. The battalion had about six hundred men and required some time to get into position. We wanted to cover as much area south of the road as possible without spreading ourselves too thin.

By late afternoon our troops were all dug in, and only sporadic fire could be heard along the front of eight to nine hundred yards. The terrain wasn't the choicest place for an engagement. The Japanese had the advantage of a small ridge. They could keep down and fire at us when we moved. We were ordered not to move, but to dig in and wait until communications were established with the regiment.

With everyone keeping down and not moving, the activities of the Japanese slowed. Only sporadic rifle fire could be heard off somewhere to the southern end of our battalion. With this slowdown, our communications personnel were able to tie in with the regiment.

During the time that communications were being established Broughton was gathering information from all of us as to how many enemy personnel were in the area, how much support they had from the beach side, and what type of combat units were available. With all this information, Broughton contacted the regiment and requested artillery support from Corregidor. After some time, Corregidor pinpointed our position, and the twelve-inch guns from Battery Way zeroed in on the Japanese.

When shells started falling in the target area, I ordered the men to dig deeper. I knew as long as these shells were dropping the air woud be full of shrapnel. Even though the rounds were exploding some 1,000 to 1,500 yards away, there was danger. If any one got his head out above the ground, he would likely be killed by flying shrapnel. As far as I had seen, these weapons had killing power second to none, as far as the guns on Corregidor.

The initial landing of the Japanese was at Quaninauan Point and as far as I could tell they had met with no resistance at all. They had moved four to six miles inland from the landing point before we engaged them near the Anyasan River. It seemed to me this force had landed near the mouth of the river, had come up the riverbed from some distance, had moved south of the river, and had taken up position out on the tablelands away from the river and some distance south of the cobblestone road at a point where the road swung back to the north.

In this area the jungle was very thick. We couldn't see anything, only hear the blast. One round fell about five hundred yards from us and the jungle cleared for two hundred yards and the ground shook like an earthquake. Everyone went down. From that time on we didn't have to worry about the men keeping below the surface of the ground or having to order the troops to dig deeper.

For the next hour it seemed a round exploded every thirty seconds. There were other explosions out there also. Between the rounds of heavy artillery, I could hear the exploding rounds of field artillery. This incoming fire was from the direction of the lines just north of us. Hearing that sound I felt better just knowing that our forces were holding in that area.

In spite of all the shelling of the Japanese position, at about four o'clock in the morning of February 27, the bastards struck us with all their might. Ironically we received an order to mount our offensive at the same time, and we were fully ready to push them back to the beach. Their commander seemed determined to break through and we were just as determined to drive them back into the sea. With a situation like that there had to be a classic fight, if there is such a thing.

We had every machine gun in position. We had adequate ammunition. Even though some of our people were far from being seasoned veterans, they were ready and willing.

During the next two days, the battle raged on and the land changed hands many times. We would drive the bastards back almost to the edge of the cliff, then they would counterattack and drive us back to the base of the hill. This seesaw battle, which was supposed to be an easy task, lasted through February.

During this time, the Japanese attempted to reinforce their units from the sea. This attempt was thwarted by our navy torpedo boat, the only one left now. With this torpedo boat, plus artillery fire from shore batteries, their convoy was either sunk or had turned its tail and run. In spite of this, however, some of their troops got ashore. Because of this reinforcement it became necessary for some of the "I" Corp troops to drop down and take up position just north of our line.

From the time we arrived until the last of February, the ground in the area changed hands so many times I found myself watching for Japanese booby traps in the foxholes. There were times I would think about how a Jap soldier had sat in this same hole protecting himself from me just minutes before. Sometimes I would dig a new hole out of pure superstition. This superstition soon passed. As time went on and the fighting got worse, I would just get down anywhere that was below the surface of the ground.

At one point, the Japs made an attempt to drop supplies to their beleaguered troops. The wind was not in their favor, and these supplies dropped to the back of our lines. This drop contained food supplies and ammunition. We were afraid to eat the food, but there was a particular type of grenade that I liked. It could be armed simply by striking it sharply on the heel of a shoe. A hammerlike handle allowed it to be easily thrown.

Even though we had increased artillery support and some armored tanks we could call on, the little bastards continued to fight with ferocity such as I had never seen before. The temperature was holding at 100 degrees with the humidity at 100 percent. The dead, especially the Japanese, were everywhere. The stench in the area was worse than the fighting. We continued to press the bastards day and night until at last they started giving way. They started to withdraw, inch by precious inch, toward the cliffs. From the appearance of the dead soldiers I saw as we advanced slowly over them, it was evident that they had been and still were fighting on spirit alone. They were starved to skin and bone, yet they fought on. They definitely were the best soldiers I had seen anywhere.

Finally we forced the remaining Japanese into an area no more than three hundred yards wide, with nothing behind them but the China Sea and a two-hundred-foot cliff. Some of them, rather than surrender, elected to jump from the cliff to their death. Others slipped over the side into the caves only to be blasted out by our water-borne troops who had joined us from Corregidor and were in the bay. The others charged directly at us screaming, "Bonzai! Bonzai!"

When this final charge was over, the Battle of Quaninauan was over. All that was left to do was count the dead, tend to the walking wounded, and evacuate the seriously wounded. We had 250 dead, and over 1,000 wounded. Most of the wounded would live to fight another day.

Chapter 4

When our unit was withdrawn from the Quaninauan area our forces were depleted to the point of ineffectiveness. Our unit was inactivated, and I was once again assigned to the service area. I had no idea what the unit was, nor did I care. All I wanted was hot food and a place to take a shower. The smell of death was in my clothes, in my hair, in my skin. I could even taste it. I couldn't talk to anyone about the events of the past three weeks. I just wanted to sleep, dream if possible, eat, and try to wipe out the horrors of the past month.

During the next three weeks there wasn't any action along our part of the front. All I had to do was to scrounge food to supplement the half-rations we were on. The Filipinos were faring much better than we were. They ate the dogs and the monkeys in the area. They also trapped iguanas in the jungle for food. Before long I acquired a taste for this delicacy and spent a lot of time trapping in the jungle for my dinner.

Days passed, then weeks. Still there was no convoy of troops or planes. Food was getting scarcer by the day. At least the goddamn Japs were leaving us alone. Morale was still high. Hell, the Japs probably blocked the shipping lines temporarily. When that was cleared the convoy would get through. That was the thinking, at least on my part. Little did I know the whole goddamn fleet had been sunk at Pearl and the brass sure as hell didn't aim to let us, the ground soldiers, know that.

On March 12, 1942, the bomb shell dropped that would break the morale more than anything the Japs had done up to now. Word was received that General MacArthur had left the islands to assume command of all forces in the Pacific. I began to realize there was to be no convoy, no troops, no food, no guns, no planes. If this war wasn't finished before all our supplies ran out, only God could predict the ending.

By March 15, the Japs were again shelling the entire line, day and night, almost at will. Individuals walking could expect to be fired upon with artillery as well as small arms. I began looking for an assignment at the front, out of the headquarters area. I felt that there, at least, I could fight back. That was more than I could do here. The only thing here were the 240mm shells coming in.

This time I reported to the 11th Division of the Filipino Army and was assigned to an infantry company. This company, like most of the other units of this division, was understaffed. Its personnel had either been killed or could not be accounted for. Once again, the company was staffed with a larger number of Filipinos than Americans, and, for the better part, all were now considered combat troops. However, morale was low. Many of the Filipino troops had been told of the departure of MacArthur and were stunned. Most felt they had been deserted and were angry. This hostility was vented openly on the Americans, making for a rather unhealthy situation.

During the latter part of March 1942, the unit had very little contact with the Japanese. Most of us caught up on our sleep and tried to establish ourselves with our Filipino counterparts. On March 28, at around 4:00A.M., the Japanese struck, first with artillery for almost an hour and then with mortars and small arms. The pinpoint accuracy of their mortars, as well as their field artillery, led me to believe that this was not just another probe, but rather an all-out attack across the entire line. I could hear artillery far to the west and all the line on the eastern flank was under fire.

Our unit, being a machine gun company, was situated along the crest of a small ridge facing generally to the north, with extra guns on each flank. The two companies on our right and left flanks were undermanned and needed increased firepower in the event of a frontal assault. The commander gave me four gun positions with Filipino crews. These positions were in cement pillboxes, built with this final stand in mind sometime before the war started. These concrete gun emplacements were about thirty-five feet in length and some eight feet wide with no roof. We had only the jungle growth to conceal us from any aircraft spotters, and this certainly didn't provide us with any protection if we became a target for bombers. The walls were of thick concrete, which gave us excellent protection from small arms fire. The machine gun mounts were permanent and about thirty inches from the floor. This allowed the muzzle of the water-cooled machine guns to clear the casements by some six inches and afforded an excellent traverse action for these weapons. The field of fire was unrestricted. I could see as much as half a mile across the rice field to my direct front.

Considering the increased firing in the direction of Manila Bay, I felt that the bastards were intent on breaking through. It would give them the best access to the port area of Marvelious and, with such close proximity to Corregidor, would allow them the unrestricted use of all their artillery weapons when and if they decided to attempt a landing on the "Rock."

They struck in the early morning hours, first with heavy mortars and then with machine gun and rifle fire—lightly at first and then increasing in intensity as the dawn grew near.

It wasn't quite daylight but I could see the silhouette forms clearly in the early dawn as their infantry started moving in. When they were within fifty yards and moving closer we opened with all guns. Still they came. Nothing we did stopped them or, for that matter, even slowed them down. As we cut the charging bastards down, more filled in where they fell and continued to charge. As they got to the barbed wire and were cut down, the bodies seemed to form a bridge over the wire for the ones that followed.

The water started boiling in our weapons. We held our fire to the left side until they cooled enough to take over for those on the right. Then the right side took over while the left cooled. By alternating in this fashion we were able to keep a steady rain of fire on the advancing horde.

By nightfall the machine guns had fired so many rounds that the spent cartridges were piling up under the tripod mounts to a point where it was necessary for us to take them from their mounts and set them atop the brass cartridges. Time after time the barrels had to be changed as the old ones were burned out from excess firing. There were times when the barrels became red hot as the water boiled away in the water jackets. Soon water became a problem, and we had to use our drinking water to cool the weapons and keep them firing.

During the night, the charges stopped. There was only sporadic firing by the Japanese and very little return fire from us. On the second day, the charge was resumed by the Japanese, and our day started as it had the previous morning. It was apparent we were going to run out of ammunition before the Japanese ran out of troops. Sometime in the afternoon, the order came to dismantle our machine guns and fix our bayonets. The order made my blood run as cold as ice. I turned, put the field phone back in place, and relayed the order to Marcos, who in turn repeated the order to his men in Tagalog. Then, with silent acceptance, his men started removing the firing blocks from their guns and tossing them from the emplacement. With one single click, I heard the bayonets snap into place on the Springfield rifles. The click of the bayonets as they were placed in readiness seemed to cause the circulation in my body to stop. Never before had I experienced such fear.

The screams of the charging enemy at the front of the pillbox could be heard over the other noises of battle. We could either engage the enemy or attempt to get away and cede the position.

We started slipping through the side door of the pillbox. Within twenty-five feet of the door, we were met by the Japanese. No command was given, nor were any commands necessary. The crew of eighteen men raised their rifles to port position and moved toward the oncoming hordes of Japanese soldiers.

I started to fire into the charging mass of humanity, and I saw the others following suit. We slowly spread across the front side of the pillbox. When we saw a Jap, we shot him; if he was too close, we used a rifle butt or bayonet. I didn't dare look to either side. I knew our people were there, so I just protected myself from the front, letting the others do the same. It wasn't possible to assist anyone who might be having trouble. Each man had to handle his own problem. Within seconds, my ammunition was gone and there wasn't a chance to reload. The only thing left to do was cut, slash, jab, parry, and dodge.

There wasn't any way of knowing how long this charge continued—ten minutes or ten hours. It seemed like an eternity. Finally, their charge seemed to just fade out. I didn't see any of them withdrawing; there just didn't seem to be any left to charge anymore. There was complete silence as I looked toward the rice field where they had been charging for the past thirty hours.

All was quiet. No hordes of Japs running this way. There was only the dead, most of whom were at the bottom of the hill near the edge of the rice field. The ground was covered by them. Christ! What a sight!

Turning away, I walked toward the crest of the hill in back of me where I could take cover from any artillery that might start coming in. I was sure it would start soon. Marcos came from somewhere in front of me. As we started to speak, I realized that once again I had survived an ordeal.

Walking to the rear of the emplacement, I could see that Marcos had a bayonet wound in his left forearm, but with the aid of a tourniquet, he had the bleeding under control and was able to function. Seven of our men had been killed.

Marcos and I began collecting the dog tags of our dead. We searched the bodies of the dead Japanese near the gun emplacement for intelligence information, then started looking for our command post to report.

There certainly wasn't any need to return to the machine gun position. The guns were dismantled and the blocks were thrown away. We had no spare parts, and possibly none were to be had. I took one last look around. All I could see were dead soldiers from both sides.

Chapter 5

At headquarters all the information was turned over to command. We were ordered to regroup with our unit and form into an organization that could, at a minimum, defend ourselves if the need arose.

During this reorganization, my orders were to assemble all the walking wounded. These men were to be moved to the rear of the command post and would be moved later to the field hospital.

For the next three hours, I moved from one company to the other to pick up the walking wounded who could still shoulder their personal gear. I sent them to the assembly area in the rear of the command post. During this break in the fighting, about 150 men were assembled and rosters were made up and turned over to the sergeant major of the command.

With the number of men to be evacuated to the rear and the number killed during the last attack, it was evident, even to me, that this unit would never again be able to form any type of effective combat unit. If the Japanese should mount another offensive soon, this sector would surely break.

My orders were to take the wounded men to the hospital for treatment, and when they had been treated, to bring them back to duty and get rosters of those who would be retained in the hospital for further medical treatment.

The trip back to the medical facility was about four or five miles, and with some seriously wounded men, the pace would have to be slow with many breaks.

Shortly after midnight the column was stopped once more for rest. We had taken breaks earlier, but we needed more time now for our people to check their wounds, retie their field bandages, and in general put themselves back together in order to finish the trek to the hospital.

We walked, rested, and then walked some more, until the sun was rising over Manila Bay. We were still two or three miles from the field hospital. Many of the men had lost so much blood they were becoming very weak. I wished there was something I could do to make the trip easier. All that could be done was watch and make sure none were left along the road alone, and to break as often as we could to prevent anyone from dying from exhaustion.

At around nine o'clock, we stopped for our last break. We were far enough that an attack was improbable. Those who had field bandages could change them. Those of us who had hard tack could eat. There wasn't any need to hold back anything. We would arrive at the hospital within the hour.

After some twenty minutes we were strung out along each side of the road again, as was the military custom of the time. Just when it seemed as if we might make it, I heard artillery fire. The guns were clearly Japanese and as I was trying to determine what target they might have, there was an explosion some two hundred yards ahead. Without command everyone left the shoulder of the road and started digging in or taking cover where they could. Over to my left on the north side of the road was an old, open trench, and I made a running dive for it as another shell exploded nearby. Within minutes shells were exploding all around me, and I buried my face deeper into the mire.

That feeling of being totally helpless came over me. I remembered Fort Hughes, when all that artillery was coming in. All I had wanted then was a chance to fight back. Yet, here I was, in this goddamn trench, face down in the muck, praying with all my heart there wouldn't be a direct hit.

I have never been able to explain it, and I have had other soldiers tell me similar stories of their fears under combat. Some of them seem silly. My fear came each time I found myself face down in the dirt with shells or bombs falling everywhere, and I couldn't do anything—not even run. I just knew that the next one was aimed directly between my shoulders, and it was just a matter of time until it hit.

During the heavy artillery bombardment, which I was convinced was aimed at the column, all I could do was keep my head down and dig as fast as I could. It seemed like hours that I had been down in the muck. Still the shells exploded all around me. My ears were ringing and the concussion got worse with each round. My eyes were burning from the powder smoke, and still the shells continued to come in on us.

After what seemed like an eternity the shelling slowed. A round exploded someplace back down the road a few hundred yards. Then nothing. My ears were still ringing. I knew the shelling had stopped, yet the sound of the explosions were still in my head. At last I felt I could chance looking over the top of the slit-trench. The smell of smoke was everywhere. There was something burning. There must have been some incendiary shells. Slowly I got to my feet and at the same time felt to see if I was still all in one piece. I was just shook up from the concussion—no cuts or shell fragments that I could find.

Standing up and looking around the area, I couldn't see anyone. No one raised from a hole. I picked up my rifle from the muck. Nothing was coming in. I never heard anything. No whistling, no whoosh of the shell, just a tremendous explosion right on top of me.

My rifle flew from my hand. The concussion pulled at my steel helmet, and the strap under my chin felt as if it would pull my head from my shoulders. Grabbing my head in both hands, I tried to get down. Something was holding me upright. Why in the hell couldn't I get down into the trench? For a moment I thought I was losing my mind. Try as I might, I couldn't get under cover.

I felt the blood running down my face. There was severe burning at the back of my neck and head, and still I couldn't get down. Then I realized what had happened. The slit-trench had been filled in around me and I was buried in the dirt up to my hips. The shells hit on each side of the trench and forced the sides in on me. There wasn't any trench to get down into, and I couldn't get my feet loose until I dug my way out. I wondered where my rifle was. It wasn't anywhere in sight. Hell, what difference did it make? I didn't need a rifle. I needed out of this mess. If another shell came in I wouldn't have any protection at all.

That damn burning at the base of my skull—what in the hell had happened? Reaching back, I felt the blood running down the back of my neck. Also there was something sticking out of my neck, hot to the touch. That's what was burning. I made an attempt to pull it out. It wouldn't move. I couldn't get hold of it. The burning was driving me wild and there wasn't a damn thing I could do. The concussion had made my nose bleed and I didn't have anything to hold over it.

At this point, I was standing waist deep in dirt and was unable to get out. The concussion had damaged my lungs and I was having trouble breathing. The burning at the base of my skull was throbbing with every heartbeat, and the blood was running from my nose like water. I was somewhere between conscious and unconscious. My head began to spin. I could hardly see the blood as it ran down my forearm. I could feel myself falling forward—then nothing.

Some time later, I heard voices. They seemed to be miles away. Then I realized someone was digging me out of the dirt. My breathing was hard. The pains in my chest were choking me as I tried to get oxygen, and the pain in the back of my head wouldn't let up for anything.

The next thing I remembered I was being placed on a stretcher and two soldiers were carrying me away from the trench. As we were leaving, the medics strapped me to the stretcher, then pulled a sheet up over my face and started the long trek back to the medical facility. After some ten minutes we passed some other soldiers and I overheard one ask, "Is he dead?" I had been resting quite well up to that time, but that statement sure as hell brought me back to reality. I pulled the sheet from my face and asked the medics to set me down.

When this had been done, I asked if one of them would look at the back of my neck. They did and found a large fragment of an artillery shell sticking out from the base of my skull. One of the medics believed he could remove the fragment, while the other one thought it should be left for the doctors to remove since there was no way of knowing how long the fragment might be.

After what seemed a long time, I finally said, "I don't give a damn what either of you think. I want whatever is in my neck removed if either of you know how to do it." The pain was more than I could stand. That ended the argument between them, and the fellow who was against taking the fragment out said, "To hell with it, take it out and let the son-of-a-bitch bleed to death, if that's what he wants." With that, the shrapnel was removed. Fortunately, the fragment wasn't very long. The medics were able to bandage the wound and stop the bleeding. Even though there were many more small pieces of shell fragments in the upper right side of my body, that burning pain was relieved. Except for the problem with my breathing and the pains in my lung, I was able to stand on my feet. I felt I could make it back to the aid station on my own, so I told them to leave me and give their assistance to any of the other injured who might be more in need of their services than I.

When these two medics were gone, I joined the men on the road and walked for another five or ten minutes. I then found a good shade tree and got out of the sun. I sat down and watched the men as they marched by on their way to the aid station. I thought I would probably be evacuated to Corregidor and taken out of combat. I didn't think I could fight. From what I could see this command had been beaten. I continued to sit and think.

There didn't seem to be anyone in charge of this bunch. All the troops that I brought out to the evacuation area were already gone. Everyone seemed to be as I, stragglers, dragging themselves along the best way they could. They seemed to be in some kind of daze. Damn, we had taken a beating this time. Much worse than any other. If help didn't get here soon, this war was going to be over for us. We would either be captured or killed. I sure as hell didn't see anyone around me who could muster enough strength to fight. We were finished.

No unit, no ship,
no help and no hope

Chapter 6

When I arrived at the field hospital, my hopes for fast evacuation to Corregidor faded. There were so many wounded people there, the doctors weren't able to give proper attention to all of them. Just to care for those who were in desperate need of medical attention was keeping each and every one of our doctors at a dead run all the time. Those of us considered "walking wounded" would have to wait until critically injured patients had been tended to and evacuated before we could be cared for.

Walking away from the hospital area and from the noises of wounded and dying men, I found a good spot. I was protected from the sun and also near a foxhole where I could get down in the event of a shelling. I got a field blanket, made myself a place to lie down, and rested and slept the rest of the day. Sometime in the early evening, long after dark, I got to see an army medic. He dressed all the wounds on my neck and back, especially the bad wound at the base of my skull. I was then directed to an area where the walking wounded were being housed and cared for.

The field hospital was the closest I would get to the hospital at Corregidor. I was told that their hospital was filled to capacity, and that this was the best we could expect for now. I was disappointed to say the least, but I did understand how impossible it was for our medical personnel to adequately handle the number of casualties coming in all at one time.

For the next three or four days the medical people dressed my wounds and cleansed my cuts each morning and sometimes twice daily. All in all, the care was extremely good under the conditions. I was resting and eating well, and, being young, I healed quickly. Before long, I was more scared to remain at the field hospital than I would be out with a unit. So I started looking for a way out of the medical area and back into the jungles.

I knew these people were pushed for beds and they probably wouldn't look too hard for me if I walked away from the hospital. So along about the sixth day, I picked up my gear and walked out, making my way west, back toward my old outfit. It was my feeling that this place would be overrun by the Japanese if they should decide to attack that section. The thick jungles looked better to me than the chance that things would get better where I was. So, on April 2, I walked away from the medical tent and back into the jungle.

Chapter 7

My breathing was better now and the pain in the back of my head and neck had eased up considerably. As I walked along the jungle trail toward the mountain, I knew I must find an infantry unit and attach myself. At least if I were attached to a unit I wouldn't be unarmed if the Japanese tried to over-run the area.

I had been walking some three miles when I came upon a group of men under the command of a navy officer. It was evident these men were like myself, lost from their command or their units had been overrun. Like myself, they were looking for any kind of an organization that could give some kind of guidance.

The officer was like us. His ship had been sunk, and not having anything to do, he had found this bunch of men and had formed them into a unit. From what I could see, they were very well armed; each of them had as many ammunition belts as they could carry. Even though a lot of them were injured, for the most part they were walking and had their wounds bandaged and could move about quite well.

When I reported to this officer he said he was Lieutenant Bridges from the navy, and that he formed these people into a unit mainly for personal protection in the event the Japanese came this way.

I explained that I had just left the hospital, and had no idea if I had a unit or not. The outfit I was in about a week ago had been shot to hell, and when I went to the medical area, I lost complete contact with them.

With that he asked if I would assist him in organizing the men into a unit, if for no other reason than to defend our own asses should the Japs come our way. I agreed, and for the rest of the day, we gathered ammunition and weapons of any type, from any place they could be found or stolen. These men were so adept in appropriating supplies and food, that by nightfall we had quite a supply of rifles, bayonets, ammunition, and hand grenades—we even had an anti-aircraft gun with over three hundred rounds of ammunition. By nightfall all the men were well armed, and steps had been taken to establish a command post.

During the day, Bridges had picked up army Lieutenant Barclay from the artillery. As second in command, he instructed me to organize the outfit into six platoons, and when this was completed I was to report to him with the names of our ranking noncommissioned officers. Some time around nine in the evening I had completed this organization (with all the ranking NCOs).

41

We then assembled at the command post, ready for our first briefing by the commander and his executive.

Bridges informed us of the existence of what was left of the 31st Infantry, just to the west of us. As far as he could tell, communications with parts of that regiment had been established, but at the moment he was not able to tell us if that unit was complete and intact. There was also an infantry unit of the Filipino army located to our east toward Manila Bay. The strength of either of these units, however, was not known. It was known that the desertion rate was due to the fact that they had run out of ammunition as well as food. They also were able to survive in the hills, and without the proper weapons they could do very little to help us anyway. Nonetheless, he said we had to consider this in our planning because that command could fall apart at any time, and we wouldn't have anything on our right front but the Japanese.

With all this in mind, all we did for the next two days was scrounge ammunition and pile the stuff inside the perimeter, not bothering to store anything but issuing it to the troops to make sure that every man got an ample and equal share. There was also the problem of food. We had access to some rations from the command on the east flank of us and had drawn as much as they would allow us to have. Our Filipino element had received some rations from their command. All of this food had been brought in and was under the control of our mess personnel, who had established a kitchen near the center and to the rear of our troop position.

From this "pack ratting" it would appear we intended to stay right here. No more running, no more hiding. Here we stood, come what may, and those fucking bastards had better know if they wanted this ground there would be a fight like they had never seen before.

The position had been taken by the Japs before and had since been retaken by our people. There was a lot of ammunition scattered about. We found many bandoleers in foxholes and trenches throughout the area. All of these had been picked up and reissued.

During the second day I looked the anti-aircraft weapon over and found it to be in good condition. I was proud of this. I knew this weapon very well. With the ammunition I was sure we would find a use for the gun if the Japanese came through this sector of the line, especially if there were any dive bombers. If I could get a crew together, this gun could be a godsend.

As I looked the gun over, I began to wonder about the possibility of depressing the barrel and using it as an artillery piece, as low-angle fire. The thought kept running through my mind and intrigued the hell out of me.

Before the day was over I was getting sandbags and having them filled with dirt and brought in to form a gun pit for the weapon. The pit was situated up near the command post, just to the rear of our infantry positions and slightly behind the little knoll. In that way the gun crew would have some protection from small arms fire and would be able to concentrate solely on operating the gun, if the time came that we would use it.

The gun pit was about five to six feet high and three feet thick. We brought the sides in rather close. Since we had only about three hundred rounds, we felt we should keep the parapet as small as possible, yet large enough for three men and all the rounds of ammo. By the close of the day on April 3, we had the artillery gun in place and all was in readiness. This fact and that I would man the weapon in the event it was needed was reported to Bridges. I had already selected two of our men, Corporal Mullins and Private First Class Livingston. These men were from an artillery unit and had some experience with artillery.

By April 4, 1942, we had prepared rosters of all the men in the provisional battalion. The roster was in the hands of our commander. Our platoon leaders had been assigned. The platoons had been designated as first, second, and third platoons with about one hundred men per platoon. They had been broken down further into squads. NCOs had been assigned to each of the small units. Communications were strung along the entire line, with telephones at certain key spots within the perimeter.

While things were relatively quiet in this area, action had started to build up along our entire front. Shelling could be heard, especially next to the base of Marvelious mountain, with occasional incoming rounds just east of us. Over on Corregidor, the big guns opened up periodically. As the big shells went over my head, I sometimes wanted to get down in a hole, especially when the base plate loosened from the projectile. That whistling and roaring scared the pure hell out of me. I couldn't tell if it was a short round, or if it was a base plate gone. The longer I could hear them, the louder they got, and even though they were five to eight miles away, it sure was scary in the shallow holes. I dug deeper as I thought of the possibility of a short round.

We were now deployed along a four-hundred-yard line, facing generally to the north and northwest. As each man was assigned to his position, he was instructed of his field of fire in that area. He was made aware of the soldier on each side of him, and cautioned about firing in such a way that might cause problems for the rest of us. Most of these men were combat soldiers in every sense of the word. Even though some had never been in the infantry, all had been under fire, and for the most part, each had experienced, to some degree, the horrors of war.

Each and every one of us were aware that we were no longer defending a military strategic location, but rather were fighting to save our lives or to avoid being captured by the Japanese. Real estate meant nothing now.

All during the day of April 5, the noises of combat in every direction increased the tension. We started tying strings together and stringing them from rifle position to rifle position, creating our own signals to be used during darkness. One jerk on the string tied to the nearest soldier indicated he should wake up or pay attention; something out of the ordinary was out front. Two jerks meant "watch to your right; something is moving." In this manner we could communicate without alerting the enemy to our presence. All during daylight, hour after hour was spent perfecting this method of communicating.

We had been issued some condensed milk from somewhere and canned salmon. The cans had been accumulating around the foxholes. Someone came up with the idea of tying these cans into bunches of two or three and stringing them some distance out in front of our line, leaving them very close to the ground. If a Jap should try to sneak into our position, he might make a noise and we would detect him before any damage could be done. This kept our minds off the shooting that was going on to our right and left flanks.

Down on the east end of the line where the commander had established his command post was a sharp drop into a small stream, where some fresh water flowed. Taking two men, I went to this area, and we made a small dam across the stream. We dug out some of the bottom and formed a pool so we could dip water out. Every man needed a full canteen before dark. The word was spread for them to fill up with the water in the lister bags that the mess sergeant had hung in the kitchen area. The cooks were told that when everyone had filled a canteen, they should refill the lister bags with water from the stream and be sure it was heavily chlorinated.

By nightfall I was so damned tired, I could hardly move. I knew that sleep would be hard to come by. The Japanese were intensifying their artillery along the front. Who could sleep, not knowing if they might decide to change their target, or some silly bastard on Corregidor might cut a round short, letting it fall in the general area?

I went up to the command post some time around sundown, found a place near the command tent, and got into a foxhole. I closed my eyes and waited for sleep to overtake me.

During the night of April 5, it became apparent that the 31st Infantry was under a general attack. From the sound of the artillery a breakthrough had been made over near the base of the mountain. Either the Japs had broken the line or the flank on the west was giving ground. The explosions were coming from farther south than they had been in the afternoon. Over near the shoreline of Manila Bay, the fighting with the Filipino unit was intensifying. Except for a few rounds falling about a mile away, the Japanese were ignoring us. It appeared there was heavy fighting underway on both our sides. There was nothing to do but sit and wait.

Early the following morning I went to the command post and was informed that communications had been lost with the units in our general area. We were on our own, and were going to hold position until word was received to do otherwise. If nothing was heard by noon from the 31st or the Filipino command, a runner would be dispatched to the rear to try and make contact with higher command.

Around mid-morning one of our observers spotted what turned out to be Japanese infantry, some three to four hundred yards out from the eastern end of our line. We had one machine gun at that point and one about fifty yards farther west. Both of these guns opened up and so did our riflemen in that area. Our fire was returned and for the next three hours this exchange of fire continued until the Japanese broke contact. Somehow I knew this was only the first, and that the worst was yet to come.

Within an hour it happened. The little bastards had us spotted. They had brought up their automatic weapons, machine guns of all types. One was only two hundred yards away, directly to the front and center of our line. There were at least two more farther south on our left flank. I was never able to positively locate where they were coming from. All we could do was keep down until the Japanese position could be pinpointed. They opened up with short bursts. The dust flew around our trench, but by the time we got our heads out they had stopped firing. This went on until darkness; then when they fired we could see the tracers and flashes from the guns. We brought fire on that point until we either knocked the bastards out or they decided they had had enough and packed out.

In spite of what we did they continued to raise hell with us. Nothing we did even slowed them down. Either they kept bringing in new crews or guns, or they were protected to the point we were not hurting them. In any case, nothing was slowing them down. Each time we opened up on the tracers, they picked up on our tracer rounds and brought more fire on us, either from the position we were firing on or from another gun along the line. They seemed to have rapid-fire weapons all along our front.

The artillery fire over to the northwest was increasing, and I could hear the return fire by our troops. I was confident that our lines were still holding in that area, but it was apparent they had been forced to pull back, as their return fire was much farther south than it had been yesterday. Over to the east, there was a fire fight in progress, and since the firing seemed about equal, I had to assume that line was holding also. There was some satisfaction in that thought. Things were still holding, and I was still breathing. That was something to be grateful for.

By 0400 on the morning of April 7, 1942, heavy fighting could be heard along the front in both directions, from the base of the mountain to the coastline of Manila Bay. At our area, in addition to the rifle fire, we had picked up some mortar fire as well, and since we had no mortars with us, there wasn't a damn thing we could do but sit, wait, and keep under cover the best we could.

At daybreak the Japanese infantry struck us. They came charging in with little or no regard for their lives, and in some cases the bastards got as close as thirty yards in front of us before being killed. We had had three days to scrounge ammunition and had a fair supply stored in our trenches before the Japanese knew we were there. The soldiers certainly didn't have any intention of letting these little sons-of-heaven take them without a fight.

At the beginning, the firing seemed to be the heaviest at the right end of the line. For the next hour I spent all my energy getting from one position to the other until I had talked to each of the men along the line. We had held this time, and the shooting had stopped. There were a few men who had been injured, but as far as I could tell no one had been killed in this assault.

The men were instructed to fill canteens if needed and take advantage of this lull to care for their equipment. "Make sure all of you have ammunition. If you are short, come up to the command post. There is some stored in that area up near the anti-aircraft gun."

45

The wounded were looked at, and about ten to twelve men who would have problems defending themselves were found. They would have to stay in a foxhole or trench. They couldn't even be considered for medical evacuation, and our medical supplies had long since been depleted to the point that only bandages could be had. These were being handed out by anyone who wasn't in a foxhole with his rifle. Our medical personnel had either been wounded or killed, and there was no one to care for the wounded. If a soldier wasn't hurt too badly, he tended his own wounds; if unable to do so, he had a buddy assist him. The order was to stay in your position, and keep your head down until you had to use your weapon. We were to conserve our strength; we might need it more later than we did now; we were to realign the troops and make sure that all had ammunition. Since we had hurt the enemy in their last attack, they were almost certain to regroup and attack again. We still didn't have any word from regiment as to what we were to do. The runners had not made any contact with us. We had to be prepared to stay with what we had.

Around 0900 hours we spotted movement at the northeast end of our line. At first I felt the Japs were mounting another attack. Then I saw they were American troops trying to get back from somewhere forward. As it turned out they were Americans and some Filipino soldiers from the division to our east. They had been cut off from their unit, and were attempting to get back south to join an American unit. There were some twenty to thirty troops and they were glad to join with our unit. It was the general consensus that our line to the east had broken sometime that morning.

During the early afternoon, there was fighting some four hundred yards to the west and just slightly forward of the northern position. This was unusual, as we had driven the Japanese back from that area earlier in the morning and were unaware of any American or Filipino units or troops in that area. But they were sure raising hell in that sector. All we could do was stand off for the moment and watch.

It wasn't long until I could see that some of our troops from the infantry unit on our western flank were falling back through our unit. They apparently were caught between the Japs who were on the offensive against the 31st and the rest of the unit we had engaged in the morning. As these American troops were breaking out our machine guns opened up and gave them cover fire until they were within our perimeter.

Those Japanese had either picked up more troops or we hadn't done the damage we thought. They were charging in on us, yelling and screaming and firing everything they had at us and the retreating men. Each time a man would raise to run, there would be a hail of fire in his direction and our men would answer them with rifle and machine gun fire. God, what a hell of a mess. These men were shot to hell and just when it looked like we had all of the men in and under cover, those bastards opened up with mortar fire. Christ, I hated those mortars. They went straight up, then came directly down at you. All a person could do was get in a hole and hope and pray there wasn't a direct hit.

After a short time, the mortar fire lifted and you could at last look over the edge of your trench or foxhole without the fear of having the hell blown out of you.

When all the new soldiers were in position and had been issued ammunition to defend themselves, it was necessary to find out why they were in this area and what unit they were from. Most of them seemed confused at first and were unable to give us much information. They were from the 31st Infantry, and had gotten themselves cut off from the main force. They were trying to get back to their unit when they were hit from behind by the Japanese.

It was near five o'clock before I could report to the commander. He wanted to know about the new troops and to decide if anything could be done to improve our situation.

A burial detail was formed and placed under the control of Sergeant Saunders. He was to go out in front of our position and retrieve the bodies of those who were killed trying to get in earlier. This would require exposing himself to the Japs, if any were still out that way. Nonetheless, it must be done. While this chore was going on, I would take a detail and find a suitable location for burial as the bodies were brought in. I was grateful for the darkness that had set in. At least I wouldn't have to look at those who had found their final resting place in a godforsaken jungle ten thousand miles away from home, where not even our own commanding generals knew they had been killed.

My detail began digging shallow graves to receive the dead as they came in, while other men cut back the undergrowth and cleared a spot some two hundred yards to the rear of our closest troop emplacement. It was my feeling we should make the place larger as these wouldn't be the last to be buried here. So, without explaining why, I just asked the men to clear back a little farther. As we cleared back some thirty to forty feet farther than Saunders had requested, the soldiers looked at me. I knew they understood what I was thinking. No words were spoken; we just understood that if we were to occupy this spot, we would want it clean. As the digging went on, the stones were piled to the side to be used as markers for the men who would be listed as "missing in action" by our commanders. There was no way death could be reported to Corregidor. We didn't even have communication with the units on either side of us. We would have the only record.

The stench of death was driving us mad. The sight of the dead soldiers, some of whom we had known and fought with, lying out in the sun bloating, certainly wasn't conducive to high morale. And high morale sure as hell would be needed before this thing was finished.

My part of the burial detail was finished and I reported to Lieutenant Bridges. I.D. tags were to be brought in to him by Saunders.

"Skipper, have we any word from higher command of the current situation?" I asked.

"No," he said. "There hasn't been a peep out of our runners since they left this morning and all I can get on that radio is static."

"Then you think we are cut off?"

"That's all I can assume at this time, but it is my decision to hold this position until our forces counterattack and we will again join our major command, or until I receive orders to withdraw." He then asked what our strength was since the new bunch came in.

I said, "I don't have the exact strength, but I believe it to be 300 or 325."

We had plenty of ammunition for at least two days at the rate we had been using it. Food was our biggest problem. All we had left was cream of wheat and some condensed milk, maybe some hardtack. We had adequate water in the stream, and plenty of chlorine tablets for purification.

The provisional battalion had formed along a slight ridge, with a slow dropoff to the front and a very sharp dropoff on the northern end of the line down to the stream where we got our water. On the southern end of the line, some three hundred yards away, the ridge seemed to disappear, and was replaced by a low flat table, spreading out to the front and to the south.

The Japanese could get in at the south end much easier than at the front or by the north. If that part of our line had in fact fallen, we sure as hell were open for an attack from that direction. It seemed reasonable to believe that American forces on our west had retreated. Otherwise why would those troops have been cut off and forced in this direction? We had to draw our line a little closer and extend the southern line around into an inverted "C." That way we could guard against the Japs getting in back of us by way of that flat strip. The woods could be full of Japs and we wouldn't know it until they hit us. Then it would be too late.

With that in mind as many people as we could find were moved to our south end, and dug in facing directly south. This gave them a field of fire that covered not only the south but also the east.

We had seven thirty-caliber machine guns, one anti-aircraft artillery weapon, and some two hundred rifles placed in an invereted "C" guarding three sides of our area. The mess tent was located almost in the center of the "C" and the lister bags of water were in the area of the mess tent.

There were a number of men with wounds who could not be left in the forward trenches. They had been withdrawn to the rear of the half-circle and had dug in facing the east. Even though most of them could not be counted on to defend our position, they would be able to defend themselves better and would alert us of anything to the back of us. This posture was complete by 2200 hours on April 7, 1942.

I then went to the mess area and was met by Sergeant Miller. As we sat down, he said, "Sergeant, we have less than a thousand pounds of rice, a dozen cases of condensed milk, some canned salmon, about one hundred cans of corned beef hash, and enough hardtack for three days for three hundred men. After that, something will have to be done."

"Miller, I don't know if we will get out of here in three days or if we will get help. If I were you I would cut the rations even shorter. Try to make it last for five days. We will be out of ammunition by then anyway if the Japs strike."

Most of our men had in their possession a number of cans of "canned heat"—alcohol mixed with wax and canned for issue to soldiers in the field to cook with. When this can of wax was lit, water could be boiled for coffee or tea. If our troops could get coffee from Miller, they could use their own water and make coffee; the light was so minimal, they could not be observed from any distance.

It was my job once more to report the grim facts to the commander. Around midnight I went to his tent. I had counted our injured and placed them in categories of no longer effective, just barely effective (if his life depended on it), able to defend or assist another soldier with ammunition, and fully able for combat.

At this point the subject was brought up of letting the wounded attempt to break out. It was agreed that any who were able and desired could leave in order to find medical attention. If they got through they should report our position and status to any command in the rear. They would be given rifle ammunition and a small amount of food and allowed to leave the area. Since they were already at the rear of the line in the morning, there would be no difficulty in contacting them individually and telling them they could try and get out.

For the next two hours, each man was cautioned against bunching up and advised to travel alone or no more than two together. Each must be sure he had a canteen of water, keep off the main roads, use all the natural cover possible, and above all, keep the noise to a minimum. Sometime around three o'clock on the morning of April 8, this bunch of men started their journey for medical aid. Hopefully, someone would get through and alert the command as to where we were and have them instruct us in what we were to do, or better still, send a relief column and get us out of there.

When these men had cleared the area, I realized how tired I was. I had to get some rest, and soon, or it wouldn't make any difference, at least for me, if the Japs attacked or not. I slept until around seven o'clock, when I was awakened by the complete silence. Nothing could be heard, no gunfire, no rifle fire, no talking by men—just eerie silence. It had been some time since I had experienced this. I sure as hell couldn't sleep.

Arising from the short sleep, I felt rested but in need of a shave, which I knew I couldn't get. I walked in the direction of the place where the stream was dammed. At least I could wash up a bit, get the sleep out of my eyes, and walk the stiffness out of my joints. The sun was rising over the bay. I walked farther down the hill away from the company, where there was an opening in the jungle. I could see far out across the bay toward Manila and to the south, over near Lagung-de-bay, a small village south of Manila where I used to go on weekend passes. Gazing farther to the south I could make out the shoreline all the way down near Fort Frank. Right at the end of the mountain range on the southern end of Luzon, smoke was hanging low over the water—probably from the heavy artillery guns on Corregidor. They fired until the early morning hours. This morning was quiet, and the crews were resting. The east end of Corregidor was plain now, as the sun broke through the gun smoke and shone down on Monkey Point, at the east end of Milinta Hill. God, how I wished I were back on that "rock." With things the way they were here, I couldn't see how we could pull this off without getting captured. Help had to come. There wasn't any other way.

The ominous quiet caused me to move back to the edge of the jungle. I felt as if someone might be observing me from above, or could observe me from out there across the bay. Backing in farther, I was looking out under the limbs of the trees. The sky was clear of clouds, except for the low-hanging smoke of the battle of yesterday. Looking across the flat land at the bay, the water looked like glass—not a wave, not a ripple. Nothing broke the stillness. Not even the fishing boats I remembered from before the war were out. It was if all living things were waiting for something to happen.

Off to the east, I could make out that old rust-colored ship, with its bow protruding above the water. I wondered when it was sunk. I could recall stories of how it was sunk when Admiral Dewey brought his fleet here early in the century, around 1900. Another war, another time. It served as a monument to what was. I wondered what we would leave to remind others that here also a battle was fought for some kind of principle that was decided upon by our generation of politicians. When it was all over, quite possibly the only thing left would be a rusty gun, a sunken ship, or maybe someone would erect a stone monument that would tell others that here on this ground American soldiers fought and died.

As I sat under the protection of the limbs of the tree, I had the first chance I had in a number of weeks to think of where I was and what the hell had been going on. This was the first time I had thought of home in longer than I liked to remember. These thoughts, during such a precarious time, were wrong and I knew it, but nonetheless, my mind drifted on. Would I survive this ordeal? I wondered how anyone would ever know what happened to me if I should be killed here in this godforsaken place. If one of those soldiers didn't get through, I doubted if anyone would even know who was here. More than likely those on Corregidor didn't even know we were here. Hell, it was a wonder they hadn't opened up on this area with those long-range artillery pieces. If the Japanese showed up in any strength and the American forces didn't know we were here, they might decide their target was here. That thought sent chills up my back.

With that I took my notebook from my pocket and began scribbling the things on my mind, thinking that if I didn't survive, maybe someone would find my body and forward these notes to my mother. If this should be the case, the notes would get in her hand, and at least someone would know where I was killed. Possibly that would be of some solace to her. Suddenly it became very important that someone knew what the hell was going on here.

After two or three pages were finished, in which I explained our position, how many men were boxed in, and the hopelessness I felt, I also decided to write that I didn't want my parents to feel any guilt over allowing me to enlist in the army. It took me six months to convince them that they should

50

allow me to enlist as a minor, get away from the Ozark hills, and start my own life. I thought the army offered me that opportunity. I wrote that the reason for my being here was my own choice and that no one should feel any guilt. I was sure that if relief wasn't received very soon, the end was at hand one way or another. Either I would be killed or captured by the Japanese, and in either case, my future looked very bleak.

I was brought back to reality by the squawking of a tropical bird. It seemed as if it too had been taking time off from the events of the past few months. There were other noises now, an artillery gun firing off to the south toward Marvelious. It sounded like Jap artillery. But they shouldn't be that far south. If so, our line had broken somewhere.

I sat listening to the exchanges of artillery from both sides for a few minutes, and I suddenly realized we were at least three miles in back of the fighting—and not behind our lines! We were behind the Japs. Those bastards had passed on both sides of us during the night, and we were an island in the middle of hell.

Leaping to my feet, I ran as fast as I could to the command post. As I was running, I heard the rifles firing somewhere out in front of our position, and I could hear our people returning the fire. I didn't have time to contemplate what had happened to the other sections for the front lines. I would have my hands full here. Before arriving at the command post, I could hear the tempo of rifle fire picking up from the northeast end of our line, and one of our riflemen was answering them.

The command post had sand bags. They were about four feet high and the soil had been dug out from the floor until we had a good protective parapet around us. By sitting or squatting one could work knowing the rifle fire would not get through. When I walked inside the tent, Bridges had the situation map spread out on a table and was pointing to this spot as he explained it to Barclay.

"Has there been any word from higher command, Lieutenant?" I asked. Bridges turned and from the grim look on his face, I knew his answer. Barclay shook his head. Bridges just pointed to a spot on the map.

"From the sound of the Jap artillery, we are caught here in a pocket, and that rifle fire we hear out there is troops they have left behind to more or less mop up. There is no way of knowing what their strength is, but we will have to assume they will attack in force at any time. They have gradually picked up their firing for the last half hour.

"Barclay, you get over to the southwest end of our position and take charge there. Make sure every round of ammo we can get our hands on is in the trenches with those men. Sergeant, you take charge on this end near the gun. Be sure you have your gun crew near the weapon. As for me, I will take personal charge of the two machine guns and rifles along the stream. Be sure both of you have a runner appointed who understands who is in charge of whom, and where we are. Send those names to me as soon as you are in position. Each of you will act on your own if and when the bastards decide to take us over."

51

I detected a certain finality in Bridges' last statement. "That is it. Get your men." Glancing over his shoulder, he motioned, "Things are getting hot out there." Lifting the flap from the tent, he was gone. I looked over at Barclay, and as I met his eyes I could see he knew that this was our only chance—fight like hell and probably be killed, or try to get out of here and be killed. A losing situation in any case. We left without saying anything.

As I left the tent on the run, all hell broke loose. The machine guns in back of me opened up, and at the same time a mortar round fell some fifty yards to the front of me. Shrapnel, dirt, and smoke was everywhere, but I continued to crawl and run on all fours toward the center of the line, where I was ordered to be.

I dove into the trench near the center of the company position and started moving among our troops until I located the men who would be my crew on the three-inch anti-aircraft gun. Within minutes the mortars were going off all around us, and any further planning had to be delayed. All we could do was keep down and observe the Japanese activity as best as we could.

Suddenly the mortars ceased and only rifle fire was coming in. I peeked over the top of the trench and could see we were under a general assault by the Japanese infantry. They were charging all along the front, from the machine guns in front of me as well as to my left flank where Barclay was in command. There was no need for commands. All riflemen were firing as fast as they could. Machine guns were blazing away at anything moving in front of them.

Looking to the south of me I could see the little sons-of-bitches charging in hordes toward our flank. They were being met with blistering fire from all quarters, including the rifles in the center. Right in the center, they started pouring out of the undergrowth of the jungle and into our position. Almost before we could change the direction of fire the bastards were within fifteen yards of our trenches and foxholes, screaming at the top of their lungs that god-awful "Bonzi! Bonzi!" Some had jumped into the trenches with knives and bayonets. All we could do was defend our lives with anything at hand.

This charge lasted no more than ten minutes, and as suddenly as it all began, it was over. Those who weren't wounded or killed started backing away and melting back into the jungle undergrowth.

Chapter 8

Lest one get the impression there were a lot of heroics, I can assure you, this wasn't heroics, nor were there any cases of extraordinary bravery. Most of us would not have been there at all if there had been any other place we could go, or if there had been any other way. We were boxed in a corner, with no place to hide and no place to run. We had to fight in order to stay alive and to keep those fanatic bastards from killing or capturing us. Each of us had long since conceded that we were not fighting to maintain any sort of military posture or strategy. Instead, we were doing the only thing we could—just keeping alive. At the same time we were praying that our commanders would find some way to get us out of there, or that there would be a relief column.

When there was a lull in the incoming fire, I listened for the sounds of battle elsewhere in Bataan, and as always, the artillery guns were farther away. I heard the explosions off in the distance, and it wasn't as clear as it was the last time I had listened. It appeared our forces were retreating farther south and that feeling of being deserted, being left behind to fend for ourselves returned. I knew there wasn't any hope. We were trapped.

As I looked at the determined faces of the men and watched them dig even deeper, it was evident that they also were listening to the distant rumbling of te artillery and were fully aware that there wasn't any hope of a relief column. We were as wild animals, trapped. These weren't heroes. These were scared men, desperate in the knowledge of there being no help on the way, but with full knowledge that to stop the fight meant sure death. We must fight on because to stop was to stop living. My personal feelings were the same. I was cornered, and I was mad at both our commanders and the Japanese. By God, if I must die, there would be others who would not live.

There wasn't time for further contemplation of my fate. The battle was raging once again, with the Japanese trying to overrun our position at all cost. Each time they charged, they were driven back, but each time some of our people were lost. Our ranks were slowly but surely being destroyed, yet we remained in place.

By nightfall things were heating up again. I heard rifle fire on each of our flanks, and even with all this noise, I heard their rifles.

The mortars began again to rain their hell down on us. Those bastards kept low in foxholes with their mortars, and dropped rounds on us any time they wanted. All they had to do was point the damn thing where each of our positions were.

There were only yards between us and the Japs. In some instances it was feet. At times the activities of the Japs could be heard as plainly as our own. In spite of this close proximity, it wasn't the Japs in their foxholes that scared me. It was the mortars. Sometimes I imagined those mortars having eyes in their nose cone, and up there, they were searching out my back.

Not being able to see but a few yards out made all of us edgy. I was so damned scared I could hardly think. Just when I was getting ready for some rest, another round exploded very close to me. It shook the hell out of me and some loose dirt fell into the hole. I picked up a clod and hurled it from the hole as one would a grenade. Someone shot at the noise.

If Bridges, our commander, could have known beforehand that things were going to turn out this way, he would have acted differently. He would have pulled us out of this place, even at the risk of court-martial. It was too late for speculation. There wasn't anything to be gained by thinking of what might have been. It was far too late for that. Our fate would be determined right here. Either we would be captured or killed, and at the moment, neither of those likely events were very appealing. If they would only lift the mortar fire for awhile. Another round exploded very close by. It shook the dirt loose on the side of the foxhole. I picked up a dirt clod just to have something to do and tossed it from the hole. Then I started digging deeper and prayed that the next one wouldn't find me.

We took shelling after shelling and at the same time their infantry kept us pinned down so close we couldn't even return their fire. All we could do was keep our heads below ground level and dig even deeper.

The only return fire from us was one of our machine guns up at the northern end of our position. That fellow managed to keep firing all during this barrage. The mortars, along with an occasional round by field artillery, kept coming. Still that fellow just chattered away with his machine gun. As I listened closely to that chatter, it seemed to relieve some of the fears inside me. At least someone was able to keep some pressure on those bastards. Late in the afternoon the mortar fire and the artillery stopped. Only the rifle fire continued. Staying low in the foxhole, waiting to make sure the artillery had stopped before venturing out, I listened for any sounds of an all-out attack. I slipped from the hole that had served me so well and by keeping to the side of the hill, I could walk about without fear of being hit by rifle fire. God, I needed to get the kinks out. I wondered how long I had been cramped down in that foxhole. I felt like I had sat in one position for a week.

Soon all was quiet. The rifles ceased firing. There weren't any mortars going off. They had broken off the attack for reasons of their own. We sure as hell hadn't been able to do anything that would make them break off. However, it was quiet. God, what a welcome event. But even with the mortars quiet, I could still hear them inside my head.

Before it was totally dark, Bridges asked me to check our position. "Find out how many people we have lost. Also, we need to know how many are seriously injured," he ordered.

I found the medic, the only one we had. He was an enlisted medical corpsman from the navy, and was frantically patching up as many as he could. He was giving first aid where needed, but with his limited medical supplies he wasn't able to give anywhere near the medical attention the men needed. Nonetheless, he was doing his best. He had formed a burial detail and they were carrying our dead back down the hill toward the area designated as the cemetery. Those who were wounded but could still defend themselves had been given first aid and returned to their trench or foxhole. The men took from the dead their rifles, ammunition, and any other items that might be useful in keeping them alive. They stored this equipment inside their own positions. The check of our position was complete, and I reported our current strength to the commander. He shook his head as I related all my information to him; then he made some notes in a book and turned away.

Darkness fell very fast. At first I felt some security in the dark, but the stillness was almost as bad as the noise was that afternoon. Nobody was talking and the Japanese were as quiet as we were.

I started thinking. I was secure in the thought that they couldn't see me and I would be able to move about. Then, as time passed, I started thinking about the possibility of an attack. With it being so goddamn dark, we wouldn't be able to see them. Hell, they could be right inside our trench before we knew they were attacking. Damn, I hoped they didn't decide to attack. I felt that fear returning. I must move about. With that, I walked back down the hill away from the line. Some of the fears were calmed and the security of darkness returned.

I found a good hole, one big enough that I could lie down in the bottom. I was so tired. I had to get some rest. I couldn't remember when I last slept. All the events of the day passed through my mind as I dozed off. When I awakened I saw some light. Raising up in the foxhole, I saw the moon had broken through the clouds and the smoke. I supposed the smoke was from the guns that had been firing almost continuously for the past twenty-four hours, but I couldn't tell where the clouds stopped and the smoke began. Somehow this fascinated me.

Climbing from the foxhole, I saw for some distance out front. My first thought was to get the hell down. Those bastards would see me and open up. The quiet was so good, I sure as hell didn't want to be the one who broke it up, so I moved farther down the hill and out of sight from the Japanese positions. Finding a place that offered some protection, I watched the clouds and smoke float around. Our people had some rest, but I knew they were, like me, moving zombies. What the hell could we do? That question went unanswered. There wasn't a goddamn thing we could do but fight if they decided to charge. At least with the moon out we would be able to see them before they were in our trenches. Finding a position where I could observe without being observed, I lay back and waited and listened.

Down south toward Marvelious, I heard the artillery guns in action. Not a lot, just enough to let us know that the war was going on. They seemed farther away, even farther then that afternoon. I was sure they were Japanese artillery pieces, probably firing blindly at Corregidor or some other fortresses in Manila Bay.

Once again I dozed off for a time, but was awakened by the sound of the giant coast artillery guns over the "Rock." First I heard the loud explosion of the gun across the bay, then that whistling sound of the projectile as it passed overhead, then the loud explosion of the round as it hit its target. God, what a reassuring sound! Just to know that those giants were yet intact and giving those bastards hell was something. Even though I was sure we were cut off with little hope of getting back to the beach where we might be able to swim over to Corregidor, the sound of those heavy artillery pieces from Corregidor certainly was reassuring.

It was nearly midnight, April 8. The guns on Corregidor had been going steadily for hours. The target, however, was to the south of us. The Japanese here remained silent—no mortars, no rifles, nothing. I hadn't been able to get much sleep but at times had been able to doze off. I was awakened by a voice coming from a loudspeaker somewhere out front and to my left. First there was some music, then someone broke in on the music and started talking in a rather personal way to anyone who might be listening. In English the voice told us how the rest of Bataan had already surrendered or had been captured, that we "might as well do likewise and stop fighting." The speaker said, "It is useless to resist. You will all die for nothing if you continue, but if you surrender you will be treated well and given hot food."

The word was passed to stand by for another attack. Most of us had heard this time and time again, and understood that this was nothing more than confirmation that we have hurt the bastards worse than they would like. To surrender would only serve the Japanese cause on Bataan. Most of us ignored the suggestion and listened to the music during the lull in the talking.

This continued for the next two hours—music for a while, then a personal plea for us to surrender before we were all killed. Then one of the soldiers down near the southern end apparently spotted the loudspeaker that had been hoisted into a tree, and he opened up with his machine gun on the speaker, blowing the thing to bits. As his firing stopped, I could hear the pieces as they fell to the ground. Our gunner was spotted by the Japanese. One of their machine guns started firing in the direction of our pillbox, then another, then the rifles. Soon the whole line was ablaze, tracers going everywhere. The fire was so intense, nobody could get an inch above the ground. All we could do was keep our heads low and pray they didn't decide to charge our position. If I could have gotten ahold of that son-of-a-bitch who started this shit, I would have personally shot the bastard. For Christ sake, that speaker sure as hell wasn't that bad.

We were so goddamned tired we could hardly keep awake, and that bastard had to start something. We sure as hell couldn't do anything, and as far as I could see the Japanese were just making a hell of a lot of noise. Nobody dared raise his head up in this mess. The rifle fire started to ebb a bit, then after a short time stopped altogether. Still no one wanted to raise up or let himself be seen in the moonlight. The word was passed: "Just keep your head down."

Near daylight another check of our positions had to be made. I was ordered to check our total effectiveness: the number of men, the supply of ammunition on hand in the trenches and foxholes, and water availability.

Our original numbers since coming to the area had been reduced to about half. Some had left trying to get back to our lines, while others had been killed and were buried back down the hill. Many had been wounded, but were still trying to defend themselves, refusing to leave. Down on the south end of our position, Barclay had been killed and was replaced by Miller, the mess sergeant. There wasn't enough food to warrant a mess sergeant. With all this information I started back toward the command post. Goddamn, what a mess. This bunch had had hell beat out of them. Still, they knew there wasn't any place for them to go. All we could do was protect ourselves if and when the Japs came our way. There was no choice. I noticed some of the men with severe wounds were off the line and sitting farther back in the trees. They had the protection of the hill. When the commander was told of the numbers wounded, it was decided that anyone who desired could leave before daylight and make an effort to find some medical unit. When I relayed this to them, surprisingly, only a few left. Most felt they couldn't make it back to safety and were willing to let this war be decided for them right here. Either our commanders would get a relief column in, or the Japanese would bypass this group, or we would be taken prisoner.

At daylight the Japanese made another attempt at overrunning us and once again they were repulsed. This was more than an attack; it was intended to see how effective their tactics with the speaker had been. From what they saw, we were still willing to fight. If that's what those heathen bastards wanted, then a fight they would get. It looked as if every weapon on the front opened up at the same time. They pulled back once again and the place was quiet.

At the south end, the Japs started pouring out of the jungle. As we turned our attention to that direction, they hit us directly in front. Within minutes, the entire front was ablaze again, and this time I saw everything happening. We couldn't keep down. There were too many of them. They poured out of the jungle, and we had to fire everything at them or be overcome. For Christ sake, I had never seen so many men in such a small area! They seemed to be everywhere. They were crawling on their bellies and charging at us. The only advantage we had was the fact that their machine guns were firing over their heads and this forced them down where they couldn't see how close they were to us. We were able to stop them before they could get into our holes. At last, the charge stopped. Those who could, retreated back into the underbrush out of sight and out of range.

While we were not under fire, a count of our losses was taken. We hadn't suffered many losses and very little damage had been done, primarily because we had the advantage of being in foxholes and trenches. The rifle fire passed overhead or fell useless in front of us in the dirt. Only when Japs came real close did we have to expose ourselves, and then just long enough to take care of them. Nonetheless, our ranks were much thinner than when this siege first started.

Sometime around 0630 hours on the morning of April 9, the mortars started. They knew our position as well as we did, and for the most part, we knew theirs. We knew where each and every one of those mortars were and how accurate they were. Most of their guns were about two hundred yards out and could hit us at any point. At first there were only occasional rounds of mortar fire. It gradually became more intense, until I couldn't tell how many mortars were firing. They didn't seem to have any certain target, but just fired at random. The shells fell into our position all along the line.

At about 0700 hours the mortars stopped. There wasn't a sound anywhere. Total quiet again descended upon us. I heard the command as it was passed, "Make ready for an all-out attack." This came from the command post. Everyone was tense. We knew that it was only a matter of minutes until the hordes came out of that jungle, screaming and running. Without warning, an artillery shell exploded close by. I heard someone scream and knew he had been hit. My head was down and I couldn't tell where the shell hit, but from the sound of that explosion, the bastards were shelling us with 105mm guns. From the sound of the explosion and the way it came down on us, I suspected howitzers. They had a very high angle of fire and were much like mortars except they were much heavier and did more damage. That old fear returned and I got lower to the ground. I felt completely helpless and got as close as possible to the front of the hole. Good God, why was I trying to get to the front? If that thing hit my hole, it wouldn't make any difference. Still I dug in and tried to get my head farther down. Another shell exploded very close by. My head rang from the concussion and rocks and steel came flying through the air. A large piece of shrapnel hit the edge of my foxhole and I smelled the burning debris around the top of the hole. Damn, I wished I could get lower. As I went forward, face down in the dirt, with the stars shooting in my eyes from the blast, I grabbed my head with both hands and tried to block out the noise from the exploding shells. Nothing kept that noise away. The more I held my hands over my ears, the louder the explosion seemed.

The barrage lifted for short periods, then started all over again. Each time they stopped, I feared the infantry would come charging at us. During one of the lulls I heard our artillery from Corregidor. It seemed like a million miles away, but there was no mistaking it. It was our people firing. God, I hoped they spotted this Jap artillery and zeroed in on it.

I wondered what the American observers over on the "Rock" were thinking about the artillery up this way, especially if they didn't know we were here. If that was the case, they might think the Japanese were firing on their own troops, or they might decide there were some troops here and open fire on the artillery pieces. At the same time there was a possibility that the commander over there would send a relief column in for us. Somehow, I still had faith that our command would get out. It was very small, but maybe. . . .

My thoughts ran wild with the idea and for just a moment I had a little hope.

I began to move toward the sandbagged anti-aircraft gun. It was about two hundred feet up toward the northern end of the line. My mind was made up as to what I intended to do.

Inside the gun pit were about three hundred rounds of special ammunition. It had been manufactured for use in defense against aircraft, and had been used back during World War I against aircraft that had fabric material on the fuselage and wings. In the nose of the projectile was some 250 small pellets, and there was a fuse in the nose that had to be set with the fuse cutter on the gun. There was a few seconds' delay after the shell was fired until the fuse caused the shell to explode. Then the high explosives would shoot these pellets out from the nose of the shell, much like a fan. Presumably these would cover a wide area and damage the fuselage or the engines, forcing the plane down or otherwise rendering the craft useless.

I had received instruction on the ammunition, particularly about this fanning action when the shell exploded. I figured that if this was effective against planes, it should be equally effective against ground troops, providing that the gun would fire from a flat trajectory position. I was aware that there was a minimum of five men required to fire the weapon on airplanes. But again, I figured that since I was not going to fire at planes, but at ground level, we should be able to operate the gun with three men. The elevation would remain essentially constant while firing on ground troops. Therefore, the only requirement would be to move the gun barrel from left to right. If this could be done at flat trajectory, and with this type of ammunition, I was sure we would get in some licks against the bastards that they sure as hell weren't expecting.

As I made my way along the line toward the gun pit, I picked up my crew. From all I knew about these two men, they were the only people who were crazy enough to try this harebrained scheme. As we approached the gun we met Bridges, and I explained our intentions to him.

As we entered the parapet we saw that some changes would have to be made. The gun was too high. The rear outriggers would have to be lowered. This could be done by digging out some of the dirt, lowering the platform from the rear. With our trenching tools we started digging. When this was completed, the next thing was to take some of the sandbags down from the front of the parapet. They had been originally set up as an anti-aircraft measure; we had tried to build up as high as we could for protection against falling bombs or incoming artillery. Now we needed low-angle firing. The barrel had to have room to come down almost to a flat trajectory. The sandbags were taken from the top and placed on the front of the steel platform of the gun. This made the front wall very thick and offered very good protection from rifle fire. We then lowered the barrel and traversed from side to side and at the same time aimed along the barrel judging how high the shell would travel when fired. At the same time we checked our field of fire, making sure that we were not going to explode a projectile over our own people.

59

Everything seemed to be in order. There was about a six-inch clearance over the sandbags and the barrel would move in almost any direction.

I walked to the rear of the weapon, opened the breech, then closed it. This was more to relieve the tension than anything else. I pulled the lanyard out toward the rear. It was flexible. The knot on the heavy cord seemed tight. All along the line firing was heavy. I walked over and traversed the barrel from side to side. Near the entrance was a box of ammunition, still unopened. I took a few steps in that direction as Mullins stepped in. He saw the closed case the same time I had and was opening it. That machine gun out there, I wished that bastard would stop. He had been chattering away since we started working. He was far enough away that he didn't do any damage, but he was always there. As I moved about, I bent over and kept low. I moved the gun barrel around to that direction. I fully intended to blast the hell out of that son-of-a-bitch with the first round. I flexed my hands as I stepped back to the front of the gun. The sweat in my palms felt cold, and I had to wipe them on the legs of my pants. Where in the hell was that gunner's glove? I knew we had one when we first brought the gun in. Goddamn, I remembered the first time I tried to fire one of these weapons, how nervous I was. Remembering that fear, I felt the sweat running down inside of my clothing. Still that son-of-a-bitch chattered away with the light machine gun. I located the leather gunner's glove under some sandbags that weren't used and I placed it over the breach of the weapon.

Bridges entered the parapet. The chin strap on his helmet was loose and hanging down on his shoulder, and his helmet was at a rakish angle on his head. He didn't look scared, just angry. A mortar round exploded somewhere down the way and he ducked, more from reflex than from fear. Turning to me, he said, "Hold up on your fire until you are sure they are ready to charge or are into their charge. Your judgment is as good as mine in that regard, but again, hold your fire. We are short on ammunition for this weapon and, as you know, our riflemen are also critically short on ammunition."

The firing had slowed at the south end of Bataan. Only sporadic artillery fire could be heard. Also, the giant guns over on the "rock" were not firing. There was an eerie quiet. Nothing was happening. Even that bastard on the machine gun had stopped. There was a knot in the pit of my stomach.

As I sat down on one of the outriggers, I saw an old communications line strung between two trees. It swayed in the air. The line would get very straight, then sway almost to the ground. The earth started shaking. What the hell? There wasn't any artillery fire and there wasn't any wind. As far as I could see there wasn't any Japanese activity that would cause anything like this. Someone yelled, "An earthquake!" Never having experienced anything like this, I had no idea what was happening. I rolled off the outrigger onto the ground and just rode the thing out. After what seemed like an eternity, it was over. I was no worse for the activity, just mentally shaken. "What strange omen is this?" I wondered.

During the next half-hour the voices of the Japanese could be heard.

They also seemed to be confused. With all this confusion, there wasn't any rifle fire and all over Bataan and Corregidor the guns were silent.

Near 1200 hours, they started their move. First, they opened up with their 105mm guns. It wasn't as heavy as we had before. Still, this was a prelude to something bigger. I got down inside the gun pit and hoped none of the shells found the mark. I had a better chance than most. The gun hadn't been fired since we brought it in. In all probability, the Japs didn't know we had it, so if a shell landed inside the pit it would be just a random shot.

The ground shook from the explosions. It wouldn't be possible to tell if we had another quake or not. The whole area was shaking from artillery. Then, as suddenlty as it started, the shelling stopped. I had seen this before. The Japs would charge at any moment. It was mid-day and the sun was beating down on us. Not a cloud anywhere, just the smoke from the exploded artillery. I had an acid taste in my mouth, either from the powder smoke or from the thought of what was about to happen. Damn, my mouth was dry. I pulled the canteen from the pouch as the first of the charge emerged from the edge of the jungle just out front and slightly to our left. At first there was only one or two. Then, as if from nowhere, they seemed to be all over the place, screaming, holding their rifles high, and charging in our direction.

Stepping up to the weapon, we laid a shell into the breech and fired point blank into the charge with a two-second fuse, the shortest time on the fuse cutter. The ammunition was very old and some of the stuff exploded almost as soon as it left the end of the gun barrel. The pit was full of smoke and the explosion was so close that no sooner did I hear the gun fire than the shell exploded. It was difficult for me to tell who was taking the worst beating, the Japs or us. Still we continued to fire.

Livingston was handling the ammunition. Mullins continued to move the gun from side to side, wherever he saw the charge coming in. Hell, I couldn't see anything. All I knew was that the round was laid into my hand and my gloved hand smashed the shell forward. Where the round went was up to Mullins. My actions were totally mechanical. I pulled the lanyard, heard the breech explode, felt the flame burn my face from the fire coming from the end of the barrel, and when I saw another round being laid in the breech, drove it home, then pulled the lanyard once more. My world was very small. The mechanics of the weapon had me in its grip. I was in a trance, and it wouldn't let me go. Mullins was the only person who knew if we were hitting anything or if we were just making a hell of a lot of noise.

As I reached to push another round into the breech, my face and Livingston's were almost together. As I looked at him I wondered if the same fear that I saw in his eyes was showing in mine. I slammed the shell forward and felt the projectile seat into the barrel. The breechblock knocked my hand free of the weapon as once again I snapped the lanyard as hard as I could. I heard the explosion and felt the fire from the end of the barrel. Livingston's face was blocked out of my mind.

The thought of being overrun passed through my mind for just a second, but I knew my actions were no longer under my control. I was like a zombie

61

in action. First there was fear, then nothing, no feeling at all. There wasn't time for feelings or fear. Another round was in place. I didn't even look, but acted automatically.

An eternity seemed to pass and still we kept firing. We had only three hundred or so rounds of ammunition. We couldn't have been firing very long, but God! It seemed like forever. There wasn't any chance it would stop. My right arm seemed like it had been burned. Still another round was ready to be loaded. I didn't dare turn my head to see if we had any ammunition left. It must be about gone. We had been firing as fast as possible.

There it was, the last round. I chanced a look in Livingston's direction. He had the last projectile in his hand. The nose was in the breech and with my gloved hand I slammed it forward. Livingston was reaching for his rifle with the bayonet fixed. The weapon swept left and the round was on its way. As the gun exploded, it came back into its recoil and stuck in that position. The spent round did not eject. The weapon was frozen at the rear recoil position, forever silent. It was as if the gun also knew the battle was over.

Stepping away from the weapon, I reached for my rifle. Livingston and Mullins were leaving the pit through the entranceway. The ringing in my ears was unbearable. I was standing alone, rifle in hand, bayonet fixed with the whole world collapsing around me.

As I stepped toward the exit port behind Livingston and Mullins, there was a blinding flash and explosion and I slipped into a state of unconsciousness. When I came to, I was in complete darkness and total silence. Nothing, just darkness. In the unbearable heat I was having difficulty breathing. I could move my hands and feet. My arms felt all right. At this point I started feeling around and at the same time wondering where I was. There was tin over my head. Also, there was a large piece of timber over my back, which was keeping me from being able to sit up. I was covered by dirt and tin. I tried, but I couldn't get up because of the timber. I wasn't pressing against me, but it was holding me down. It lodged across the area and acted as a protection from the dirt. The timber crossed over my head and kept the sandbags from covering me, leaving enough room for an air pocket. But it had me trapped in a very uncomfortable position, with my head bent down almost between my knees. The air was stifling and I had to find a way out of here or I would die. Frantically digging, my hand felt my rifle, and I remembered the bayonet. Taking this off, I dug much more effectively and in only a short time I broke through to the outside. I drank in the fresh air.

As soon as I made the hole large enough, I stood and I saw that we had taken a direct hit from an artillery shell. I had caved in the sandbags, and this protected me from being hit by flying shrapnel. All I suffered from was the concussion. That is what knocked me unconscious. Just outside the pit were the torn bodies of Livingston and Mullins, only a few feet from the entrance. There was no movement, no voices, not even any rifle fire.

I had such a damned headache; I wondered where everybody was. Hell, there wasn't even a Jap. I sure as hell didn't aim to look out front for fear of what I'd see. I did glance to the south. Good God! What a mess! There wasn't anything worse than the sight of a battleground after the battle. I didn't know what had happened, but I had to get out of his mess.

I extracted myself from the tin and debris, made sure I had my canteen, then started toward the command post. Nothing was there. I walked toward where we had dammed up the little stream. I'd need water. On the way down the hill, I found an automatic rifle and two clips of ammunition. Exchanging my rifle for this one I proceeded down to the water hole and filled my canteen. Then I remembered I had no chlorine tablets. Nonetheless, I had to have water, potable or not.

The sun had long since dropped behind Marvelious mountain, but I still walked—anything to get away. I would try to reach the bay. I had no idea why I wanted to walk back toward Manila Bay. I suppose because that was the only place where I felt I could find someone I knew. Suddenly, from someplace, I felt I had been hit in my left knee. There was a very sharp pain and as my weight shifted away from the pain, I fell. Moving until I got into a sitting position, I found that I had been hit by a rifle shot from somewhere. I didn't even hear a shot, so this was more than likely a stray bullet and was more by accident than by design. Nonetheless, I had been shot and there wasn't anything I could do about the bullet. I'd have to walk with the thing in my knee until I found someone to remove it. I sat until almost dark. Then, taking the automatic rifle and using it as a crutch, I started looking for a safe place to stay for the night. Far off to the south were some artillery pieces firing. I listened closely and heard them as they exploded over on Corregidor. I continued to drag forward toward what I believed to be the direction of the field hospital. I had to find a place to lie down and sleep. I needed rest and the pain in my knee was killing me. If I slept, maybe things would look better in the morning. Right now it looked grim. At least there wasn't any fighting near me. It had been so long since it had been this quiet, I didn't know if I would be able to sleep or not. The ringing in my head had slackened, but I still heard the noises of battle as I traveled ever deeper into the jungle. At last I could go no farther and I fell, almost totally exhausted, to the ground.

I was so goddamned hungry I could eat anything, but there wasn't anything to be had. All I could do was lie down for the night. Damn, I wished I had looked closer around the area for something to eat. Even iron rations would be welcome. But as that thought ran through my mind, I recalled the sight when I got out from under that tin debris. I couldn't bear the sight of what had happened. All I wanted then was to get the hell away from there. The torn bodies of Livingston and Mullins were clear in my mind's eye. I wondered if anyone got away. But how could they outrun the little bastards? Maybe some of them got the opportunity to surrender. I wondered. Hell, I didn't know.

I didn't have the slightest idea what I was supposed to do. Here I was, a bullet in my leg, nothing to eat, no command to which I could report, no way of letting anyone know what had happened. If I found an American unit, I'd most likely be court-martialed for desertion. With all these things running through my mind, I finally went to sleep.

Chapter 9

In the morning I was awakened by the sound of voices I was unable to understand. It sure as hell wasn't Tagalog and as far as I could tell it wasn't any of the other native dialects. "This must be Japanese," I thought. I must not let them know I was awake. With partially closed eyes I saw wrapped leggings and black tennis shoes near my face. What now? Those bastards were right on me. How in hell did I let this happen? I couldn't see the other man. I wondered how close he was. Damn, I must be careful. I remembered the Browning automatic I had when I came here. If I could locate it maybe I could get to it. The only chance I had was to get the rifle and kill the bastards before they realized I was awake. I heard the Japanese soldier that I couldn't see get up. He was talking to the other fellow. He walked around me. I saw just the lower part of his legs. Then he sat down. There was his rifle and the bayonet was fixed. I was all the more convinced that I must find that Browning, but where in the hell was it? Both men were in full battle gear. They continued to talk. From the corner of my eye I finally spotted my rifle. It was about four feet away and I noted the ammo clip still in place. I had just made up my mind to jump for the rifle and hoped I could bring it to bear on these soldiers when the one nearest me laid his hand on my forehead. It was obvious that he was checking my temperature. At that moment, a million thoughts ran through my mind. Why had they not shot me and moved on? They sure as hell could have. If they were as hard as I had been led to belive, why the interest in my temperature? Where in the hell was I anyway? What should I do? I wasn't sure they intended to kill me.

I lay there trying to think the situation through, coming up with no satisfactory answers. I decided that there was a very good chance I could surrender without fear of being killed. At that point, I rolled over, pretending that I had just now awakened and seen them. I glanced toward the Browning and one of them saw this and kicked the weapon farther away. I raised myself up on my elbow, then started to get to my feet. There was a sharp pain in my left leg. I had forgotten about the gunshot wound. Sitting back down, I waited. Then once again I tried to get to my feet. This time I made it to a standing position and tried to step off when I fell. My left leg went out from under me and that god-awful pain seemed to run from my knee right up my back into my brain. I rolled over and got back into a sitting position. At this point, one of the Japanese soldiers took his canteen from his belt and offered it to me. I hesitated and he indicated I was welcome to drink. Taking the canteen, I found it was tea. I took a small amount and he indicated I could drink as much as I wanted.

The soldiers assisted me to my feet, then gave me a short piece of tree limb to use as a crutch. We started off in the direction of where the American field hospital was. For the next thirty minutes or so the three of us walked — that is, they walked and I staggered along. They stayed right with me, and as I stumbled, one or the other of them would catch me, keeping me on my feet and walking. It was downhill, and at times I saw the bay through the trees. The whole terrain had been blown to hell. There were shell holes everywhere. It appeared that there had been a terrific battle along the jungle flatland.

When we arrived at the hospital, it was occupied by the Japanese army. They were bringing in their wounded for treatment. Our medical personnel were working their tails off treating wounded people, American as well as Japanese. The hospital had been bombed in the past forty-eight hours. Some of the patients who were there for wounds or illness had been reinjured by the shelling or bombs.

Along with many others, I was placed in an area to wait for treatment. The worst were being taken care of first. I saw others being brought in, some with limbs blown off and others, like myself, with minor injuries.

I hadn't eaten anything for two days. I think I went to sleep or again slipped back into unconsciousness, but at any rate, things went black and when I awakened the crowd around me had diminished and it was dark. Someone was shaking me and handing me some rice.

It wasn't until the following morning that I received any treatment, but during the night I had been able to get some pain killers and as a result, rested quite well. When I did get treatment, I was seen by a corpsman who gave me a shot of something. He put some medication on the gunshot wound, then wrapped the knee. He then told me that I should find somewhere to rest until somebody was available to remove the bullet. It was a flesh wound and had not damaged any of the bone in my knee. Aside from being sore as hell, I would be all right.

Sometime during the afternoon, I was rousted by one of the Japanese soldiers who marched me out of the building toward the main gate of the hospital compound. There he gave me a crutch and started screaming at me, motioning me out of the gate. I took the crutch and ran as fast as I could away from the area. Not having the slightest idea what I was supposed to do, I saw the mountain and headed in that direction. As I looked back I saw others were being hustled out of the gate.

Chapter 10

Leaving the hospital area, I started walking toward the mountain, sure that I would find food and water in the jungle. I was not yet able to accept the fact that the American army had surrendered. I kept looking for someone who could tell me what had happened. I continued walking, ever deeper into the jungle and in the direction of the mountain, with only one thing in mind. I had to get the hell away from here and away from the Japanese.

I knew that I could survive in the hills, especially when I got away into the mountains where the land hadn't been picked over. There were always growing things for a person to eat, and with luck, there might be an animal to kill for food. If our forces had surrendered, I wanted to get as far away from here as possible while I had the opportunity. If I could get away from this part of Bataan, there was a chance I could join with some friendly Filipinos. Anything was better than becoming a prisoner of war.

With my sore knee, I had to walk slowly, but in the past three or four hours I certainly had put some distance between me and the Japs. I hadn't seen anybody—American, Jap, or Filipino. I had the jungle all to myself, just me and the monkeys and the ever-present tropical birds.

In pain, I wanted to stop, but decided to continue walking. There were several hours of daylight left and the more distance I put between me and the Japs, the better I would feel. I trudged on until at last I was overcome by exhaustion. I found a place where I could hide and make a bed of leaves so I could rest and sleep for the night.

For the next two days, I trudged along, searching for food in the old mess areas. Sometimes I found rice left in the bags, and by turning them inside out I got a few grains to cook. There would sometimes be cans of condensed milk that hadn't been punctured. This went very well with the rice.

The deeper I got into the jungle and the farther up the mountain the better the water. There were many small streams and with no one to bother me I could search out the best places to stop. I tried finding places where there was water and natural cover overhead. I didn't want any spotters seeing me if any should by flying over the area.

I kept my canteen filled at all times, and with all the new growth of bamboo, I got bamboo shoots to eat.

Out here alone, I had time to regroup my thoughts about the past few months. I had been so preoccupied with the actions of the war, that I hadn't fully realized the dangers around me. The noises of battle dulled my mind to the point where the stillness up here on the side of this mountain was as frightening as anything that might be lurking out in the darkness.

That night I selected a spot far up the mountain with an opening in the jungle growth that allowed me to see Manila Bay, some eight or nine miles away. Corregidor was plainly visible off to the south. At that moment, there wasn't any noise at all except for the birds. The large guns over on the "Rock" were silent, and the Japanese were not firing. If a war was going on, I couldn't hear it up here.

During the morning of the third day, I climbed up the mountain until it was getting difficult for me to walk. I decided to change direction and start walking the side of the mountain going toward the north. I had no idea how far I had come from the coastline, but I had been walking inland, so I should be well into the jungle and away from the main road that ran north to south through Bataan. I felt that it was safe for me to turn north.

At times I saw Manila Bay, but because I couldn't see the shoreline, I couldn't be sure how far I had walked. It would appear that I had come inland some ten miles since leaving the hospital. I continued along the side of the mountain, picking the easiest trails. There were no signs that Americans or Japanese had been in the area and the only food I had found was bamboo shoots. This wasn't a new experience for me. I had been scrounging for food since February.

By mid-afternoon I saw the main road leading south through Bataan. I saw convoys of trucks moving south toward Marvelious, the little village at the southernmost part of Bataan. I couldn't make out what type of trucks they were, but they must be Japanese. They were too far north to be American.

Without realizing it I had descended the mountain farther than I liked, and I was scared of running into a Japanese patrol. Before dark I had to get back farther into the jungle. The aftermath of war was everywhere. There were rifles, web equipment, canteens, and even some artillery pieces that had been deserted. I sat down for a rest and gazed at the weapons with their barrels elevated as if they were waiting for the crew to return. I picked up a good belt, another canteen, and a good mess kit. "I'll find food somewhere and when I do, I'll need this mess gear," I said to myself.

Moving toward a small stream, I stumbled upon the body of an American soldier. Someone had placed him in a sitting position against a tree trunk with his rifle across his lap, bayonet fixed, steel helmet down over his face, and his hands gripping the stock. From what I saw he had been dead for several days. The fact that the soldier was dead was of little consequence because the past few months I had become accustomed to sights such as this. What bothered me was a note scribbled on a piece of scrap paper and tacked to the trunk of the tree just over his head. It read, "Only those who are not afraid to die are fit to live." As I read this inscription the words were indelibly stamped on my brain and I knew they would remain forever. During the past few months I had experienced the fear and terror of being killed at any time and watched men as they were torn to bits by shell fire. I wondered, "Who in hell has the right to make such a judgment about this soldier?" The son-of-a-bitch had time to write the note after he had taken the time to set him up against that tree, but somehow didn't have the time to bury him. I bent down once more and read the note, and the anger filled me more and more. I took the entrenching tool from my backpack and dug a shallow hole under the great tree. There I left this soldier with no marker, just his rifle and his helmet.

When I finished, I walked until I could walk no more. Still I couldn't erase that scene from my mind. There was only one consolation. The man was buried and would not be bothered by animals. This helped very little. Those words on that piece of paper kept haunting me.

At last I was so exhausted from walking, I had to stop for the night. Somewhere there in the darkness of the night, I came to the conclusion that cliches are useful only for the people responsible for the man's death. It was something that eased their guilt. Most certainly I could find no glory for this soldier, lying in the damn jungle, eight thousand miles from home. Just one of those thousands of other Americans destined to be listed as "lost in action" for all time. I was overcome by sleep at last.

When I awoke, I found that I had bedded down near the road. Because there wasn't any activity along the road, I walked the shoulder. If a Japanese patrol came this way, I could step off the road and be under cover quickly. The morning was quiet, and I would hear any vehicle before it got near enough to see me. For the better part of the morning I continued walking north, listening for noises. When a vehicle came, I stepped back into the brush until it passed, then resumed walking.

After a while I realized that in spite of being out here walking for the past three days I hadn't come very far north. In fact, I was not much farther north than where I was when the Japs overran my unit. From what I could see in the area, there had been a furious battle. Pieces of equipment were everywhere. During the past three days I had been able to avoid the sights by going around them, but today, without realizing it, I had walked right into the center of a battleground. There wasn't any way of avoiding it. The best thing I could now was stay on the road. No telling what mess there was out in the bush.

It had been five days since my last encounter with the Japanese army. I'd just as soon not have to look at any more of war's aftermath, so the road seemed like the better of two evils. I moved faster. I wanted to get away as quickly as possible. Still I had to look forward. A Jap patrol could come by at any time. Also, I had to listen for any sounds coming from behind. Picking up my pace and not looking to either side, I moved into a trot. Up at the bend of the road, I saw a large heap of dirt and debris, something that had been pushed into a large mound by a bulldozer or some other type of heavy equipment. Tree trunks and downed trees, shattered equipment, and other material were in a large pile some twenty to thirty feet high. The heap was directly in front of me and there was no way I could avoid looking at it. I had to pass and then the road bore back to my left. When I was only thirty or forty yards away, I saw what had happened and the sight startled the hell out of me. The bastards had used a dozer and pushed the dead, along with all this other debris, into a great heap. Instead of them dozing out a place and pushing the bodies in it and covering them, they pushed everything into a large pile. There were bodies mixed in with dirt, blown-up pieces of equipment, and other debris. Even an old command car was there. The smell was worse than anything I had ever had to endure. There were so many flies, they nearly blocked the sun. I was afraid to open my mouth, there were so many of them. I was still trotting and as I came closer the sound of the flies was like a swarm of bees. They were hitting me in the face as I ran. When I was only a few yards away, I saw that these men had either been gunned down on the road as they were trying to retreat, or had been taken by surprise by a large number of Japanese soldiers and were killed right on the road. Then, when the rest of the army came through, they pushed them off the road with the dozer along with other things blocking the way.

I came to a full halt and looked at the very top of the heap. There was an American soldier, his body covered from the waist down with dirt and debris. His eyes stared toward the heavens and his right hand pointed in that direction as if to say, "That is the direction you must look." This I understood as a personal message for me. I became so spellbound by the figure that I didn't hear the truck. The damn thing was right on me before I heard anything. I heard rifle fire and saw a Japanese soldier standing on the back shooting at me. So much for the message. With one great leap, I was off the road and into the brush. I lay still as the truck disappeared around the bend. I waited, wanting to make sure there were no more vehicles behind that one before leaving my place of safety.

Getting deeper and deeper into the jungle, with only the chatter of monkeys and the sound of tropical birds for company, I soon realized that I was once again feeling better. My nerves had come back to earth; only the mental image remained with me. Walking slowly now that everything was quiet, I suddenly felt hungry and I had very little with me. There was a small amount of rice and a can of condensed milk in my pack. This didn't seem like enough. I began looking for bamboo shoots. As I searched, I found plenty for the night. Bamboo shoots were very nourishing and could be eaten many ways—boiled, fried, raw, or cooked with rice.

Darkness was coming on fast, so I found a good spot where I could make a small fire. Within minutes I prepared my meal for the day. When finished, I realized that I was exhausted. I would have no problem sleeping. I would be alone with the night noises, which I had become accustomed to over the past few months.

There are few places more eerie than the tropics at night with all its noises. But for the first time in weeks I had peace of mind, something I hadn't experienced in a very long time.

I slept well, but was awakened by something before daybreak. I couldn't make out what, just something. I remained silent, not moving, just listening. There was nothing. Just the jungle coming alive from its long night's sleep.

I felt rested, but also hungry and there wasn't anything in my pack. I would spend the day scrounging for food. I tried standing and found that I had slept on the leg with the wound. I hadn't noticed the pain until I tried standing. I would have to find some way of dressing the injury in spite of the fact that I had nothing to put on it. If I could find a stream, I'd boil some water and wash the wound. That should help keep the infection down until I got medical aid. Medical aid? Good God, what in hell was I talking about? I was acting as if I could walk into a doctor's office and have him take care of me. How damn stupid could I get? The only care I would get was what I did for myself and then hope and pray that it would be all right. With that thought I picked up my gear and started searching for fresh water.

By nine o'clock I came upon an old abandoned command post. The first place I started looking for was the kitchen area. I had become very proficient at this by now. I could just look at the area and could tell where things were.

It wasn't long until I spotted two field ranges the mess sergeant had dug in. He had dug out the dirt and placed it around in a square and set the stoves down inside this hole. The dirt made for good protection against small arms fire so the cooks had a safe place in which to cook. In one corner of the parapet was a stack of burlap bags, folded neatly as if they were to be taken along when the unit was ordered to withdraw. However, it appeared that they had to move out quickly without taking the ranges or anything with them.

I searched the area thoroughly. Finding nothing, I started turning the burlap bags inside out. In the bottoms of the bags I found some grains of rice that stuck in the folds of the burlap, especially in the corners. I ended up with more than a pound of rice. While I was wrapping it, I thought about how I would find some bamboo shoots. Feeling very good about my find, I started my search for the fresh water that I so desperately needed. Before leaving the area I took one last walk around, looking for anything I might be able to use. During this search, I found a pair of khaki trousers, two khaki shirts, and some underclothing that had been discarded. Folding these items, I placed them inside my pack.

Turning once again down the mountain, still going in a northerly direction, I picked up any bamboo shoots I found. It wasn't but a short while until I found the stream of water that I had been searching for. Looking down the stream I located a spot where I would be under cover and out of sight from any spotters and built a small fire. With some stones, I made a place where my mess kit could sit over the blaze. I would eat first, then take care of my wound.

When I finished eating, I refilled the mess kit with water, then brought it to a boil over the hot coals. Using one of the canteen cups for a container, I soaked some pieces of the underclothing and cleaned my wound. After I had washed the wound thoroughly, I saw no infection. At least there wasn't any redness around the wound. It was sore, but all in all, I could move about very well. I supposed I should be grateful. I had had all this time alone, which allowed the wound to heal.

I spent the better part of the next morning at the little stream, changing clothes, washing those I had worn since before the fall, and of course, moving around. Since I had washed the wound, I could walk much better. I didn't bother waiting for the clothing to dry before packing it away in my pack. It was hot and they would dry inside the pack almost as fast as they would in the sun. Picking up all my gear and filling two canteens with fresh water, I started out. For reasons unknown to me, I continued on north. I felt a need to be moving in that direction.

The rest and sleep plus the opportunity to clean up at the stream cleared my thinking. I became aware of the absence of combat noises that had been so much a part of me for the past five and a half months. There were no explosions, no bursting rounds of artillery, no bombs, no chatter of rifles and machine gun fire. The yells of "Bonzai, Bonzai" had ceased. No longer did I hear the call for help and the cry of the dying. All this had been replaced with the sounds of the tropical birds and the chattering of the animals scurrying about as I passed. The noises of the birds and animals stopped as I neared them; then after I passed they began all over again. I realized that nature would replace itself. Everything would be restored. The jungle would renew itself and the forest would be restored. Only the humans who were responsible for the damage would have problems recovering.

Far off to the south, there was the faint echo of artillery. The large guns of Corregidor could be heard for miles, but the answering fire from the Japanese, though closer to me, could barely be heard. Whatever they did, I sure as hell wouldn't be part of it. It was over for me. All I could do was keep moving away and hope that I was doing the right thing. The thought crossed my mind, "I wonder if I will be court-martialed when this is over?" I sure as hell didn't have any orders to do what I did and those Japs didn't put me in any prison camp back there at the hospital. As far as they were concerned, they wanted me away from them, out of their hair.

Trying to climb higher up the side of the mountain was out of the question. My leg was hurting so badly it wouldn't stand the strain. So I walked along the side of the mountain, selecting the easiest trail. Finally I decided that I could hide as well down lower as I could up that way. Gradually I was back near the bottom of the mountain and moving north, parallel to the road, but staying well back in the brush and jungle where I couldn't be observed by anyone who might be passing along the road.

After two hours of trudging through the thick undergrowth, I came upon an opening, an area that looked like it had once been cleared for cultivation. Staying back under cover, I saw two men walking in the same general direction as I, but at the edge of the clearing and near the road. They were only about one hundred yards away. They were Americans. My first reaction was to get the hell out of there, but instead I stepped out and they saw me. One of them raised his hand in recognition. Waving back, I started around the back side of the clearing, but when I came out on the north side both of them were waiting for me and it was impossible for me to avoid them further. One of them asked, "Do you have any idea what has happened?"

"Not the slightest. I have been wandering about for the last four days and haven't seen anyone who can even tell me whether we have surrendered or not," I replied.

"That's the same with us. We were overrun and have been out in the jungle since the ninth of April."

"Me too. I wanted back in the mountains where I could join up with some Filipinos, but hell, I can't find any of them either," I said.

We continued to exchange what information we had and it was generally decided that in all probability Bataan had fallen to the Japanese and unless we kept out of sight we would be caught as well. After this the three of us started moving once again, keeping well off the road.

We ran into people walking everywhere. I didn't see where they came from. The harder I tried to keep away from the crowd, the more I ran into them. Before nightfall there was a large contingent of Americans and Filipinos, all of them wanting information about what had happened. I wanted to be away from the throng, but we had come together at a very bad time. It was getting dark, and this was much farther north than I had ever been. I didn't know anything about this part of Bataan. The jungle was there, inviting me, but the fear of the unknown kept me from going back out into it. I moved away unnoticed. I soon found a good place to sleep. Hoping everyone would go on their way, I stopped and prepared for the night. A number of people had done the same.

After about an hour, I moved around among these men inquiring about the possibility of there being a medic in the group. I soon learned of an enlisted man who was a medic, so I sought him out and had him look at the wound in my knee. In a very short time he had cleaned it and put some sulfa powder directly onto the affected area. He then took some new bandages and rewrapped my knee. When he had finished, he gave me four small packages of sulfa powder. He told me, "When you find that this bandage needs changing, you can put at least one of the packages of powder on the wound." My gratitude toward this man cannot be overstated. If I had not received this treatment, I could not have finished the long and arduous march that was ahead.

Back under the cover of the brush, I watched the stars. I had done exactly what the Japs knew I would do. In my attempt to get away, I had walked northward, the only way out of Bataan, and had wound up as all the others who had been overrun, in one group marching out of Bataan. Little did I know that I had joined that large contingent of captured American and Filipino soldiers and sailors who would soon take the "death march of Bataan."

Chapter 11

Early the next morning when I awoke, the people around me had gone. I got my gear ready and once again started moving north away from the sounds of that artillery over on Corregidor.

I kept off the road out of sight of anyone who might be in the area. I had every intention of avoiding the Japanese. Also, I didn't aim to get mixed up with any more Americans. The ones I saw last evening knew less than I.

I still believed that if I could make it up to the northern end of Luzon, I could get into that mountain range and stay until the U.S. army came back and drove the Japanese out of the Philippines.

The more I tried to avoid people, the more I ran into them. Everywhere I turned there were Americans and Filipinos, and all of them seemed to have the same idea as I. By eight o'clock it looked like a march of stragglers. We had picked up some officers, and even though there wasn't any organization, our sailors and soldiers were flocking around the officers, trying to get information as to what was expected of them.

I overheard one ask, "What should I do?" The stock answer became, "There isn't anything that can be done. We are all prisoners of war." When those words rang out, even though spoken softly, they sounded like they were shouted. I knew it was over. Why didn't I get the hell out of here last night and into the mountains? Even though I didn't know this area, at least out there I could make my own decisions. Here there was nothing I could do.

I was nothing more than another prisoner marching north. Nobody was paying attention to anything or anyone. We were just marching north, walking head down, spirit broken, and with little or no hope. I could still hear that officer say, "Nothing can be done. We are prisoners of war."

Before an hour passed, a Japanese truck pulled alongside the marchers, and two Japanese soldiers dismounted. They were the first guards I had seen since leaving the hospital. As the truck pulled away, the two soldiers started moving us in the direction they wanted us to go. We no longer were able to move on and off the road.

The two men started yelling and slapping the hell out of anyone near them, and I heard more yells back of where I was. There were more guards on the truck and they were dropped off farther back before the vehicle arrived at this point.

As one of them prodded me with his bayonet, I cursed under my breath for having waited so long that morning. Now, I didn't have a choice. I had to deal with the situation on their terms. Still angry as hell at myself I continued to walk, and the longer I walked, the more impossible it was for me to extricate myself from the long line of American and Filipino marchers. Also, the Japs had increased in number, making it impossible for anyone to escape.

Watching the helplessness of our officers and the broken spirit of those near me, I became fully aware that the war was over for me. Resistance would be useless. My fate was in the hands of the Japanese. This awareness was both a relief and a sense of despair. A relief because all doubts about what had happened in Bataan were erased. I could forget about being relieved and taken out of here. Those thousands of planes and thousands of troops were not coming. Despair because there was no doubt that I had no control over what was to happen to me. I stumbled on, neither talking nor wanting to be talked to. If I fell back, a Jap prodded me in the back side with his bayonet. If I stepped out of line the son-of-a-bitch slapped the hell out of me or hit me in the face with anything he had in his hand at the moment.

On the first day on the "death march of Bataan," I hadn't been under the direct control of the guards more than a couple of hours when another column started merging with us. This bunch seemed to be coming from the direction of the shoreline of Manila Bay and from what I could see, they had been under the control of the guards for some time. It appeared we were stragglers and had more or less drifted in with this column. The men were in very bad shape. Many in this group didn't even have canteens, and even though it was only about eleven o'clock, they were dying from thirst and the Japs hadn't indicated they intended to ration any water. There wasn't anyplace where a person could find water. Watching these men, I reached down and clutched my water bottles, remembering how I had filled both canteens the night before and had gotten water that morning before I started moving. Once again I was grateful that I had that time out in the jungle before getting caught.

As time passed and thirst became more of a problem, I took one of the water bottles from the pouch and, removing the lid, I tried to get a drink. The canteen was grabbed from my hands by someone near me. I struggled for the canteen, and got it back after wrestling the man to the ground, but he had nearly emptied the bottle. As I put the canteen back in the pouch, knowing that we had been seen fighting over the water, I started falling back. A guard grinned at the episode and moved forward. I let two men pass, then more. I wanted to be away from anyone who might know that I had another canteen of water. I had some water, and the fact that I had a drink that morning enabled me to make it the rest of the day.

The thought of that man trying to take my water away angered the hell out of me. What was happening? Surely the guards could see what was going on and would get water to us soon.

The afternoon dragged on with no indication of the Japs giving us a rest break or water. We just trudged ever forward, putting one foot in front of the other, knowing that if we fell it was sure death and if we stumbled outside the line of march, we would get the hell beat out of us. We trudged on. The tropical sun beat down and I heard some of the prisoners begging the guards for water, but I hadn't seen anyone get anything.

Things were racing through my mind about what had happened to the American forces in the islands, and as people were talking, I listened — especially to the officers. By nightfall I gathered that General King, who was the commander at Bataan, surrendered all the forces under his command back on April 9. Since that time the Japanese had been moving the American and Filipino prisoners out of this area. Also, I learned that Corregidor was still intact and had not surrendered. The war was still going on.

Thinking about that date, I realized that I had been wandering about out there in the jungle for at least four days. It must be April 13. My mind seemed to play tricks on me. I had lost track of how long I had been out there. There was one thing certain: during that time I was able to get some much needed rest. From what I could see that was something these men hadn't had, especially these who merged with us that morning.

The time out in the jungle gave me another advantage. I had had the time to regroup my thoughts and had cleared my mind of the exploding artillery shells and the bombs. I had become so used to them that their absence almost drove me out of my mind. Without the time for rest and a chance for the wound in my knee to heal, I wouldn't have had a chance in hell of making this march.

I had been busy with my thoughts and the sun had dropped behind Marvelious mountain. It was cooler. I heard the guards screaming and yelling, and in general, raising hell all over the place, urging us to pick up the pace. I detected an urgency in their action, a fear that they would be caught out in the thick jungle with a large number of prisoners and only a handful of their people guarding us.

Our ranks were being closed up. The prisoners behind me were gaining while we were closing up on the marchers up forward. Near me were two Jap guards yelling in broken English, "Speedo, Speedo, water very soon." At the mention of water the prisoners picked up the pace. I knew some of them hadn't had water all day and in some cases it had been longer. It had been several hours since I had had any water and I was thirsty. I could imagine what it must be like for those who had walked all day with nothing.

Darkness fell very quickly, and the Japs managed to get us bunched up into groups of two hundred men, with about ten of their guards to control us. Soon we were directed off the road and out into an opening. The guards were slapping hell out of everyone in reach and screaming as loudly as they could. They wanted us in a smaller group, bunched together as close as possible. Then they spread themselves around the group. Everyone was so damned tired and weak from no food or water, we lay down as soon as the guards backed away. There was no way to escape from this area. Those bastards would shoot you before you could get ten feet outside the circle. Even if I could get away, how far would I get without food or water? Not far,

I was afraid. I had no map, and only a small amount of water in one canteen. At any rate, there were more than likely Japanese units everywhere. The way things were going, I'd probably stagger around out there and wind up right in the middle of a Japanese unit. With all this running through my head, I found a place out of reach of the guards and lay down, waiting for the chance to sneak the canteen from the pouch and get a drink without being seen. After the experience of the morning, I didn't dare let anybody know that I had water in one of my canteens.

It was nearly ten o'clock when I was awakened by a truck being driven into the area and from the noise being made by our people. I knew something must be happening.

Grabbing my canteen belt, I ran toward the truck. The Japs had brought water, and the prisoners were pushing and shoving each other to get into the line for water. Some people were standing at the rear of the truck where they could open the spigot and fill their canteens, while others at the front opened the spigots and drank from their cups.

The water tanker was capable of holding several hundred gallons of water and the Japs were allowing us to drink as much as we wanted and fill our canteens if we had them.

It was almost impossible for people to get near enough to get water. Everyone wanted water at the same time, and were cursing and shoving each other while the Jap guard was doing everything he could to keep things orderly, making us stay back and wait our turn.

The truck remained for what seemed like hours and those with canteens filled them for later. Others carried water away in mess kits or anything they could find. Each time I woke during the night I could see people standing at the spigots drinking. I know what they must be thinking, "Get all I can while I have the chance."

When I was sure that all were asleep, I dug deep inside my pack for loose grains of rice. The small amount of rice plus the water helped. I was much more fortunate than most.

As I chewed on raw rice, I thought about those who had no way to carry water and automatically I reached for my two canteens. Finding them and assuring myself once more that they were full, I lay back. I knew some of the men saw me fill two bottles. This might cause me problems tomorrow.

I was brought out of my sleep by the guards yelling. I had slept some, and was startled, to say the least, by their screaming. They were ordering us out on the trail. Hell, it was still dark, and I had no idea what the time was.

The guards made no attempt to feed anyone. The only thing I saw was their shoving and slapping hell out of anyone close to them and pointing in the direction they wanted us to go. Remembering yesterday and how difficult it was for me to get to my water, I took one of the canteens from the pouch and drank deeply before I picked up my pack and gear and moved out on the road.

Before we had traveled a mile, the brutalities started. The guards were

76

different. They were fresh, with clean uniforms. They were determined to vent their anger at being assigned to this degrading task.

It was not yet sunrise, and I remembered the possibility of someone seeing me fill two canteens. Now was the time to get away from anyone who might have seen me before daylight. So I stepped out quickly, mixing with people already on the road. When I walked out from the area where we slept, there were men on the road. I had no way of knowing where they came from or, for that matter, how long they had been marching. I just stepped out to the road and melted in with the marchers. Soon I was with faces I hadn't seen before. All I could hope for was that no one recognized me. What a damn mess. I had to hide from my own people the fact that I had water.

The guards were driving us hard. Anyone who stumbled was prodded in the back and forced back onto his feet. If he fell he was run though with a bayonet or sabre.

The end result was always the same: death. Be it instant or lingering, suffering by bleeding to death from untreated wounds inflicted with a bayonet or sabre.

Nobody was allowed to stop and assist those who fell. They would be finished off by one of the guards behind us. When a prisoner fell dead or was murdered, he was left where he had fallen, where he was trampled into the earth, or covered by the dust that accumulated as the marchers passed.

I had no way of knowing how many men there were to follow, but it was evident that thousands had preceded me.

There was hardly a time when I didn't see the body of someone who had either been killed or had died, left where it had fallen along the road, where it was covered with dust. Some had been trampled until they were barely recognizable, but I knew what that heap was. They were ever-present and an awful odor let me know they had been there for some time.

The Japs were pushing hard and the tropical sun was bearing down on us. There was no indication that we would be given a break or water. In the heat, I needed some water soon. I knew that if I was seen opening my canteen I would be mobbed by men around me who were slowly dying from the lack of water. Still, with the heat and the dust choking me, soon I would have no choice.

As the march continued, I just kept putting one foot in front of the other, not wanting to take chances until I must, looking neither left nor right, hearing nothing, blocking out everything, trying not to think of my surroundings, doing only the things I must to keep from falling and becoming another one of those dust-covered forms alongside the trail. At last, I could wait no longer. I must have water or die. Up forward were a number of prisoners who had canteens on their belts. They seemed to have closed in on each other for some reason. If I could get into that group—melt in where everyone had a water bottle—perhaps I wouldn't be too conspicuous when I took the canteen from the pouch. Quickly, I moved forward and within a short time I was among this group. I moved over to the left side of the column, away from the guard that suddenly appeared. I had not seen him earlier. I slipped the canteen from the pouch and opened the top. Then quickly, one, two, three deep swallows, the canteen was jerked from my hands and before I could do anything a soldier had emptied the canteen. For a moment I could have killed that son-of-a-bitch with my bare hands. Instead, I took the empty bottle, turned it up so all could see that this man had taken my water, at the same time pretending that this was all I had. In doing this I had turned a very bad situation away from myself and toward the man I knew must have been dying of thirst.

I decided to get the hell away from these men before my deception was discovered. So, with renewed strength from getting water, I picked up my step and soon was out of sight and out of reach of anyone who might discover that I still had water. If it should be necessary for me to have additional water today, the men around me wouldn't know.

The screaming continued, with a new phrase added: "Only two more miles, only two more miles."

Some one yelled, "only two more miles," and at the same time they prodded the marchers with their bayonets for emphasis or slapped hell out of the person closest to them. Occasionally I was treated to some of their discipline, especially when they decided that we needed to be reminded that our lives were meaningless, as far as they were concerned. The sooner we were dead, the sooner they could get back to the task of winning more battles for their emperor.

The end result of this kind of thinking was visible alongside every foot of the road, where the bodies of American and Filipino soldiers and sailors lay in the dust. They had lost their lives at the hands of barbaric bastards who seemed to glory in their abilities to murder and slaughter helpless men.

Some ten to fifteen yards directly in front of where I was walking, an American soldier was reeling from side to side. He fell to his knees, then managed to rise to his feet and continue on. He was making the maximum effort to remain upright. He knew the end result if he could not keep pace. He continued to struggle. There was a guard near him, and he glared at the unfortunate man. Once again he fell. This time he could rise no more; he was finished. The guard calmly ran him through with his bayonet. The guard stepped back out of the line of march, took a cloth from his back pocket, and wiped the blood from the blade. At that moment a military command car pulled alongside. The guard stopped cleaning as an officer jumped from the car. He had witnessed this atrocity. The officer stepped in front of the soldier, stood him at stiff attention, stared directly into his eyes, then removed his sidearm and placed the barrel directly between his eyes and pulled the trigger.

The Japanese officer glanced at the body of the American, then at the slumped figure of his own soldier, and returned the pistol to its holster. He swiftly turned away, got into the command car, and was soon gone in a cloud of dust.

It was once more quiet, and as I took one last glance at the two lifeless forms, I wondered if the Japanese soldier would also be listed as lost in action.

The swift military justice I had witnessed seemed to be commonplace in the Japanese army.

Sometime during the afternoon, I became aware of an American officer walking alongside me. I noticed that he had the insignia of a lieutenant colonel. He walked slowly, but was managing to keep on his feet. He was muttering over and over, "I can't make it any farther." His left arm hung loosely at his side and there were injuries to his left shoulder. He was in great pain, and had been walking for some time.

As we walked he told me that he was wounded the last day of the war on the morning of April 9. He had not received any medical aid since the surrender. He believed he had been walking for at least four days. He also told me he had difficulty keeping pace with the others and that the guards had reinjured the wound at least two times since the start of the march. He had been given rice and water that morning, but nothing for the wound.

After some time, I saw that the officer was in so much pain, he would never survive unless his burden was eased. I asked him to let me carry his pack and give him some relief. He seemed determined not to discard any of his load, even though it was much too heavy for him, especially with the wounded shoulder.

"I may have to discard everything I have later, but not now," he stated. "I have some underclothing in my pack that I can use for bandages, if we get a break, and if I don't take care of the wound soon, I won't make it anyway."

"If you like, I can give you a short break. You can have the pack back anytime you like," I said.

At last he reluctantly let the pack slip off his shoulders, and I took it and hung it over my shoulder. The damn thing seemed to weigh seventy or eighty pounds, but I took it all the same and the two of us continued along this trail. Even with the load off his back, he continued saying, "I can't make it any longer, I can't make it any longer."

At one point I informed him that I had been shot though the knee the last day of the war, but I sure as hell intended getting through the day, and with the load off his shoulder he should be able to make it until nightfall. "Just you hang in there for a while longer. Things will look brighter in the morning," I said.

The afternoon dragged on with the Japs becoming meaner all the time. The column was closing up; something was happening up forward. It wasn't late enough for a break. There was some other reason for the column closing up. Damn! I hoped it was for water.

The trail entered a rough spot. There were trees and some large stones at the side of the trail. The road was narrow, no more than a wide path. We had been climbing and were now going down the other side. On this side, the terrain was rough and covered with large trees. The trees were not the tropical variety, but hardwood. There were many small trees and grass along the ground. There were small outcroppings like stone ledges and on the trail were small rocks that rolled underfoot. The hill dropped off quite sharply on

79

the right. At the bottom, I saw water; there was a stream running back toward the direction from which we had come.

Soon I saw what slowed the marchers down. There was a walk bridge. The Japs held us back, allowing only two or three on the bridge at the same time. If one of the guards was on the bridge, we had to wait until he was on the other side before we could start across.

Walking a few feet, then stopping, gave us a chance to rest. The guards were preoccupied with the crossing so we leaned against the high bank on the left side of the trail without them seeing us. Many of the prisoners got some respite from the torturous march, even though we knew that if the bastards saw us there would be hell to pay.

As we came near the end of the bridge, I saw far below, the water running clear and fresh against large boulders at the bottom of the ravine. The view of that water would drive some of the men out of their minds, especially those who had had no water all day. We moved closer to the bridge. Slowly the line was thinning in front of me. The colonel was right in back of me as we approached the walk bridge.

There were three men on the bridge. As I approached I saw the thing sway in the air from side to side. The trail had narrowed until we were in single file. I moved ever closer. I assured the colonel I would wait at the end of the bridge for him to catch up. He nodded his assent and I stepped onto the approach and started across. When I was some ten to fifteen yards from the end and near the center of the bridge, I looked back over my shoulder and saw the colonel on the bridge about ten feet behind me. The damn thing was swaying and I hung on to the cables used for hand rails. The boards under my feet squeaked from the strain of the load. I heard a scream, and as I turned, I saw the body of the colonel as it hurled through the air toward the jagged rocks at the bottom of the ravine. I gripped the cables tighter as I saw his torn body on those rocks and could almost hear that statement I heard from him for the past three hours, "I can't go on any farther, I can't go on any farther." Before the scream I had heard no shots; he had either been shoved over the side or decided that he, in fact, couldn't go on any farther and had jumped to his death.

I stepped off the bridge onto solid ground. The marchers hadn't even slowed. They wouldn't be allowed to check if the man was dead or alive. He was just one more soldier who would end up on the rolls of the United States army as lost in action, probably for all time. Hell, I didn't even ask his name, nor did he ask mine. We were just two soldiers who met on this march, walked together for a few hours, then it was all over.

The bridge was behind me, and I still had his heavy pack on my back. I had become so preoccupied with the events of the past hour, the extra weight went unnoticed. Just as I decided that I should dump the entire load, the Japanese ordered us off the road for a break. Damn! If the colonel could have held on for just another hour.

During this break, I ran through the contents of the pack. I sure as hell didn't aim to carry it any farther. Inside were some underclothing, two pairs of socks (filled with loose tobacco), a large bar of soap, a razor with blades. But best of all, there was a large chocolate bar—solid chocolate that doesn't melt when kept wrapped. When I had separated the things I wanted and packed them inside my own pack, I tossed the rest of his things aside.

I had to be careful about the tobacco and chocolate. I had learned enough in the last two or three days. One could be killed for a hell of a lot less than a chocolate bar.

When we started again, my spirits got higher. I had extra supplies. I still had water, and when we stopped, there would be something to eat.

Each time we stopped there were some who didn't return to the road. They had gone as far as they could. They died in the rest area from wounds or from total exhaustion. They were either murdered or left where they were to die. This stop was no exception.

Picking up my pack, I moved out as quickly as possible and as I was leaving I made every effort to block out the screams in the background. I knew men were being murdered. I still heard the screams, even though I was far away from that spot. Those sadistic bastards felt compelled to demonstrate their superiority over us, and those of us who were too weak were their victims. We meant nothing to them, only numbers, nothing more. Those who were sick or wounded were slowly being eliminated.

The afternoon dragged on. I managed to keep on my feet somehow. I didn't look at what was happening around me. I didn't want to see. I had all I could do to keep upright, so the guards wouldn't kill me.

We were now entering some small Filipino barrios, and as we passed through the natives stared at us. When we came near them I saw tears streaming down their faces. This display of affection was overwhelming.

The tropical sun had dropped behind the mountain range and it was somewhat cooler. Then, at last, darkness. The guards were directing us off the trail. They closed up our ranks and divided us into groups of about two hundred men. Ten guards watched over each group. We had been herded off into a rice paddy that had not been planted in some time.

The water normally in a rice paddy had long since dried up, leaving large clods of dirt as hard as cement. By moving these large clods around, I was able to make a spot where I could stretch out. The only thing I could think about was getting off my feet.

I felt hunger pangs; the chocolate bar was safely hidden away in my pack, and that relieved the feeling for the moment. Just the knowledge that I could eat at any time took much of the hunger away.

I opened my eyes. It was completely dark. I'd been lying flat on my back for God knows how long. It was quiet in the rest area. No one was talking.

With total darkness around me, I picked up my pack and moved to the outer part of the group. I found a spot where I urinated, but the action was more to allay any suspicion as to my real reason, which was to find a spot where I could get that chocolate bar and some water. I dug deep within my pack, taking out the candy bar and breaking off only a small part. Even if the

Japs didn't bring in more water or food, I would live for yet another day. I fell asleep again.

After a while I was awakened by loud noises in the rest area. Getting into a sitting position and working my stiff joints until I could make out what was happening, I listened. The Japs had once again brought in water, and the men charged the truck. I was alone at the outer edge of the rest area. Slowly I removed my canteen from its pouch, unscrewed the top, and drank the water left in my canteen. I had no fear of being seen. Everyone was at the truck trying to get to the head of the line. I drank all the water in the one bottle and waited. After some time, I walked to the truck and found the end of the line. At the truck I refilled both bottles. I drank more water while at the truck.

Back at my sleeping area, I lay for some time looking at the stars overhead. Again I dozed, knowing that whatever tomorrow brought, I would have water.

Later that night I was again awakened by a truck entering the area. This truck pulled alongside the water truck and when I arrived at the vehicle a Jap handed out a rice ball to each prisoner as we passed in front of him. This rice ball was about the size of a baseball, and packed very tightly. As I started eating I found it had sour taste as if it had been cooked for some time and had been outside longer than it should have. Nonetheless, I ate. It was food and for some, it was the only food we had had for two or three days. It could make the difference between living or dying. The fact that the rice was partially spoiled was of no consequence. No one refused it.

Taking my rice ball, I went back to my pack, and there in the darkness finished what I had left. I watched the others as they finished theirs and looked back at the truck to see if there was more.

I suddenly realized that my knee was sore. I had been so preoccupied with hunger that I had forgotten about the knee or had not noticed the soreness. Reaching down and rubbing the bandage, it felt stuck, so I opened one of the canteens and let some water drip onto the wounded area. Then, by flexing the leg for some time, the pain eased, and I was once again able to go back to sleep.

The sun was already up when the guards started yelling and kicking at us. When we were awake, they started moving us back onto the road.

When one of them got close by and yelled, I wasted no time getting my gear on my back and away from there. I sure as hell didn't need one of them kicking my knee. That is what they did—busted up anyone who was injured. Those slow in getting to their feet were perfect targets. My pack was on my back, and I was on the trail in seconds.

The road was filled with marchers as I stepped into the line. It would appear that some had been on the road for several hours.

There was no organization. I just merged into the mob as they walked past and started walking northward, always northward.

The guards wore fresh uniforms and for the most part they looked rested. They weren't wearing their steel helmets. They had on little khaki caps, with short bills. On the back a piece of fiber hung down over the back of the neck. The silliest damn thing I had ever seen, especially when they wore glasses. The flap then came around to their temples and covered the earpiece of the glasses. The little bill at the front of the cap covered the top of the glasses. Somehow all this made them look about five feet tall. Those who carried sabres had to hold the end off the ground.

There was no way of knowing how this bunch would treat us. We had to wait to find out what their attitude was.

I hadn't been able to figure out what type of organization the Japanese had for this forced march. There weren't any rosters, no head counts, nothing. They just pointed with their bayonets in the direction they wanted us to go, and we moved in that direction.

We were being driven like cattle along a trail. We were slowly being reduced in numbers by starvation and the lack of medical attention for our wounds. In addition were the murders of those who were unable to keep pace with the stronger ones.

I was pleased that I was away from anyone who was with me the night before. As I looked around, there wasn't one face that I recognized. For the present I didn't have to worry about people knowing that I had two canteens. One was nearly full and the other was full to the top. Also, if someone should have seen the tobacco or the candy bar, I was out of their sight as well.

This bunch of prisoners looked as if they had been through hell. They walked with their heads down, looking at their feet. I could understand this to some extent because of the rapid pace the Japs had set for us and with all the dust. All of us must watch where we stepped for fear of falling. But damn! We looked beat. I wondered how long we would be able to continue this pace, yet we continued to plod onward. I tried blocking out what was happening around me by keeping my eyes straight forward, or, as the others, looking at the ground. The thought crossed my mind, "Why, if these people have been on the road all night as they look, didn't I hear them last night? I was only a short distance off the trail and should have heard people walking past." I hadn't heard anything. But, I suppose that as tired as I was when we were ordered off the road, they could have walked right over the top of me and I wouldn't have known it. By letting this puzzlement run through my mind, I was able to keep from thinking about the dust and the screaming that was going on. I plodded forward.

That damn guard! Where in hell did he come from? He sure wasn't there the last time I looked. The son-of-a-bitch seemed to have just materialized out of thin air, and the way he was eyeing that Filipino soldier and gripping the hilt of his sabre, I knew he was bent on killing someone. If that soldier didn't watch himself, it would be him. Slowly, I let one man pass, then another, until at last there were four or five men between us. At the same time I let the men pass, I was easing my way across the ranks, until I was at the far side of the column.

That Filipino stumbled and I saw the Jap's fingers grip tighter on the hilt of his sabre and the muscles in his face tighten. The soldier regained his footing and the Jap relaxed some but stayed right back of the man. He was hanging on, waiting.

I kept my eyes looking straight ahead, but watching from the corner of them in such a way that I wouldn't be detected by the guard, and also where I could see every move that bastard made. I wouldn't dare stumble, and I saw the others near me were aware of what was about to happen. They also straightened up.

Five minutes passed. He was still right behind the Filipino, who didn't even act as if he were aware of the Jap being there. The man stumbled once more; he was almost to his knees. I saw that the man had been wounded. There was blood on the left leg of his trousers. Again the guard tightened his grip on the sabre hilt. When the soldier struggled back to his feet he saw the guard and faltered once more. This time the guard didn't wait. His sabre was withdrawn from its scabbard as the soldier fell forward. That long blade was over the guard's head, and he turned as the soldier fell and brought the blade down with full force across the neck of the falling man. His head was nearly severed from his body.

Without so much as breaking a step, I kept walking, my eyes straight ahead. The guard was wiping the blood from the blade with his back turned away from the marchers. I saw this and glanced toward the fallen warrior. The body was lying face down in the dust, legs sprawled apart and that grisly slash that nearly decapitated him plainly showing for all to see.

The guard remained standing with his back to the column as I passed his victim. Within minutes the scene was behind me. That blood-covered body would become yet another unrecognizable form along the trail of death, and just one more solemn reminder for those who passed of the atrocities being perpetrated upon us by the conquering army.

I quickened my pace. I wanted to be away from this place as fast as possible. I wanted to erase that scene from my mind; also I wanted as much distance between me and that son-of-a-bitch as I could get. Try as I might, I still saw that form with the head lying askew on its shoulder and that guard with his back turned wiping the blade of his sabre.

The terrain was changing now. We were leaving the mountain area and moving out onto more level land. There were still some rough areas, but off to the left and far out I saw green fields and areas where crops had been planted.

There were more people alongside the roads and small barrios some distance from the trail. On occasion I saw people standing in doorways. The Japs made us go around these populated villages, forcing us to skirt the towns.

The natives had made attempts to give food or water to their people as well as the Americans, but when they were caught they were severely punished.

By mid-afternoon, we changed direction. We had been walking north ever since leaving Bataan, but from the direction of the sun we had changed and were now moving more toward the east. The surface of the road was

84

hard and in some places there was blacktop. This reduced the amount of dust in the air. We had left the secondary roads and were on one of the main roads leading away from this part of Bataan. This road was more traveled than the trails we had been walking over for the past few days.

On each side of the road were unplanted fields and far off in the distance I saw patches of green. From here it looked like corn or sugarcane, but it was much too far out for me to identify.

Later, perhaps four o'clock in the afternoon, we came upon some artesian springs. They were spurting water into the air. These wells were only a few yards from the road. As I watched this phenomenon, I wondered if this might be a mirage. I hadn't had anything to drink since morning, because of my fears of being attacked by my own people. I still remembered those fellows who took my water bottle from me earlier on the march. The sight of that water spurting from the ground when everything had been so dry caused me to question my sanity. Nonetheless, it made me even more thirsty. I had to have water soon.

I watched the other men along the line of march as they looked longingly at that sight. I recognized that look in their faces. If I should take one of the those bottles from the pouch now, I was sure I would be killed. Besides, I knew how they felt. With all that cool water just out of reach, my throat had become so dry I could hardly stand not getting water some way.

Some of the water had found its way alongside the ditches. Some of our people caught the guards not looking and dropped down and drank from the hoof tracks of the farm animals or from the ditch alongside the road where small puddles had formed. Some of our group had been granted permission to leave the column for water, but other guards reasoned they might be attempting an escape and opened fire on them with their rifles.

Having witnessed the shootings, I was convinced the acts were done purposely, that those who did the shooting knew damn well they had been given permission.

Even with all this taking place, I knew I must have water soon, although I knew that if I opened one of my canteens, there was a good probability that I would be in trouble. With all this running through my mind, I contacted the nearest guard and asked him to accompany me to the nearest well. First he said, "Go on, it's okay."

"Hell no, you have seen the others with their rifles," I said.

With that he went along and the other guards never shot at me. I was able to get fresh water and in addition was given permission to fill both water bottles. The guard never knew that these bottles were already full and neither did the people in the ranks.

With my thirst taken care of and my deception intact, I felt good. Also, I still had that chocolate in my pack. The knowledge of having something to eat relieved some of the pressures of the moment.

We were back on a dirt road and the dust was in my face. The ranks had closed up into a tight march, causing the dust to worsen. We were now walking right on one another's heels and with no wind at all the dust was choking the hell out of me. Still I plodded forward.

Some of the Japanese guards who were alongside the column that morning were still with us. The bastards didn't look so damn fresh now. They also were feeling the effects of the heat and dust. If we were on this dusty road for long they wouldn't get any relief either. Perhaps we would be taken off the road soon for the night. It was getting late and even though the sun hadn't gone behind the mountain, it would be sundown soon.

I tried not to hear anything. Every ounce of strength that I had was being used to keep upright. The alternative was death—swift and certain.

At last! The sun fell behind the mountain range, and I felt a light breeze starting to blow against my back. My shirt was soaked with perspiration and that breeze seemed to hit and cool me all over.

The straps on my pack felt as though they had cut into my flesh. Even though this pack wasn't heavy it hung like lead across my shoulders. I noticed this especially because of that cool breeze. Before, I had been so preoccupied with the heat and the dust I had not noticed how the straps were cutting into my shoulders.

The breeze picked up more. I wished there was some way I could lift the bottom of the pack and let some of this cool air underneath. If only these bastards would stop. Hell, with this change in temperature, one would think even the sadistic bastards would want to stop for a rest.

Then, as if in answer to my prayer, the guards started closing the ranks as they had done before each night in preparation for stopping. "Hiako, Hiako," the screamed. "It's only a little farther." I kept on my feet, moving forward. I stumbled, almost going down, but managed to regain my footing. I was aware of the consequences if I fell. Once more I stumbled, and this time I fell all the way to the ground. Try as I might, I couldn't get back onto my feet. I tried once more. It was no use. I could go no farther. Then I became aware that others were all around me, face down in the dirt. We were off the road, stopped by the Japanese guards.

I was face down on the ground, breathing deeply of the cool air. For the longest time I lay there, just breathing, thankful to God that I had not fallen while on the road, that I had, in fact, made it to the rest area.

I took in more of the cool air but the heat on my back and shoulders made me aware that the pack was still there. I hadn't had the energy to remove the straps, nor for that matter, had I fully realized what had happened. At first I believed I had fallen on the road. I must have been completely unconscious on my feet.

Finally I got into a sitting position. When I removed the straps, it was as if skin was coming off with them. My shirt was soaking wet, especially under the pack, and when it was removed, the cool air hit my back like the air from an air conditioner. I turned so my back was facing the breeze, and with my head down between my knees, I closed my mind of all the day's events and just let Mother Nature relax my tired muscles and my weary mind. When I finally lifted my head, it was dark. Everyone was quiet.

It was very dark. No one was watching or paying attention to anything. I decided to drink water from my canteen. With everyone being tired, in this darkness, I wouldn't be noticed.

Taking one of the canteens from the pouch, I drank deeply. The heat being as it was this day, I was terribly in need of water, so, before returning the bottle to its pouch, I drank again, almost emptying one canteen.

When the bottle was safely back in its pouch, my mind turned to food. I opened the pack and found the chocolate bar. Breaking it in half, I ate the hard chocolate. I felt the energy surging through my body; if only there was something for bulk that would fill that great hole I felt inside.

After another hour, I took the canteen from the pouch. This time I emptied it. I still had another full bottle, so even if the Japs didn't bring in more water, I had enough for another day.

With the thought of having extra water, I fell asleep. Hell, my leg didn't even hurt, so I stretched out on the ground and slept.

Some time later, I was awakened by another truck pulling inside the rest area.

This time there were two trucks. One was rationing rice balls, while the other was a water truck. Most of the men were at the water truck, so I made my way to the rice ration, knowing that I needed food worse than water. Once again, we were rationed that same rice ball that they gave us before. It was a little sour, but I returned to the area where I was sleeping and ate it anyway. When this was finished, I went to the water truck. I drank as much water as I could.

Sometime in the early morning hours, I was awakened by sharp pains in my knee. Apparently with it feeling so well last night, I had not paid enough attention to it. Either I had slept on it or infection was starting. That medic back at Bataan warned me about infection. I searched the pack and found the sulfa powder. Then, after I unwrapped the wound I let the cool night air flow around the injured area. Taking my fingers I pressed around the wound, finding the whole area tender to the touch. I then took one of the water bottles, and with some of this precious water, I washed the wound. I dampened part of the bandage I made with some cloth torn from a pair of the shorts from the colonel's pack. Then I sprinkled the sulfa powder on the damp area and placed this over the wound and wrapped my knee with the rest of the pieces of underclothing.

All this took about thirty minutes. When I was finished, I stood and moved my leg, flexing it up and down for some time. The pain was gone and I was able to return to sleep.

It seemed as if I had just closed my eyes, when the guard started yelling that it was time for us to get back on the road.

I had grown used to this way of being awakened. I knew what was ahead. Almost without thinking, I took the partially filled canteen from the pouch and drank. Right now there was little danger in opening the bottle and I was fully aware that this might be the last opportunity I'd have for several hours for water.

It was much cooler compared with the past few days. As usual, though, these were new guards—well-rested and well-fed. They wanted us on the road fast, and those who were already marching by were being pushed hard.

I stepped out onto the road and melted in with the marchers. I wanted to be away from anyone who might know I had water. I hitched the belt up, making sure I let it wiggle the canteen around as if it were empty. Soon I was just another marcher who might have rested last night or one who could have been on the road the entire night; just one more body putting one foot in front of the other. I was fully aware of how fortunate I was. I had had the good fortune of staying out in the hills for four days. I had had extra water most of the time, and of course, that piece of hard chocolate.

We had been on the road for some three hours when a truck came alongside the line of marchers and then swung off the road into an opening. The guards ordered us off the road, and we were again given an opportunity to get water. If we had canteens, we could fill them.

The men up forward didn't have to be told. They charged the truck as soon as it stopped. I watched from a distance and while the men were getting water, I, along with a number of others, rested. Back of me, I saw nobody. The road was clear.

While we were getting water, another truck arrived and again we were issued one rice ball each. All this took no more than fifteen minutes.

The guards rested while we ate the rice; then again they screamed, "Hiako, Hiako," and the mob was on the move again. I hadn't even finished the rice, but ate as I picked up my pack and got back to the road.

Stepping out onto the trail, I glanced back. There were people some two hundred yards back now. They had caught up and we were once again strung out as we had been since I started on the march.

As we stepped out, very briskly now, with the added energy from the rice, my first thoughts were, "Perhaps we will be getting more rice today." What a hell of a way to think! I had just finished one of their damn sour balls of rice, and here I was wondering when they would be kind enough to issue more.

By mid-afternoon, we were still marching and hearing that same phrase, "Only two more hours." The heat had begun to be a major factor. The breeze was gone; there was nothing to move the dust. It was about head high and choking the hell out of us.

We were climbing a small grade and I saw the opening in the low trees up ahead. As the men walked through that opening they seemed to disappear over the ridge out of sight.

Soon I was approaching the top and could see far out into the flatlands below me, stretching for miles. I saw mountains in the far distance.

As I started down the grade on the other side, there was a small village only a few hundred yards out into the flatlands. Perhaps that is where we would stop; maybe that is where they had been driving us. My hopes rose. Then I looked closer and at the other side of the village, I saw the prisoners leaving. Then I followed with my eyes and saw them strung out for miles from the north edge of the little town. They looked like ants crawling out across the flat land as far as my eyes could see. I had not noticed them at first. I was so preoccupied with the belief that the guards had been pushing us hard, so we would be at our destination before darkness. Otherwise why would they have kept telling us, "Only two more hours"? Of course, there was no way of knowing how many people were in front of me. We had been in the rolling hills where there was timber or brush and couldn't see more than a few hundred yards forward or in any direction for that matter. What the hell did that bastard mean—only two more hours? It would take more than two hours to get out there where I could see the farthest man. The son-of-a-bitch was deceiving us, just to keep us moving.

As all these things ran through my mind, and as the anger rose within me, I found we had entered the village I saw from the top of the hill. We were entering the southern edge of the town by way of a dusty street. The dust was ankle-deep and hung in the air, refusing to move. It had settled on the sides and roofs of the bamboo houses.

In back of this main thoroughfare, people watched as we trudged along this trail of death. I saw tears running down their faces, and read the hurt in their eyes as they wept unashamedly as we passed. The Japs were more aggressive now that the people were watching them. They slapped and beat anyone in their reach in their attempt to show the natives their superiority.

Near the center of the village, a Filipino woman in the last weeks of pregnancy had been pushed or shot and had fallen in the narrow street where the marchers were moving. This woman, unable to drag herself from the line of march, had been trampled to death by us. Nobody was allowed to drag her from under the feet of the men and most assuredly the prisoners would be killed if they tried to assist this helpless woman.

The woman's unborn child had been trampled from her body and lay in the ankle-deep dust, gasping for breath in its effort to live. I saw the infant's mouth opening in a great struggle for air. The American and Filipino soldiers had been forced to walk over, step on, and trample these two forms in the dust until life was no more.

I suddenly became aware that, even though we had been forced to march over that woman, we were guilty of participating in her death because we didn't do anything to prevent it from happening. In later years, I would ask the question, "Wasn't there another way? And yet, I know that had there been anything that could have been done, it would have been done.

Passing on through the village, the guards did everything they could to prove their superiority over the Americans by beating hell out of us at every turn. The thought of that unborn child, choking, struggling for life amidst this torture, I wondered, had it the knowledge to fully understand what was being perpetrated against these men, had it the understanding of man's inhumanity to man, would it have struggled for life so desperately?

My sector of the march was clear of the village. The guards were pushing hard, as they had done each evening before ordering us off the road for the night. East of us I saw some automobile traffic. We were nearing an intersection with one of the main roads running north and south through the countryside. Also, a rail line ran parallel to the highway. The guards were rushing like mad now. They seemed to know where we were heading and wanted to get the trip over before the night. I saw several rail cars parked some distance from the buildings. I didn't know which town this was. I had never been this far north of Manila and had no idea where we were.

As we got closer to the buildings the guards kept screaming and beating anyone within their reach. It wasn't possible for me to think about where we were. It took every bit of effort to keep out of reach of the bastards. I had learned over the past few days that in order to do that I must always keep two or three other prisoners between them and me, so I tried staying in the center of the line of march.

I kept moving this way for some time, but others were doing the same. So when I moved from one side to the other, I sometimes found myself right in the face of a guard. While watching the guards, I fell. I had stepped into a small depression and before I could regain my footing, the guard near me slapped the hell out of me, knocking me half-way to my knees. I staggered forward and again I was hit in the mouth by the son-of-a-bitch. Getting myself upright again, I didn't even look at him. With blood streaming from my mouth, I picked up the pace, moving out of his reach. I had nothing but utter contempt for the bastards. What I had seen had convinced me that they had no place in the human race. They were nothing more than animals.

The prisoners had closed up ranks until we were walking right on each other's heels. I could see in all directions. We were being separated into smaller groups, with five or six guards per group. Marchers were being herded off the road toward what looked like an old burned-out building. Parts of the walls were still standing. There was a large, concrete floor covered with ash about an inch deep. There was an area across from the guards where part of the wall stood near the northeast corner of this building site. I scurried for that area while others just fell where they were.

It only took a few minutes to find out we couldn't move. If we did the ash swirled around, making so much dust we had difficulty breathing.

Getting to where I could put my back against the wall and where I could see those guards, I removed my pack and sat down. I needed water, but I'd have to wait. It was not dark enough.

I put my head down on my knees and closed my eyes, blocking out the day's events. When I opened my eyes again, it was totally dark. No one else had taken a place in this corner. The area was completely quiet.

Pulling my shirt up over my head as if I were letting air onto my bare skin, I removed one of my canteens, then lowered my head under the tail of my shirt and drank long and deep from the bottle. After several large gulps, I pulled my pack under my head and waited. I just didn't give a goddamn what might be ahead.

I lay there waiting for the ration of rice. It never came. Sometime around midnight one truck entered our area. It had water but no rice. I refilled my canteen and returned to my little wall. The Japs told us there would be no rice tonight.

Finding there would be no food, I went into my pack and found the piece of chocolate. This time there would be no holding back. There was only a small piece remaining, so I ate that. The candy bar saved my life. Without the extra energy given me from this hard chocolate, I would not have made it this far.

When I awoke the following morning, the sun was high in the east. We had been allowed to sleep later than anytime before. I wondered what the little bastards had in store for us.

I sure as hell didn't trust them. "Something is up," I muttered under my breath. "Hell, don't knock it, relax and enjoy it," someone said. I ignored the son-of-a-bitch. There was little enjoyment sitting in the goddamn ashes, but I supposed the man was right. It was better than being out on the road getting hell beat of you at every step.

The sun was high in the sky and the heat was unbearable, so at last I left my position to stand where I could see the activities.

There seemed to be much activity near the railroad yard. It was some distance away, but I saw people moving about in that area. Also, prisoners out in the open areas were moving in that direction.

It wasn't long until the guards told us to get ready to leave. I picked up my pack and stepped from the building. I saw marchers behind me on the move. Out at the road a guard stopped us while another group moved ahead of us. While this was going on I chanced getting some water, especially since these men all had water last evening. Taking the canteen from its pouch, I started drinking. I felt the eyes of these men watching, but that was it. They watched, nothing more. When I finished and the canteen was returned to the pouch, I felt a sense of relief, both that I had been able to get some water before getting out on the road and also that I had not been jumped.

The line started moving. We were out on the little trail going toward the rail yard. I couldn't imagine where we were. The only thng I knew is I had been walking north ever since I left that field hospital, but because of those four days walking and wandering around in the hills, I didn't think I was more than fifty miles from Bataan.

The guards were shoving and screaming. There seemed to be a sense of urgency about getting us away from here. I heard "Hiako, Hiako" everywhere. The prisoners were closing in on the boxcars fast. As my group came alongside the tracks, the guard directed us back down the tracks to the freight cars and away from the buildings.

I didn't see an engine in that direction, nor could I see any down this way. The cars seemed to be parked for loading, and as yet there was no locomotive to move them.

As we walked alongside the string of cars, I heard voices from within. There were moans as well as cursing. The sliding doors on the cars had been closed, and there were pins in the locks. Up to now, I had no idea what the Japs were going to do, but now it was obvious. They had been loading men in the boxcars and locking them inside. It sure as hell didn't take long to figure out that this wasn't going to be any pleasure trip.

My group was alongside one of the cars, and the door was open. The men moved forward to be loaded inside. The guard was yelling and threatening the men with his bayonet as they clambered inside. Before I knew what was going on, I was climbing up over the edge and into the dark railcar.

I remembered seeing an air vent on the end of the car as we were walking alongside the track, so I started crawling on hands and knees toward the end of the car.

The cars were small, no more than forty feet long. From the smell of manure, it would seem we had been loaded onto boxcars used primarily for shipping livestock to and from the markets. The guard standing at the door placed his sabre between my shoulder blades as I crawled past and screamed something I didn't understand. I made one lunge under the feet of the men standing in the car, and I was out of his reach and out of his sight. I felt the back end of the car. I was against the wall near where I had seen the air vent, so I pulled myself to my feet and for the moment was content just to stand there and get my breath.

Chapter 12

I had been inside the boxcar for more than an hour. The temporary blindness caused from coming in out of the bright sunlight was gone. Still, I couldn't make heads or tails out of what was in here. It was as dark as a dungeon inside, and men were jammed in like sardines. Those along the ends or the sides had an advantage. We could lean against something. Those in the center were compelled to stand and hold on to each other to keep from falling to the floor.

I had managed to squirm my way over until I was standing in one of the corners at the left side of the car. We waited; another hour passed. Still nothing. There was no indication that the train was going to be moved. The only sound that could be heard was the moaning from the people inside the car. Some were cursing, others were crying. The heat was unbearable. Still we waited. The air was stifling and the smell had become so bad I dreaded the thought of breathing. Some people had diarrhea. Most of us were stripped down to nothing, wearing just shorts or cutoff trousers or a G-string. Nothing between them and whatever was under them. I caught myself slipping down the side of the car, and I made a grab at the top for something to hold onto. Finding a cross-member along the end, I pulled myself back to my feet.

My thoughts were about that locked door. What happened if the car should get derailed? Worse yet, what if one of our bombers spotted us and thought we were just another Japanese supply train? There were no markings that I could see. They would blow the hell out of us. We could be burned to death in this thing. There wouldn't be a chance of getting out.

With the thought of fire, I started thinking about the chance of one of us accidentally setting the place afire. It was doubtful that anyone would try smoking even if they had something to smoke; they would be scared to let anyone know they had tobacco for fear of being mobbed. I remembered the sock filled with tobacco inside my pack. I sure as hell wouldn't try getting that out.

This bunch of crazed men had degenerated to the point they thought only of survival. For them to kill for water or food, or for that matter tobacco, would not surprise me in the least. Fear of fire from inside didn't seem to be a concern—but from outside, that was another question.

It was in the middle of the afternoon. It seemed like I had been standing for hours. My legs were like lead, and my knee ached. I wished I could remove my pack, but that would be impossible. I must leave it on my back.

The men in the center of the car had nothing to lean against, only each

93

other, and that caused problems. I heard someone say, "Goddamn it, don't lean against me," or "Get the hell away from me, I can hardly stand myself." These men were now starting to fall. Their legs had given away from standing too long in one place. Heat exhaustion was also taking its toll. The men had suffered from starvation, thirst, combat wounds, and tropical diseases, such as malaria and dingue fever, and were falling like flies in this sweat box.

The groans from the ones who had fallen to the floor could be heard plainly. They pleaded in vain with the men around them to help. Nobody was able to render any assistance. As they cried louder and the numbers increased, I tried blocking out the cry for help. The moans and wailing rang loudly inside my head. The sobs roared inside my mind as I put my hands over my ears. It was no good. It was a roaring river ever increasing in intensity, until I myself felt the urge to scream. Pulling hard against the cross-member, I remained upright.

Those on the floor were dying. They were at the mercy of those yet standing, and they too would be on that same floor dying unless something was done, and quickly.

I felt myself slipping again, and with all my strength, I pulled myself up. My hand moved across the timber and I grabbed the edge of the air vent. In doing this I felt some bolts that held the cross-member to the end of the car. There were also some large steel rings bolted to the timber. They were on a swivel that allowed them to lay flat against the wall when not in use, but could extend out on sort of a hinge.

I had my face toward the wall, hanging onto the ring for dear life with my left hand. There was very little light inside here, but I saw three rings placed at intervals across the cross-timber.

After testing the strength of the rings, I removed my belt, then ran it through the ring. Then I brought it under the straps of my pack and buckled the belt. In this way, I was able to hang with most of my weight suspended by the belt, giving my legs and feet some rest. At the same time, I could protect myself from falling to the floor and into the slimy human excrement where I would most assuredly be trampled to death.

I relaxed in this resting position for some time. I could raise onto my toes and tighten the belt, making it shorter, and then let my entire weight hang on the ring. God, how my legs ached from standing in one position and struggling constantly to keep from slipping down into the slime on the floor. Being able to hang was a blessing. I wondered why I didn't see the ring earlier.

I had no way of knowing how long we had been here. Time had very little meaning. I hung from the ring for awhile, until circulation became a problem in my arms, then I let myself down and rubbed myself until the tingling left my arms. I could only stay up for short periods. But by rotating, I was able to withstand the torture.

Sometime later, I noticed there was no light coming through the vent. It must be dark outside. Inside it was as dark as any dungeon. I couldn't make out any faces. There were only forms near me, and since my back was to them most of the time, I could only sense their nearness.

I wondered if I should attempt to get some water from my canteen? I sure as hell needed it. But if I were caught, there was no telling what would happen—I must wait a while longer.

Taking the belt back through the ring and under the straps of my pack, once again I suspended myself, taking the weight off my feet and legs. I was thinking about the water, and was wide awake, my eyes searching this mass of humanity in the darkness and listening for any signals from them. I knew I needed water, but also must use every caution at this point. My arms were tingling, so I let myself down and at the same time turned my face into the corner of the car. Then, very carefully, I removed the canteen from the pouch, took the lid off, and quickly drank this life-giving liquid. When I swallowed, I heard the noise and was scared that it was audible over the moans of the dying men. I took one more swallow, then very slowly put the cap back on and returned the canteen to the pouch. Everything I did seemed to roar, even screwing the cap back on and closing the pouch. I snapped the fastener on the pouch; I waited for someone to grab me. Nothing. I had been successful. I was aware that this water was the only thing that would sustain me. Keeping it hidden from the dying men became the most important thing in my life. I still had water for later. I was convinced that the men with me would kill or be killed in an attempt to get water. I kept this knowledge uppermost in my mind at all times. My survival depended on whether I got water from the canteen without anyone seeing me.

With the water safely back in the pouch, I ran the belt back through the ring and lifted myself off the floor again. I had barely let my weight down into the straps when I felt a jerk of the car. Was it me swinging back against the wall? I waited. There were some noises from somewhere forward. I waited some more. I was almost holding my breath. I felt the car move. My God! Was my mind playing tricks on me? No, it was moving! Slowly at first, now picking up speed. It was moving and as it did, I felt some cool air coming through the vent over my head. God had taken a personal hand in our fate. There was fresh air. It was gushing through the vent. The odor of human feces was blown away from me.

I let myself down onto the floor and held onto the ring for balance. While the train sped along and cool air streamed through the vent overhead, I used all the spiritual knowledge I had to thank God just for air to breathe.

The direction of travel was north, and I was at the front end of the car. People had stopped moaning; or if there were moans, I was not able to hear them over everyone's talking. The cursing had ceased and only low murmurs could be heard as the train sped through the night.

After an hour, some of the men on the floor regained their senses. I heard the pleas for help somewhere in the darkness. I heard low muffled weeping near the center of the car.

Once again, my legs were tiring from the jolting of the car as it sped along the track, and I slipped the belt through the ring and turned my back on those crying, trying desperately to blot out their sobs. It was no use, even with my hands over my ears.

I slipped the canteen from the pouch and drank a small amount of water, fixed the belt through the straps of my pack, then relieved the weight from my feet. There was water for yet another time.

Sometime along about daylight the train slowed. It had slowed a number of times since leaving the station, but this time it was apparent that it was going to stop.

When it came to a complete stop, the air stopped flowing and the smell was back as bad as before.

We waited—nothing. Then from somewhere forward, I heard voices. Prisoners were yelling at one another.

Outside the car, there was some activity. Suddenly the sliding door was opened.

It wasn't quite daylight but some light entered the wide door and outside guards were telling us to get off the car.

There was no hesitation. We all tried to get out the door of this hell pit at the same time. We almost fell out the door.

Being all the way back in the car, I waited and was one of the last to leave the car. I replaced my belt in my trousers while I waited for the rest to get off.

Making my way toward the door, I stepped over bodies on the floor of the car. As I turned to slide from the sliding doorway, I saw a number of bodies remaining inside. There was no effort to check if these men were dead or unconscious. Our people were rushing away from the car, and the Japs weren't paying any attention. These men would be left where they were for someone else to care for. Who? Hell! God only knew.

I took one glance at the inside as I slid down to the ground. As I turned to walk away, I could almost hear the typewriters at some distant office back in Washington, as the clerk tried sorting out what had happened to those left inside the boxcar. They would be placed in that ever-growing list of "lost in action."

All the cars had been unloaded, and the survivors were some distance from the track in an open area, with no guards near us. I could still smell the train, or was it just my imagination?

I found a place to sit and rest. Then I took the canteen from the pouch, opened the lid, and emptied the contents. With everyone looking, I turned the bottle where all could see it was empty before returning it to the pouch.

It was still cool, and the Japs weren't in any rush. They were allowing us to sleep or rest as we wished.

After two or three hours there was a water truck in our area, and I saw more a few hundred yards away. We would all get drinking water.

When I had filled both canteens and found a good spot to rest, I had a good opportunity to look over these prisoners.

I was particularly interested in the American prisoners. I was unable to tell much about the Filipino soldiers. They were small, but I could make a much better judgment about the Americans.

The men had been able to survive thus far, although in poor condition.

Those who were seriously injured in combat hadn't made it. The rest were walking quite well. They were tough, they were mean, and they were determined. There were a lot less injured now than when we were put inside that pit of hell. Many of the sick and wounded had died and their remains were still on the freight car, especially since I didn't see the Japs separating the sick and injured before we boarded the cars.

Nobody was talking. There was no conviviality among the prisoners, especially the Americans. Some of the Filipinos had congregated, but even they were not talking as much.

I didn't trust anybody. I didn't expect anything from anyone. From what I had experienced over the past few days, if I was going to live, in all probability it would be at the expense of some other son-of-a-bitch. I was sure they felt the same as I.

Before the truck left, I went back once more and began filling the bottle I had been drinking from. I took more time than someone thought I should. Someone yelled, "Get you damn ass away from the water and let someone else get some." I just glared back at them and continued filling the bottle. A Jap stepped up and slapped the hell out of me, forcing me away, but I had one full canteen and the other was over half-full. My face was bleeding and one eye was partially closed, but I felt the satisfaction that I had enough water for yet another day.

It was well into the morning before the Japs were ready for us to move away from the area.

Those groups toward the front of the train moved out first. The guards were busying themselves by prodding at prisoners with their bayonets and yelling as loudly as their lungs allowed. The yells of "Hiako, Hiako," were everywhere.

I managed to get away from that group where I filled my canteens. I rubbed my swollen face and almost smiled at the thought of having so much water on my belt and knowing that the prisoners around didn't know it.

Soon my section was ordered onto the road. Before we walked fifteen minutes, we entered the southern edge of a small village. Over on the right side of the road was a sign painted red. There were some numbers and small printed words I didn't understand, then a large word: "CAPAS."

We passed through this part of the village in minutes and were out on yet another secondary road leading almost directly west.

It didn't look like a road used by automobiles or trucks, but was more of a farm road, used by wagons and carts pulled by animals. For the most part it was dirt, with deep ruts worn on each side. In the center of it were weeds and grass, now trampled by the marchers.

It was much cooler, and I welcomed the opportunity to walk. Only a few days ago, I didn't think I would ever say that.

The Japanese guards hadn't altered their attitude toward us. It was just good to be out in the open air, away from that boxcar and away from the awful smell and where the air I breathed was clean.

Walking along, watching these men stepping rather lively in the cool

97

breeze, it was apparent that only the strong had survived. Few men were falling now.

Because there were fewer men falling, the Japs had to use more force and their atrocities were more open. The bastards didn't have the excuse that the prisoners were not able to keep pace and must be eliminated. Those who got bayoneted now were being slaughtered for the sake of murder.

This group of guards seemed harder than those who started the march, and were much more determined to eliminate us with or without provocation.

The guards walked on the right side of the column, so, as I had done all along, I moved over to the opposite side, always keeping other prisoners between them and myself.

In the short time I had been a prisoner of war, I had learned to read the bastards quite well. They were looking for an excuse to kill someone. By my keeping people between them and myself, there was less chance of my provoking them into using their bayonets on me.

We had walked for some time. I dodged from side to side as the guards moved. Then I noticed the column closing up, and I heard more guards yelling, "Hiako."

Were we going to get a break this soon? It didn't make sense. We hadn't been on the road that long, but we had been moving quite fast.

"Hiako, Hiako," they screamed. "Only a short time now." I wondered if I dared believe this was the end of the ordeal.

I remembered back in Bataan, when that son-of-a-bitch kept telling us over and over, "Only two more hours, only two more hours," and when I saw that long line of marchers across the flat land. Was this just another hoax? I sure as hell didn't trust them. We were closing ever tighter, and were right on each other.

The march had slowed now and at times we had to wait for short periods for the people ahead of us to move.

This went on for another hour. Then I saw some buildings about a quarter of a mile ahead of us. They appeared to be on the right side of the road and stretched back east for some distance.

The buildings could be military barracks. They were single-story structures placed in rows and large enough for forty or fifty men.

Getting closer, I saw they were built of bamboo. There were openings on the sides like windows with no glass and at the ends there was another door-like opening.

Within minutes we were alongside this compound. It had been fenced with barbed wire and inside Americans and Filipinos were milling around. As we passed, they barely gave us a second glance. It was as if they had seen this activity for some time.

The column stopped. Up ahead was some sort of commotion. Listening, I heard someone screaming. No one moved. I listened for that scream again. Stillness. Nobody was talking, not even the Jap guards. Slowly the column started moving forward.

Up ahead and to my right was a tower about thirty feet high. Inside this tower were Japanese guards with a machine gun trained in this direction.

This was the end of the march. The men up ahead were entering the compound. A smaller building on the right obscured the entrance from my view, but I saw men running who had passed through this checkpoint.

The column stopped once more. There was another commotion. I heard muttering from the prisoners ahead of me. There was muffled grumbling coming from the people up ahead that ran back through the ranks.

I was on the outside of the column, nearest the guards bunched up just forward. I moved slowly back into the mob. I must keep people between me and the Japs so as not to be conspicuous.

I had no idea what was going on up there, but I had made it this far and sure as hell didn't intend to be killed right at the front gate of this prison by being stupid.

I saw now what caused that commotion. The gate post on the left side of the entrance had the head of a Filipino soldier, while the one on the right had the head of an American soldier. The guards had placed the heads in such a manner that they stared down at us as we entered the gate.

I turned my head to avoid the stare, and alongside the fence was the body of an American. He had been murdered in the last few minutes, bayoneted, and was still bleeding from the large hole in his chest.

Goddamn, they prepared this entrance well for us. I felt the hair on the back of my neck crawl.

Seeing this grisly mess, I tried to get as many people around me as I could and at the same time move faster toward that gate.

The Japs were scared someone might run amok and try killing one of them, so they made us crowd in closer.

Some twenty-five yards inside the compound, an American officer stood directly in front of the men who were entering and moved us in the direction we should go. This was the greatest thing I had seen. He was the most courageous man I had ever seen.

He had no plan; he just wanted us away from this place. I am sure he witnessed that murder just a few short minutes before and knew that more would be murdered if we didn't get away from the gate.

When I came through the gate, under those heads, with no guard inside or in front of me, I bolted forward toward this officer. He saw me coming and stepped aside, pointing to where I was to go, and said, "Get the hell out of here fast!" There was no waiting. With increased strength, I broke into a run and didn't stop until I was well inside the compound.

More people inside told us where to go, but none of them stood out like that officer.

There wasn't anyone taking names and with all the confusion at the gate, I understood why. I wondered how anyone would ever know who was here or, for that matter, how many. I had run for more than two hundred yards and was deep inside the barracks area out of sight and out of earshot of the Japanese.

There was no screaming by the guards, no sounds. Nothing, except the echo from the scream of that dying soldier. I could still see the limp form at the side of the barbed wire fence.

I was now inside one of the bamboo buildings, not knowing who directed me there.

Finding a place to sit until my eyes adjusted to this light, I waited. It was quiet here. Good God! I was in a concentration camp. Would I at last get some rest? Were any medical facilities here? What about food and water? There were a million questions and no answers.

Looking down the aisle, I spotted one of the bays that wasn't occupied, so I walked in that direction and, without asking, crawled back near the wall, took off my pack, placed it where it could be used as a pillow, lay my head back, and closed my eyes.

At last I was off my feet. I could rest and give my injured leg a chance to stop aching.

I still heard noises outside. Men were still coming. They were moving deeper into the barracks area. Sometimes one entered this building, looked around for an empty spot, but finding none, moved on through and out the other end.

I was accustomed to the light, and could see the interior of this barracks.

It was about sixty feet in length, and no more than thirty feet wide. There was no flooring, only a narrow strip of bamboo slats forming a walkway through the center of the building. Every six feet or so were bamboo upright poles. These ran from the floor to the roof. About eighteen inches above the ground, another pole ran parallel to the ground. There someone constructed pallet or bamboo in a square about six by eight feet and tied this pallet at the front and at the wall, forming a bay about six feet wide by eight feet deep. In these cubicles there was room to accommodate two prisoners.

The outer walls were constructed in much the same way: a framework of bamboo poles, with bamboo fronds covering the frames. The roofs were of native nipa, a grass-like material.

While this type of construction seemed rather primitive by American standards, it was effective as a method of protecting the people from the rains during the heavy rainy seasons. During the dry season, the thick walls retained a certain amount of dampness that kept the heat out.

Soon the noises subsided. It was getting dark. Nobody was talking. Most were resting.

After an hour or so, I awoke and my leg was aching. I leaned against the wall and removed the dirty bandage. There was some infection, but the aching let up some with the bandage off, and the cool air felt good.

To hell with it. I'd rebandage it later. With that I lay back with my head on my backpack and let the last five months pass before my eyes.

Chapter 13

The events of the past five months were hazy, especially that period of combat. Those events were overshadowed by the actions of my captors during the past few days.

I hadn't had the time to contemplate what had occurred in my life. It had been a time of self-preservation, with little or no time for rational thinking about what had happened to the American forces.

I wondered if I should consider myself fortunate that I was alive, or were those killed in the Battle of Bataan the fortunate ones?

Most of the men with me at the fall had been killed during that battle. They wouldn't have to spend the rest of their lives with the knowledge of the deaths and tortures on the "march of death."

But who was I to make such a judgment? Thinking of that great heap of bodies with the one pointing toward the heavens, I found little in that scene as it flashed across my mind that would cause me to want to exchange places.

The mental stresses of not knowing what moment I would be blown to bits by bombs and shelling had been exchanged with the images of the tear-stained faces of the Filipinos who lined the roadsides.

Had I lost all self-respect? I sure as hell didn't have any respect for anyone around me.

At this point I knew that I was alive—"survival of the fittest"—and I couldn't find any satisfaction in that fact. It sure as hell didn't help that I knew it after the fact.

Had I lost all respect for mankind? As far as the Japanese were concerned, I couldn't even see them as a part of the human race. The events of the past few days had altered my attitude toward life and death.

For a fleeting moment I saw those pure mountain streams and small creeks back in Bataan, where I fished and hunted before the war. I drank from those streams without the fear of becoming ill. Now, those same streams were polluted with bodies. No one in this generation would be able to fish those streams without thinking about what had happened there.

When I thought of those who were wounded but lived and all the broken bodies that I had seen strewn along the way, I found them all secondary to broken minds.

I felt betrayed by my government. How are the people in my government explaining this back home? Why am I part of this tragedy? Both questions went unanswered.

101

My mind turned toward the people touched by this war and this battle, who in all probability had had little or no consideration about their great loss. The family of that expectant mother who was trampled to death by us, the Americans along with her own people, even though we were forced to march directly over her. What were the thoughts of this family? What would their answer be, if asked where their loyalties lay?

Who would blame them for their anger or even hatred at their own government, or of course, the government of the United States? What possible interest could this family have in the goddamn war?

While I pondered these questions, another image arose: that colonel who jumped to his death. Certainly, he didn't have to concern himself with survival. His broken body was at the bottom of that ravine as a monument to the broken spirits of those who survived.

I wondered if any unit had accounted for him. Did the United States army know what happened to him? Had his unit dropped this officer from its rolls as "killed in action" or "missing in action"? If so, missing to whom? Certainly not missing in action by my account; I knew his status. All too well I knew what happened to him. I lived because of his death. That chocolate bar I got from his pack was the reason I survived and was now in Camp O'Donnel.

Should I be grateful that I was afforded an opportunity to live by having life-saving chocolate, or should I despise the colonel for robbing me of my right to die?

First day in a
concentration camp

Chapter 14

Long before daybreak, on my first day in the concentration camp, I was awakened by people entering the building. All of them seemed to be searching for a place to lie down. I assumed they were more marchers coming in to camp and needing a place to sleep. It became quiet again, and I realized they belonged in this barracks and had been outside for some reason. As it turned out they had been out for water. The Japanese would let the prisoners turn the water spigot on only once during the day, and if you missed getting water, there would be none until the spigot was turned on the next day. No one had bothered to wake me when the word was passed. I went back to sleep, vowing that they could all go to hell as far as I was concerned. Before I was asleep, I remembered how I hid in order to prevent anyone from seeing me while on the march. I realized that was how we all managed to get here alive. A new breed of Americans was in the making. Like it or not, this was the environment I must learn to live in—or die in, as the case might be. I took the canteen from its pouch and drank, then returned to sleep—my first in over a week. That seemed more important now than anything.

Once more I was awakened by the cleaning of mess gear and this time I would not be left behind. Since there were no facilities for cleaning up, I fell in with the mob without asking where they were going. Soon I was in line waiting for whatever food might be available.

Ahead was a very large building, 150 feet long and 50 to 60 feet wide. It had a low roof and was open on each side. Toward the southern end the bamboo closed off an area where ranges were situated. Out in front of these stoves was a serving counter. As we walked in front of this serving counter, we were given our rice. I spent a lot of time picking out little white worms and other bugs from this watery rice. It had no seasoning or salt.

While I was picking out the bugs and worms, I noticed a number of prisoners eating and not looking for the worms, just eating and ignoring them. Soon I would be doing the same.

On my return to the barracks I saw another line and went in that direction. I learned another water tap had been turned on. Once again my luck was holding.

With the knowledge that I had adequate water and some food I returned to my barracks with the full intention of resting up. I damn sure didn't aim to get too well acquainted with anyone. Right now, I owed allegiance to no one and I expected none from anybody around me.

It wasn't until the afternoon that I decided to walk around the camp. There was more honesty here than I expected. I could leave my gear in the sleeping area without fear of having anything stolen. This gave me freedom to look the place over, move about, and see what facilities we had in camp. I was in need of medical attention, and wanted to find out if there were any medical facilities. Even though my wound felt much better, I knew of the danger of infection.

Over near the south end of the prison compound, I located what served as the dispensary. I entered and asked to see a doctor. Instead, I was directed to an enlisted corpsman who unwrapped the wound, cleaned the area as much as possible, put some medication on the wound, rewrapped it with clean bandages, and released me.

As I was leaving, I saw many sick and wounded people that needed attention much more than I. I was fortunate indeed to get any attention at all.

Walking along near the barbed wire, I saw soldiers who had given up and lain down along the fence. They could go no farther, not even to their barracks, where they could get out of the sun and away from the flies. Most would die where they lay.

I was determined not to get involved in anything. Unless some goddamn Jap forced me to do otherwise, I'd get inside the barracks and rest.

I needed to sift things through my mind, try to make some sense out of what had occurred over the past few weeks.

Crawling back into the sleeping bay, bracing my back against the wall, I had my first chance to get a good look at my surroundings.

There were only about a dozen men inside. Most were resting or just staring at the wall. A lot of men were out of the barracks. Their gear was stashed in the bays. I wondered if some were out on detail or just looking the place over as I was a bit earlier.

I hadn't seen anyone I knew. I let my eyes drift across one face on to the next, not letting them catch me looking at them. Eventually I became very tired and sleepy and blissfully dropped off.

Late in the afternoon, I was awakened by the rattle of mess gear and it was apparent we were to be given more to eat. Once again I asked no questions. I just fell in and followed along in the same general direction as the others, not talking to anyone, just looking ahead toward the large bamboo building where the watery rice was served.

Passing along in front of the serving counter, I was served a scoop of steamed rice, and again without comment followed the others out the side of the building. Finding a place to sit down, I ate this mixture of rice and worms and bugs. I tried to get them out, but at last I gave up and like the rest of the people, ate every grain from the mess kit and pretended all was well.

We were served rice two times a day and were given no water for clean-up. We barely had sufficient water for drinking purposes. I found an area not far from the barracks where there was some sand. I cleaned my mess kit with sand and a piece of cloth torn from a pair of shorts.

104

There were no latrines, just slit-trenches for toilets. The cases of dysentery were increasing by the minute. The slit-trenches became the center of attraction. At any given time fifty or sixty men were either using these trenches or waiting in line to use them.

These facilities created their own health problems, especially with flies. They became so thick they seemed to obscure the sun at times. They were everywhere—in the barracks, in the mess area, out in the barracks area. The only respite from them was darkness.

After eight or nine days inside this prison, I heard rumors about getting on details outside the camp. The Japanese would increase the rice ration and also there wouldn't be any limit on the amount of drinking water. I felt my leg was healed enough now that I could consider this option. I sure as hell didn't aim to sit here and starve to death, as was the case with many prisoners. Either they couldn't or wouldn't eat the rice with the insects in it and as a result they died. The lines taking the dead away grew longer and longer each day.

I had to find a way to get assigned outside the camp. Hell, I might even get the opportunity to escape if I could get outside the barbed wire. My spirit was running high at the thought. If I should be able to get out of sight of these monkeys I wouldn't be taken by them again.

With all these thoughts running wild through my mind, I started looking for someone who could get me on some sort of detail.

Up near the front gate, the Japanese allowed the American officers to get together a small staff to assist them in controlling the prisoners.

When I arrived at this building, I began looking the place over from the outside. Some small flat tables were up near the front of the building, and just inside the front door an American noncommissioned officer sat at one of the tables. He looked as if he would be the one who could give me information on any details outside the compound.

After some time I entered, walked over to the sergeant, and said I would like to volunteer for a work detail, one that offered extra rice and water. He took my name and my barracks number. He then instructed me to return to the barracks and remain there until I was called. He would send someone for me as soon as a determination was made on the detail to which I would be assigned.

Sometime during the afternoon of the following day, a soldier entered the barracks and called my name. At first I didn't answer, not knowing what he wanted. But when he called once more and stated I was wanted for work detail up at the administration building, I came forward and accompanied him outside where there were three or four more prisoners. Together we proceeded to the building where I was yesterday.

Entering the building, I was motioned to a chair and after a short time the sergeant asked, "Do you still want a work detail?" When I answered affirmatively he directed me to report to the medical dispensary the following morning, as soon as I had finished my rice.

As the word was spread that the water spigot had been opened, I fell in with the rest for my ration of water. Standing in this line in the heat and fighting off the goddamn flies, I wished the sun would get behind the mountain. I inched forward in line until at last I could fill my canteen. Then I saw the line forming for the rice. It was dark now so I just fell in.

Long before daybreak, I awoke and proceeded to the mess building for my rice. I was finished and at the dispensary by the time the sun was up, anxious to learn what I would be expected to do.

Chapter 15

I arrived at the medical facility early, with some apprehension about asking to go to work, but with the full knowledge that if I didn't keep busy, my fate would be, as it had been for so many, to waste away both mentally and physically. So I entered the building and presented my work card to the Japanese guard, who motioned me through the back door to the dispensary.

Inside, I was met by an American medical corpsman. I presented my card to him and was directed toward the rear of the building, where a detail of some fifty men was waiting to be sent out when needed. As I came through the door I saw an American captain standing near the door. Assuming him to be in command, I reported to him for duty.

"Thanks for coming, Sergeant," he stated. "We have the dubious honor of disposing of the dead. With that limp you will have difficulty carrying bodies to the burial area. You can go out with the first crew and work with the detail digging the graves. Those men over near the gate are ready to move out now. Go ahead with them and relieve the men who have been digging all night." With that I joined the others at the gate and passed through. Outside another Jap was waiting to escort us to the designated area.

About a dozen of us marched for a mile and a half southeast to the gate, where we relieved the crew on duty. It wasn't until now that I found out we would also have the responsibility of assuring that a maximum number of bodies were in the burial site before the hole was covered.

The holes were twelve feet by sixteen feet and in most cases were at least six feet deep. Sometimes we struck stone and weren't able to get that deep.

Two of us would be stationed down inside the site and as the bodies were dumped down, our job would be to lay them in such a manner as to get as many as possible in the pit. The first layer would be in one direction, the next would be changed from the head to the feet. This way the head of the second layer was between the feet of the layer below.

After receiving these instructions, I moved off toward the site that had been finished. I saw the Japanese guards moving away from us. Some of them were putting face masks on. As they moved away my eyes caught sight of movement from the direction of the compound where a column of men was coming this way. "Yonder is the first bunch," someone said, A noncommissioned officer touched my shoulder and said, "Get your partner and get down in that first pit." At that point I took the arm of the man

107

standing next to me and down into the pit we went. I waited for whatever was to come.

The first two men were at the edge of the site with their cargo, and as I reached for the body they rolled it over the edge, nearly knocking me off my feet. Before I could right myself the second body was rolled in. The man with me grabbed the first one and dragged it to the far corner so I followed suit with the one that had just fallen from above. These first two or three bodies had faces. I even saw that they were Filipino. Then, as the pile at the edge grew, they lost their faces and I knew there was no personality to these forms. There were no feelings. They came from nowhere. No kin to mourn their passing, no priest to say words over them. Nothing. For a moment I felt something. I knew if this didn't leave, I would be the one being dragged across the bottom of the pit.

For the next half-hour to forty-five minutes I dragged, tugged, and straightened limbs in the common grave until they were ready to be covered. I reached for an outstretched hand and was assisted from this pit. I looked down, and I could see I had been standing on top of bodies. I moved away some twenty or thirty yards, sat down with my head between my knees, and the nausea overcame me. But with only water and watery rice in my stomach, I only had the dry heaves until I was completely exhausted. No one even bothered to look in my direction. They all understood.

The temperature had risen very quickly since the sun came up. It was beating down. The damn Japs refused to let us cover the dead in the last hole. It wasn't full as they thought it should be. The smell was so putrid we could hardly breathe, and the flies so thick I was kept busy keeping them away from my face. The fucking Japs had on their gas masks. I hoped the bastards smothered to death. I'd gladly push their damn asses down in that hole and finish filling the space they so badly wanted filled.

The Japanese guards moved back away from the site, and as they pulled back we did the same. Very shortly another group arrived with more dead. At least the hole would get covered.

It was nearly noon when the last of the dead had been disposed of, and we were on our way back to camp. I didn't feel clean, so I left the rice line and went back to the spigot to wash and clean up once more. As I returned and received an extra ration, I looked at it and thought, "What a hell of a price!" I ate it anyway. Then I went to the water spigot and filled my water bottle and returned to the bamboo barracks for a much needed rest.

This was the procedure for disposal of the American and Filipino dead at Camp O'Donnel. My duties were working down in the pits or bringing the bodies from the dispensary area out to the burial site.

On the days when I was assigned to pick up bodies, I found I had to get up early and eat my watery rice as quickly as I could so as to be first at that fenced-in area behind the dispensary. My partner and I could select a body and carry it to the gate and wait until the Japanese guard was ready for us to proceed.

These mornings seemed to be the most degrading of all. Everybody was run down both physically and mentally. If we were unlucky and got a heavy body, we would be near death ourselves by the time we arrived at the burial site. Consequently, there were fights over who got the lighter bodies. The persons who got there early had the choice of the light ones. When you lost the fight, you got the heavier load and, weakened by the fight, had an even bigger problem.

As I watched, as well as participated in these acts, I became convinced that when the human animal has been stripped of his dignity, he will revert to the level of other creatures in order to survive. Since he has the ability to think and make decisions, he is worse than a lot of the other creatures. Somehow, I had become as much a part of this animal-like behavior as any of them. I also had engaged in the fights for the lighter loads.

On one of the mornings when I overslept and came to the area after everyone had already selected the choice cargo, I searched back under the bamboo building for one that might have been overlooked. The hopelessly ill had been committed to this area by our medics because they had no chance of living and the medicines were so scarce. They must be used for those who had a better chance. These men had crawled in and out of the sun and had been trying to get out through the bamboo latticework around the building. Some had died in their efforts while others were still living. As I crawled over or around the dead as well as the living, I saw a soldier near the rear of the place tearing at the latticework, trying to make a hole big enough that he could get out. In his weakened condition he was unable to pull the slats loose. When I got near him, I saw he was half-crazy. I grabbed the bamboo with him and together we tore a large hole for him to get through. When I had selected my cargo and was waiting to be allowed to leave, I saw him crawling away from the building toward the barracks area. Maybe he would make it back to his barracks.

When I had washed for the evening meal, I encountered the army captain in charge of the detail. He informed me that one of the Jap guards told him that Corregidor had surrendered. With total disbelief, I went to my barracks carrying heavy thoughts and sadness. I now knew there was no fight left in me. How long could I endure? With the death rate increasing by the hour, the number required to dispose of would only increase. That may well be all we did. Those of us able to move would keep taking the dead to the burial site until, at last, some one would carry us over that same road.

Within two weeks prisoners captured on the "Rock" were brought into camp. Most of these men were more healthy than we who had been in camp since the fall of Bataan. They were getting one hell of a shock at seeing what was going on here.

It was now June 1942, and the rains started. I was still on the burial detail, rationalizing that someone had to do this job. Since there was extra rice and plenty of water, I would continue this ghoulish task.

Death and disease were everywhere. It was doubtful if anyone was capable of keeping a record of the numbers dying; and if anyone was making records, I was sure the fucking Japs would kill them if they were caught.

The burial detail had increased in number to about five hundred men. We were split into two shifts, a day shift and a night shift. At least one hundred of us were assigned to digging the pits. This detail was now permanent. My bunch brought them in and the men at the pits took over.

At the end of each shift when I had finished cleaning up and eating my rice, I returned to the barracks. My fellow prisoners did their damndest to avoid me, keeping as far away as possible. When I inquired of one of the other prisoners as to why, he replied, "You smell of death and we see so much of it around us during the day, we sure as hell don't like to smell it at night." It seemed that I had become so accustomed to the stench that I no longer noticed it, nor did I care that the odor might be offensive to people near me. At any rate, my preference was to be left strictly alone. Friendships, it seemed to me, were a liability rather than an asset.

Sometime in the latter part of June 1942, I was awakened early in the morning hours by a loud clap of thunder, and I could hear rain falling outside. Somehow I knew that the day would be a bastard. The rain was coming down in torrents, yet I knew I must report to the dispensary for more of the same as the day before, and the day before that. The death rate was still going up and even with five hundred men on this detail, we were not able to keep up.

Arriving at the mess area, with the rain falling in sheets, I felt cleaner than I had in months, but I could see the cooks weren't impressed at all with my cleanliness. They didn't want to be any closer to me than absolutely necessary. They let us serve ourselves, while they stood back and observed. If one of us took more than they thought we should have, they yelled at us to lighten up. I moved away from them to the far end of the building. I finished the watery mess as fast as possible so as to get to St. Peter's ward ahead of the others. I didn't feel like fighting for a lighter load.

Back in May when the weather was dry, we had a blanket in which to carry the bodies. The blankets had long since been replaced with the doors from the bamboo buildings. These could be used over and over again but with this method of carrying our dead, there was no way we could avoid looking at them. Still nobody bothered much about this. It was just another load to be disposed of the only way we knew how. I wished they were covered with something, especially with the rain falling. There was something about their faces looking directly into the falling rain that bothered me.

My partner and I selected our load and had it on the door, waiting for the goddamn Jap to let us out of the gate. Even though it was not yet sunup, I saw several men ahead of us. Soon now the word would be received to move out. Fifteen minutes passed and still no word. What the hell was the holdup? Finally I sat down and let the rain fall. After all, this was the best shower I had had in a long time. Not talking, I thought, "I wish I had some soap." Good God, what had happened to me? Sitting in the mud, with rain coming down in sheets, ten thousand miles from home, with a dead man lying on a door, his head touching my back side, and I wanted soap to wash with. What kind of an animal had I become? All this in order to be rationed an extra ration of rice, something I didn't give a damn for in the first place. Starvation certainly had caused me to do strange and heartless things.

Whatever had been holding the Japanese up had been cleared. I heard the son-of-a-bitch ordering the column forward. It was day break and I could see better, but the rain was still falling.

Walking alongside the fence with our load, I saw where last night's wind had blown the walls off some of the buildings. I wondered if anyone was inside. There wasn't any movement. If anybody was inside they had found something to get under and out of the weather. We had become accustomed to situations like this.

The load was getting heavy and my shoulders ached from being twisted as I hung on to the front end of the door. The mud was ankle-deep even on the solid road bed. I could just imagine what it would be like as we made our turn at the end of the fence on the way out to the burial site. I wished that Jap would give us a break before I dropped this door. I stumbled on, tugging at the door in order to hold on. Then, just as I thought I couldn't hold on another step, the column stopped. I damn near ran into the man ahead of me. Taking a step backward we sat the door down in the mud. My fingers were tingling from the way my arms were twisted, and I had to rub until the circulation returned to my hands and arms. As was the routine, my partner and I changed ends before the column started moving again.

Today's partner didn't even grumble when asked to change ends. This had to be his first day, or he was a nice fellow, I thought. I might try to talk to him later. He seemed to have realized my arms and shoulders were killing me, somewhat unusual for this detail. Most of us would have done our best to keep the rear of the door.

When we arrived at the place where we turned off the road, I heard a lot of noise near the right side of the road. Two hundred yards forward the column moved and I saw a pack of wild dogs growling and snarling at us. The Jap guard was facing these wild beasts with his rifle, bayonet fixed and at the ready. I was certain the only reason he was doing this was because he was fearful the dogs would attack him. I wished they would. I needed a little entertainment. I caught myself smiling at that thought.

The mud was half-way to my knees, and it was almost impossible to keep moving. The column stopped. I heard a Jap screaming somewhere forward. We sat our load down and waited, the mud oozing through the bamboo slats. The two of us sat down on the edge of the door and waited. I chanced a look at my partner and detected a slight grin—the first friendly face I had seen, possibly because I needed to see a friend. It may be that I hadn't taken the time to notice if anyone wanted to be friendly. I'd make it a point to look this fellow up when today's detail was finished.

The screaming continued up forward, and I got to my feet so I could see what the commotion was all about. Twenty-five yards ahead I saw that one of the carriers had fallen down in the deep mud and the corpse he was hauling had fallen off the door on top of him. The arms of the body had become stiff overnight and had gone on each side of him as he fell, pinning him to

111

the ground. In his weakened state, he wasn't able to get out from under the body. Other prisoners were laughing at him. The guard was so mad I thought he would blow up completely. He was screaming and pointing his rifle, motioning for someone to assist. Then I heard someone holler at the pinned-down man, "Come on, get him tiger!" Then the man began pleading for someone to please help him, and he started crying. At that point someone pulled the body off this poor man, and as the Jap allowed him to get out of the way and rest, the column moved on. As I passed, I couldn't look in his direction. I just kept walking.

We arrived at the site some fifteen minutes later, and found more problems. The pits had filled with water and the diggers were having problems keeping the bodies from floating out as fast as they put them in. This floating problem was solved by having the carriers bring their load up to the edge of the pit and at a given order dropped the cargo into the water-filled hole at the same time. In this way, the water was displaced and the people in the holes had a chance to hold the bodies down until another load was dumped. When the prescribed number were in place, the diggers would then start shoveling the mud over them.

With our part of this ghastly detail completed for now, I joined the others for the return trip to camp. The guard made us walk farther toward the south end of the site where the walking would be better for them. Also, it wasn't as far to solid ground. The rain had washed all the dirt from the grave sites in that area, and those damn dogs were tearing the bodies apart. God, I was grateful for the wind and rain. I could imagine that putrid odor, especially if we didn't have the wind. What a nightmare!

There was to be one more trip to the burial site that day, with the same results and the same events.

Walking rather slowly back to camp that afternoon, I broke my own rule and engaged in conversation with my partner. I introduced myself, and in return he told me he was Julian Roberts, a former member of the infantry in Bataan.

Before returning to the barracks, I stopped at the dispensary to let a medic look at my knee, which had swollen during the day. The wound was essentially healed. The swelling was caused by the heavy loads I had carried through the mud. The wound was cleaned and a new bandage was applied.

As I was leaving the dispensary, I found Roberts waiting for me just outside the door. He signaled me to come around behind the building with him, where he pointed to a water spigot that I hadn't seen before. It was partially hidden from view but as the valve was turned there was water. Later, I learned that Roberts knew of this spigot for some time, but until now had not revealed its location to anyone. Since we were out of sight of other prisoners and the Japs, we turned the water on and even with the rain coming down we washed over and over again. There wasn't any soap but I felt cleaner and we were able to fill our canteens and drink as much as we wanted without having to hurry.

That evening, as the rains continued to fall, I visited and talked with this newfound friend, and as we talked long into the night, I began to feel that, just maybe, everybody on the face of the earth wasn't out to kill me.

Roberts, like myself, was a farm boy from the Midwest. Like me, he didn't understand what in hell was going on in this hell-on-earth place. We were in complete darkness as to what the United States government was going to do to get us out.

I never asked what he did in Bataan, or on the march out of that area, nor did he question me. Without knowing it, we seemed to have formed a pact. Whatever had happened to us in the past was in the past, and the only thing we concerned ourselves with was the present. I fell asleep more at ease than at any time since the early part of the war.

Roberts and I teamed up on the burial detail and neither of us would leave for St. Peter's ward without the other. In this way we didn't have to fight or argue, and the other people left us alone.

During July the rains continued. By the end of July those seriously wounded when they came in and those with diseases had long since died; only the strong remained. There had been a marked decrease in death due in part to the fact some of the prisoners had been transferred out. The Americans who had left were mostly commissioned officers, especially the high-ranking people. But a few enlisted men had been allowed to accompany them.

The Japanese were also releasing many of the Filipinos, allowing them to go home.

I had heard of some enlisted personnel being sent from here on details, but hadn't been able to confirm if the rumor was true. By the second week of August the prison population had been reduced to where our detail had been cut back to less than one hundred men. Now even with the rains, we were able to take the time to bury our dead.

Sometime during the middle of August, I heard a rumor that Japanese were looking for some men to work on diesel engines. This was to be some type of special detail.

I didn't know a thing about diesel engines, but since they wanted a detail to work on them I presumed that they probably didn't know anything either and maybe I could bluff my way through until I learned enough to get by. Anything to get away from here.

That evening I told Roberts of this rumor and together we started looking into the story. This was one time I didn't have any apprehension about volunteering.

The next day, Roberts and I went to the administration. I was going to look up that sergeant. Not finding him we talked to an officer who took us to a Japanese soldier who spoke some English. Somehow we convinced the son-of-a-bitch we were right for the job, and our names were put on the list as volunteers for this detail. Two days later we were called to the Japanese guardhouse. The man who summoned us told us to get our gear, that we would be leaving Camp O'Donnel.

113

Making an effort to comprehend
man's inhumanity to man

Chapter 16

The main gate was only a few yards away. I wanted to charge through to the outside, leaving this place far behind me. I had to contain myself. Just outside of the main gate a Japanese military truck was parked. Five American soldiers were standing near the rear of the truck. Walking through the gate, my eyes turned toward the gate post. Remembering the two human heads used to decorate this entrance on my arrival caused me to move in closer behind. I felt somewhat safer with the people around me. While we waited to be told what was expected of us, I remembered that it had been four months since I first entered that gate and my first concentration camp. During that time I had been compelled to witness the worst atrocities ever perpetrated upon the American soldier in the history of our country.

Standing here ready to leave Camp O'Donnel, a place where death and torture had become so commonplace, was like getting up and going out into the field back on the farm. Death was everywhere, and I had witnessed so much I had paid no more attention than I would if I had found a dead animal en route to the fields.

I tried to think in terms of how many had died in this concentration camp. The numbers were so astronomical I couldn't even hazard a guess. Again, I found myself wondering who was attempting to account for these dead soldiers. In my mind I could hear the typewriters clicking away somewhere in the far distance as someone was attempting to make sense out of this chaos, and in their frustration, dropping them from the military rolls—"lost in action," never to be accounted for.

But what about right here? In this camp, with the ragtag remnants of what used to be the only outpost of the United States in the Far East, what had happened to us, the living? Why would I hide water from my fellow soldier, when just a small amount might save his life, and why would they hide water from me?

I could still see the scavengers taking the rings from the fingers of the dead. If a ring was too tight to be removed, they would simply cut off the finger and take the ring off the other end. They would furtively hide this jewelry from the other prisoners until they could barter the stuff for food. I saw us degraded to the point where we had no respect for ourselves or our fellow man. There was only survival. This was the rule of the day.

I saw the agony in the eyes of the American doctors when they must make decisions, that this man would not survive, regardless of anything they might do. He must be consigned to St. Peter's ward, so as to conserve the precious little medicines they had for those who had a better chance of living. The same question was repeated over and over by those selected to go: "Why me? Why does it have to be me?"

Then that pleading question changed to hate. It could be read in the eyes as they burned holes in you. I saw them as they began their struggle to get out of the sun. I saw those who had gotten back far enough and were trying to break through the slats of bamboo skirting, those hardy ones who fought to get back to their barracks, while the carriers walked on past, not offering to help. The hate that showed in these faces would remain in my mind forever. That look that said, "You will understand when your time comes. When it is your turn, you will want someone to stop, even if only to say, 'I am sorry I can't help.'" Again I tried to think if there was anything I could have done differently.

Their pleading rang in my mind. They asked for anything that would ease their pain or relieve the torture. I asked myself, "Will this ever pass? Will I ever again be able to sleep without these pictures floating through my mind?"

There were those who escaped the fate of St. Peter's ward and made it as far as the barbed wire fence, where they struggled to make it back to their barracks. They clung to the wire, half walking and half crawling, doing all in their power to get inside their barracks. Others failed in these efforts and fell where they were, to be gathered by the burial detail and transported to the pits.

I wondered why I had been allowed to live? Why was I being spared from the pits? Did God want me to live in order that I would have to remember what had happened during the past few months? I found nothing that I could be proud of during this period. Again I wondered how God in His infinite wisdom could permit human beings to perpetrate such inhumane atrocities that would cause them to turn on each other in the manner they had.

I was suddenly brought back to reality by a Japanese guard who directed us to climb aboard the truck to leave Camp O'Donnel. For where? Hell, I didn't give a damn. Anyplace but here as far as I was concerned. Nothing those little monkeys could do to me could be worse than what had happened here. Anything was better.

Chapter 17

I was completely surprised when the guard asked me to climb onto the truck. This was the first request by the bastards since my capture. In the past it was always a beating or threat if I didn't move as fast as they thought I should. As I climbed into the back of the truck, I thought things were improving.

The truck was moving as I took a last look at the gate posts. The vision of those heads was still in my mind, although they had been physically removed. I must concentrate on removing them from my mind as well. That along with the death stares from the eyes of those men who remained here must be placed in the past. Deep inside me I knew this place would never be completely erased from my memory.

The truck was moving south and east toward the little village of Capas, where I had gotten off the train when I arrived.

Even though it was raining and there wasn't any roof over us, I felt the jubilation running through me as we left that place behind, heading for God knew what. I refused to look back.

As our truck entered the small village, I noticed the absence of the natives. No one was outside. It was rather early and I supposed with the rain people were remaining inside. There was a young pig rooting in the muddy ground at the edge of the village. The truck was moving slowly. I would like to have that pig in a pot. The truck picked up speed as we left the village and got on the main road that led south toward Manila.

As we continued on toward Manila, I saw the burned out machines of war left behind by the American forces as we retreated back into Bataan. Except for these destructive signs of war, there was a certain serenity in this countryside.

Soon I was drenched from the rain. I removed my shirt and enjoyed this natural shower, and once again I found myself wishing I had some soap. Instead, I rubbed the upper part of my body and let the rains fall.

Two hours had passed since we departed from Camp O'Donnel. Still we were going south. It was evident our destination was Manila. Soon we entered the northern edge of the city. I recognized some of the landmarks as we moved through the city. The truck turned sharply back to the right onto a pier in the port area. When the truck pulled up the guard dismounted and told us to get off and wait. For the next hour, I sat and listened to the noises associated with port activities — the whistles from the ships, cranes squeaking, dock workers hollering at each other, seagulls crowing.

Far down at the end of the pier Japanese military personnel supervised the loading and unloading of equipment. Out through the opening on the west side of the pier, I saw out into the bay. There were some small boats moving about. They seemed to be coming and going at will with no noticeable restriction on their movement.

I had become so accustomed to the Jap guards screaming and threatening me, it seemed unnatural that this port should be operating so smoothly. Hell, these people were acting as if nothing had ever happened. Even the Jap guard that brought us here had left us alone.

As for us, we were enjoying this brief respite from the beatings we had been subjected to for the past three months.

I saw a Filipino coming our way. He had a bag of something under his arm. After looking up and down the pier he took some pieces of candy from the bag and gave each of us a large piece. This candy was almost black, but I remembered that the Filipinos fed candy like this to the small ponies they used to pull the carameta carts before the war. At any rate, I took the candy and ate it as if it were chocolate.

After about an hour, the Japanese guard returned and ordered us to move farther down the pier where a small boat was waiting for us. As we were boarding, I noticed other American prisoners sitting or standing on the deck of this boat and when we got on we took our place among these men. I assumed these men had been brought here from other camps like ours.

The little interisland boat was approximately sixty-five feet long with the pilot cabin near the center of the ship. There was space for standing or sitting on the deck, both forward and aft of the cabin, with walkways along each side.

As I stepped onto the deck the Jap guard that brought us from Camp O'Donnel ordered us forward to where another Jap guard was watching over some twenty or more American prisoners.

This guard didn't check any names, nor did he seem to give a damn one way or the other who we were or what we were here for. The son-of-a-bitch just stared at us and motioned with his sword for us to seat ourselves on the deck. Nobody was talking. All seemed somewhat puzzled.

Down on the pier I heard the dock workers as they removed the tie lines.

As the small boat moved out into the deep channel, I felt the sea breezes blowing in from the south. The rain we had this morning was gone. This was the cleanest smell I had ever known. I almost forgot that I was a prisoner of war.

After we cleared the harbor, I walked over near the rail. About a quarter of a mile off the port bow was the old rusty bow of a ship sticking out of the water. I recalled someone telling me that this ship was sunk when Admiral Dewey came at the turn of the century. I had seen the thing every time I came to Manila on passes from Corregidor.

As the ship cleared the breakwater and entered the main shipping channel, it started picking up speed as we headed directly toward the island fortress of Corregidor. I waited and watched for any indication that we were going to dock at Corregidor. Roberts then joined me at the rail.

"Sergeant, do you have any idea where they are taking us? I know that is Bataan off there to the north, and Corregidor should be out here someplace."

"I don't have any more information than you, Roberts, but my guess is that we will be put off somewhere on one of the forts here in the bay. There are four of them, you know."

"It's only a few miles until we can see Corregidor, but if we go past there, it's the China Sea and no way of knowing where these bastards will take us."

"I can't imagine what they would want us to do on Corregidor, but it sure would be great if that is where we're going. I was stationed there when the war started."

"I never got to the Rock, but I have heard a lot of talk about it," he replied.

"Roberts, when I arrived in the islands I was sent to Corregidor, and I served there until a month before the war started. I then was sent over to Fort Hughes. Those forts were the cleanest places I ever saw. It sure would be a godsend if that is where we are headed."

Both of us fell into silence, just watching the shoreline off to the north. There were a lot of low clouds ahead, and the visibility up that way was bad. As is the case here in the islands, it could be raining like hell one minute, then the sun would burst through the next.

Ahead and to the left, I could make out the outline of Corregidor, just south of our course. We were skirting far to the north near Marvelious. It looked as if we were going to go out to sea or stop at Marvelious. Then, when we were about midway of the "Rock," the little ship turned directly south toward the north mine dock of Corregidor.

The old concrete pier had been blown to hell by the bombs. The Japs had built a wooden pier in its place.

As we pulled alongside the pier, I saw a number of American soldiers. Some of them were busy securing the lines from the ship to the pier. I assumed we would be taken in tow by this crew of Americans and moved to their camp. Instead, we were turned over to another guard who started moving us to an area about a quarter of a mile west of the entrance of Milinta tunnel.

That night we were issued rice cooked in the Japanese kitchen. It had some cooked fish in it. This was the tastiest meal I had eaten since my capture, and the ration was adequate. As I prepared to go to sleep, I realized I hadn't been beaten and had had a good ration of rice also. The Japs hadn't even threatened me to any degree. Things were looking better.

The following morning we were awakened by a Jap guard and once again fed rice from their kitchen. No sooner had we finished when a guard called Roberts and me, along with five other men who had left with us from Camp O'Donnel. He ordered us back down the hill toward the dock area, this time over to the south side of Corregidor, where we boarded a small harbor craft manned by Japanese marines.

Fifteen minutes later we pulled alongside Fort Drum, a giant hulk of concrete, built in the structural design of a battleship with large fourteen-inch turret guns, the type used on battleships.

Before this fort was built, this was a small island called El Fraille. The United States converted this small rock into a fortress, with crew quarters, mess area, ammunition storage for all the artillery, and open storage area for the other supplies necessary to run a garrison of this type.

The small boat pulled alongside the sally port, and we were put inside the fortress.

The Japs had placed a small garrison of their troops here for purposes that I never understood, as the Americans destroyed everything before they were taken prisoner.

Down at the bottom of this concrete ship were four diesel generators, the source of electricity for running this post. Before and during the war all four of these generators were sabotaged by our troops before the Japs came aboard. We soon learned that it would be our job to repair the engines our troops had so effectively destroyed before they were captured.

There were other Americans at this fort. They, too, were brought here from concentration camps throughout the islands. They set up quarters for themselves for sleeping and a rather nice place for everyday living.

I spent the whole night talking to anyone who would listen. I felt as if I had been freed from bondage, a bondage that I couldn't even explain. It wasn't the Japs. They still had me prisoner but something else far more important. I felt I could trust these men, something I hadn't been able to do since the days of Bataan.

We were taken below deck, where we found steel bunks fastened to the wall by hinges. By unlocking the hook at the top of these bunks the bed would drop down and a chain on each corner held the bed level as well as solidly in place.

As I was looking the place over, an American sergeant entered the large room and introduced himself as Sergeant Humphries. He told us we could draw blankets from the supply room after we took one of the beds and stowed our gear. "You won't have to carry a canteen here," he said. "There is running water for drinking. It is brought in from somewhere and stored on the fortress." Reluctantly I hung the canteen on the wall above the bunk, then went to the supply area where I was given a blanket and a piece of canvas to lay over the bed spring. That night I slept better than I had for five months.

Early the next morning I was awakened and told the showers were open. We could stay under these showers as long as we wanted because the water was pumped directly from the sea. Needless to say, there was much jubilation among the seven of us who had just arrived from Camp O'Donnel, where there was only drinking water always in short supply.

After the salt water shower, the new men were ordered topside for a briefing by the commander of this detail, a sergeant in the Jap army. I was somewhat surprised at his command of the English language. Also his attitude toward us was different. He seemed to respect us as soldiers. He spoke to us as human beings and was forthright about what he expected of us.

He informed us that we would prepare our own food under the supervision of the Jap cook, that our ration of rice would be the same as that of his soldiers. If we wanted fish with the rice we would have to catch them from the side of the rock when not working.

"Your only purpose for being here is to work on the diesel engines, restore electrical power for the post. Since the American commander was responsible for the destruction of this equipment, I feel it only proper that you, the Americans, should restore it to operational order," he said.

We were dismissed and ordered below to the engine rooms.

When I entered, I was sure glad the Jap sergeant wasn't around to see me. I was completely taken aback. At first I thought these were the biggest engines I had ever seen. My only hope now was to fool these people long enough to learn something about them. Hell, I hadn't even seen a diesel engine. These were the largest engines I had ever seen. Each piston was separate, and there were six large pistons in a line. They had had explosives placed alongside them and were blown to hell; parts were all over the floor. In most cases, as far as I could see, they were broken. How in hell could we ever get this place operating? Even if I knew what I was doing, I doubted that I could fix this mess. Along the bulkheads the electrical wiring had been torn out of the walls, and the Japs had brought in their own wiring from the generator they had set up somewhere on the top deck. I couldn't even tell the difference between their wiring and the old wiring. Theirs had been wired alongside the old system. My only hope at the moment was to keep the Japs from finding out I didn't know a damn thing about diesel engines. With a mess like this, it shouldn't be difficult. No one could make these things run. The thought that I had convinced these people that I understood the principle of diesel power amused me. I wondered if they knew any more than I did.

Walking along the catwalk beside these monsters, I was pleased with the skill of our people in their efforts to render this equipment useless. They certainly did their part at making sure the Japs would not be able to use this engine room. There was enough work here for a long time; it might be possible to stay here for the duration of the war and that wouldn't be a bad deal. It sure as hell was clean here, especially with those salt water showers. I let these thoughts run through my head for some time before coming down to the main floor, where the others were picking up parts from the deck.

I didn't even know the principles of diesel motors, but fortunately for me at least, two of our seven men did. One of them, Private Reed, had served on Fort Drum, not in the capacity of mechanic, but had worked in the engine room crew, so he had seen these monsters running and would know—if we ever got one ready to run—a hell of a lot more than I knew. Reed also knew something about the electrical system leading from generators. This, too, would help if and when these things were repaired.

Corporal Sanders had operated diesel tractors before entering the service.

The rest of us had been around gasoline engines, and we would have to learn as we went.

I felt that I could do this; there weren't any skills required in moving equipment and cleaning the place so I didn't aim to spoil this detail by letting anyone know about my lack of experience with this stuff.

I didn't give a damn about getting the place operating, and the others felt the same. With a mess like this there was plenty of work just cleaning, and I didn't intend to ever get the place operating again. Unless they got mean as hell, the only thing they would find down here was a clean engine room with great big shiny pistons standing up in the air.

We cleaned and we polished and we cleaned some more. As the pile of broken parts grew larger we would take it topside. The Japs would have us place metal in boxes so they could transport the stuff away. At the same time all the unbroken parts were being placed in an area so we could use them later. We would use these engine parts when or if we were forced into starting them.

The work continued for some time. We learned the Japanese on this island didn't want to start the engines. It wasn't our job to start them. We had played right into their hands. We had separated the good parts from the broken ones, and were no more than a salvage crew taking parts from there to be sent somewhere else to be used on other engines that were as damaged as these.

After a week or more of cleaning and moving things around in order to get close enough to the engines to work, I felt I should come clean with the two men working with me, let them know that I knew nothing but was willing to listen and to learn. This came as no surprise to them.

At this point I started to wonder if this type of work would be considered as aiding the enemies of the United States, but soon dismissed this from my mind. This was the first detail where I had to work directly for the Japanese army, and it caused me trouble.

It was my opinion that working on this job would not be aiding the enemy, and I am sure if there had been any hesitation on my part, I would have justified it by the rationalization that I was aiding myself. This detail had got me away from the worst place I had ever known. I was in a position where I had a chance to live. Also, I felt better about myself than I had in a long, long time.

Here on Fort Drum, in the middle of Manila Bay, sitting on a rock with water all around us, the doldrums of long and lonely days with no entertainment soon caused us to seek something to divert our minds from the situation of being prisoners of war.

It wasn't long until we learned that the Japanese soldiers, being extremely young in most cases, were also very gullible. So we fabricated a hypothetical dog and named him "Bismarck." When the Japanese were near, especially the very young ones, we would pet Bismarck. When anything went wrong, Bismarck got the blame. This always baffled the Jap guards. They would stare at us and attempt to see this dog, then walk off shaking their heads in disbelief.

121

The Japanese commander soon learned what we were doing and became so amused with the idea that he joined with us and even volunteered to lead Bismarck around the deck, much to the astonishment of his subordinates. This helped pass the time and certainly relieved a lot of the boredom.

It became the custom to rotate the task of walking and caring for this dog. This care consisted of feeding him and giving him baths, always when the Japanese soldiers were observing us.

I was working the detail in the kitchen with the Japanese cook. On this day there was an officer from one of the other forts inspecting the post and the cook was fixing his meal. They had fresh eggs for this officer's breakfast and the Japanese cook, being no more than sixteen years of age, was a perfect candidate for trickery. So when he broke the eggs in a saucer and turned to do something else, I ate them and then continued on with whatever I was doing. The cook started looking for his eggs. When he couldn't find them, he asked what I did with them.

"Hell, I don't know what you did with them," I said. He kept looking around, and I reached down and petted Bismarck on the head. He stared at the floor, then again said, "Did you eat those eggs?"

"Hell no, I didn't eat any eggs. What the hell, do you think I could eat raw eggs?"

Our food was always rice, nothing else unless we could catch some fish. So we were always looking for any kind of food the Japs might leave lying around while we were on duty in the kitchen.

The Japanese soldier broke another egg, and again as he turned away I ate it. When he saw this egg was also missing, he was completely beside himself. He started screaming and yelling, "You ate them." I asked him, "How do you figure I ate them? Did you see me cook anything? For Christ sake, I don't eat raw eggs." He slowed down, but still looked confused. After some time I told him, as I petted the dog, "You know, I'll bet old Bismarck got those eggs." At that, a smile a mile wide crossed his face, and as for me, I was four eggs better off. So I decided I shouldn't carry this joke too far, but all day long that little bastard watched me as I walked the dog and petted him.

This was the only entertainment on this detail, and with the place being so small, the only exercise we got was walking around the deck. I did this as often as possible. When I was on the march out of Bataan, I had the opportunity to see firsthand what happens to a person if he isn't in good physical condition and is forced to march for long periods of time. So in spite of the fact that the food was limited, I continued to walk around the deck each morning and again in the afternoon or evening.

On this detail, we always got the same ration of rice. Not as much as we needed but much more than the normal ration at Camp O'Donnel. The Japanese liked fish and often joined us at the rail with their fishing gear. Because of them needing this extra food and fishing alongside of us, we were able to get equipment to fish with from them without any trouble.

Fish and camote (sweet potatoes) peelings scrounged from the galley made up our diet. This diet sure as hell beat the watery rice I was getting at Camp O'Donnel.

After some two months at Fort Drum, the Japs decided that some of us were needed elsewhere. Nothing had been accomplished here. We hadn't started any of the diesels, nor had we produced any electricity. The Japs had taken a lot of parts off the fort, and the place was cleaner.

They gave no warning. They just told me that I was leaving now. This was a shock for me. I had envisioned myself being right here when Mac-Arthur returned.

The stay here had allowed me to regain some of my health, even to the point where I believed there was a chance to survive this prisoner of war experience. To be once again moved to another concentration camp was shocking to me. I had started to think of Fort Drum as a sort of heaven, a haven from the O'Donnels and death marches, and a place where I could trust again. Now, I had been told I must leave.

Returning to the sleeping quarters, once again I packed what things I had. Strapping my pack on and putting my web belt with the canteens attached on, I was ready to go wherever the bastards wanted me to go.

Passing the mess area, I filled both canteens, then proceeded to the loading dock, where a small boat was waiting. When I boarded I was so depressed I could hardly bear it, but nonetheless resigned myself to whatever eventuality was in store for me. I took one last look through the sally port inside the concrete battleship, thinking of what I was leaving behind. God, how I wanted to stay! I wanted to remain there until the war was over.

After boarding the interisland boat, I found a place where I could get comfortable. Then I was taken by surprise by the guard who said, "This will be a short ride. You are being taken to that island over there." He pointed toward Fort Frank, four miles away.

I was stationed on this island for a time before the war and was somewhat familiar with some of the equipment used on that island. I started wondering if these people had found out some way that I had been on the island, and were expecting me to solve some problem they were having. If so, I might be in for trouble, especially if they thought I knew something about the diesels there. Hell, I hadn't even seen them, and all I knew was what I learned on Fort Drum. I hoped I didn't fall into a trap and they found out I had been fooling them all this time.

This small island is known as the island of Caribou. It's more than a mile wide and is almost round. It lies about two and a half miles off the coast of Luzon, and about ten miles south of the island of Corregidor.

As it turned out, there was a crew of American prisoners working and and all I had to do was join them in their attempts to start the engines.

There was a Japanese major in command here, the same one who was at Drum for inspection and whose eggs I had eaten. At the sight of him, I had to chuckle at the thought of the cook and Bismarck.

The Japanese soldiers on Fort Frank were different. They were combat soldiers. With this island being just two miles from the mainland, these men were defensive. In their minds we were enemies and dangerous to their lives. I could see this in their dress, in their faces, and in the way they made us keep our distance from them.

I knew I would have to be extremely careful and try not to do anything to anger the bastards or the result would be death.

As I stepped onto the dock, I saw an American soldier about one hundred yards from the pier filling sandbags, while other Americans were carrying them up a flight of steps to the top of the solid stone wall where they were placed around a machine gun emplacement. A Japanese soldier was on the machine gun and the fucking thing was pointing right at me, or at least that was what it seemed to be doing.

As one of the soldiers put down his sandbag, one of the guards slapped the hell out of him and he fell to the ground. There was something about the sandbag the son-of-a-bitch didn't like. I felt the hate returning. As I turned to walk toward the end of the pier, a Jap guard screamed at me and at the same time I felt the point of his bayonet in my back. I turned to see what the son-of-a-bitch wanted, and in so doing I could see as much hate in his eyes as was inside me. I knew he was reading my mind. If he was, he would push the bayonet through me at any second. There wasn't anything I could do but start walking and at the same time hoping I was going in the right direction.

The five of us were on the steps with the guard pushing and shoving us toward the top, reaching the point where the machine gun emplacement was, then back along the level area until we were at the bottom of more steps and up these until we reached the top of the island.

Over to the right were some wooden structures inside barbed wire fencing and a gate over to the east side. I headed for that gate with that son-of-a-bitch screaming and slapping all the way. When all of us were inside the bastard turned and left without another word. It was like herding cattle into a corral. As soon as they are in and the corral gate is closed, there is no further need for hollering.

In front of the only door in the wood building, I reached for the door knob when the door opened and there stood an American sergeant, in full dress. He introduced himself as Sergeant Gray, the ranking sergeant on the island.

"The Japanese briefed me this morning on your coming. They also told me that you people were to assist us in getting the generators operating."

"Sergeant Gray, we have been working on the diesels at Drum for the past few weeks, and none of them are running, so if I have anything to say about it we won't get any running here," I said.

"My sentiments exactly. We will work as hard as hell on the fucking things, and if one should be fixed, we will destroy it again. I have been here since the surrender, and from what I have gathered this is a good place compared with other camps. But I can tell you, these Japs are an angry bunch of bastards and will kill you as soon as look at you, so I advise all of you to be extremely careful," he warned.

124

"Is this the only building where there are Americans?" I asked.

"Yes, and we have managed to accumulate some blankets and things like that to sleep on, but the Japs have taken all the steel bunks and either used them themselves or have shipped them out. The only thing we have to sleep on is the floor or on some lumber that we have managed to bring in to get us up off the ground. For now just find a spot to sit until you dry off."

He then motioned me to come with him to the room where he slept.

"First of all, I don't see how these old generators can hurt the Americans, if and when they do return. The only thing that bothers me is why they have such heavy emphasis on the defense of this island. They don't seem to give a damn about Fort Drum," he said.

The meeting broke up with us both agreeing to work like hell and pretend we were going to get this bunch of engines running. In reality we would either not repair them or if we did get one operating we would find some way of destroying it.

For the next few weeks our people worked on the engines, mostly by gathering the spare parts, either from the other islands or by cannibalizing one unit for parts for another, telling the Japs we needed it. The idea of sabotage seemed like too much risk weighed against the damage we would do to the Japanese.

With these thoughts in mind, I felt another private talk with Gray concerning the planned sabotage was in order. The only problem as I saw it was that there were two of those big engines in the main plant that were nearly ready to start. If they had to be started then the plan for sabotage would have to be implemented.

Should we decide to sabotage them it wouldn't be any problem. The dumb bastards didn't have enough brains to know if the engines had been sabotaged or if they were broken. Even so, should we be caught, it would mean torture or even death.

As Gray and I were talking, he asked if I had discussed any of the details of our plan with anyone. He seemed to feel that even if we got every one of the damn things running, it wouldn't help the Japs' war effort one bit. Since we had adequate food, maybe we should hold off that plan until a more opportune time.

At this time in late 1942, rumors were running wild. I never could figure out where the rumors originated, but from what I heard the Americans could be retaking this island at any time, and if this were true, there were a lot more ways for us to assist the American army than just sabotaging those damn diesels and generators.

About a week after my talk with Gray, during the first week of December, I received word that I, along with nine other men, was to move off this fortress. We should be ready to leave at once. By now I was getting quite proficient at moving from one place to another on short notice.

Friends were left behind without notice or even a second thought. It was much better to keep acquaintances, never to get close to anyone.

I was ready. I looked at the faces of the men around me who would be

125

going on this trip. They were without expression. Some of these men I talked with or had seen around on different details since coming here. Others I recognized by face only. None meant anything to me, only they were Americans, and were the only contact with civilization at the moment.

Somebody said, "Sergeant, do you have any information as to where we are going?" "Not the slightest," I answered. Then no more conversation.

I took one last look around where I had lived for the past few weeks, then walked toward the front of the building and to the outside where a Japanese guard was waiting just outside the gate.

This Japanese guard was in full battle dress, steel helmet, backpack carried high on his back, rifle, jungle netting on the helmet, crossed web straps over the shoulders and down to the web belt, extra ammunition in the belt pouch, and that ever-present small bag the bastards always had hanging on their belt. It had some religious connection, and contained some religious trinkets. The way the son-of-a-bitch was scowling at me I would like to take the bag and ram it down his damn throat. He was the meanest looking bastard I had ever seen. He sure as hell hadn't been on this island since I had been here, or I would have remembered him.

Since I hadn't seen him before and since he was in that battle gear, I assumed he had been sent for the purpose of bringing us to wherever we were supposed to go. I hoped it wasn't far. I'd hate to have to travel far with this man, especially with a small detail like this one. I knew he could kill the whole bunch of us just for the hell of it or just to get us out of his hair.

As he turned toward the steps leading down toward the pier, I whispered to the soldier next to me, "Be very careful with that one. Don't give the son-of-a-bitch any excuse." At that moment he saw me talking and charged into the group, hitting me squarely in the face with an open hand.

He slapped me so hard, it felt as if my head would come loose from my shoulders, and at the same time he was screaming at the top of his lungs. Again, he slapped me with his open hand. This time I went down. As I started to rise, I felt his boot between my shoulders holding me to the ground. Another guard grabbed my hands. They tied my hands behind my back. Then, that ugly bastard removed his foot and pulled me to my feet by pulling on the rope they had used to tie my hands. With a shove, I was pushed toward the top of the stairs where one of the American soldiers grabbed me, preventing me from falling some one hundred feet down the steep cliff.

By the time I got to the bottom of the stairs, both my eyes were swollen nearly shut and the blood from my nose and mouth covered my clothing from my neck down to my feet. That bastard was still at my back, pushing and hitting me with his fist and open hand. I finally managed to step onto the deck of the little interisland boat, but not before he gave one last shove, pushing me headlong onto the deck. I started pushing with my feet until I was at the nearest bulkhead, where I twisted into a sitting position. He was still slapping the men coming behind me and was still screaming as loudly as he could. Over the side on dock side eight or ten Japanese guards

126

were laughing as if this were the best entertainment they had had in a long time.

When all of us were aboard, the motor started and the small boat slipped slowly away from the dock. That damn monkey placed himself forward near the bow of the boat where he could best guard all of us. I wondered why I was all trussed up while all the others on deck were not. I couldn't move from where I was. All I could do was sit and make every effort to get comfortable.

The small ship slipped out into the south channel of Manila Bay and headed north.

Through my half-closed eyes I saw Fort Drum over to my right, and up forward Fort Hughes came into view. It was just to the left of our route. I hoped that we were heading there. As the distance closed I felt my heart beat faster with the anticipation of stepping off on this little island once more.

After about ten minutes another Japanese guard came forward. Seeing the blood all over me, he started jabbering away with old Frankenstein. Shortly after he came over and untied my hands, allowing me to stand.

I turned my back on that son-of-a-bitch and stood looking over the rail at Fort Hughes and Corregidor, growing ever larger in the distance.

As I stared through the fog and rain, I kept wondering what was in store for me and where we were going. The hate inside me was so strong, I knew that if either of those monkeys gave me the slightest chance I'd push the miserable bastard over the side and to hell with the consequences. They more than likely would kill me before the day was over anyway.

Standing with the light rain blowing in my face and blood still oozing from my mouth, Fort Hughes loomed up ahead. The boat was pulling very close to the east end of the small island. It seemed like the engines were slowing as if to pull into the north mine dock. The elation I felt about returning to the fort where I first started this war was more than I could stand.

Just when I was sure we were going to stop, the pilot throttled the engine. The small boat raised in the water as we sped away from the pier, heading north toward the south mine dock on Corregidor, just two miles away. God, I hoped they didn't swing around toward Manila. The thought of Camp O'Donnel flashed through my mind. Suddenly I felt cold. I glanced at my hands. They were trembling. The boat slowed and pulled into the pier and I relaxed. At least I would not be going toward Manila this day. They were going to take us to the south mine dock on the Rock. Perhaps we would be assigned a work detail on this island for awhile.

That ugly son-of-a-bitch directed the others to leave by way of a small gangway that had been pushed aboard by some Americans and Filipinos working on the pier. As I started walking toward the gangway, he hit me squarely in the mouth. By now my face and head were so beaten I didn't feel the blow. When everyone had departed he grabbed my arm and shoved me through the opening in the rail and down the gangplank. On the pier he stopped me and retied my hands behind my back, then shoved me toward the land end of the pier. I looked around me and saw other prisoners, those working on the pier as well as the people who came with me. They were looking away from us as the bastard shoved me forward toward a waiting truck.

At the truck, my guard, with the assistance of the driver and one other Jap, lifted me off the ground. The three of them shoved me into the back of this truck. Then the two guards boarded and the driver sped away from the dock area.

The driver took us up a narrow roadway, bypassing the bottom side barrio. Soon we were in front of the long enlisted barracks at an area known to me as "middle side" on Corregidor. The truck moved along very slowly and both my guards talked with each other in hushed voices, ignoring me altogether. My head was ringing so badly from the beating I couldn't hear them, but I could see them through swollen eyes. I didn't have any idea what they had in mind for me, only that something had this ugly bastard in one hell of a mood. At the moment he was leaving me alone, and for that I was grateful. I sure would like to have the son-of-a-bitch in my sights for just a second. I'd blow his damned head off his shoulders. The truck was barely moving now, and one of the guards looked out around the canvas cover and yelled at the driver.

When they stopped, I was told to get off. Somehow, I managed and by staggering forward ran into a large tree that saved me from going down.

I was taken inside a door and the new guard remained with me while "Frankenstein" went inside to report to someone. I tasted blood in my mouth and the salty taste caused me to become thirsty, but I knew better than to ask this guard for anything. So far he hadn't beaten me, but I noticed he was grinning like a damned hyena.

Some twenty minutes passed before the guard returned to take me through another door into a small office. Inside was a small desk and a chair. This room was well inside the old barracks. There were no windows. There was only one more opening through a closed door leading still farther into the building. The other guard was told something and left, leaving me alone with this ugly bastard. I was sure he was going to start beating me again.

He stepped back and locked the door behind me, then went through the other door and I was left standing alone.

There was an electric wall clock behind the desk. Was it because of the quietness that it sounded so loud? Still that roaring might be from my head. I was so confused I didn't know anything. I waited and listened. Nothing. Just the roaring from the electric clock and the pounding in my heart, which I was convinced could be heard over the sound of the clock. I waited, then after what seemed an eternity, a Japanese army officer entered the room and the guard was dismissed.

For the next few minutes I stood and waited while this officer walked around the room, first in front of me, then behind me, not saying anything, just walking. Sometimes he would look at me, then turn away, but most of the time he just walked, looking at the floor as he paced around. Then he stopped, standing directly in front of me. Looking straight into my eyes and

128

without blinking he stated, "You are recommended for execution." I started to open my mouth to speak but he raised his hand to silence me, and again in perfect English he said, "Execution—do you understand?"

"Yes, I understand what you are saying, but I don't understand why," I replied.

He continued, "I must advise you the less you say at this time, the better it may be for you." At that I clammed up and said nothing more.

This officer left and went back through the door, leaving me standing alone, more scared than ever before.

After some ten minutes, which seemed like ten years, the officer returned with an American army major. This officer was dressed in a khaki uniform, pressed and clean as if he had just come from reporting to General Mac-Arthur. Without speaking to me at all, I heard him pleading my case before the Japanese officer.

"If you will release this soldier to me, you can hold me personally responsible for his conduct," he said.

I had never seen this officer before, but at that moment (even if the son-of-a-bitch should go ahead and execute me) I couldn't have been more proud to be an American.

The two of them went out of the room leaving me alone. The clock on the wall ticked away. The noise was deafening. Total silence—just my breathing and the clock. I waited. What the hell could they be doing? It seemed like an hour since they went behind the door. Buzz, hiss, buzz, hiss. Damn, what if that major couldn't convince the Jap officer that I shouldn't be killed?

The door opened. The major was standing there alone. He removed the rope from my hands and motioned me to follow him through the door. I held my breath for fear that I would be lined up and shot, or worse. Once on the outside, I was placed under his care. For the first time I knew what it meant to be indebted to another man for my life.

We walked without talking until we were over a sharp bank out of sight of the building. Then I realized we were totally alone, no Jap guards, just the major and I, and he seemed to know exactly where he was going. I just trailed along, still not saying anything.

Soon we were at a flight of stairs leading down the side of the hill, down toward the lowest part of Corregidor.

My eyes were almost closed from the beating I took that morning, and I was so tired I could hardly walk, but with the major assisting me I found the railing to the stairway and was able to guide myself down the steps to the first landing. I told the major that I didn't think I could go on until I rested.

We sat down and for the first time he spoke.

"I am Major Grayson, the senior American officer on this detail, and that Japanese officer has placed you in my care while you are here."

I made an attempt to express my gratitude to this officer, but was unable to find words. Finally, I just said, "Thank you for saving me from their execution squad." He nodded and the subject was closed.

Grayson explained that some of the soldiers who came with me had been assigned to his detail. They had told him of my being herded away from the pier. When he heard this he started trying to find out who I was and why I had been singled out for special treatment.

The two of us sat in silence for a time, then continued on our journey down the long staircase. At the bottom the major took the lead and started moving off to the left along a trail that went over toward the cold storage area of Corregidor. I had been on detail here before the war, and was somewhat familiar with this section of the Rock.

Over to my right I could make out the water towers for the storage area, and just a little farther I saw the beach and the long pier where we came in when I came back from Camp O'Donnel. I stumbled and we both paused momentarily. Back to the extreme right I saw the gaping opening to the Milinta tunnel, some five hundred yards away. The pockmarks where the shell hit were plainly visible, and there were shell holes all over the place. Hardly an inch of ground had been untouched. Even in this trail, someone filled in the shelled-out places. I commented to the major, "This place sure as hell took a beating before the Japs took it." He nodded, and once again we started walking toward a building that had come into view ahead.

The trail dropped off sharply and we were on a dirt road. I heard water running. Moving on farther up this little draw, I saw some activity inside the camp. To my right was the sound of motors running, and just ahead of me was the entrance to the tunnel. It ran back inside the hill I just came down. The major indicated this was our camp. Much to my surprise there was no barbed wire around the area, just some small buildings with good roofs to keep out the rain. At the entrance to another small tunnel I saw the kitchen ranges and some American cooks busying themselves with cooking.

Grayson turned me over to an American sergeant and told him that I was to be assigned to duties within the camp and for him to see that I got to the doctor and have him look at my wounds.

Sergeant Park, the acting first sergeant in camp, took me to a small building where I found a G.I. mattress on the floor. He told me that this would be my area. "Keep it clean," he said. "I will call you when it is time to eat. Also you will find running water in the shower building, just to the rear of this building. You look like you need to clean up. Then see the Doc. He has a small dispensary here in camp over near the major's office. Maybe he can do something with those cuts." He turned and was gone before I had an opportunity to thank him.

I went to the shower and cleaned and washed the cuts and bruises, then was told I could eat as soon as I got to the kitchen area. When I got there I was fed corned beef hash, rice, and some hot tea.

Goddamn! What a day! Last night I was reasonably content with being a prisoner of war, working for the little sons-of-heaven. Then, without warning, I was moved from Caribou Island, beat half to death, trussed up like a wild animal, shipped fifteen miles to another island, and sentenced to death for reasons completely unknown to me. Now, suddenly, I had been given a

130

reprieve from death, placed in the custody of someone I had never seen before, had a shower, cleaned up, and was fed a good meal.

It was almost dark when I entered the dispensary and found the doctor. He cleaned the cuts and applied some antiseptic and told me to see him in the morning.

As I walked toward my sleeping quarters, I couldn't see any activity of any sort. No Japs, not even any Americans. I sensed a feeling of freedom. Was this feeling a release of the trauma of the day, or was this, in fact, a prison camp where I would receive treatment as a human being?

I did not attempt to talk to anyone. To hell with it. I was so damn tired and so sore from the beating, all I wanted was to sleep. But this first night wasn't a restful one. I awoke at all hours of the night. The nightmare of yesterday was more than I could endure. That statement by the Japanese commander kept ringing in my head, and I would wake up hearing him say, "You have been recommended for execution." Finally, morning did come as someone woke me early for breakfast. Again, I was served a rather substantial meal of rice and hot tea.

By noon I was able to accept my surroundings as well as demonstrate a small bit of trust in the other prisoners. Yesterday I sure as hell didn't trust anyone or anything. I felt I had been betrayed by my own people, and I was suspicious of everyone. I just knew someone had told the Japs that I was going to sabotage their damn equipment and that was the reason for them sending me over here to be executed.

After I had visited our camp doctor, Captain Russel, I met Grayson out in the area. He inquired about my injuries and asked if I had been treated. Then he told me to come to his office in about an hour.

When I talked to him later he informed me that I would be assigned to a detail within the compound assisting other men with the maintenance of the large generators that supplied the power for all the personnel and equipment on the Rock. This, he reasoned, would keep me out of sight for a while and away from that Jap guard who beat me on the way over. He felt that the fellow had most likely lost face by my not being killed, as he had recommended, and the best thing we could do was keep out of sight of him if at all possible.

For the next few days I worked inside the motor rooms and followed instructions from the other Americans. I soon healed and became used to the area. I wanted to stay here as long as I could. The work wasn't hard and the food was good. Best of all, the fucking Japs left us alone.

I decided during this period that in order to make sure that the Jap didn't recognize me, I would grow a beard. So for the next few weeks I let my beard grow. When all was quiet and my beard had altered my features radically, the major placed me on another detail.

This was a new adventure, being organized by our officers in camp and in all probability at the urging of the Japanese as well. We were to search the island for bodies, both American and Japanese.

This detail was headed up by Captain Long, an officer of the engineers, a very tall, distinguished gentleman. He was a person that I knew I could trust, and my admiration grew as the weeks passed.

When anyone would locate a body, especially an American, this captain wouldn't allow it to be moved in any way until the debris or soil from around it was removed. Then he would take a log and record the name from the ID tags, always making sure this was witnessed and signed by another prisoner. After all the data was recorded in the ledger, then and only then would the body be moved.

These remains would then be placed in a wooden box and the lid nailed shut. One of the dog tags was nailed to the top of the box and the other was taken to the burial site at the east end of Corregidor. A wooden cross was used to mark the grave site and the other tag was fastened to the cross.

Any Japanese body found was turned over to them in these boxes. As far as I know, Long didn't keep records of these remains.

In early 1943, while on this detail, I was searching the eastern side of Malinta hill just north of the eastern entrance of the tunnel, near the main water tower for Corregidor. I came up a slope from the beach. I found an unusual number of Japanese bodies that had been overlooked in our previous searches. They were more or less bunched into a small area in very heavy grass and brush. I wondered why so many and why in this particular spot. I hadn't seen any pillboxes near hear. Also there were many shell holes from the Japanese artillery. Some of the dead Japanese soldiers were down in the holes, indicating that they had come in after the shelling.

Finding one I could get to easily, I examined him very closely and found several .30 caliber bullets inside the rib cage. At once I checked some more of the remains and found the same in all cases. They had been mowed down by American small arms fire, but from where? I sure as hell would like to know where that soldier was when he did this. Looking up through the brush and the trees, I could see a water tower, so I started walking in that direction. It was some two to three hundred yards away and the going was slow through this mess of vines and grass. At last I was at the bottom of the tower, standing near the ladder leading to the top.

Glancing down toward the area where I located the bodies, I saw that it was not possible to have covered that area from ground level. So I mounted the ladder and started climbing. About half-way to the top, I stopped at the first landing to rest and get my breath. I could see all the way to Bataan, even though it was cloudy and there were some rain squalls over in the bay.

Up above the tree tops the air was clean and sharp. I had become accustomed to the stench down there in the jungle. I had forgotten how clean air could smell so fresh and feel so good in my lungs. I breathed deeply, and for a moment I forgot what I was up on this water tower for. I began climbing once again to the top. At last I was at the edge of the top of the tower, and climbed through the small gate that opened onto the top surface of the water tower. There it was, the answer to my question as to how the large number of Japanese soldiers had met their death.

There at the north edge was a .30 caliber water-cooled machine gun, its barrel pointed in a rakish manner toward the sky, with expended rounds of ammunition everyplace, scattered for seven or eight feet around the gun. At the rear of the machine gun were the skeletal remains of a soldier. His right leg was partially covered with the expended ammunition, his uniform still intact. The collar was open at the neck; a hole was torn through the shoe on the right foot but still tied to the ankle bone. His finger bones were extending from the sleeve of his khaki shirt, his flesh long since gone, blown away by the winds and rains. The finger bones were groping to the inside, as if in defiance. His steel helmet was some four or five feet away, the chin strap broken in the middle. A large gash was cut into the steel where shrapnel had hit.

On the belt side of the machine gun were the remains of a marine, in the marine corps green fatigue uniform. His right arm had been blown some four or five feet away. Part of the shoulder bone was still there, but the sleeve and the rest of the arm was torn off completely. His left arm was folded across the front of his shirt, as if he were feeling for his right arm or his shoulder. These two soldiers had rested here since the fall of Corregidor, their flesh wasting away in the sun and the heat and the rain and wind.

I found it impossible to look any longer. Turning away, I walked to the far edge of the tower, where I leaned against the rail guarding the edge and stared into the distance. I couldn't erase this scene from my mind. Why, my God, why?

Turning once again I walked to a small structure used as a service entrance to the tower. This structure had been hit and partially blown apart by exploding shells. A gaping hole had been opened into the water reservoir. Turning away from this structrue I noted another torn out part of the top of the tower at the northern edge, just to the right and in front of the machine gun position. The Japanese had landed two direct hits on top of this tower. The bastards sure as hell wanted to be rid of these two soldiers.

Returning to the machine gun I noticed that the front of the army sergeant's uniform had been ripped in the chest area and the shirt had sunk through the skeletal remains almost to the surface of the tower top. He had been killed by shrapnel from an artillery round instantly. He had either been knocked back from the trigger of the machine gun, or had fallen backward when hit.

Without touching or disrupting anything, I started the long climb down to the ground. I must find Long and report this find to him.

It wasn't until the following morning that I was once again climbing the water tower. This time, however, the captain and a detail were with me. We had containers to bring the remains of the two warriors from their lofty perch.

When we reached the top, no one moved but just stared at this scene for what seemed like a long time. Scenes such as this were a once-in-a-lifetime thing, and I must never forget, not even the smallest detail, what I was viewing. Here were bravery, honor, total commitment, the ultimate price.

In the midst of these thoughts I was brought back to reality by Long. He requested my assistance in identifying the remains.

The soldier's shirt was carefully opened and inside the rib cage was a piece of shrapnel about six inches in length, weighing at least one-half pound. This had broken the entire left side of the chest and lodged in the backbone. I lifted the dog tag and read aloud, "King, Wilbur, serial number _ _ _ _ _, United States Army, blood type." This having been recorded and verified, the remains were then placed in the wooden container and one of the tags affixed. The box was then closed and another soldier moved the box away from the machine gun.

In much the same way, the marine was identified. His remains were placed in another box to be removed from this place, where I had had the opportunity to view enough heroism to last me a lifetime.

The boxes would be removed from the top of this tower and buried only a few hundred yards from where the men fell.

I continued on the detail until the latter part of February 1943. During this period some three hundred American dead were recovered and buried in the small cemetery at the east end of the island.

During this assignment I found there were many advantages, in spite of the nature of the work. For one thing, while digging around in the tunnels and the defense positions throughout the island, we would find canned food. This was always brought into camp and kept in the food storage area. The Japs didn't care for American food so we didn't have to compete with them for the stuff we found.

The Japanese wouldn't allow radios, but while out in the areas where the Americans lived before and during the war, some were found that could be repaired. These were hidden in a tunnel near the camp.

It wasn't long until we learned when we could pick up news from Australia or from San Francisco. We could have one or two men listen in on these newscasts and relay the information to us. In this way we could guard the tunnel and make sure that if a guard came around we could get the listeners out and hide the radio so they wouldn't find it.

When it came my turn to listen in for the news, I would tune the radio to shortwave and start searching the dial for the newscaster from San Francisco. His name was Winters. God! What a thrill to hear that voice! That newsman, it seemed to me, knew just what I wanted to hear. Always after one of his broadcasts morale within camp would soar. We would talk until the wee morning hours about what he said of the progress of the American army and navy throughout the world and particularly throughout the Pacific.

It had been five months since I returned to the islands in Manilla Bay. The horrors of the death march and the tragedy of Camp O'Donnel were in the past. Even though those events were still in my mind, I had regained my health. I felt good about myself and was convinced that MacArthur would soon arrive.

Chapter 18

A few days after the burial detail was finished, word was passed that two Japanese officers were coming inside the camp. Everyone was curious about their presence. In this camp, only a few Japanese had ever visited us, so it was with some apprehension that we waited for news of the visit.

We didn't have to wait long. They wanted two men for a special detail. The nature of this detail was not explained, but they told our officers we would remain under the control of this camp. However, for the next few days we would be outside the camp.

Grayson had no idea what the detail was all about, but did caution me to be extremely careful, remembering the events that brought me to this concentration camp in the first place.

Inside the building I gathered my gear in preparation to leave. I was scared, to say the least, but I was becoming more fatalistic concerning my destiny as a prisoner of war. In less than thirty minutes we were marched from the camp toward the north mine dock on Corregidor. There a small boat was awaiting our arrival.

The two of us were ushered aboard, where we joined more Americans and Filipinos. Some of these people were working with equipment and appeared to have been aboard the ship for some time.

Wilson and I were taken below deck to the sleeping quarters, where arrangements had been made for us.

There were open portholes alongside our sleeping quarters well above the water line, making this area well lighted and also very cool.

Within the hour we were moving out into the main channel. When we were well out away from the pier the ship turned back east toward Manila. We only went a short distance toward the eastern end of the island when we stopped and dropped anchor.

We were told to come up on the main deck, and I saw some of the Filipino crewmen bringing diving equipment out on deck. As they started laying the diving gear out on deck, it was obvious the Japanese intended this equipment to be used by some of the men aboard. Surely they didn't intend or expect me to do any diving! Hell, what would we be diving for in the first place?

I didn't have to speculate long. A Japanese who spoke flawless English was ordering everyone to gather around him.

"It has come to the attention of the Japanese Imperial army that American officials dumped a large amount of silver into the bay before the

135

island was captured, and it will be your job to recover that silver. It is also known that some of you here on this detail have knowledge as to where this silver was dumped. Therefore, you are expected to locate this treasure for the Japanese Imperial army," he said.

"For you prisoners who have no knowledge of diving, you will be instructed on the use of the equipment, which is captured American diving gear and shouldn't be difficult for you to learn."

He continued, "In case some of you are worried about this operation, I want you to know that all the equipment will be operated by you: the diving gear, the air pumps, the whole works."

I took one look at those old bell heads the navy used for diving, then felt my heavy beard and wondered just how in hell I could handle this. I didn't have any shaving equipment and my beard was much longer than it should be with that bell over my head.

"What the hell difference does it make?" I asked myself. I couldn't dive anyway. By the time I had been taught to dive, I would have solved the beard problem as well.

As soon as the Japanese finished talking, he walked over and tapped a navy man on the shoulder. "This man will be our instructor in the proper use of this diving equipment." As it turned out, the first class petty officer was a qualified diver, and he, like the rest of us, was completely mystified as to how this fellow knew of his background as a diver.

When I saw this I realized that they probably knew as much about the rest of us. I would surely have to play this one close. It appeared that there was an informer. But who? And was the son-of-a-bitch on the boat? I still hadn't forgotten how I was snapped up over on Fort Frank and brought to Corregidor to be executed. I'd let them tell me what to do and not volunteer for anything.

I slept well the first night and the following morning started receiving my instruction in sea diving.

First, we were told we would not be deeper than sixty feet, in most cases less than that. All we had to do was go down to the ocean floor and search for the boxes of silver. If any were found, we were to signal the top by pulling a light rope attached to us. All the technical things would be taken care of by our personnel at topside. All I had to do was trust the people operating the air supply. Since they would be Americans, some of my apprehension was eased. But still, I was scared as hell about being inside that bronze bell, with my life support coming from the people on deck whom I didn't know. I asked about the beard, hoping it might disqualify me, but was told that I could find some scissors and clip as much off as I could. A short beard wouldn't cause any difficulty. Then the bell was set over my head several times to acclimate me to the feel of the damn thing. Also it was to prove that I could breathe the air coming from the pump. I was a full-fledged diver in the service of those moronic bastards.

As the days passed I found the Japanese had no knowledge of diving so they wouldn't be checking us. While on the bottom we could do as we pleased.

136

The first few days were spent letting us use the equipment. We were only a short distance from the pier, where the water was calm and shallow, no more than forty feet deep. Our air hoses were long enough to allow us to move about over the bay floor.

It was during one of these test runs that I came upon a large yacht sitting on the bottom. It looked like it had been scuttled. I couldn't find any sign of it being hit by shells or bombs. Everything was intact. So I decided to do a bit of exploring on my own.

Climbing aboard, I could see this wasn't just another sunken boat. Everything aboard spelled money. I found the bar area where there were a number of bottles of whiskey and other spirits. I reasoned that I might get an opportunity later to retrieve some of this if I could take some of it over near the end of the pier.

Inside one of the sleeping quarters I found a cache of jewelry. There was an old Spanish comb with a string of diamonds across the top, two or three rings of different types, and a hat pin with a large pearl.

I took some of the bottles and all the jewelry and left the yacht. These things I stashed at a piling near the end of the pier. We were often allowed to swim in this area when in camp and not on a work detail. With this in mind, I signaled for the crew up on the boat that I wanted to come up.

That night I talked about finding the boat with some of the people. I didn't tell how I had taken the things off and stashed them at the pier. Someone suggested that, in all probability, I had come upon the scuttled yacht of President Caison. The yacht had been sunk before he had left the islands with MacArthur. At any rate, I had something from that yacht.

A day or so later we were moved from the north side of the island over to the southern side between Corregidor and Cabello Island, where we would start diving for silver.

As far as I could tell, this whole diving detail was a complete farce. The Japs certainly weren't equipped to pull this type of operation off. They had no detecting equipment, just a handful of Americans who were ill-trained at best, prisoners of war with the attitude that anything they got from us they could stick in their ear.

We dove down and tried to locate the silver. When we found anything that wasn't split open we sometimes sent up a box. We broke others and scattered the damn stuff over the ocean floor. Many boxes had been opened by the currents or had been partially opened before they were dumped. In that case we just scattered the coins around and sent up just enough to keep the bastards off our asses.

This search and recovery continued for the next month. Then the Japanese gave up and returned us to the prison camp, where we would be housed to wait for yet another detail.

Chapter 19

The major gave me a day to rest up, then called me in. He explained that he was in need of someone to work at the pumping station located near Battery Way, on the north side of the Rock where some fresh water wells were. This water was the fresh water we drank and the Japanese cooked with.

It was apparent that the Japanese didn't have the technical abilities to run this pumping station, and that the Americans would be the ones responsible for furnishing the water for the entire population on the island. This seemed to me the safest way in which to handle the situation. With this explanation I was assigned to the pumping station with another American, a Sergeant Garrison.

The pumping station was about a half-mile from our compound, and I had to climb a very sharp incline to the end of a little point that jutted out from the island. Up here I could look down on the pier at the north side. God! I could see almost into Manila. The sun was out. No storm clouds today. What a beautiful view, and I was here all alone, the first time in so long I couldn't remember. No guards, no Americans, no Filipinos, nobody to worry about, not even me. The grass was so green, I saw the beauty of nature for the first time. It had been so long, I had forgotten that out there somewhere this world had something to live for. Even though I was not an active participant, I was alive and I was grateful.

I was told by Grayson before I left that I would be sleeping at the station, so I had packed all my things and had them with me.

I slipped the pack from my back and found a place to sit and think awhile. As I was daydreaming of some distant time when I would once again be home and this nightmare would be over, I remembered that I had some tobacco in my backpack. I rolled a cigarette, then just lay back into the grass and tried to forget the war. The hell of O'Donnel, the death march, the cannon roar from Bataan. To hell with it, let it die for now. The singing of that bird, what direction was it? I'd try to find it. It might see me and fly away. My God, I could almost hear the running water in the creeks back home in Missouri. I wondered if it were possible for a person to send a message by mental telepathy. My parents must wonder what had happened to me. I couldn't for the life of me remember when I wrote them the last time. Sometime in March 1942, and it was March 1943. At least a year, even if they got that letter, but as I recalled there wasn't much moving out of here then. Hell, they probably hadn't got any word from me since the war started. I

138

wished I had written more back then, when I had the opportunity. God only knew when I'd get another chance.

I was awakened by the low drone of a ship's whistle and returned to reality.

A small trail led down the side of the hill and at the end of the point I saw a tin-covered building that I presumed to be the pumping station.

I found Garrison, who was working on some equipment. After our normal greetings, I was given a walk through the station and shown what I would be expected to do.

Walking through I noted that this plant not only pumped water, but there was a large generator that produced electricity for the central part of the island.

"Watch your step," I was advised as we walked along a catwalk toward the rear of the building. "Don't touch any of that stuff over your head. I have been down here since the fall of Corregidor and I can assure you that there is enough electricity running through those bus bars to burn you instantly," Garrison said.

"Yesterday as I made my rounds through here I saw a greasy looking place on the floor," he said. And looking up, he pointed to what was left of some small animal that had fallen on the things he had warned me about. Just the charred remains of what appeared to have been a rat. I felt a shudder run through me as we passed. To think that was only two feet above my head, and I was walking along as if everything were okay. I wanted out of there and I mean right now.

We continued along, however. When I got to the end of the building I saw a small door leading to the outside, and I vowed right there that if the water pump was to be checked by me, it would be from outside. I would not walk that catwalk again.

God! If I felt I didn't know anything about those diesels when they brought me out of O'Donnel, I knew one hell of a lot less about electricity, and I'd be a son-of-a-bitch if I got myself killed with something I didn't know a damn thing about. I'd keep my distance.

Garrison turned and started back to the front, and I just kept walking on out the door and around the building.

I had seen enough. I asked to be shown where we slept. I wanted to get the pack off my back.

Garrison led me down a little trail toward old battery Morrison Tunnel. Just in front of the main tunnel was a small shack that had been thrown together out of pieces of tin and some salvage lumber. Inside were two bunks built from the scrap lumber, one on top of the other, and since Garrison had been here longer, I got the top bed. Each of these bunks had a thin GI mattress and two blankets.

Garrison pointed to the bunk and informed me he had to return to the motor room, and he would see me when I got settled. He turned and was gone.

Here in the shack the noise from the pumping station was hardly audible.

139

I felt serene. Not a Jap anywhere. I wondered how long this could last. Hell, Garrison said he had been here since the fall. That was nearly a year. I might be right here when MacArthur returned, and that could be any day now. It had been some time since I had heard any war news. Making another cigarette, letting this thought sink in, I tried to envision what it would be like when the general came marching back to Corregidor. There wasn't the slightest doubt in my mind that he would. I intended to start gathering some ammunition and some rifles and hiding them where I could get hold of them.

A person should be able to find any type of weapon he wanted around this place. The Japanese knew we were helpless as hell, and hadn't even looked around this area. They knew that for us to attempt to use any weapon around here would be suicide. Besides that, there were only two of us. What harm could we do? If I could hide some weapons and ammunition until America came sweeping back to the islands, they might just be in for a little surprise.

During my stay at the pumping station, I continued searching for firearms and ammunition, storing this material in a room far inside the tunnel where I hoped they wouldn't be found by the Japanese. Since I didn't know anything about Garrison, I determined not to let him know of this arms cache.

During one of these excursions, I came upon a manuscript someone had completed and hidden underground. This manuscript was wrapped in a protective oilcloth, then placed in an army footlocker and buried.

Taking this manuscript into the small quarters where we slept, I began reading. At first I thought the writer had written about his experience on the Rock, but soon found this story had nothing to do with the Battle of Bataan or Corregidor. It was a fictional story he had started before entering the service and from the notes inside the locker, it would seem, the writer had enlisted in the military service for the sole purpose of finishing this book. The title of the manuscript, as I recall, was "Long, Lean, and Narrow."

After reading through this, Garrison and I rewrapped the manuscript, placed it in the footlocker, and buried it back in the same hole where we found it.

Garrison and I continued to run this pumping and generator station for the next few weeks, he on the night shift and I on the day shift. We were on twelve hours and off twelve hours. Even when we worked we had a lot of time when we could look around the area. Most of this equipment ran by itself and we just watched for trouble. Most of our time was spent either cleaning the area or just sitting. The latter gave me too much time to ponder my situation, so I usually found something to clean or something to read.

Garrision was a stickler for keeping dust and spider webs out of the building. Many times when I came in I would find him climbing around up over the equipment, up near the roof. I remembered his warning to me about the high voltage in those bus bars and the animal that fell from the ceiling. I wondered why he took chances.

The electricity to our quarters ran directly from the pumping station to our shack, and one evening while reading, I saw the light dim, then go completely out, then come back on again. Since I had been here long enough to know something must be amiss in the generator building, I thought it best that I check to determine if Garrison needed assistance.

When I entered the building, no one was at the desk. I hollered for Garrison. No answer. Again I called and still no answer. Then I saw him, just a charred form on the electrical bus bar. He had fallen from the ceiling and electrocuted himself. This was the cause for the short in the electrical system. There was no need for me to shut down the generator. I just picked up the phone and rang Grayson to inform him.

There wasn't anything left to take to the cemetery out on Monkey Point, just his identification tags and some bones that didn't burn. A record was made of his death by Long. If and when we got out of this, someone would know how Garrison died and where his remains were buried.

Not long after Garrison's death, I became very ill from malaria or dingue fever, possibly both, and had to be relieved from this detail. I returned to the main camp where I was given quinine. I was kept out of the weather until the camp doctor was able to get the fever under control.

Chapter 20

While at the main camp recovering from malaria, I became a part of a group of four people who were making plans for an escape to contact American forces with information about the personnel on Corregidor. We also hoped to make an attempt at organizing a guerrilla force to assist the landing force that would surely be coming back to liberate the Philippines from the Japs and return what was left of General Wainright's command to the United States.

Sergeant Harrison, Chief Petty Officer Decker, Sergeant Gray, and myself had the blessing of Grayson in this endeavor. He and the other officers in the camp were active in assembling equipment, preparing rosters of personnel, and in general, making ready anything we might need. Also, they were preparing us with orders that we would be required to carry out, when and if this venture was successful.

Grayson as well as some of the others knew whom we could contact on the mainland in order to get an effective guerrilla force organized. They had instructions for us to take along. We still had to get a boat to take us off the island. At this point we only had the outboard motors. They were hidden in one of the old blasted-out sections of the cold storage area. The current plan was to build the boat in this area and with the help of other prisoners, carry it to the beach when ready.

During this period, we lived for rumors about the American forces— where they were fighting and whether they were winning. It was my feeling that the war would be back in the islands soon. I remembered Mac-Arthur's promise, "I shall return," and of course, I expected him to keep that promise.

It was the feeling that when this happened, we should have a force over on the main island with some knowledge of where there were American prisoners, and also let the commanders know what defenses were here on the Rock. This was the driving force behind Grayson's action in getting the four of us to the main island before MacArthur returned.

I worked with the three men any time we had an opportunity, always remembering that if we were caught it would mean death. Always, one man was on guard while the rest of us worked. To this end, the commander and a few of the officers had been brought in on the project. I was still suspicious of Gray. He was with me at Fort Frank, and I still felt uncomfortable around him. I told the major of my feelings. He assured me that my suspicions were unfounded, and that he personally would vouch for Gray's loyalty. I owed my life to this man so I took his word, and from then on I felt better.

We were now authorized to swim off the pier of the north mine dock, and most of the time the Japs were nowhere in sight.

On one such day, I was able to dive under the pier and recover the items I took from the sunken yacht. I slipped these things out of the water and took them back to camp, where we divided the alcohol up and had a little party. The labels were gone from the bottles, but it didn't seem to matter to anyone. We just mixed the whole batch together, whiskey, scotch, and brandy, and some grapefruit juice from the kitchen. We had a great time until all the booze was gone.

I took the jewel box to my building where I concealed it with every intention of eventually smuggling the jewels out of the Philippines after the war was over.

For the next few weeks we went on details all over the island of Corregidor, looking for food or anything we could use or thought we might be able to use. During these weeks, I found several thousands of dollars in paper money, and stashed this with the jewelry to be smuggled after the war.

The currency I had accumulated over the past month or so now reached somewhere around sixty thousand dollars and it, along with the jewel box, was becoming harder and harder to hide. It had become an obsession. The fear that someone would steal my treasure, as well as being scared the Japs would find it, was preventing me from concentrating on my primary mission of getting off this island and over to the mainland. Something had to be done. I started looking for some way to hide this loot permanently.

On one occasion I opened the jewel box to check the contents. Inside was an old Spanish comb. The teeth were some three inches long, and across the top mounted in a silver base etched with a flower design was a row of diamonds, each at least one-third karat. Spaced in between these diamonds were stones of purple or red. There was also a hat pin, with a natural pearl directly in the top center of the head of this pin. Amidst the jewelry was a man's ring with a stone of black onyx and a small diamond set near the center and over in one corner, away from the carved head in the onyx, was a large diamond (about one-half karat). I treasured these items because I believed that if I could get them out, after the war, I would be set for life. It mattered not that these items belonged to the family of the president of the Philippines, and in all probability, had great historical value, especially to the Philippine government. Right now it was my feeling that if I could get my cache of dollars and jewelry concealed well enough, to hell with the government of the Philippines, or for that matter, the United States. I wanted this treasure for myself and intended to keep it if at all possible.

By now I had had time and the materials to make myself a new backpack. I told the major that I would need this large pack when we were ready for our escape. With a pack this large I could carry any records out of here that we wanted and since it was constructed of waterproof canvas it would protect any paper in my possession. The truth is I was thinking more of the money and the other treasure than I was thinking of documents.

During this time the Japanese warned that I, along with several others,

143

would be going over to Fort Hughes on a special housekeeping detail for the Japanese on the small island of Caballo (old Fort Hughes).

I gathered all my personal things, including the treasure, into my new backpack. If the Japs should decide to search this, I was in deep trouble. I had managed over the last few weeks to assemble some clothing. Here on the Rock there were tunnels everywhere and our troops had left things much as they were when they surrendered. The Japanese had either been ordered to leave things alone or were reluctant to enter the places because of booby traps. So, inside the dry tunnels, I found all the khaki uniforms I needed and even a pair of shoes. From a clothing standpoint, I was well off.

Along with all this, I wrapped the things I got from Caison's boat and the money, and placed them inside the pack. I was scared as hell that the Japs would find it, but I was also aware that if I didn't get the stuff out, especially the jewelry, and the Japs found it, it sure as hell would be lost forever.

Over on Fort Hughes we were housed in an old bombed-out building at the foot of the only hill on the island. This building was just north of the fourteen-inch gun battery on the south side of the island and about one hundred yards from the rail line that ran up into the tunnel leading to the mortar battery.

Being on such a small island, with the number of Japs being about the same as the number of Americans, we had full run of the island. They knew we couldn't go anyplace. As long as we kept the area clean and someone was always there to do the dirty work, we could come and go as we saw fit.

With this freedom of movement, plus the fact that I had once served on this island, I was able to get into areas that normally would be overlooked by the other Americans.

I kept my treasure hidden and was able to keep it out of sight of the Japs until I could find a suitable site for hiding it permanently.

It was during one of my tours, searching for just the right spot, that I became interested in what had happened to my old unit, and began searching around the eastern end of the island in hopes of finding out anything I could about I Battery, 59th Coast Artillery.

Even though I had walked every inch of the island many times, the place was so overgrown with tropical growth that I couldn't recognize anything. I remembered burying one of our men at the south side of the low part of the island, and I started in that direction, hoping that I could tell something about what happened at the fall. The Japanese hadn't cut anything. They just came in from the pier and stayed right in the center of the island. The undergrowth was so damn thick that when you got in twenty or thirty yards you almost felt as if you were lost. I went in the direction I believed the burial site to be and hoped it was the right direction.

At last I found the markers that my unit put up for our people. I recognized some names. I knew Private Masters and Staff Sergeant Blunlett. There were others from G Battery, names I recognized as people I had talked to before the war.

Farther down toward the east end I found the old three-inch guns, still intact, with their rusty barrels pointing in the air, waiting for a new crew to come along and take over. Some of the sandbags had rotted and the sand was spilling from them. Inside the parapet spent rounds were all over the area, and weeds were growing up through the metal platform of the gun.

Standing here I could almost hear the first order, "Stand by for action." A chill ran down my back and I shuddered at the thought of the bombs bursting all around me. I glanced into the air, almost wishing I could see the puffs of smoke from our bursting shells. Almost unconsciously, I listened for the drone of the Japanese bombers. No sound, just the buzzing of insects around my ears. I moved outside the parapet and over toward the barber's area. The trenches were caving in and the grass and weeds obscured the ground. There were the tree limbs that were torn down by the bomb that killed our barber, and the old barber's chair still askew in the shell hole. It hadn't been moved since that fateful day back in December. The rains had washed a lot of soil down around the chair, but it still could be seen. That wasn't just a chair to me. Hell, I sat in that damn thing and talked to its owner about his wife and family, about his home over on the island of Mendora. I wondered what his family was doing since his untimely death. Did we get the word over to them of his death? Or was he, like so many I had seen since then, just one more person to be listed in the government records as "missing in action"? The question bothered me, to the point that I vowed that I would make every attempt to see his wife and children when this thing was over and inform them of just how he died.

Moving away from the battery area and farther up the hillside toward the tunnel where the dispensary was located, I passed through the field kitchen with the old field ranges still as they were at the beginning of the war, only rusty as hell. The canvas was falling apart and dropping down around the cast-iron stoves.

The tunnel looked like a good place to hide my treasure, except I doubted if I could find any place that I would recognize when I came back. But I'd keep this place in mind when I decided to hide it.

It was during one of these excursions back to my old unit area that I found one of the battery guidons and brought it back to camp with me, knowing that the Japs would take a very dim view of my having any part of the regimental colors in my possession. The problem for me was how to keep this guidon.

Knowing that the Japanese were very sports-minded, I figured to fool them once again by sewing this guidon on the back of my shirt, then telling them it was a baseball shirt. This worked so well that I would only wear the shirt when the guards allowed us to participate in sports. I took some of the cash I had and slipped it inside the pocket created by sewing the guidon onto my shirt. I thought I might be able to use the money at a later date.

As the weeks passed it became obvious that something had to be done about the stuff I had managed to keep hidden. It was only a matter of time until I would get caught, and then there would be hell to pay. So I started in earnest to try to find a suitable spot.

I obtained two gallon buckets with good lids, and while cleaning up the area over at the old gun position, I managed to find some tar that was used to waterproof doors to the powder passages within the battery area. By heating this tar I was able to place the money and the jewelry inside and pour melted tar on top. Then I sealed these two cans and made my way up through the tunnels toward the upper side of the island. Up near the center where the twelve-inch guns (mortars) were, I entered through what had been the island medical center and found an area of the cement wall that had been cracked by Japanese shells or bombs. A crack was running down the wall of this gun emplacement. It was about twenty feet from the northwest corner of the wall. The shells had torn out the dirt, leaving a cement wall standing with nothing behind. I climbed up on the outside and made my way back to that area and just dropped the cans with their contents down into the bottom of this bomb crater. Then, with my hands, I pushed enough dirt on top to cover the objects, not wanting to fill the hole completely, for fear it might be noticed, and figured that the rains would cover them up further. With that crack in the cement, I would be able to find my buried treasure any time I got back to Caballo, which I felt wouldn't be much longer. The American army would be back soon and I could recover these items at will. I departed and returned to my area feeling very good that I had been able to do all this. I was sure no one had seen me.

Our job was to keep things clean and to dig wells for the brackish water that the Japanese and ourselves used for bathing. Also, we would meet the water barges that hauled the water for drinking and assist the Filipinos and the Japs in loading this fresh water and pumping it into water towers.

In June 1943, the Japanese decided we were no longer need on Caballo, so without notice we were ordered back to Corregidor. For the next few weeks I was assigned to drive for one of the higher-ranking officers on Corregidor. During the day I would drive this officer wherever and whenever he wanted to go, and at night I was returned to the prison camp at the old cold storage area under the control of Grayson.

During the evenings we would plan our escape. This was always the main concern for the commander as well as the four of us who were going to the mainland. We made up rosters of the Americans on the island, including the names of personnel on the detail on the top side of the Rock. The major knew the officers and most of us had a few names of the enlisted personnel, but by no means did we have a full accounting of that detail. There were twice the number in that detail that were at the bottom side. We got the names of as many as we could. The commander was to certify the authenticity of the list, and I would be the person who would carry this list of Americans. When contact was made with the returning forces or if by chance I came in contact with anyone who could get information to MacArthur's command, I was to turn this information over to them.

While I was on Caballo, the other three men had gotten the boat and the gasoline needed to get us over to the mainland.

Even though we still had the radio hidden and could get news via short

146

wave from San Francisco, the news was very inconclusive. We couldn't find out anything about the progress of our troops, and with this in mind the commander kept delaying our departure. So the preparation continued. This was Grayson's project, and I had the utmost faith in his decision. He didn't feel that the Americans were anywhere near making an invasion of the islands, and wanted our escape to coincide with the return of MacArthur.

I continued to drive and work on the escape plan until the first of July, when we decided it was time. We would make the attempt on July 12. This would be well before the rainy season started, and we would have weather in our favor to get back from the beaches and into the mountains before the rains started. If we waited any longer the bay would be rough and with this small boat there could be trouble just getting across the twenty-mile stretch of water to the mountain area south of Manila.

Our craft, assembled from three outboard motors, was more of a raft than it was a boat. A navy man built it in such a manner that it would cut the water and increase the speed. This was very important, as we wanted to leave after dark and be some twenty miles out by the time the sun was up.

Everything was in readiness. We even had a canvas sail we could use in the event the motors failed.

Just as we thought things were ready, the Japs pulled the rug. I was taken off the driving detail, and all of us were restricted to the camp. Before I knew what was happening, I, along with about half the Americans on the island, were herded aboard one of the interisland boats for movement off Corregidor.

This was a sudden move, and without warning I remembered the sudden move from Fort Frank when the bastards had singled me out for execution. I wondered if this was more of the same. I was not being beaten like then, but the thought scared the hell out of me just the same. I knew of no provocation, except the boat, and I wondered if the bastards had uncovered our plan. If so, I'd had it for sure this time. I'd watch their every move. If it looked as if they were taking me someplace for execution, I would try to swim to the mainland. All I could do was wait and watch.

The boat started toward Manila, and as it picked up speed, I watched the island of Corregidor slowly grow smaller over the fantail of the little boat. God! What a sad day. Yesterday I was going to escape to freedom, today I might be on my way to a firing squad.

Observing the guards, I saw they were in a very good mood. I didn't trust the bastards, and kept close to the rail. The boat continued toward Manila with still no indication that they were up to something. Corregidor disappeared from view over the horizon and we were still moving toward the city. Ahead, the skyline was coming into view, and the port area was visible to the naked eye. If they tried anything now it wouldn't be far to shore and I'd sure as hell give it a try.

The boat entered the port and we pulled up to pier seven. The Japanese were pushing us off as fast as we could make the gangway. I was shoved into a line by another Japanese guard and the ones who brought us ashore left toward the end of the pier and into the city, their chore finished.

147

Chapter 21

The new guards were still on the boat. Those who came in with us left us standing by ourselves on the pier. It was as if they had finished their job and then to hell with it. If they left it wasn't their responsibility. We didn't know what was at the end of the pier, so our only choice was to wait until the guards aboard were finished with whatever they were doing.

Soon they emerged from the cabin and came down the gangway to the pier. Each was armed with a rifle and had bayonets fixed. The one who seemed to be in charge motioned with the point of his bayonet. He wanted us to march toward the land end of the pier. Two guards led off and we fell in behind.

At the end, several trucks were waiting for us, their drivers watching as we approached. With no delay, we were loaded aboard. I was near the front of the group, and first on the truck. When we were all loaded with one guard on each truck, the lead vehicle moved out through the streets of Manila. Our little convoy passed through the old "walled city," then suddenly stopped at a large gate. Glancing up, I read the inscription over the gate, "Bilibid Prison." I had known about this prison since my arrival in the islands. There was a branch of it on the Rock before the war, but this was the first time I had seen the main facility. I recalled having guarded prisoners from here. Some of them were serving sentences of more than five hundred years.

Now the guards were unloading us at the gate of this maximum security prison. What in hell had I done to be sentenced to this place? I knew damned well I hadn't committed any crime that would warrant a term here. I also wondered if some of those prisoners I had guarded might still be here. If so, what would be their reaction to seeing me?

When I was off the truck, I looked back at the other trucks. The guards were slapping the prisoners around back that way. I got the feeling they wanted to impress the guards inside the gate.

The gate opened toward the inside and was controlled manually by a single man. It had steel bars more than one inch thick, running up and down, only about six inches apart. At the center, running crosswise, was a flat steel plate with holes drilled through it. The steel rods ran through the holes, then the plate was welded at the end. I was totally spellbound. I had never seen anything in my life comparable to this. On each side of the gate was some kind of ivy that covered the wall. The wall was made of large stones with cement between each stone. The height of the wall plus the size of this gate

148

made the place seem more ghostly. All the stories I had heard about "old Bilibid" scared me more than anything. At the right side of the main gate and some twenty feet down the wall, was another smaller gate. It had the steel bars but was small enough that it could be opened easily, allowing anyone having business in or out of the compound.

The prisoners were being accounted for by the guards, and inside the gate, I heard the guards as they got ready for us. I could see only a few feet inside, but I knew there were more than a few people in there.

As I waited for them to enter, the thought went through my mind that a person could be lost inside this prison system for life. My God! I wished I could run. I knew that was impossible. You wouldn't get thirty feet. If you weren't shot, they would club the hell out of you with their rifle butts.

I took this thing personally. They couldn't be bringing all of us here because of crimes. Some of these people I didn't even know, and those I did sure hadn't had any problems with the guards. I remembered when I was moved from Fort Frank and found myself under sentence of death with no idea what I had done. I had many questions and not one answer. I was here and there wasn't a chance of escape, so there was nothing to do but wait.

My mind was running wild. I was as scared as I had ever been in my life. I heard the lock being worked from the inside. The huge gate swung open. I paused for just a moment, not wanting to go inside. I waited too long. One of the guards pounded me between the shoulders with his rifle butt, knocking me forward. As I stumbled and tried desperately to remain on my feet, someone grabbed me from behind, preventing me from falling. I moved much faster now and that guard had another prisoner to beat on. I was inside "old Bilibid," not knowing if I was here as a prisoner of war or had been sentenced for something they had trumped up. At the moment it didn't seem to matter one way or the other.

I heard the squeak of the gate behind us. We slowed and ahead was a large building with huge glass windows. Inside were several people. On my left were some long one-story buildings. These ran out from that glassed-in building like the spokes of a wagon wheel. These were cellblocks and that place in the center was the guard control building. This part of the prison was like one half of a wheel. The inner wall of the cells was only a short distance from the guardhouse. At the other side was a wide walkway running parallel to the wall. With this kind of construction, only a few guards could watch over many prisoners.

We hadn't walked more than fifty yards inside the compound when I saw American prisoners. This sight decreased my apprehensions to some extent, especially when I saw some U.S. navy officers in uniform moving about. There were American prisoners in the cellblocks. Some were standing in open doorways as we marched past.

I soon learned this was not a prison in the sense I had thought, but another prison camp for those who had been injured in the war or were otherwise physically unable to work on the hard labor details.

We were halted near the north end of the glassed-in building and were told by one of the navy officers that this place was a prison hospital and was staffed by navy doctors. I could hardly believe it.

I was to learn that these doctors had convinced the Japanese of the need for a place where people who were crippled or disabled could be cared for. My first thoughts were that the doctors must have a talent for persuasion to have accomplished this. In the past we had had only the slightest of medical attention. If one needed major attention, he usually died. From what I could see, this place had every appearance of being a hospital.

There were many handicapped people here. The place had been kept remarkably clean. In fact, if you could forget that great steel gate and those high stone walls, this would be a good place to await the return of MacArthur.

Some guards inside the glassed-in building ordered us to move farther into the prison compound. Marching in front of the cellblocks toward the northern end, we passed through a large opening through a divider wall into another section of this complex. In this part of the prison there were only buildings and no cellblocks. We were away from the patient population. Prisoners stayed here until shipped to a work detail. The guards were not part of the hospital, but monitors.

I learned quickly that they were like all the others. Their hostility toward the American prisoners was no different than those on the Rock. They screamed at us as we entered their area, pointing their bayonets or sabres in that familiar threatening way. I hoped this attitude was because of the worsening of their war efforts. If so, I could endure.

We were ushered inside a building, then divided into smaller groups and assigned a building where we would remain until our next work detail.

In this building there were prisoners lying all over the floor. Several spots of floor space were vacant. As I searched for a spot, I saw an individual I had known for a long tme, even before entering the army. We had grown up together in southwest Missouri. I had no idea he was in this part of the world. Joe Blair had enlisted not long before the war and had come out here with an armored unit, arriving only weeks before the war started. His unit was captured in Bataan the same day as I was caught.

Blair made room for me and the two of us talked. He had an army mattress spread out on the floor. I had one of them on the Rock but couldn't figure how he managed to get one in this prison camp. I was sure the Japanese wouldn't issue such an item.

There was a small enclosure inside the building made of steel bars. There was a lock on the single door. When I asked about it, Blair told me that it was a jail cell where prisoners were taken for disciplinary problems.

During this stay Joe and I renewed our long friendship, talking about people we knew at home.

We were able to move about quite freely. As long as we remained inside this northern section and stayed away from the Japanese guard area, we could move about as we chose.

150

Chapter 22

I became accustomed to the place. Being allowed to sit around and renew old friendships was a real treat. We listened to the rumors about the war, how near our forces were to the Philippines. In general, morale was good. When I was not visiting with people I knew before the war, I sat and daydreamed about when it would be over and I would be on my way home. This vacation was not to last.

The Japanese decided that I was much too healthy to remain here, so I, along with some fifty other prisoners, were readied for movement. Where? God and the Japanese only knew. The word was passed by our officers that we should get ready for departure at once.

Packing my backpack, I noticed Blair had also been alerted. He was nearly blind and was brought in because of his physical condition. He was on a detail at Nichols Field and couldn't stand the torture there. During the past few days he told me of the atrocities going on there, how one couldn't stay there for any length of time and how the Japanese had to continue to draw laborers from the hospital complex in order to keep the detail on schedule. He told me about the Japs extending the main runway and at the same time building a new one. He was fearful that we would be sent to that construction job.

During my stay I heard of other concentration camps where they used slave labor by the POWs as well as at the main camp at Cabanatuan. As Blair kept talking about Nichols Field I kept hoping we would get one of the other details.

My pack was ready; Blair was tying a rope around that mattress. I wondered why he would burden himself with such a load. Hell, he would have all he could do just keeping up with the others, especially with his eyesight as bad as it was. When I mentioned this to him, he laughed. "If things are as they were when I left Nichols, you will soon learn why I am taking my mattress." Since he had been out there and knew the conditions, I accepted this without further comment.

Turning back toward my own gear, I recalled the problem I had with the straps cutting into my shoulders on the march out of Bataan, so I busied myself adjusting these for a long march.

It was mid-afternoon when I heard the screaming of the guards. Without waiting, I picked up my pack and moved outside where others were already lining up to be accounted for. What a motley crew. Some had backpacks, others had nothing but a water bottle. And of course there was Blair, with his mattress on his shoulder and a small roll under his arm.

151

We marched inside toward the gate, that same steel gate I came in through the first day. This time we were halted in front while the gate people took a head count.

The great gate swung open. On the outside, the guards wore full battle gear: rifles, steel helmets, full web gear, and netting on their helmets. They also had a small piece of canvas hanging down over their neck and part of their back. One would think they were going from here right into combat. I saw one of them eyeing Blair, so I stepped to the outside of Joe. When I was sure I hadn't been noticed, I whispered to Joe to step faster and soon we were away without incident.

They started beating us as soon as we started walking. They seemed determined to demonstrate their superiority over us to the Filipinos who gathered around to watch. For about an hour they screamed and yelled and beat us while we marched away from the prison, but as we moved outside the residential area they stopped their torture.

The pace slowed as we came alongside a railroad. I heard the squeal of hogs coming from the car nearest me. Once again, I was reminded of that trip out of Bataan and that boxcar I rode in toward the village of Capas, near Camp O'Donnel. At that thought, a shudder ran up my back. Surely we weren't going to be taken back into that hell-hole. Ahead, I saw the first of our group loading onto a waiting car. As I approached the car I would be riding in, I saw two guards. One of them was screaming for the men to hurry. "Hiako, Hiako," he yelled. Joe was in front of me now, scrambling for the door. He was having problems with the mattress. The guard started for him with his sabre drawn. Seeing him, I shoved Joe through the door onto his face as the blade of the sabre hit the edge of the door. Joe rolled toward the opposite side of the car, and before the son-of-a-bitch could redraw that sabre, I grabbed the side of the door and scrambled through out of sight. The two of us were safe for the moment.

I took Joe by the arm and started him toward the front of the car. My arm felt like it was broken. I didn't know if the Jap hit me or if I hurt it when climbing inside. I slipped to the floor as soon as we were near the front wall. Both of us were out of breath. The car was moving almost as soon as I settled onto the floor. I felt that cool air from the forward vent. Within minutes we were leaving Manila. There wasn't a chance of us being sent to Nichols Field, but the thought of returning to Camp O'Donnel was on my mind.

The heat was bad in the car, but compared with that ride out of Bataan on my way up to Capas, it wasn't bad at all. We didn't have nearly as many men in the car as we had then, and this group had water and didn't start out half-starved and thirsty as we did then. There wasn't the sound of men begging for help. Also, there was enough air for all of us.

The train was going full speed and the air was pouring in through the vent. Still, Blair and I remained sitting on the floor. Blair, with his matress, was leaning back against the front end of the car with me. My backpack was tugging at my aching shoulder. I must get the straps off. Someone was raising hell with Blair for taking up more room than he thought he should. Joe squirmed over into the corner where he could see any movement in front of him and at the same time have his back protected by the corner. He said nothing, but glared in the direction of the complainer. The sliding door had been closed and we were locked inside.

The train stopped several times, and each time we waited for the guard to open the sliding door. During the stops, the heat nearly suffocated me, but by remaining quiet it was bearable.

After what seemed like several hours, the train once again slowed. When we had totally stopped, there was a noise at the door. As the door opened, the yelling started for us to get off the train.

Climbing down from the car I noticed a light rain falling. The air was fresh and cool. The guards moved us out very quickly and in a short time we neared a low building. Alongside the aisles and over the main entrance I read the words, "Angelese." I knew where we were. We had been assigned to the labor detail at Clark Field. It was a great relief for me to know that we would not be going to Camp O'Donnel.

All the guards left us and entered the building. We sat and waited in the slow, drizzling rain.

There was no protection from the rain, and Joe's mattress was getting wetter and wetter. I wondered how he would carry it. If we stayed out here all night, that thing would weigh more than he did.

At last the guards finished their chores and told us to get to our feet.

After we had been walking for about a mile, I took the mattress and gave my pack to Blair. Joe took hold of the rope that he tied around the bedding to keep up with me. It was very dark and his blindness didn't matter as long as he held onto the rope.

The rain was coming down in sheets and the mattress was getting heavier by the minute. I wished he had this damn thing where the sun didn't shine. Still, I knew I was better off than him, so I continued walking. Why anyone would put so much stock in a goddamned mattress, I didn't have the slightest idea.

At last we were at the front gate of the camp. From each side of the gate I saw barbed wire and inside were the shadows of buildings.

Chapter 23

A Japanese guard came from nowhere out of the darkness just inside the gate. He acted as though he knew we were coming. Taking a key from his belt, he opened the gate at the main entrance and admitted us without checking numbers or anything. The Japanese soldiers who brought us here lined us up and counted us as we passed in front of them. Soon an American captain was standing in front of us talking with the guard, and we were turned over to him. He said, "I can't take any names tonight. I'll get all of you out of the rain, and in the morning your names will be added to the camp roster." With that we marched away from the guard shack along a row of bamboo buildings. Each time we passed one of these buildings the captain dropped off a few of us; then we went on to the next. This continued until everyone was inside. The rain wasn't cold but we were all soaked through and through, and I felt a chill running through me as I patiently awaited my turn to be selected. Blair hung onto the end of the rope as we marched along until at last there were only a few men behind us and the captain was directing the men in front of us to break off and enter a building.

I shed the mattress and handed it back to Blair and he in turn handed me my backpack. Glad to have that load off my back, we crowded through the door.

Inside the building, it was dark and water was dripping from everywhere. I wondered how we could sleep in this mess.

The water was coming through the roof almost as much as it was outside. Why in the hell didn't we just stay outside? Then I heard the wind whipping against the bamboo walls. Hell, I should be grateful just to be out of that. All I could do was make the best of things until it was light.

If I could find a spot where it wasn't leaking, at least I would be able to rest.

Seven or eight men from the detail had been told to sleep in this building. All of us were stumbling about in our attempts to find space. I stepped over someone and was told in no uncertain terms to watch where I was walking.

My explanation that we had just arrived in camp and had been assigned to this building got very little sympathy from the prisoner, but he did tell me that there was space at the east end and that it leaked like hell down there. I was so damned worn out, I could have slept out in the rain so I started making my way in that direction.

I took my pack from my shoulders, pushed it back toward the wall, and stretched myself out on the cold bamboo floor. The others were still stumbling about in the dark, cursing each other as well as the darkness. To hell with them. My body ached from head to foot. They would have to find their own spot. Each of us needed light to find a dry place, but there was no way of knowing how long it would be until morning.

After I had lain there for sometime, I felt that gnawing inside my stomach. I hadn't eaten since early in the morning before we left Bilibid, and it must be after midnight. I took my canteen and drank several gulps of water. This relieved the pangs somewhat. I considered saving the water until I knew more about this place. Then I heard the rain falling, and I knew I could catch that if need be, so I drank again.

Snores could be heard over the rain and wind. I couldn't sleep. There was a chill running through me, but there wasn't anything dry in my pack that I could use for cover. I listened, and the drip, drip, drip near my head seemed to have a soothing effect on me. At last I fell asleep. The last thing I recalled were the events of the day and the barbed wire at the main entrance of the camp.

I kept waking up. I was either shivering from the cold or burning and sweating. When daylight finally came I was completely worn out. During one of the times when I was not freezing I fell asleep again and when I awoke, the barracks was empty. At this point I realized I had been running a high temperature and probably some of our people noticed this and didn't bother waking me before they left. As I lay there listening, I heard people outside the barracks. They were yelling at each other as they went to their assignments.

Even though I had a high fever, I had been around long enough to know that if those men out there were going for rice, I had best get out there and get whatever was available.

Taking my mess gear from the pack, I left the building and followed some people. Soon I was at a very large bamboo building at the southern end of the camp where they were serving the morning rice. The first thing I noticed were two lines, someone told me which one I was supposed to be in. One line was for the men who worked outside camp on different details. Those men got more rice than those kept inside because of sickness or other reasons.

When I had drawn my rice, I knew that when I was able to work I would again volunteer for outside work, no matter how difficult the detail might be. I recalled that detail at Camp O'Donnel, but as I watched some of the men come off that rice line with heaping dishes of rice, any doubts were erased. Compared with what I had been issued, it looked like a feast. My ration wasn't enough to keep a person alive, much less satisfy hunger. Taking what I had, I walked away, looking longingly at those filled mess kits. Right now, my stomach would hardly tolerate the food although at the same time I was hungry. I made a mental note to find out all I could about the details as soon as possible.

I walked through the crowd with my rice until I found a spot where the wind wasn't blowing. I tried to eat my rice. My entire body shook from the cold. I felt a queasiness in my stomach. I wondered if I would be able to eat this meager ration. I knew I must.

When I finished, I returned to the barracks where Blair was talking with some of the prisoners who had been there for a while. There was an American doctor and a small dispensary. Most likely, they had something for my fever. Also, if I should have malaria, there was some quinine there.

After some discussion, I decided that I should get the hell out of here quickly and find the doctor. The guards who ran the details wouldn't let anyone leave once they had you outside the compound. The doctor had a much better opportunity to keep me in sick quarters now than at any other time. Heeding their advice, I left the barracks without delay and found my way to the dispensary. The doctor diagnosed me as having dingue fever, a form of malaria. He gave me some liquid quinine along with some aspirin and told me to stay in camp until he released me. He would clear my staying in camp.

Taking the medicine and expressing my thanks, I returned to the barracks. Everyone was gone—even the men who came in with me. I wondered what in hell they thought they could get out of Blair, yet his gear was there and he was nowhere around.

I rolled his mattress out in a dry spot, knowing he wouldn't mind. As I stretched out on the damp bedding, I felt the aspirin had taken over. My headache was better but had been replaced with a roaring from the quinine. Suddenly I was sleepy.

Waking sometime later and finding the building still empty, I had time to think, especially about the leaking building. The Japanese would do nothing to make the place more comfortable, so I started looking for a dry place.

Everywhere the floor was wet from the leaks. The bamboo walls had soaked through. On the leather gear of the men out on detail were large spots of green mold, indicating it had been raining for some time.

At the west end there were no windows or doors, but I could see the place was empty. If anyone lived in that area, they hadn't left any gear around. Also, I noted that it was dry there. Picking up everything I had and dragging Blair's mattress behind me, I made my way into the dark corner of the barracks. When I was fully settled, I took everything from my pack, placing it where it would partially dry.

The aspirin seemed to be wearing off and the chills returned. I took everything I could from my gear to keep me warm, and even tried getting under the damp mattress. Nothing seemed to help. The roaring in my head was getting worse, and the chills were driving me crazy. As I looked toward the east end of the barracks, I saw the rain coming through the roof all the way to the end. This was the only dry spot in the building.

At last, I could stand it no longer. I had to return to the dispensary for more medicine. Pulling myself up from the floor, I started flexing my arms, trying to get warm and at the same time making my way down the aisle. As I passed along the bays where the prisoners had been living, I noted the arrangement for sleeping was much like the bays at Camp O'Donnel. Bamboo slats were tied at the wall, then allowed to lie flat toward the center of the building. Inside each cubicle was room for two prisoners. Some had GI blankets while others had none. At the eastern end of the building were two canvas cots. This was not often seen in any camps I had been in.

I explained my chills and fever to the doctor and the fact that I had nothing to cover myself with. He went into the back of the building and when he emerged, he was carrying a heavy blanket. He gave me two more aspirin and then handed me the blanket and said to take it but when my condition improved, he must have it back. Thanking him, I left the building. I ran all the way to my barracks. Once there I took off everything I had on and wrapped myself in this clean blanket. For the first time in hours I was completely dry. Pulling my pack away from the damp wall, I used it for a pillow. I then pulled the blanket over my face and within minutes I was sound asleep.

It was late in the afternoon before I was awakened by noises of men returning from detail. I felt wet and clammy from the perspiration. My temperature had subsided. The warm blanket, along with the aspirin, had given me the opportunity to rest and get the sleep I so desperately needed.

Outside men were hollering at each other. Their labors for the day were over. From somewhere near the front gate, I heard the guards screaming as the men entered the compound. They wanted a final opportunity to get their licks in on the prisoners.

I needed to know what the men did on the details. I listened very closely as they talked. It was dark in this part of the building, so I could listen without being seen. My main concern was what they had to do and how much extra rice they got for doing it. I knew, when I was well enough, I would volunteer for the detail that offered the most rice.

Near me some men were talking about cutting bamboo near the airfield and how fast the stuff grew. Others were talking about screening gravel somewhere on the south side of camp. This information struck me as odd — screening sand in this rain? Still, the one thing about that detail that registered was, "I don't give a damn about how hard the work is, the extra rice is worth it." "Extra rice." The words stuck in my brain and I knew then that this was the detail for me.

I watched and listened for some time. All the time I watched for Blair to return. I had his mattress and should he get in and find it moved, he would raise hell. For the next half-hour I listened and watched. Another group was dismissed by the guard near the guardhouse. Soon men entered the barracks, and I saw Blair talking as he entered. Before he could start raising hell about his gear, I called him from in the back of our new area, letting him know I had moved us during the day to a spot where it was dry. He walked in the direction of my voice, feeling more than seeing.

"Where the hell did you go this morning while I was at the dispensary?" I asked him.

157

"You had just left when one of the guards entered the building and the bastard roused everybody in the barracks out," he replied.

"Didn't you try telling them you had problems seeing?"

"Hell, they could have cared less. They took all of us on a detail handling barrels of airplane fuel. I didn't have any problems and besides, the rations are good. We got a big ration of rice out there on the job," he said.

I moved from his mattress so he could sit. He saw that I was wrapped in a blanket and felt the material and asked where I had gotten it.

I told him about my fever and going to the dispensary and told him I was not to work any detail for awhile.

Blair told me about his day and what he had to do on the fuel detail. It was near the Jap garrison and the extra rice they had received had come from their kitchen. I had heard the sand detail come in at noon for rice. We talked until evening rice, and then got in line. I received the same ration as before while the sand detail went through the special line and received extra rations. A Jap guard stood at the serving counter checking IDs. Each man got as much rice as he wanted. The men with smaller containers went through the line as many times as they wished, but were watched carefully to make sure they didn't give any rice to their friends. My line was watched by another fellow, who made sure the cook didn't give out extra.

Back at the barracks, Blair and I talked the situation over. People in camp were getting appoximately 300 grams of rice per day; those on the sand detail were getting as much as they wanted. This certainly created an incentive to get on that detail. I thought about this all night long. The Japs sure as hell could care less about the health of the prisoners, so the only reason for giving as much rice as people wanted was to make it easier to get men out on that job.

All I could think of was getting well enough to get on the sand detail. I never gave a thought about the difficulty of the work. The only thing I knew was that these men were given all the rice they could eat. What the hell! It couldn't be any worse than that detail at Camp O'Donnel, and I liked the idea of getting outside the barbed wire fence. Outside there was a chance of talking to a native and hearing something about how the war was going. Inside the only thing we heard were rumors.

I must have patience. The doctor wouldn't let me go on detail, and he continued me on quinine. I learned as much as I could about the sand detail—where it was hauled, what the hours of work were, how the treatment was. The sand was being used to construct another runway. We screened the stuff and another detail at the main air base mixed the stuff into cement. I hadn't been able to learn if that detail was from this camp or if another camp was near here. During the day, I could see for miles in every direction. The place was certainly large enough that there could easily be two concentration camps. I was sure the Japs wouldn't let us know if there were other prisoners nearby. If we found out, it would be because we accidentally ran into them, and they volunteered the information. That was unlikely. Most of us wouldn't talk to anyone we didn't know.

158

Finally, the doctor released me to go out on detail. The problem was getting the detail I wanted and not being assigned to where there wasn't extra food. When the Japs learned I could do hard labor, they would be after me, each detail competing with another for me. I'd have to be careful.

Most of the men in this barracks were on the sand detail. Once assigned, the Jap in charge screamed through the door, and they went out and were counted off. If anyone was left, another Jap picked them up and assigned them where they were needed.

On my first day off the sick roster the guards were around all day, so all I could do was stay out of sight, waiting until morning.

The following morning, when everyone was getting ready for work, I fell in with the sand detail as they were called. When they left the main gate they had a new member.

The guards marched this detail south from the main gate, some two miles. I saw several screens set up on angles and under the screen I saw where sand had been screened from a pit alongside. The guards were splitting the detail up, but I learned quickly that the prisoners had more or less formed their own groups and I found myself standing alone. One prisoner stared at me and grinned. He motioned me in his direction, and I joined his detail without saying a word.

When I was down in the pit, he pointed to a shovel. No one talked. The crew started shoveling the sand onto the screen. Two other men moved the sand around, causing the smaller particles to screen through while the larger rocks collected at the foot of the screen. Yet another prisoner was assigned to shovel them away, making room for more to fall.

I learned that when you didn't know what was expected, it was best to follow along with the others. These men weren't talking; the work was done in silence.

We were keeping our heads down and pitching the sand, when suddenly I remembered where I knew this man from. Hell, he and I served in the CCCs together before entering the army back in 1938. I wondered what in hell he was doing here. I supposed he was thinking the same about me. The thought of meeting someone else from home in this damn place almost boggled my mind. The only person I had met over here since my capture that I knew was Blair. And now this fellow. What kind of goddamn war was this anyway? Hell, I didn't know how to handle anyone from home. I had operated alone for so long and only recently ran into Blair. Even though I was scared to talk now, I knew I would converse with this man soon. I tried recalling his name. Jacobs. That was it. From Moutainview, Missouri. I glanced in his direction. He returned my stare with that grin. He also knew me and knew I remembered him.

I learned quickly there was a quota. This crew and the one next to us screened a certain number of truckloads each day. This information was obtained from the guards. The crew wasn't allowed to talk at all while working. This seemed rather odd, but I must go along with it until I could learn why. We worked in total silence. Near noon we were ordered out of the pits and

159

marched back to camp for the noon ration of rice. That was what I had been scheming for, that extra rice.

When we were in line at the mess building and that cook was piling the rice on, I held my mess kit in front of the cook until it was heaped with the rice. I planned on going back through the line for a second helping. Good God! What a sight! The rice was so high on the pan it was almost falling off. When I was finished with the first ration, I found there was no need for more. I was full for the first time in months.

The guards wouldn't allow any talking on the march back to camp, and I had been much too preoccupied with the extra rice to talk with Jacobs. I sat down and started talking.

"How long have you been in this prison camp?" I asked him.

"I came here more than seven months ago from Cabanatuan," he answered.

"You are the last person in the world I expected to see in this place. Hell, I wouldn't have expected to see you in this part of the world," I said.

"When I left the Cs, I couldn't find work, so I joined the army and was sent here in July 1941. I was captured on Corregidor."

I told him I had arrived in April. He went on to say, "There is another man here who was with us at the CCC camp. Remember James Cantrell? As I recall, you and Cantrell were rather close friends there."

"Cantrell? How in hell could he survive? The Japs hate big men like him," I stated.

Jacobs started laughing at that and before I could ask anything further a Jap was screaming at us to fall in for the march to the sand pits.

That evening after my first day on the sand detail we were given all the rice we could eat. I was aching from head to foot but the thought of yet another man from home being in this camp haunted me. I must find Jacobs— and Cantrell. I was anxious to see him.

"Where does James stay?" I asked.

"Near the north end of the compound."

We walked from his building. As we were walking along, I asked if he knew why there wasn't any talking allowed on the detail.

"I think it is a punishment. A few days ago the bastards started beating the hell out of us if we talked, so we stopped," he replied.

"Punishment for what?" I asked.

"I don't know. A few days ago something happened out on another detail. The guards all are mad as hell and started beating everyone who came in reach. Anyway, we have worked in silence since. I also heard of some prisoners being beaten badly from other details. There has been some on this detail but nothing like I have heard about," he said.

We located Cantrell, and the three of us talked way into the night. He related that he had arrived on the islands in November, just in time for the war, and was captured on Bataan. After the march he was in Camp O'Donnel during the same time as I. We wondered why we had no seen each other.

160

Stories were exchanged for the better part of the night—how each of us had decided we would enlist in the army, and how we had managed to get to this part of the world.

I learned we were generally divided into seven groups in this camp. This was done so we could all get a fair shake at showers. The Japs would only allow the shower to be turned on once a day, and then for a rather short time. Before we were divided into groups there were fights and other problems and as a result the stronger of the prisoners got the baths. In this way, we could expect to get a shower once a week, and on that day the guards agreed to let the detail come in early. Jacobs suggested that I made sure I had everything and get in the shower as soon as possible after arriving in camp. If I should miss for any reason, it would be another week before I got another opportunity.

The men told me that the Japs issued soap but cautioned that this soap would melt in the rain. One shower was about all you could expect from one issue. I hadn't received my issue since my arrival, but had heard people swapping for soap, especially the men who remained in camp. They seemed to be trading the stuff all the time. When we decided we should knock off and get some sleep I returned to my barracks with the knowledge that I could expect to be clean once a week. I also understood the odor of the prisoners, and why so many men stayed outside, especially when it wasn't raining. Some slept on the ground rather than stay in with the smell and the heat.

One thing bothered me. Something new. In the past I had operated alone in the camps. I hadn't trusted anyone. Now these men had changed that. I had known these men for several years. And Blair I had known all my life. Jacobs and Cantrell were telling me what I could expect and I was listening. I had thought when I ran into Blair that he would be it. He was nearly blind and needed someone to assist him, but these men came from the same part of the country as I. I knew them well. One would expect I would be happy seeing someone I knew. Not so. I supposed I was scared these men would see right through me and some of the things I had done. I'd just as soon not have someone from my hometown know about that.

The pits

Chapter 24

I had been at Clark Field for a little over three weeks and during that time I worked the sand detail. The Japanese assigned me a number. The number wasn't just for identification. It also placed me into an escape squad. The Japanese at Camp O'Donnel wanted us to try escaping. This way they could eliminate us. Here the guards needed our skills and would do anything to prevent us from escaping.

The escape squads were designed in such a manner that if anyone got away five men on each side of his number would be executed. The numbering started from one and went through the total number of prisoners. If the man was caught he would be executed alone. In a real sense, each of us was the prisoner of the other, in addition to being a prisoner of the Japanese.

We worked twelve to fourteen hours a day, with any overtime it took to meet the assigned quota. We left camp and belonged to the guard in charge, body and soul. The work foreman didn't give a damn one way or the other if you were sick or not. If you had been assigned to him, you would work as he saw fit. If you were unfortunate enough to be sent out sick or if you became sick on the job and couldn't meet the standard set by your guard, the sadistic son-of-a-bitch slapped and beat you, forcing you to work until the quota was met. It was a foregone conclusion that when we left camp, there would be beatings. It was just a matter of how bad.

On the west side of the concentration camp, the Japanese had built some bleachers around cockpits. The pits were dug into the sand four or five feet deep, with bamboo poles stuck into the ground close together and tied at the top. These poles held back the sand and formed the wall of the pit. At one side of the pit steps led down inside.

If a prisoner was caught trying to escape or was found guilty of insulting one of the guards or degrading the Japanese government, he was sentenced to be executed, and the pits were where the sentence was carried out. No matter if the accusations were real or imagined, the sentence was always the same. The bleachers were for the men on the same detail or group of the man being executed. These men watched the man being forced down into the pit, where three or four guards were waiting with fixed bayonets. They had been driven into an angry mood. They were told how this man had insulted the emperor of Japan and how it was their sacred duty to eliminate him. They had been told how this man had the audacity to insult the Japanese nation and must be eliminated.

In most cases, the Americans who entered these pits, entered believing and hoping that their lives would be spared, providing they showed some remorse. They knew their sentence was unjust. They prayed for some divine intervention on their behalf, that at the last minute they would be spared. But the result was always the same: murder, slowly but as surely as all hell, murder. When an attempt was made to evade the sharp point of one bayonet, they were caught by another, until at last, they slipped into death from loss of blood. All of us in the bleachers knew there would be no last minute reprieve. A man was as good as dead when he stepped into the pits.

Not all Americans sentenced to death were so submissive. On one occasion at least, when I was brought into the bleachers, I watched an American fight back.

When all were seated, the prisoner was brought into the area. This man was known to most as "Tony the Greek" and considered by most of us as one of the meanest men you could ever expect to meet. He had been found guilty of an infraction of the rules—we were not told which rule—and was sentenced to the pits. I did know he had been a source of irritation to the Japs for some time. We were curious as to how he would react when placed in this sure death situation. The guards down in the pit had become accustomed to the Americans accepting their fate without resistance and expected the same with the Greek. They were caught off guard when Tony showed absolutely no fear. Instead, he sneered at them at the bottom of the stairs. Every muscle in his body flexed as he opened those big hands, then closed them into large fists. His eyes were only slits as the muscles in his face contracted. He waited, his back against the stairs. He was forcing the bastards to come to him, wanting them to make the first move. Every eye was on the Greek, and I knew each and every one of us were whispering a silent prayer, yet knew he hadn't a chance in hell. One couldn't help admiring his courage. He faced certain death and knew it; still he held his ground waiting, watching their every move. Suddenly, without warning, one of the Japs lunged forward. The Greek nimbly stepped aside, letting his bayonet slide by and into the bamboo stakes. With the head of the guard only inches away, he took one of those great hands, and with the strength of a cornered rhino, he smashed into the side of the Jap's neck, snapping it like a match. One lick and the son-of-a-bitch slid into the sand dead, never again to murder and maim. It was nearly impossible not to applaud, but remembering where I was, I remained silent.

The other guards saw what had happened. Their fear could be seen even from the bleachers. There would be no fun and games this time. There was a roar of a rifle. I lowered my eyes, knowing what was happening. There was another shot. I opened my eyes and saw the limp forms of the Greek and the Jap on the floor of the pit. Tony the Greek never felt the bayonets as they were plunged through his lifeless body. The source of irritation for the Japs had ended.

There was much confusion around the pit. The dead Jap was still in the hole alongside the Greek. The other guards were yelling at each other. They were at a loss as to what they must do. The report of the rifle brought

163

the Jap commander to the area as well as some of his staff. Something was said and the guards entered the pit for their lost comrade. The officers looked on as he was carried from the pit.

Taking advantage of all this confusion, I moved away from the bleachers. I was afraid there would be reprisals when they had had time to regain their composure. If that should happen I wanted to be away from the area.

Soon their man had been pulled from the hole and every one of them had left the area. They left without saying anything about what we should do with the body of the Greek. Someone had informed the American commander and he was on the scene. He had the body carried toward a small gate leading out to the east side of camp.

Another Jap ordered everyone to the barracks, except the three or four men designated to bury the body. There was a cemetery some three hundred yards east of the camp in that same sand bed where we worked.

Several days passed. There were no murders. Still that incident would not leave me.

Some time later, I was ordered to take a body out for burial. When we passed through the area designated as the cemetery, I caught myself wondering where the Greek was buried. There were many heaps of sand and they all looked the same. The one thing that impressed me most was that there was only one person placed in a grave. There was no coffin, but it wasn't like those common graves at Camp O'Donnel. Unconsciously I started counting the piles of sand. The newest ones were no problem. The sand had been washed away from the older ones and grass was growing over many of them. In some places they were sunken and you couldn't tell if it was a grave or a natural depression. The detail finished digging and when the body was nearly covered, I realized I didn't even know this soldier's name. I didn't even bother looking for a tag. He was just a detail for me, and on my day off at that. As I scooped more sand into the hole I wondered if anyone had a record of his death, or where his remains were placed, or if he was like so many others I had seen over the past year, just another American soldier on the roll of "lost in action," perhaps for all time. Here as in those other spots where the rain had washed away all traces, so would his memory fade in time.

During my stay here I had managed not to get involved with the guards. I had gone out on the details, filled my work quota, and kept myself away from threats of the pit. I had had my share of beatings, been slapped about and humiliated by the bastards. But I was alive and although my health was bad, I felt extremely fortunate compared to many others.

Malaria had taken its toll on me, and I had to seek lighter work. I was at my lowest weight since my capture at Bataan, about 110 pounds, and I couldn't keep pace on the sand detail. I was forced to get on another detail where the work was lighter.

The camp commander asked the Japs to pull me off the sand detail and place me on the detail cutting bamboo at the concentration site.

This detail was at the northern end of the main runway and while it was

164

difficult work, it was much lighter than shoveling sand. There wasn't nearly as much rice but the chances of finding extra food were much better. The rice was of better quality because it was prepared by the Japanese for their own people. The noon meal was far superior to anything we got in camp.

I remained on this detail without incident until I was alerted to move from Clark Field some time in mid– to late–December 1943.

This alert came as somewhat of a surprise. I had resigned myself to spending Christmas here. We were cut off from the world. There hadn't been any war news. No matter how bad the conditions here, I was worried about what was in store for me when I left. However, I was ready for movement in minutes. When I arrived at the main gate, at least half the prison populaton was there. No one was taking names. I assumed the camp officers had made the selection and had that information.

Looking about for faces I knew, I saw Blair and Jacobs, along with a few others I had known casually.

Blair had that mattress over his shoulder, and was easy to spot. That damn thing had become an obsession with him. It was so dirty it was difficult to tell what the thing was made of. Still, he hung on as if his life depended upon it. Christ! I thought he had limited eyesight. What in hell could the bastards expect to gain by transferrng him to another work detail? But here he was, looking all around, confused.

I started working my way to him. When I touched his shoulder, he asked without looking, "Is that you, Dick?"

"Yes, I'll be going out with you. It would appear you are stuck with me again," I said.

"Has anyone said where they are taking us?" he asked.

"Not to me they haven't. No one has said anything, just get my gear and get ready to move out."

Somehow leaving didn't bother me. This damn detail hadn't impressed me at all. Except for going into something unknown, I was happy to be leaving. The rice had been rather good and most of the time there had been enough, especially when on the sand detail. But this had been the hardest work I had ever done. I'd be glad to get away from that.

Although there were some apprehensions on my part as I prepared to leave, there was also some security in the knowledge that I was alive because I was able to cope. What was coming was unknown.

Chapter 25

With a feeling of apprehension about leaving and also wanting to be away at the same time, I waited for the Japanese to do whatever they had to do before we were taken from Clark Field. I had time to reflect back to this concentration camp.

Every one of the guards had gone inside the guard shack, leaving the prisoners milling about and staring at each other. We all wondered what was in store for us. Some of the men had remained in camp since coming here, while others of us had been out on work details. Some were extremely ill, while others were in different stages of sickness. All were suffering from malnutrition.

The worst thing that kept running through my mind were the execution pits. Thinking about this, I saw a parade of terror-stricken men; some begging, others praying, and still others passive about the thing and just waiting for the inevitable. They had seen others before them and knew the end result of being sentenced to the pit. In my mind's eye, I saw them being shoved, slapped, and prodded along with the bayonets on their way to that stairway that led them down into the torturous spot. I saw them ask permission to pray and be laughed at and scorned by their masters as being weak. These men here seemed to be spared victims of the pit.

I thought of the cemetery. I could hear the sand as it hit the clothing of a limp form. He would rest there through eternity. No priest would say anything, no chaplain, not even a box to protect his remains, only the rag on his back. For him it was over, and soon the rains would wash away all signs of the displaced sand.

I saw the faces of the Japanese soldiers, the perpetrators of the heinous crime. I saw them walking away from the pit, laughing boisterously. They were also victims of a sort. They had been ordered to do this thing. They dared not question the orders of a superior in the Japanese army. If they did they would be butchered as they had been ordered to butcher us.

With all these things racing through my mind and the anger I felt, I realized that leaving even with apprehensions was a blessing for me. Things had to be better where we were going. Hell, for me to be somewhere where I couldn't see the fence or look in the direction of those heaps of sand would help.

I intended to survive, and those bastards would answer for each and every one of those men out there. I intended to live long enough to watch every living son-of-a-bitch involved get his just dues.

Chapter 26

I heard the screams of one of the guards near the gate. The prisoners were on their feet. As we gathered our gear, we made a rather disorganized sight. Some of the men had nothing but the rags on their backs while others had small packs. And, of course, here was Blair with that large bedroll over his shoulder.

I took one last look over my shoulder at the bamboo buildings and their thatched roofs. There was no greenery in the camp. Everything was drab and weatherbeaten. This camp held no attraction for me. I was glad we were going.

After marching for some time we were at the village of Angelese, the same railhead where I came in five or six months before. We were loaded into two railcars waiting for us. The group was split in half and as soon as we were loaded the sliding doors were closed and locked.

We ate not long before we left camp, and then had been given time in which to fill water bottles. The cars could accommodate quite well. Some were able to sit. The train didn't wait. We were barely settled when the car started moving.

The train was going south toward Manila. There were no stops, and there were no shortages of water. Within three hours we were in the city and were unloaded at the main rail station. Before really realizing it I found myself back at that great gate at the front of old Bilibid Prison. It was almost as if I had never seen this gray wall before.

In spite of my apprehension, I remembered that Americans were inside. There were doctors with medicine, something many in this group sorely needed. The knowledge that we were here and not out on another labor detail was gratifying.

Very quickly we were taken inside and out of sight of the Filipinos who were staring at us from the sidewalks. As quickly as we entered, the gate closed behind us and we were marched farther into the prison.

In front of the main guardhouse we were told to sit. We waited several minutes before an American naval officer emerged from the guard building. He told us we would be housed in one of the cellblocks, but there would be a wait.

It was hot. The rains had stopped and we sat in the dust and waited. At last we were taken into one of the major cellblocks. Within this large block were small steel cages. Each cage had a sliding door that covered half the cell.

The cells could be locked individually. Inside was nothing; no chairs or bedding were present. As we moved into the cells, I thought about sleeping on the hard floor. That mattress Joe lugged around all this time sure as hell didn't seem stupid now.

It was dark, and I had problems adjusting my sight. I started looking for Blair. I wanted to be in the same cell. But from what I saw, once I was in the cell there would be no chance of change, espcially if they locked the cell door. Joe was about five or six feet behind me when we were inside the outer door. The guard who was pushing us into the cells was ahead of me. I stepped aside and let one or two men pass until I was in front of Joe. That guard was screaming and slapping at people when they didn't get inside as quickly as he thought they should. I was where I wanted to be. All I could hope for now was room for both of us. The guard was putting four men in each cell.

There were only a few men in front of me now, but that son-of-a-bitch was mad as hell about something and was swinging at everyone who came in front of him. There was no way to avoid him. I was next. He swung his open hand at me but I was able to dodge him and jump inside the cell. As I did he hit me across the back with something. It felt like the barrel of his rifle. I sprawled across the hardwood floor and started crawling into one of the back corners. Blair was right on my heels, mattress and all, grinning from ear to ear. The Jap hit him, but the mattress protected him from the blow. He also crawled into the opposite corner. Hell, I felt secure. The bastard didn't hurt me and he was screaming and hitting someone else. The door had been shut, but not locked. I could see all the way back to the door where we entered, and the cells were filled on both sides of the aisle, with four men to each cell. The only walls between us were the bars that separated the cells. I could see everyone in this block.

Blair was taking all this in stride. He had already rolled out his mattress, staking out his area as if he had been here before. I did likewise, taking my pack from my shoulder and stowing it in my corner. Then we sat and waited. Nobody was saying anything. Everywhere I looked men were sitting on the floor inside their cell, listening to the noises around them. The noise subsided and that screaming stopped. Looking in the direction where the guard should have been, I saw he was gone. The door at the end of the cellblock was left open when he left. I kept watching that door for him to return. Nothing.

All the cells were left unlocked. Any control would be from outside the cellblock.

I heard someone slide a cell door open. Then almost as if it were a signal, doors were sliding open all along the aisle. What a relief! Within minutes, laughter returned, and I heard men talking from both ends of the block. The men who came in first had stowed their gear, and some of them had left their cell and made their way to the door at the end. I even saw one of them step out the door and out of sight. Then others did too and before long, we learned this was to be like a barracks. We could come and go as we wished.

The cellblock was well ventilated. There were windows near the roof of

168

the building. Contrary to what the place looked like from the outside, this could be rather comfortable.

The next few days we rested. The American doctors checked me over. Blair and I shared his mattress. He slept on it at night and I used it during the day. In this way, both of us were able to get the much needed rest for regaining our strength after that bone-breaking labor detail at Clark Field.

Right when things were looking up for me, I was told that I had been selected for a driving detail. The details were not known.

I was taken out of Bilibid and escorted to the area of Manila where MacArthur's headquarters were before the war. I would drive for some Japanese officers when needed.

On my first day, I was taken to the motor pool area and shown which vehicle I would be driving. It was a 1939 Buick the Japanese had confiscated. When the Japanese sergeant showed me this vehicle, I could see the envy in his eyes as well as his anger. He was gone before I could ask anything. I knew he was mad because he wasn't selected as the driver.

I had never driven anything as new or as big. Most of my driving experience was with a Model "A" Ford and an old vintage car that my father had from the early 1920s. This was going to be an experience.

In those days, the Japs never questioned if any American could drive. It was assumed he could, and when the need arose, you were assigned as a driver. I wanted to drive this big American automobile more than anything. All I could think of was being behind the wheel of that car, speeding down the highway.

All day long I cleaned and revved the engine. I took the car out of the motor pool and drove around the area. It was during this time I saw the racks for flags or something on the front, and on one side there was something written in Japanese. When I drove around the area, the guards allowed me all the room I needed. I later learned that this car was used by a high-ranking Japanese officer and was for his exclusive use.

All day long I drove and shined and checked the air in the tires, making these people believe I knew everything there was to know about this automobile. I could tell I was not making any friends with the Japanese.

For three days I worked with the Buick and at the same time got used to driving. I knew that I had not been assigned for housekeeping duties, that sooner or later I would be asked to drive someone in this car. I wanted to know what I was doing. I was told to service the car and bring it around in front of the headquarters building. I only had to wait for a short time until a high-ranking Japanese officer and his aide came out of the front door. The Japanese in the area bowed and scraped as he came by. I knew this must be an important man.

The aide told me to open the trunk and he inspected the back. I had put and extra can of gasoline, extra oil, tools, and some water in the trunk.

When he was satisfied that everything was in order, we drove toward the main highway leading north out of the city of Manila. We were barely on the main road when we were joined by other vehicles. Some of these had red lights flashing and were rushing about the road getting into position as we moved along. All I had to do was drive and let the others do all the maneuvering. We were in the midst of a rather large convoy of trucks and staff cars. In the open country I opened the thing up. To hell with it, to be out on the road with all this power under me was the most exhilarating experience of my life. I didn't even think about who was in the back seat.

The aide spoke some English. He told me to stay in line, not to try passing. Christ, it was all right with me. The only thing I could think of was how exciting this was, driving a high-powered car.

I didn't notice how far we had gone, only that we were on the northbound highway and we weren't stopping for anything.

Time passed without my knowing it. It was in the afternoon. At the speed we had been traveling we had come a good distance from Manila. Then, without warning, the convoy slowed and up ahead the lead vehicles were leaving the main road. We were being escorted into a large bivouac area of the Japanese army. These were tents everywhere and guards spotted at designated spots as sentries. As the Buick entered the compound, the guards and people moving about all stopped and saluted. I was the only American in the place. I brought the vehicle into the center of the area and parked. The aide got out and then the general. The aide turned and told me to wait in the car. There was nothing more.

It was after sunrise when we left the camp. The blacktop road was much worse than the main road we came north on. Sometimes we ran out of blacktop and were on dirt. We were heading north toward a mountain range. This range of mountains were not the same as I had known in Bataan. They were too far east of that area. We were even farther north than Camp O'Donnel.

Before noon on the second day, I resigned myself to the task at hand. I drove, nothing more, and kept my mouth shut. It was too late to make any attempt at getting out of this.

Throughout the day the convoy moved farther toward the mountain area. We drove hard for a few miles, then stopped for a conference with lesser-ranking officers.

It was late in the afternoon when we reached the foothills. We were directed off the road and into a controlled area. The first thing I saw was a fence, then a gate with two guards at each side. Along the road inside the camp, guards stood stiffly at attention as we drove past. We stopped near the center of this compound near a very large building. I was hustled into a room and isolated from the Japanese. Rice was brought to me. The orderly sat it on the floor, then left.

The third morning the Buick was filled with gas. We left the camp by a dirt road that climbed the side of a mountain very quickly. When we were well into the timber area, the convoy stopped and camp was made. This time we were in tents. This was field headquarters.

There was a guard posted near me. I had been moved some distance from the place where the officers were housed.

170

The tent was rather large and the sides were rolled up from the ground allowing the air to circulate. All in all it was rather comfortable. Up here it was cool, especially now that the sun was down.

There was water and plenty of rice and I didn't even have to line up for either. It was brought to me by one of the orderlies, who wasn't at all thrilled at the thought of bringing rice to an American.

I wished I had my pack with me, but it was at Bilibid with Blair. In it I had an extra shirt and could use it in this night air. Hell, I was led to believe I would only be out of Bilibid for a day or so.

I talked with the guard and rested. Each day large patrols were formed and went out the front gate into the hills. When they returned in the evenings there was always loud talk from the main tent.

Three days passed. I shined the Buick until there was nothing more I could do to it. The guards wouldn't let me drive it, but I revved the engine and sat behind the wheel and waited to get back on the road again. I sure had the bug about driving that big American car.

Sometime during the night I developed a severe fever. The thirst was terrible. I drank all my water in a very short time and had to get more brought around, much to the chagrin of the guard. There was a sharp pain in my lower side. It was cold and there wasn't anything to cover myself with. I lowered the tent flap. Still I felt like I was freezing. The pain persisted. I called the guard but he ignored me. I continued pestering him, and because I was driving the general's car, he decided it best to call the aide. No one came around that night, and I thought I was going to die. About eight o'clock the guard did get some blankets. He saw me shaking from fever. He went inside the big tent and brought out two of them. He could see I was sicker than he had thought, and once again reported this to the aide. By the time he was in the tent, I was begging. I had never had anything hurt so bad. This time I got results. The general himself entered the tent. He asked his personal doctor to examine me.

I hadn't known there was a doctor with this convoy. He pressed on the area where the pain was the worst, and I felt a sharp pain shoot throughout my entire body. He said I had appendicitis, that there was nothing he could do out here, and I must wait until we were back in Manila where there was an operating room. He spoke in Japanese and broken English, but I understood clearly. He left, and I thought I was being deserted to suffer. He soon returned with an assortment of medications. He gave me what he could to ease the pain. He also told me how I should sit or lie in order to reduce my discomfort.

Two, possibly three hours passed, and I started vomiting. The only thing I had eaten was rice and water. Soon the vomiting turned into dry heaves, but the nausea wouldn't let up. Each time I heaved, the pain felt like it was ripping my stomach apart. Then, suddenly, the pain stopped as I was straining. I seemed to have pulled something inside me, but the pain was gone. Also, the nausea eased off. I knew this thing had passed.

I was almost asleep when the doctor returned. I told him how the pain

171

had stopped and that I was feeling fine. Also, I told him he could forget about me for awhile; I would sleep. He felt the area in my side, then leaped to his feet and was out the door like a shot. Within minutes he was back and the general was with him. He and the doctor were talking and I couldn't understand one thing being said. At last the aide spoke to me. "The doctor believes your appendix has ruptured and that you must have surgery now." There was considerable chatter between the general and the doctor, with the doctor saying no, no, no, and shaking his head. Then! Before I realized what was going on, two orderlies entered and carried me from the tent and into that large command tent. I was laid out on some sort of table or bench right under a light. I could hear the doctor still saying no, no, no, but the general had the final word. A bottle of liquor was forced into my mouth and someone told me to drink. I took one great gulp and felt the stuff burning as fire in my throat. They hardly gave me time to get my breath until they forced the stuff down again. After I drank several times from this bottle of saki, I felt the doctor doing something with his hands, near the area where the pain was before. The bottle of saki was passed again and each time I drank deeply of its contents. By now there was no need for the order to drink. When the bottle was passed I drank as much as I could. I felt a sharp needle and knew I had been given a shot of something. In a rather short time whatever it was plus the effects of the liquor numbed my thinking. They were preparing me for surgery. I recalled the doctor saying I had to be in a hospital for that. The bottle was passed and again I drank. I hadn't drank anything in a very long time and this stuff was taking hold very well. Still I didn't know for sure what was taking place. I would like to sleep. I drank deeply of the bottle once again and started closing my eyes. From somewhere I heard chatter among the people over me. Then there was a sting on my stomach. What in hell were the bastards doing? That pain hit again, and this time was unbearable. I screamed and felt the knife as it was disemboweling me. There were a number of them holding my arms and my feet and legs. I was sure the bastards were murdering me, but struggle as I might, I couldn't get out of their grip. That bottle was pushed down my throat again. The stuff ran down my throat and I screamed from the pain in my stomach. I started to vomit again, and the saki came up into the face of one of the people holding me. I heard something, then there were spangles in the air from a blow on the head. A fist smashed into my lower face, then another blast on the top of my head. There were flashes and spangles flying around my eyes, and then nothing.

The next thing I knew, there was pain in my stomach and head. The Japanese doctor was standing over me as if he recognized that I was returning to consciousness. He pushed that bottle of saki into my mouth and again offered me a drink. I groaned at the thought of the stuff but heard him say "Drink," and then I remembered that fear of being murdered. I knew that if he wanted he could finish the job. I drank. My nausea returned, but I drank more. For some time this continued. Each time I came around the bottle was shoved into my mouth and I drank until I passed out again. I had no idea

172

or how long this had been going on. The next clear thing I knew I was being carried out in a blanket tied between two poles.

After what seemed an eternity, I was placed in the back of a truck with two Japanese soldiers and the truck was being driven away toward the south.

During this trip, one of the guards kept pouring saki down me; the other held onto the stretcher set into the side of the truck bed. They kept me unconscious until at last we were at the front gate of Bilibid. Some American doctors worked on me.

The next thing I recalled was a bright light shining directly into my eyes and hearing the people working over me speaking English. I didn't feel anything; what they gave me deadened the pain. I couldn't move my feet, but could see them and feel pressure in the area of my stomach.

The American doctors explained to me that I had undergone surgery by the doctor wherever I had been but they had to open the incision again. When I complained of the treatment at his hands, they told me that if he had not done what he did, I would have died. I was not sure if I should be grateful or if I should hate the bastards even worse.

For the next several days I was confined to a bed in a cellblock that had been converted into a surgery ward. During this time, the infection in my body kept me on the edge of death, while the doctors did everything in their power to keep me alive.

During this time and for several weeks afterward, I ate a diet of chopped corn. It had been ground into small grains, larger than cornmeal but small enough that it would cook up soft in boiling water.

My recovery was very slow. My weight was below one hundred pounds, and I required assistance to walk any distance. I could walk to the latrine and put on my clothing and undress myself. Blair brought all my personal gear into this ward for me.

It was early January now and I was still on the diet of corn, but some Red Cross packages had been received by the Japanese. These contained several food items and our doctors seemed delighted at the prospect of having something for the patients besides corn. Patients such as I who were near death were given special attention.

The only thing we knew about the war was what we could glean from the Japanese. They brought in news clips to be shown to their own troops, and they also requried all prisoners to watch these propaganda films. It didn't matter that some of us were not able to walk. We were placed on stretchers and brought out where the film was shown. We were forced to lie near the front and watch what the Japanese were supposedly doing to the Americans. I had had a problem healing and a tube was placed in my incision. I was not to try walking for a few days. During this time one of the films was shown. I was hauled up near the screen and told to stay. The screen had been stretched between the cells nearest the end next to the guardhouse. The method in which it was hung made it possible for people to view the picture from either side of the screen. From where I was, I could see under the screen and there were nearly as many people on that side as the one where I was. In the movie some ski troops engaged some Americans somewhere with lots of snow. All lighting had been doused near the screen. The only lights were those in the Japanese guardhouse. I was watching this movie with great interest when I heard noises from near the west wall. I saw the lights in the guardhouse grow dim, then get bright again. In back of me some of the prisoners were scrambling to get away. I heard some swearing and everyone started running back this way. I felt a big foot in my stomach as they ran over me. Someone fell across me and couldn't get up. This protected me from others. Whoever this was on top of me remained until this melee was over. I was carried back into the operating room. I would learn later that someone tried an escape over the wall during the movie but had touched the high voltage wire along the top. When he was knocked back inside he ran into the crowd in his attempt to get away from the guard. This was nothing more than a panic situation but it sure as hell tore my stomach open again.

The doctors tried to stop the blood, and at the same time gave me something to knock me out.

For the next several days I remained in critical condition. The doctors did everything they knew to keep me alive. I was having difficulty enduring the pain. It was worse now than at any time after coming in from the field, and there wasn't very much these people could give me that would ease it.

With the extra nutritional food from the Red Cross packages, I slowly regained my strength. I couldn't work at anything.

While on the detail on Corregidor, I had sewn some green dollars in the back of that shirt, but never had any use for the stuff. No one wanted it. But here in this walled city there were people who would deal in paper dollars or any kind of currency.

Blair had free run of the place. He was even here before Clark Field and he knew every dealer.

The Red Cross stuff had long since gone, and we were back to the corn and rice. I gave Joe some of the paper money and he had made his connections. He brought back sugar candy made from cane, extra rice, and even some strange little mango beans. On one occasion he had to pay five hundred dollars for one large goose egg. We thought this to be quite high, but since we had dollars and nothing to eat, the price was right. Especially now that the main ration was corn. Only rarely did we get rice, and with so many of us near starvation, anything that could be obtained for additional food might mean the difference between life and death.

I was released from the surgery ward, and was back in the cellblock where I was before the driving detail. There wasn't any chance of the food getting better. I had used all the money I had hidden. The only thing now was corn, not even salt. It wasn't long until the Japs moved us from this cellblock and back to the north side of the prison where we had first met. This, I knew, was the last stage before they sent us out of here. Each day when the corn was rationed and I tried eating that swill with absolutely no taste at all, I wished the day would come. Anything would be better than this.

174

The Japanese mess hall was nearby. I knew they considered us healthy enough to work. So I started trying to get a job. I didn't get the job, but in my efforts I found out where the Japanese cooks dumped their garbage. I got these peelings without being seen by other prisoners, but this was not to last. One of them followed me after seeing Joe and I eating something extra with the corn. From then on, there was a fight when I went for them, each of us wanting everything we could get with this slop. The damn Japs heard our fights and would come to the windows of the mess hall and watch as we fought for the garbage. They soon tired of the entertainment and stopped throwing the stuff out. Our source of extra food was gone.

I had been here for six months. My health was such that I knew I would soon be selected for another slave labor detail. Rumor had it that the Americans were back in this area of the world and were closing in on the Philippines. I wanted to be here when they returned. My greatest desire was to be the one who opened the great gate, letting everyone through.

As each day passed the rumors flew about the impending return of MacArthur. Someone started the rumor that a force had landed on the island of Borneo and was preparing for a landing on an island called Yap. When I asked where the island was, I was told it was near the southernmost tip of the Philippines, close to us. The guards were very jumpy now, and this added credence to the rumor. Every time an American prisoner got near one of them, he was slapped and beaten.

The prison population had doubled in Bilibid during the past two days. There were problems getting everyone inside the cellblocks. Many had to sleep on the ground between the buildings. The ration of corn decreased until there was barely enough to sustain life.

When all the prisoners were in from down south, they, along with many of us who had been here for some time, were alerted for movement.

Within an hour after being alerted, I was packed and at the main gate. Only yesterday I had fantasized about being the one who would open this gate for our returning forces.

Looking at this bunch of prisoners and the guards, I saw no changes. The faces were different, yet they were the same. The guards were as they always had been, some meaner, some not so bad.

Suddenly without warning I felt the butt of a rifle in my back. Then I was hit on the side of my head with a fist. I had not heard the order to move out, and this son-of-a-bitch was demonstrating his superiority. I was on the ground trying to get back to my feet when he hit me again. This time I fell against the wall, but quickly regained my footing. I was so damned angry nothing mattered. I stepped right in front of the little bastard and said in English, "You rotten son-of-a-bitch, I am going to survive this and when this is over, I will hunt you down and kill you, so help me God!" An American officer, seeing how near I was to being murdered, grabbed my arm and pushed me forward and away from the guard. As he did, the guard stood and watched but said no more, nor did he try hitting me again. I walked away from that great gate, blood streaming from my mouth and from a gash on the side of

175

my head. I didn't know it at the time, but that incident gave me the will to live.

For the next hour we walked through the streets of Manila, subjected to ridicule before the Filipinos lined up on the sidewalks. When we passed a large crowd, the guards increased their harassment and their screaming. When I had an opportunity to look, I saw many of them bowing their heads or looking away, not wanting to witness this demonstration.

We marched to the same railroad station. This time the cars were open with stake siding. There were plenty of them and they were not overcrowded. We were on the move almost instantly. The train was moving north, away from the port area. This meant we wouldn't be taken out of the islands—a good sign.

The train had been rolling for about half an hour; it became apparent that we were being taken to the main concentration camp at Cabanatuan. Some of the prisoners near me had been in that camp before.

Once again I was reminded of those rumors about MacArthur's return and about that landing on an island south of the Philippines. That rumor, plus this sudden movement of prisoners from down south and the edginess of these guards, could mean only one thing: they were bringing us into one area where we would be liberated as a group.

After all these months in concentration camps throughout the islands, I learned that I must keep my thoughts and plans simple and positive. I must believe this ordeal was coming to an end and soon. I would be free to do as I wish. That attitude was the greatest source of survival I had.

The train had sped across the rural areas of the island of Luzon for some time. My thoughts had so occupied me I hadn't noticed that we were slowing.

When we slowed almost to a crawl, we saw Filipinos running alongside the rails. Some of them were waving while others were off on the road just watching. There seemed to be an air of jubilation among them, an attitude I hadn't seen in some time. Their attitude added to my feelings that the war was almost over.

When the train stopped, the ranking American officer started lining everyone up to be marched away to wherever the Japanese intended to take us.

Many in this group had been in prison at Bilibid for differing periods of time, for two weeks up to a year. Many were still recovering from illness or injury.

The guards seemed to be in a rush to get us away from the natives. Unlike those in Manila who wanted to show their superiority, these guards just wanted us away from those in a joyous mood. They started shoving and slapping as soon as we started walking. If someone fell, someone else assisted him back to his feet and he stumbled onward.

Although still sore from the surgery, I was able to walk, keeping well inside the line of marchers, a trick I had picked up when on the march out of Bataan. If one of my fellow prisoners fell near me, I assisted him; otherwise,

I moved forward. I wondered how much farther. I must have said it out loud. Someone answered that it was about five miles from the railhead to the main camp at Cabanatuan, and that we should be there any time. I knew if I fell I would be beaten. I must keep moving. My right eye had closed from the swelling on the side of my face. I saw men passing me, unable to keep pace. At my left there was a barbed wire fence. This must be the main camp. If I could hang on until I was inside, I'd be all right. My head was swimming from the heat. We had been pushed so hard that there was no opportunity to get water since leaving the train. I was not sure where I was, but the yelling had stopped, and I couldn't see any Jap guards. I felt my legs crumbling beneath me, and I fell face down into the dirt and dust. Someone asked, "Are you all right?" When I asked how much farther to camp, he said we were inside. I crawled from the line of marchers. Someone came by and assisted me to a dispensary where I was given fresh water and told to remain there at least for the night.

I was at Cabanatuan. This was my first time here. I hoped this would be the last move for me before MacArthur's return.

Chapter 27

Cabanatuan was a very large complex compared with other camps where I had been held. Everywhere I looked were rows of bamboo buildings. A few wood buildings were scattered about the compound.

I was permitted to remain in the dispensary area for about a week and had a better than average rice ration. Except for the period when I was held on Corregidor, this was the best rice ration I had had when there wasn't any labor detail involved.

During this time, my face, although badly bruised by the beating I took at Bilibid, was greatly improved. The cut on my head was healing well. My doctor advised that I move about the area to get some exercise. While doing this I had an opportunity to learn about the camp and what work details were being performed here. I was not bothered by the guards when moving about this subenclosure. They thought we might be contagious in some way and were left alone as long as we didn't venture into the outer part of the camp.

This concentration camp was one of the first camps to be established after our surrender and for the most part was a holding area for prison laborers. The Japs drew from here the men needed in the slave labor camps throughout the islands.

As a general rule, officer personnel were not sent out on those details, except as supervisors. As a result the majority of prisoners were office personnel, mostly below the rank of lieutenant colonel.

They had established themselves very well. Some had been in this same location since the surrender. They still had their military uniforms and were able to keep them rather clean. Many had their insignia of rank and were allowed to wear it. All in all, the place was well organized when compared with the labor camps in other areas of the islands. Still, all the people were in poor physical condition.

A large farm was adjacent to the camp. The prisoners were charged with working it. Supposedly the prisoners were to be rationed edible vegetables. The Japanese took the choice parts of the crops and the prisoners who raised the stuff got what was left.

People given the chance at working the farm had the opportunity to get extra food even if only what they could eat was while they were working. There were always volunteers to work this detail. Anyone who could stand would gladly work in the fields, especially when they were ready to harvest.

178

It had been six months since the Red Cross parcels were received, but there was still some of the food around the camp. This camp got a much larger shipment than other places. If you had anything considered valuable, you could trade for it, but the price was very high. The camp commander had stored some of the food received in the Red Cross packages, but this was issued to patients who were very ill. Medicine was closely guarded.

As soon as I could, I asked to be released from the dispensary. I went into the main camp where I would have the best chance of getting on that farm detail. If there was one thing I had learned since becoming a prisoner of war, it was that on the details one had a much better chance to get extra food. Also, when I was working, there was less time for thinking. When I was idle, all I did was think about the time when our forces would come storming through the gates and I would be free.

I was able to get on the farm detail as soon as I put my name on the list. I learned from the stories I had been told about earlier times, that now much stricter control was placed on the detail, and it was easier to get assigned there.

First off, we were given numbers, exactly as at Clark Field. Had I known that, I might not have been so eager to get on the detail. It was hard to trust ten men. I hadn't been told what the sentence was here, but I remembered what it was at Clark Field.

Out in this area of the farm, I saw mountains off to the south and east. At the edge of the cultivated area was heavy foliage that would offer excellent cover if one should decide to make a break. That alone caused me to be a bit jumpy. I started looking about for numbers. If someone in my number bracket decided to jump the place, I wanted to go along.

Rumors of MacArthur's return came in with the new arrivals daily. I got the distinct impression that the prisoners were being assembled for the purpose of having everyone where they could be exchanged easily. In addition to these indications, the Japanese were more edgy now than at any time since I became a prisoner of war. About half the time when I went out I didn't see the numbers on each side of me. They were on some other part of the farm, and might try escaping without my knowing their plans. With the war winding down, I sure as hell didn't want to become a victim without at least having a chance of getting away. Each day we left the main gate, I was afraid. Then in early August two men slipped into the trees and brush at the southeast side of the farm. I heard about this on the way into camp at the end of work. As we walked along it became a joke that some of us might be in the escape squad, but none of us knew what the numbers were of either side of these two men. Hell, it could be that twenty men would be executed because of them. As we passed through the gate, an American marine major was just inside the entrance, and there were three or four guards with him. These people were taking men from the ranks as they entered camp. Some of these men were not aware that the Japs were pulling men out because of the escape, but I had seen this sort of thing before and knew that these men weren't being selected for any favors from the Japs. These were the numbers

179

on each side of the escapees to be executed. As I entered the gate, my pent-up nervous system sank at the sight of the first man nearest me. His number was only six away from mine. Any doubts I had about what this was went out the window. I had heard rumors about an officer who had collaborated with the Japanese, but this was my first sight of him. When he reached through the ranks and took me by the shoulder, I knew this was the end. There were several men in the group now. Some of them were totally unaware of what was happening and were even laughing with each other. I supposed they had come from other parts of the farm and had not heard of the escape. Seeing this, I moved away from the guards and farther inside near the forward edge of the selected group. I waited. Then I saw the major concentrating on another man entering the gate. They were saying something to each other, and while they were getting their victim, I stepped gingerly back into the line of marchers, removed my number, and tossed it as soon as I was around the first building. As soon as I could, I broke ranks and rushed toward the dysentery ward. I found a medical officer that I had met on another detail and explained what had happened. He admitted me into the ward and back-dated the entry. It was as if I wasn't on the detail. I could do no more, just hope against hope that this would work.

I heard nothing about my slipping away. No one asked about why I was here and I was so scared I wouldn't say anything to anyone. I was afraid to ask about the execution—if it happened or not. Just to let well enough alone was my only hope. That major who pulled me from the ranks never showed up around the ward, nor did the Japanese. I had many sleepless nights, but as time passed and there was no indication that they were looking for me, sleep did come. I was surprised since the bastards at Clark Field would have taken me from the sick bay and that would have been it.

Several days passed and the medical doctor pulled me aside and told me he thought it was safe. The quicker I got out of his dispensary, the better he would feel. I understood him clearly. Christ! What I had put this man through! My gratitude could never be expressed adequately for his act of kindness. When I was back in the barracks, I vowed that I never again would volunteer for any kind of detail at this camp, especially if it involved leaving the camp.

The prison population was growing day by day. Almost any time during the day new people arrived and none were taken out.

By not being on detail I was able to observe the other prisoners as they came and went on their details. There were men whose limbs were nothing more than bone with skin drawn so tightly it shone, even glistened in the sunlight. Some were bloated out of proportion and in many cases body fluids were seeping through their flesh due to edema. It made me much less selfish about my condition and the treatment I had received.

Some men wore slings from their necks that extended low enough to carry their testicles, which had swollen from the fluids to such an extent they couldn't bear the weight. They plodded into the camp in droves and I wondered how they had been able to survive.

At this time my weight was holding at about one hundred pounds. I had had both the wet and dry Beri-Beri. Now my problem was with dry Beri-Beri.

The hunger in the eyes of the new men coming in could be read in their every action. They brought in their quan buckets (containers that could be used for cooking anything that one might be able to beg, borrow, or steal), which they guarded closely. These containers were unusual, to say the least. I cut the bottom from a canteen, and when I was out on any detail, I could slip this from the pouch and put food inside, or anything I had the opportunity to steal. When in the pouch, the Japs thought it was an extra water bottle. It was excellent for rice or mango beans, but I brought in any number of things in other camps. I never had it checked by the Japs.

One hot afternoon I was in the barracks with only one army captain who had just arrived. He was sitting in the bay and staring at a cat that strolled into the building. This cat belonged to one of the prisoners and had become his mascot. The captain sat on the edge of the bay watching. I knew what was on his mind, but I didn't do or say anything. The cat stopped in the aisle. It stretched its long body and licked itself; it looked both ways, then walked slowly down the aisle. That stare on the captain's face left nothing secret about his intentions. I had seen that starved look many times. If that cat survived it would be because it really had nine lives. The cat moved by the captain. The captain's hands were opening and closing, his eyes never leaving the prey. The captain sprang from the bay as a tiger would leap on its victim. The squeal of that cat could have wakened the dead as it was being torn limb from limb by the bare hands of this crazed man. Then all was quiet. The animal was dead and without so much as a glance in my direction the captain left the building through the same door the cat had entered. Sometime later, he returned with food in his quan bucket. He sat and ate and I could hear him muttering about how good this rabbit was. It was obvious he had little awareness of what he had done.

That evening when the owner of the cat returned from his detail, I saw him searching for his mascot. When his search failed he began to ask questions. Three days later he asked me if I knew what had happened to the cat. When I told what I had seen, how this fellow was muttering about fried rabbit, he went out of his mind. He told me if that son-of-a-bitch ate his cat, he would kill him with his bare hands. With that he stormed from the barracks. I followed him and saw the captain cornered by this fellow.

"Captain, did you kill my cat?"

"No, corporal, why would I want to kill a cat?" the captain answered.

"You were seen cooking some meat in your quan bucket the same day the cat disappeared. Just what were you cooking?"

"Rabbit," the captain replied.

"You are lying, there aren't any rabbits in the camp and you know it," said the corporal.

"That is what I cooked."

"You bastard, you are lying. You killed my pet and ate it."

With this he lunged at the captain and both of them fell to the dirt, struggling around trying to get at one another. Fortunately, they were in such weakened condition that they couldn't do serious harm to each other. The marine, however, was in better physical condition than the captain, and soon overcame him. Some of us separated them. The fight was over and the captain still maintained he ate a rabbit. He actually believed what he was saying.

I studied the face of this officer, a man who just a few months ago would have scorned the person who attempted to serve him food of any kind unless it was properly prepared. He had convinced himself he had hunted and killed a rabbit.

Word was passed for us to prepare to leave Cabanatuan immediately. There was no time for farewells, just time to get packed and make sure my canteen was filled and I had some extra rice.

Near the gate where I had entered this camp, men were gathering. An officer assembled them as they arrived. This assembly consisted of officer personnel. This was the first time I had been shipped with only officers. They represented all the armed services and in most cases were in khaki uniforms.

The more that arrived, the more confusion there was among us. Somehow I knew that I wouldn't be in the Philippines when MacArthur returned. I felt much as I did when I left Bilibid. There were men who had been out on details, and I thought we might be going to another work detail. Most of these men hadn't been outside the barbed wire of Cabanatuan. The Japanese had either changed their attitude toward officer personnel or this group was being taken off the islands. I was caught up in an overall plan much larger than I was able to comprehend at the moment.

Chapter 28

Everywhere I looked there were prisoners. I didn't see much organization. We were more like a mob than an organized group trying to board a ship. People were being hustled up a gangway only a few yards from where my group was waiting. Farther out toward the end of the pier was another gangplank and men were being boarded in that area. I knew we were being taken out of the islands. This was a much larger ship than would be used for interisland movement. I was in a severe state of depression, the worst I had suffered to date. My mind kept racing back to the prison camps where I had been held, the beatings I had taken and the other tortures and degradations. I would prefere any of them to boarding this ship. I knew that U.S. forces would be landing in the Philippines and I wouldn't be here. Why, I asked myself, had they selected me to leave?

I felt a prodding between my shoulders and turned to see a Jap guard jabbing me with the muzzle of his rifle. I began my climb up the gangway.

Stepping on the deck, I was brought back to the reality of the moment. This wasn't a large ship by normal standards. It was rust colored and there were several large areas on the side where it had been painted with red lead paint. That screaming Japanese guard could be heard over the noises of the prisoners, and he continued slapping everyone who came near him. No one was exempt from this treatment. Rank had no privileges here. The cuts on the bottom of my feet burned as if I were standing on hot coals. There was no protection from the sun, and the steel deck was hot. Directly in front of me was a water hose, and water was flowing from it and running across the deck toward the opposite side of the ship. There wasn't a guard near, so I stepped into the cool flowing water as the people went past.

The guards were pushing and shoving prisoners toward the bow, but I couldn't see where they were going to put all the men they were bringing aboard. There wore two canvas-colored holds forward from where I was standing. They were pushing the men down through an open door into those covered hatches.

The forward hatch was loaded first. I saw the door that opened into the hatch nearest me. The lumber used for it was new, cut only a few hours before. The Japs had to rush this ship into service.

There was some sort of delay on the pier. The prisoners had slowed coming aboard and those on deck were fast disappearing into the hatch. I couldn't keep standing with no one around me. I would become too conspicuous, and if the guards should think I was stalling, the bastards would start swinging.

I passed the first hatch door. I saw a guard from Cabanatuan known as "Donald Duck" because of the way he was always squawking. People at Cabanatuan had warned me about him, and I had managed to stay clear of him until now. He was one of the most sadistic guards in the islands. I wondered if he was going to make this trip with us. I hoped he was just assisting getting the people on board.

His screaming could be heard over everything. He was standing between me and the door and there was no way of avoiding him. I didn't want him to get the idea I was stalling, so I closed ranks with the people in front. I wanted as many men around me as I could get. I was alongside him when he screamed and swung his free hand at me. I managed to duck and step inside the door, but the light was bad and I feared falling. While grasping for something to hold on to, I felt his foot in the center of my back as he shoved me down the staircase. I managed to hang onto the two-by-four timber used as the handrail, and soon I was down in the bowels of the ship, out of his sight and reach.

Men were walking around in the dimly lit hold trying to find space to sit. I heard people yelling out the names of friends, trying desperately to get back together with people they left Cabanatuan with.

It was hot as hell so I started back toward the stairwell. If the Japs didn't remove that tarpaulin from over the hatch, the only air coming into the hold would be through that doorway.

I stepped around people and over some. When I was near the stairs, I heard someone say, "Goddamn, soldier, you are taking up space for two people with that damned mattress." Good God! It could only be one person—Blair! There couldn't be anyone else who would attempt to bring a mattress into this mess. I stepped closer and it was Blair. As I sat down on one end of the bedding, I told the complainer that two people were taking the space. I removed the pack.

"Damn, am I glad to see you! I was having problems seeing and no one seems to give a damn about anybody but themselves," Blair exclaimed.

"Joe, why in hell are you still carrying that mattress?' I asked.

"I don't know, but with this steel deck, this thing will be worth its weight in gold after awhile."

My vision was better now, and I saw his face. He looked like hell. Both eyes were swollen closed and there were cuts on his face and blood stains all over the front of his clothes. Someone had beaten the hell out of him.

"What happened to you? Did you get a nose bleed?"

"Yeah, I had problems keeping up and that squawking son-of-a-bitch up on deck beat the hell out of me, then threw me down the staircase. That is why I have staked out an area so near the stairs. I wasn't able to drag myself any farther back. Some of these people have been giving me hell, but now that you are here, I'm staying right here."

The hold was filling quickly. I didn't know how many more could get in, but the Japs were still shoving people down the steps.

The heat was getting to some of us. It was over 100 degrees and the humidity was high. What oxygen we had was being used faster than it was coming into the hold.

Blair had about had it. The tussle with the other prisoners plus the beating had sapped him of everything. His weakened condition plus lack of oxygen caused him to sit.

"Look, Joe, I was on a train or two where the air is as it is here, and the best thing I found was to sit and not move for anything. It requires less oxygen and the breathing is easier." Without another word, the two of us sat, heads on our knees and did nothing but breathe.

It seemed more than an hour before the Japanese stopped pushing men down the steps. Two American officers were standing near the bottom of the steps talking to each other in hushed tones. I recognized one of them as Major Cooper. I had met him on the train to Cabanatuan. Almost at the same time that I recognized him, he saw me and motioned me over to him. Here I learned that the officer with him was Lieutenant Colonel Fitzsimmons. He and Cooper had known each other from previous assignments. The two were trying to make some sense out of this mass confusion and to get some organization out of these people who were literally killing themselves milling about. For the most part, these people had never been in a situation like this and didn't know how to handle it.

I stepped in closer and Cooper introduced me, stating that I had been out on a number of details and had been in situations like this before. Possibly I could be of assistance. "Yes, the problem for now as I see it, is blocking everyone off in such a manner that the space we have is equally divided. There must be walkways where men won't be walking over each other," he said.

From his first word, I liked this officer. The authoritative way he spoke commanded respect.

"We have over four hundred men down here. That doesn't give us much room to work. Major, how long do you estimate the hold to be in feet?" the colonel asked.

"No more than seventy feet wide and a few feet longer."

"We have to do something quickly. The way these men are milling around in this heat, there will be deaths in very short time, and I doubt if they realize what they are doing." Then he added, "Captain Mercer is in this hold. Get hold of him and have him come here."

"Yes, sir," was Cooper's reply, and he began searching through these confused men.

From somewhere I heard his voice, "Gentlemen, will Captain Mercer come forward." Again, "Gentlemen, give me your attention." The hold became very quite and every face was turned toward the hatchway. "Would Captain Mercer please come to the foot of the staircase."

Almost instantly, an officer stepped from under the stairs. I didn't see how he could have arrived as fast as he did, but what was most surprising, he was the same captain who had the problem with the marine and his cat at Cabanatuan.

185

His attitude was altogether different from at the barracks. He even seemed rested and in some strange way, in his element. It was obvious that this wasn't the first time Mercer had been in bad situations.

The colonel was speaking.

"Cooper, you and Bilyeu take the forward portion of the hold. Block those people into groups of twenty men per group, leaving about a two-foot walkway between groups. Mercer and I will take the rear portion," he ordered. "Major, don't let any officer give you any trouble. This is an order and must be done if we are to keep them alive."

For the next three hours we pushed, shoved, and forced the crazed men into some type of order. If anyone became mean or nasty, Fitzsimmons seemed always to be near and could be heard saying, "Do as you are told. Move or someone will move you." They always moved without further argument. When this officer spoke, it was with such authority that no one dared ignore him.

Late that evening, when everyone was comparatively quiet, mostly because of exhaustion, the ship got underway. I was so worn out, I hardly knew when the anchor was listed. Then I felt the ship moving away from the pier. Soon I felt fresh air from somewhere. The movement of the ship was scooping air into the hold. I felt my breathing ease and that awful stench abated.

Earlier in the afternoon, the guards had passed some pails into the hold to be used as toilets and already the smell from that area was becoming a problem. The air quieted the men but still I wouldn't want to be sleeping back there.

The ship was now well underway, heading away from Manila. The cool air was from two air scoops, one near where Blair and I staked out our area, the other across the hold opposite the staircase. One of them blew the air toward the rear while the one in my area was opened toward the bow.

Later, I heard some people yelling for water. The Japs hadn't made any effort to get water down here. The heat while we were getting organized had taken its toll and some of the prisoners had drunk all their water. Thirst was a severe problem before we had been on this ship eight hours. Fitzsimmons had made several trips up the steps asking for water and each time he had been forced back into the hold by one of the guards, who refused to listen.

It was near midnight when I noticed the ship was slowing. Either we were going to drop anchor or there was some other reason for caution. As we slowed, the air was not coming through as before. We had been underway long enough that our position should be near the edge of the China Sea, near Corregidor.

No sooner were we totally stopped when the heat got as bad as it was earlier. Only a small amount of air entered through the vents, and only those near them could feel anything. Again I was grateful that I found this space.

I was not moving, doing as little as possible so the little oxygen we got would not be wasted. Then I heard a guard yell from on deck and saw Fitz-simmons mount the steps. Very quickly he called out, "There is water up here. Will someone assist me in getting it into the hold?" Three or four were on the steps and passing buckets of water down the stairs.

There was a dim light near the spot and as the buckets were set on the deck at the foot of the stairs, I could see steam rising from the water. We had been given water, but the damn stuff was steaming hot. First I was angry. I thought this was another torture treatment; later I learned the water was probably boiled for sanitation purposes.

Cooper ordered us to wait until all the buckets were down before start-ing the ration. I heard him remark after all the water was in the hold, that we had ten buckets of six gallons each. There was one bucket for two groups plus added ration for three groups.

Each block of prisoners was told to appoint a group leader that after-noon. Group leaders were to come forward and pick up their rations of water.

Sixty gallons of water for four hundred plus men is little, to say the least. When the stuff must be rationed in the darkness and in such small amounts, someone was bound to either not get his share or feel he had been cheated. Nevertheless, when the group leaders arrived, they were told what was ex-pected and then allowed to act for their respective groups.

I felt fortunate to be in a group with the commander and his assistant. I knew the water would be rationed fairly.

When I got a whiff of the water, I nearly vomited. The water was boiled, then poured into the wood kegs used for shipping pickled radish out of Japan for the troops. The preservative was so strong it soaked into the wood and there was nothing that would get it out.

Each man was supposed to get about one-quarter cup of this hot water, but with people dying of thirst, survival of the fittest became the order of the moment and within minutes, fights broke out. In several parts of the hold there was trouble. Some of the men didn't get any water at all while others got double rations. Those small cliques formed earlier in the day took care of their little groups and what was left went to the rest of the prisoners. Soon the colonel and Cooper were breaking up the brawls. This was no easy task.

I allowed the water in my cup to cool before attempting to drink it. I had some water left from the bottle I brought aboard.

I heard people all over the hold gagging as they tried drinking, and in some cases they were vomiting on the deck. Another smell to be added to an already sickening situation.

Fitzsimmons had been shoved back down the steps and this hadn't gone unnoticed by those who believed they were cheated on the water ration. They were once again raising hell. They quieted because of Fitzsimmons' assurance that there would be another ration. Now they saw him being shoved down the stairs. He had been hurt and couldn't assist in quieting them. Cooper and Mercer were sent around and somehow they managed to quiet the men once more. There was dissension among the group now. I feared that the cheating done by a few would cause serious problems as long as we were in this hold. When the life of one person is endangered by another, distrust can be extremely dangerous.

The hold was quiet now. Those who didn't get water had given up and gone to sleep, or they stopped complaining due to complete exhaustion. Joe and I searched through our gear and found some rice. I had some I hid in the open-bottom canteen and he had a little of the corn chops he brought with him from Bilibid. This small amount of nourishment plus the putrid water gave us a small edge.

Sometime during the early morning hours I made my way through this mass of human bodies toward the buckets being used as toilets. The closer I got to them the stronger the odor. I had thought the smell was unbearable where I was. Good God! The air choked me back here. No one could bear this condition for long. It had been less than twenty-four hours since the first man entered the hold, and the air was already so polluted breathing was nearly impossible. Certainly this condition would only worsen.

Near sunrise, Fitzsimmons contacted the guards and attempted to get something done. I heard "Donald Duck" screaming. When the colonel fell onto the deck, the group below spoke as one voice for the first time. I heard a low curse under the breath of these men as the entire population surged forward. They intended to climb out and kill that son-of-a-bitch. The guards on deck sensed this and bolts of the rifles could be heard as they pushed a round into the chamber. That sound only angered this mob more and they continued moving toward the stairs.

Fitzsimmons sensed this explosive situation and with blood pouring from his mouth, climbed the steps and spoke through broken teeth. "I know what all of you are contemplating. It will do no good. Seat yourselves and keep calm. I'll try again as soon as I am able." With that the prisoners became quiet and soon were back in their groups.

Time passed and he was once again able to stand. He mounted the steps. When he was a few steps off the deck he turned toward the men in the hold and stated, "Men, I appreciate your support, but we must use common sense. If I can get by that one guard, perhaps I can make contact with someone who will listen." Something in the way he explained this brought a very dangerous situation under control.

On deck, the voices of the colonel and the guards could be heard. Most of us thought he would again be beaten by the "Duck." But his demonstration in handling us made the Japanese realize that his influence could be used in their favor. The guard saw the colonel as he emerged from the hold and screamed, but this time he was silenced by his supervisor. This Japanese officer must have recognized that there could have been serious problems if the prisoners had stormed out of the hold. He listened to the colonel as he explained the problem with the latrine facilities and the shortage or water. Within an hour, there was another ration of water. This time there would be no chances taken that some men would be cheated out of their share of this hot stinking water.

The groups who claimed they were shorted were the first called to the staircase, and the water rationing was done by the commander and Cooper.

There was another surprise that morning. It was only a short time until there was a ration of rice. The rice had been readied in the ship's galley, and the Japs asked for someone to be sent topside to assist in getting the rice below. There were hands everywhere wanting this detail, but again the colonel had to make the decision on who would be sent. He made his selection based on his knowledge of the men. Soon, two men were on their way topside and when they returned, they brought rice balls that had been prepared by the Japanese cooks.

The second day we were more organized. Lists of the groups were being prepared. These lists were brought forward to Fitzsimmons. They were printed on any kind of paper that could be found. They contained the names of the men in each group and also the names of the group leaders and their assistants. Fitzsimmons scanned each roster and approved or disapproved of the designated leaders. If he did not confirm the group leader, the list was sent back and another man was selected.

I watched this procedure with great interest. I had not known nor had heard of this officer, but it was apparent that he knew much more about these people than most of us thought.

There hadn't been another ration of rice and there hadn't been but one ration of water since morning. Nothing had been done about the latrine facilities. We hadn't even been allowed to empty the buckets. They were running over. With limited air circulation, the air was so polluted it choked you. It was worst near the latrine area. I didn't know how those people endured it.

Soon after the sun had gone down and the heat from the hot deck lessened, there was activity on deck again. I heard that familiar scream from the "Duck," but also there were noises from the ship's crew as they were scurrying about. Then there was the sound of the anchor being lifted. The creaking hoist could be heard over all the other activity. I felt the ship move forward, ever so slowly at first. This was the most welcome sound I had heard since boarding this ship. I knew there would be fresh air coming through the vents as soon as we gained momentum. This would dispel some of the foul smell and bring new air into the hold. We were picking up speed now and the air seemed to be gushing into the hold.

From the door above me, a Jap stuck his head in and hollered for Fitzsimmons. As soon as he returned from talking with the Jap, we were allowed to start dumping the buckets. Since the men near that area had suffered the most from the smell, Fitzsimmons placed them on the detail, letting them get topside for fresh air, even if only for a short period. No one complained about this detail.

Getting the buckets out and the fresh air in made the hold fresh in only a few minutes and breathing became easier. The ship was moving out fast and the air was cool. The silence that was so noticeable before we got underway was

189

broken. Men started talking, first in low muffled tones, then louder, until there was an almost constant chatter from all parts of the hold.

With the men talking once again, the tension eased. I knew the incident about that first ration of water wasn't over, but at least there was conversation.

Near the area of the latrine buckets, the men were moving away from their sleeping area and were talking to people in adjacent groups. This was good.

Not long afterwards, word was passed that we would be allowed topside. Before we could start up the stairs the anchor was once again lowered. We were stopping again.

I asked Blair to come with me, but he refused, saying he was scared someone would take our spot. I understood his feeling, but the need to get out of this place convinced me to get out of here any time I had the opportunity. I hit those steps on the run. I needed to be out of this hell-hole more than anything.

Outside, the air smelled as fresh as any spring weather I had ever known, and I felt new life surge through my mind and body as I breathed in deeply the wonderful life-giving air. I couldn't get enough. I had been below in that foul mess so long, my lungs were begging for more. I kept drawing the air into my lungs and at the same time moved through the groups of men toward the south side of the ship. It was important for me to know where we were. When I had broken through the men and was standing at the rail, my beliefs were confirmed. The silhouette of Corregidor stood out only a mile south of us. The high point of the Rock was clear against the skyline. We had anchored in the small harbor on the north side of the island. It was in this area that I had worked on the diving detail when I was brought back here some eighteen months before.

I kept staring into the darkness, but saw nothing that would indicate a village over there. I asked if we were near Marvelious, and if so, why there weren't any lights.

"I would suppose there are no lights because the Japanese have the village under blackout," was the answer.

If that were true, then we were being taken out of the islands because the United States was closing in on this place, an idea that had been uppermost in my mind since we were so hurriedly taken from Cabanatuan. This thought depressed me more. I started thinking about what chance I would have swimming to shore or Bataan. It was at least two miles away and the current was strong. I experienced some of that when I was on that diving detail. Still I might be able to make it.

I moved from the rail and out among the others on deck. I knew the majority of this group of prisoners were officers and had a better understanding than I did of current circumstances. I moved about listening to their conversations. I heard things like, "This ship could become a target for MacArthur's airplanes or subs, should he decide to bomb this far north." I heard another person remark, "The ship isn't marked as a prisoner of war ship and our pilots couldn't tell this ship from any other supply ship and would want to sink any shipments in or out of here." These were not pleasant words.

All the guards placed themselves at the bow of the ship and at the same time had strung a rope across the ship between them and the prisoners. With the exception of that barrier, we could move about the deck as we wanted.

I saw lights in the captain's bridge some forty feet above me. All else was dark.

I made my way across the deck through the throngs of men as they mingled and talked. I located Major Cooper standing alone at the rail. He had managed to detach himself from the others and was easily recognized, even in the dark. This man was one who couldn't hide.

I spoke to him as I approached and told him I was grateful the Japs had allowed us to empty the buckets.

"I don't know, Sergeant, if it is possible, the situation is worse now down there than when we came up. I have just been told that one of the men has died and the Japs won't consider letting us put the body over the side. Some of the men have taken the body and placed it in the latrine area.

"It doesn't take much imagination to predict the morale problems this will cause. It is as bad as it can be now, but when the men have to use those buckets and see the body there—I don't know what their reaction will be."

I thought about how I would react. A sight like that was enough to break the strongest of men.

The major was talking again, and brought me back to reality.

"As I am sure you know, there are a number of people aboard who haven't been through anything this bad before. When they go back below and see that, I am sure they will demand that Fitzsimmons do something, and I don't know if he can. If not, there may be trouble," he said.

"Let me know if I can be of any help," I said.

The major said, "I just wanted you to understand, we need all the help we can get. If you know anyone down there who can be trusted we will need him."

"I don't know any of these officers, at least not that well. The only person I know is nearly blind, and can't be of much help. But I do know that he can be trusted and we can rely on him to do anything he is physically able to do," I replied.

"You mean Blair?" he asked. "If the Japs should allow us to stay on deck, we could handle it. Hell, I would keep enough people up here sleeping on the steel deck to make room down there, but I know they won't. As soon as it starts breaking day, those bastards will run us below."

I felt the ship roll under me, and became aware that we were moving. I didn't even hear them lift anchor. I wished I had jumped over the side and taken my chances. Only a few minutes later I saw the faint glimmer of lights near the southern end of the Bataan peninsula. This raised my hopes. I knew this area was blacked out, but if there were lights out this far, perhaps that was a military post. Good Christ! I was letting my imagination run away with itself. There hadn't been an American airplane in these waters since the Battle of Bataan and Corregidor and I was beating myself silly just because I heard someone suggest the possibility of us becoming a target.

Daylight broke and I recalled Cooper's statement about us being forced back below.

Someone touched my shoulder. When I turned, Major Cooper was standing right behind me, his face drawn and grim.

"There are two more deaths below," he said rather matter of factly. He turned and walked toward the door leading down into the hold and I was right on his heels. I didn't know why I was following. He spoke with the authority of one who wanted me to assist. When we got down the steps, he went directly to where the two dead men were. They were from the same group. Two other officers worked over them, and he and I assisted them in dragging these last victims toward the latrine area. They were laid out face up. The smell and the sight nearly caused me to vomit. We did not want to attract attention to what had happened. I stood at one end of the row, tugging at the body, getting it in as close to the other as I could, while another man did the same with the other end. The others stared. I had already seen this picture, so I bolted from the area and went back on deck.

My physical condition was the worst it had been since my capture. The rush up the steps plus having to drag those bodies had me totally worn out. If they were going to make us go back below deck, I wanted to get as much fresh air as I could.

I was at the rail and breathing very hard. I felt the clean air go deeply into my lungs and very shortly I thought of where I had been and what I had witnessed.

Those three men were laid out where we would have to view them each time we used the buckets. What a thought! If only the Japs would allow us to toss their bodies over the side, things would be much easier. In all probability, there would be more deaths before the day was over. Hell, one would think the bastards would insist we put the bodies over the side of the ship, if for no other reason than for their own health's sake. Still, they wouldn't come down here. They would sit high on that raised deck and with the ship moving into the wind, they would miss most of the smell.

That stint with shortness of breath reminded me of my own state of health. My weight continued to fall, now the lowest since my capture. My chances of survival were very small at this time, but then, if I had to live and breathe that putrid air down below, who in hell wanted to survive.

The sun was up now. The peak of the mountain east of us was lit up brightly. Then the guards started their screaming for us to go below. Each of us was trying to keep out of their reach as we scrambled for the door. I heard someone say that rice would be rationed soon.Rice! Why in hell didn't they bring out the rice while we were all on deck? The air was better than when we were at anchor, but when I was down there a while ago, the air was thick. The only thing going for us was the fact we were moving.

Down in the hold we waited for the signal that rice would be served.

192

Fitzsimmons made sure each man got one ball of rice. No one refused. Soon afterwards many men got sick, either from the foul water or the rice. Some of the prisoners had problems eating. Some made an attempt to get to the latrine buckets. I heard vomiting in several other areas of the hold. Many didn't make it to that area. They heaved rice and water on the deck where they slept, adding to the filthy conditions. The guards refused to pay attention to our officers when asked to go topside.

The buckets filled quickly and even spilled over. Soon it didn't matter if they were used or not. All day long, I heard people gagging and vomiting.

By mid-morning, more bodies had been added to that growing pile near the latrine buckets. I made as few trips as possible to that area.

Late in the afternoon the ship slowed and the rolling ceased, or at least, wasn't as bad as before. We were near the shoreline. But where? I felt we had been moving north along the shoreline of Luzon.

The Japs rationed more rice balls. The vomiting started anew, and now that the ship had slowed less air was coming through the vents. The stench was so bad one had problems keeping his mind on the job at hand—eating this rice. I again reminded myself how fortunate I was to be near the air scoops.

Just when I thought I would go completely out of my mind, word was passed that we could go back on deck. This time I had no problems getting Joe out of the hold. We left everything where it was and climbed out of this hell into the fresh air.

It wasn't totally dark, and I could see the guards up on the raised deck. The little bastards had their face masks on. I suppose the smell had become so bad even they couldn't stand it. Hell! I couldn't smell anything up here. I wished I could shove their goddamned heads down in that hold, especially down near those buckets. They would know then what foul odor really was.

Once again the cleanup detail was mustered, as it had been each time we had been allowed above deck. I wanted to get my turn over as quickly as possible. I made it a point to let the colonel know when I dashed down the steps for my buckets. I sure as hell didn't want to make any extra runs down there. I wanted this night out on deck.

When I neared the area of the buckets I noticed the number of dead had increased, but I'd be damned to bother counting. What the hell, two, ten, twenty, whatever. It made no difference. The only important thing for me at the moment was to get two buckets of this mess and get the hell of there.

When I had dumped my pails and returned them to the head of the stairs for the next man to take below, I found a spot on the rail away from that entrance and on the opposite side from where the stuff was being thrown out.

East of us I could see land. Even in the darkness I could make out a high mountain. It was Marvelious mountain. I had seen the landmark from every angle possible. There could be no mistake. The Japs had hugged the shore-line. As I gazed at that landmark where some of the stiffest fighting took place during the war, I wondered, had I known then about this, would I have allowed myself to be taken prisoner? Hell, no one could have foreseen this.

Throughout the night the prisoners went below and returned with buckets of filth to be dumped over the side. Both Blair and I had been fortunate thus far. Neither of us had been sick to the point of vomiting, making our area as clean as it could be under the circumstances. We didn't have to go below to clean our area. We stayed near each other throughout the night, talking about everything except the ship and the conditions. Since both of us were from the same area of the United States, we talked about people we knew back in the Ozark mountains, girlfriends, mountain food — always the conversation led to the subject of food.

Sometime during the night word was passed about a latrine up on deck we could use. It was near the bulkhead separating the forward part of the ship from the crew's quarters and the prisoners. This thing had been built sometime during the day yet I had not noticed it when I came on deck. When I saw this contraption, I found myself admiring the genius of it. They'd cut a steel drum diagonally to form a pouring spout, then drilled holes in the sides and put a steel rod through the holes fastening them permanently into an upright framework. They placed a salt water hose where it would pour into the barrel. When the barrel was filled, it would tip, dumping the salt water into a galvanized trough that we had been directed to use as a latrine. The salt water washed the body waste over the side. I had never seen this before. Hell, the trough was nearly always clean.

If they constructed one of these in one day, perhaps they would have another by tomorrow and we would at least be able to get rid of those buckets below and would be allowed to come topside. With the odor from the latrine gone, the only thing we would have to contend with would be the smell of the dead. Hell, who knows, they might even let us bury our dead. My spirits were elevated to some extent after I saw this new addition to our living conditions.

It had become very quiet on deck. The prisoners gathered into small groups, talking in hushed tones. Some of them found space and were sleeping on the steel deck, while others were just taking in the fresh air.

Day was breaking. I saw the glare of the sun at the top of the mountain. I heard a guard screaming somewhere forward. He wanted us below deck. I hesitated, not wanting to leave. The men forward of me were being shoved through the door down to the hold. At the same time this guard was pushing and shoving, I heard another shouting that as soon as we were below, there would be another ration of rice. Why in hell couldn't they leave us out on deck until after we had eaten? There would be less vomiting.

The rice was handed down and distributed. The men barely started eating when the gagging began. Soon the cursing started. Someone had vomited too close to someone else. Someone had spent hours cleaning the area last night just to have someone else mess it up. We had been out on the

194

deck in the clean air so some of our energy had returned. By nine o'clock our energy was gone and the hold was once again quiet with only occasional vomiting and gagging. Again, Blair and I escaped the vomiting. I heard the colonel tell someone we would be getting another ration of water soon. I was thirsty, but I knew I must remain still and conserve my energy.

It was nearly mid-morning when I heard the Japanese on the main deck. They were screaming and seemed to be in a state of panic. Down here everyone was quiet. We heard the commotion and were just as confused. After a few minutes I heard an explosion nearby. Cooper was standing at the foot of the staircase looking toward the door. I heard the engines speeding up. Another explosion some distance away was heard. Fitzsimmons joined Cooper at the bottom of the stairs and both of them looked at the door, then at each other. I wanted this ship to be blown to hell, but there was that fear of being drowned in the process. I remembered an experience when I was on the diving detail, when I felt the current dragging me under, and I had little or no control of where it was taking me. I recalled the terror, and for just a moment that same feeling returned.

There was another crash. It was so near I couldn't tell if it was a bomb or not, but the timbering overhead blew away, leaving the canvas flapping in the wind. I smelled the powder smoke from that one. It hit near the door right over me head.

"Joe, let's get the hell out of here. This bastard is going down and fast," I yelled. I saw him already rolling his mattress and gathering his pack.

Fitzsimmons was at the head of the staircase yelling at us. "Get out of the hold as fast as you can. The Japs have left the deck."

There was a solid mass of humanity rushing the steps. I grabbed Joe by the arm and two of us were on the steps, pushed there by the mob. His mattress was rolled tightly and over his shoulder as I pushed upward against the bottom end of it. At that moment I couldn't imagine why he had that damn thing, but there wasn't time for any speculation. People below were cursing our slowness. Hell, the thing wasn't slowing him down in the least. If I didn't know him so well, I would think he had panicked. But I knew better. So to hell with it. Let him have the damn thing.

As I stepped through the doorway and onto the deck, I saw we were listing badly. The people up on deck were as panicked as those still below. Prisoners tried to get over the side all at the same time.

I took a quick look for land, then turned and shouted to Joe, "Get rid of that mattress. You are going to have to swim."

"The mattress will make a life jacket for me. I'm taking it," he replied.

Behind me I saw men climbing through the timbers as well as coming through the door. Clearing the hold, most men went directly to the rail and over the side. They were leaving everything they brought aboard behind. Their only interest was getting off this sinking ship.

I saw the shoreline just east of us, about half a mile away. Forward, directly over the bow, less than a quarter of a mile, was a pier extending out into the bay. West of us and some distance away was the shoreline of a small island. As I turned to tell Joe what I thought we must do, all I saw was his back as he dashed toward the rail and over the side, mattress and all. He disappeared over the side out of sight. Damn! I hoped he made it. I had all I could do to take care of myself.

As I climbed over the rail, I glanced toward the shoreline. A small boat was burning near the shore. It was also sinking. Overhead and east of the ship were more planes. As one came near us and banked away, I saw a star on the wing. The American forces were in the area and were blasting the hell out of the Jap ships.

I went over the rail and ran down the side of the listing ship. Then I jumped and felt myself tumbling through the air. I hoped I would stay clear of the ship. Good God! Would I ever hit the water? Down, still down, then cold water. I hit feet first. Deeper and deeper I went. I moved my arms and hoped. I made every effort to pull myself up to the surface where I could swim clear of the ship, but the more I tried, the deeper I went. Good Christ! How deep was I? My lungs were bursting. I must have air. After an eternity I burst through to the surface. I was gasping for air and spurting salt water at the same time. The top of my pack had come open and it was filled with water. It was slowing me. It had held me under the water. I struggled and finally got the top partially closed by turning on my back and pulling the back from under me.

I'd heard stories about how it is necessary to get away from a sinking ship or you will be sucked under no matter how well you can swim. With all the strength I could muster, I swam in the direction of the pier. The water was calm in spite of all that had happened. Stroke after stroke I moved away. I heard explosions from the direction from which I had come. I heard the roar of airplane engines overhead, but I didn't dare stop swimming to look. My pack had filled again with water and was slowing me down. I pulled the pack onto the other side and fastened the remaining strap. Without looking at anything else, I put my head down and kept stroking away.

I continued until I was exhausted, then turned on my back. I saw two planes coming out of a dive. As they did, they winged off over that island out of my sight. There were more explosions.

I could swim faster now. I saw men in the water near the ship. I seemed to be leaving them behind. I was clear of the ship. It was still afloat, although listing much worse than when I went over the bow. Men were still leaping down the side near the aft portion. I wondered how many had been trapped in the holds. My pack again filled with water and felt like lead on my back. I must get to that pier as soon as possible. I kept stroking and the pier got nearer. As I slowly closed the distance between myself and the pier, I heard machine gun fire on the landward side and the sound of another plane in that direction. The planes left. I still heard the machine gun fire. The planes were gone, yet they continued shooting. I kept trying to locate where the fire was coming from and at the same time kept stroking the water. Then I saw it. There was a machine gun position on the pier, about halfway back from the end. The gunner was firing at the swimmers. The bullets were going over my head and out farther toward the ship. This gave me incentive to swim faster. Behind me was another roar from the planes, then another explosion. Looking over my shoulder I saw an explosion where the ship was. I didn't know if it was a bomb or an explosion inside the sinking hull. The sound was like a secondary blowup after a bomb has exploded. I saw the bow of the sinking ship rise in the water, then start under. The stinking bastard was going under. The aircraft started strafing the swimmers. Good God! Couldn't they see we were Americans? The pier was only a short distance away. By swimming under the water part of the time, I was safe. I got under the pier. Above me was a slab of cement and under here no one could see me. About one hundred yards under was a ladder on one of the pylons leading to the top. I had no desire to go up there at the moment, but it gave me a place where I could hang on while the water drained from my pack. Also it gave me time to rest my arms. I would remain here until the machine gunner was either killed by the strafing or the bastard left the pier.

I could see far out over the surface of the water as well as along the shoreline where the aircraft had been bombing.

After about an hour, the place was quiet. The gunner on the pier hadn't made any noise for some time now. Most of the swimmers had either made it ashore or had gone under. The ship was nowhere to be seen, but there was an awful lot of smoke out that way. I felt it might be safe for me to climb out.

The entire pier was empty. The machine gun position was still about one hundred yards farther in, but there wasn't any movement around it.

I saw several men gathered on a small beach about three hundred yards down from the landward end of the pier. I couldn't see them from my vantage point below the pier. I looked for signs of the ship. It was gone. That last explosion, whatever it was, finished the filthy son-of-a-bitch.

Looking at the place where the ship had been, I saw large pieces of wood and other materials floating on the surface. I couldn't distinguish between pieces of timber and bodies. Even if they got off the ship safely after the last explosion, many people must have been hit by the strafing. I wondered if I had been here on the pier all along and that trip from Manila was only a bad nightmare. Or was I yet on the ship dreaming that the ship had been sunk?

Others joined me. If this was a dream it was becoming a very clear one. People were prostrate on the pier, resting from the long swim. I couldn't see anyone who had been injured in this group. Most were sitting or lying quietly. No one wanted to talk. It was a very somber moment. All of us were aware that any of those floating objects could just as easily have been one of us.

Many survivors had crawled from the bay onto the sandbar, and more were arriving all the time. Farther down the shoreline I saw men wading ashore. In most places the people had gathered in large groups, but on this pier there were only fifteen or twenty people. I knew it was only a matter of time until the Japs saw us standing out against the light between the land and the open water. I was grateful that they had left me alone this long. With the thought of being caught out here with this small number of men, I gathered my gear and began searching for a way off the pier. I wanted to join the larger group on the sandbar some two hundred yards away. Ignoring the others I made my way down into the water. It was rather shallow and I waded. Soon I was on the beach where a large number of people had gathered.

Before I walked fifteen yards down the beach, I saw Blair. He had all his belongings spread out on the sand. He hadn't been injured. He was lying alongside his mattress, allowing it to get full exposure to the sun.

"Joe! How the hell did you make it with that damn load you had to carry?" I asked.

"Hell, I made it fine. That thing makes a good life jacket," he exclaimed.

"I don't suppose any of the bullets from the planes hit you."

"No, I knew we were being strafed, but I just kept paddling," he replied.

"I don't know how close they came to me, but I did hear people screaming like they had been hit."

The conversation about the strafing was nothing more than something to keep our minds off what had happened out there, and both of us knew it. Still we chattered away about everything but what was deep within us—that large numbers of men were lost in this tragic incident.

For some time the two of us laid back on the sand, the sun baking us, letting time pass, without the Japs around us. The bastards were busy down the beach looking for their own survivors. I saw them running about the area. They seemed to be as confused as we. They were more confused than I had ever seen them.

I was hungry and thirsty, but I felt better than I had in some time. This day, I had seen the United States of America knock the hell out of these barbaric bastards.

Someone located fresh water over the retaining wall at the edge of the beach. I took my canteen and Joe's to fill them. After a few minutes the two of us were drinking fresh water. Then I realized how thirsty I was. We emptied the bottles and I returned to the water spigot and refilled them once more.

For several hours we remained on the beach, drinking water and refilling the canteens. Late in the afternoon, I saw the survivors south of us being moved off the beach. The guards were roughing up everybody they came near. It took some hard convincing, but I got Joe to see it would be better for the two of us to move in that direction and find where they were taking the men than to wait until they came to us. At last he rolled the mattress and we moved off the beach, taking one last swallow of water and refilling the bottles. We walked south along a narrow street for two or three hundred yards, then the street turned inward toward several large buildings. To our left were smaller native buildings. The larger structures appeared to be American. This place was the home port of the United States navy before the war. We were in Alangapo.

We hadn't gone far before we were joined by other American prisoners.

We entered a large gate. Inside a guard was screaming at the prisoners as they approached the gate. As the men entered the guard slapped and banged them with his fist. I wished for just a moment that I had not come off the beach, but headed into the mountains. I was sure some of our people had done that. Yet if the Japanese caught us slipping through the village, it would be sure death, and I had no idea where their guard positions were. As we passed the guard I heard Blair curse under his breath. I understood his feelings, but it was too late now. We were back under their control.

Inside the compound more guards were directing the prisoners as they came through the gate. They wanted us to move toward the eastern fence. This had been the perimeter fence for the U.S. navy yard that was here before the war started. It was very high and made of heavy mesh wire with two strands of barbed wire along the top. The posts were steel and some twenty to thirty feet apart; this was a typical security fence for an American military installation.

I entered the large group of men unnoticed. Men were coming in all the time, making it difficult to tell when one was arriving or moving from one spot to another. The Japs had put us in tennis courts. There were marked lines on the cement and although it had been many months since the courts had been used, the paint was still visible. I sought a spot off the cement but all the space between the courts was taken, and the Japs had lined themselves along the fence. I sure as hell wanted as much distance between then and me as I could get. I found a spot big enough for both Blair and myself. We placed our gear where it could be watched. Then I started looking for someone in charge. Mercer or Cooper were nowhere to be found. I had always gone through them when I needed information from Fitzsimmons. So I went directly to Fitzsimmons. He was scurrying through the mob trying to reassert himself as the commander of this group, attempting to learn who had been killed and who had survived. His leg had been injured and he limped among the men, placing them in groups and instructing them to remain in smaller groups until they could be accounted for. I marveled at his strength. Most men would be content to let the damn thing fall apart, but still he continued to make an effort. He didn't have paper or pencil, but was pleading for the men to remain in smaller groups. The men were as confused as any bunch I had ever seen.

Sometime late in the afternoon someone obtained some paper and something to write with, and we moved about trying desperately to get the names of the survivors. Fitzsimmons managed to save some of the roster that was made in the hold of the ship, but we had people from both sections of the ship, so it was of very little value. We would barely get a fix on a group when another influx of people would arrive from out of nowhere. At last, he gave up.

Several hours had elapsed since we started assembling on the tennis courts. The Japs lit the place up and placed guards all around us. The numbers of men entering the area had dwindled to a trickle. I couldn't tell if we were getting a few more or if the men were moving in and out of groups,

199

but, for the most part, there was very little movement at the moment. I looked over this section of people and saw small groups huddled and talking. In the morning the colonel would have a chance to get the men into groups again and get their names.

I recalled the long lines of men on the pier in Manila, how I thought about us getting on that ship. It wouldn't be nearly as crowded when we boarded another ship. Our numbers had been reduced enormously.

Before daylight, I was awakened by Fitzsimmons. He was once again attempting to get control of the situation. I saw him in the middle of my group, paper in hand, asking people their names. Seeing me he asked if I had seen or heard of either Mercer or Cooper. When I told him they weren't in with any of the survivors I had seen, he said, "Perhaps they escaped into the mountains." I was asked to assist him and it wasn't until mid-morning that we had what passed for an accounting of the men.

New officers had been appointed and instructed that they must remain with their assigned groups. They were told not to allow the men in their groups to move about. Two times during the day, new rosters were prepared by the group leaders and turned in to Fitzsimmons. Each time the officers were instructed to keep updating their accounting. This procedure was time-consuming and required the men to stay in one place, or get permission to visit other groups. Many became angry. The new group of leaders managed to keep control until there was some accounting of the survivors. We recorded only the names of the ones present.

I walked away from the area and into a group of new leaders who were talking with Fitzsimmons. I overheard one of them say, "There are less than nine hundred of us remaining." About 1,600 had boarded ship.

The guard force had been increased until everywhere I looked there was one of the little bastards. Along the fence they had placed a guard about every hundred feet. This increased security indicated they thought a large number of prisoners had escaped. They beat the hell out of anyone within reach. They were combat-ready and their bayonets were fixed. They even wore their field packs. There was every indication that the United States had returned to the islands, or was certain to do so at any time. On the tennis courts work went on, counting and changing rosters, reassigning men from one group to another. I noted a great sense of urgency on the part of Fitzsimmons. It was as if he were aware of something that we weren't. All day long he moved among the groups, assigning commanders or assistants and making them keep the men in their respective areas. This caused some of them to become angry. Fitzsimmons stopped moving about, letting his junior officers handle the situation.

Before it was completely dark, I got permission from our group leader to move about. I want to see the men for reasons I couldn't explain. There were many faces I hadn't seen before or at least didn't recognize. We had been reduced by considerable numbers since leaving that main gate back at Cabanatuan. As I walked among them, I became aware of that feeling back on the dock when I felt there would be several who would not finish this trip.

200

When I returned to my group and let my group leader know of my return, I saw that the counting had stopped altogether. The men settled in for the night.

I heard men talking about an invasion somewhere south of us. There was no effort to stop these rumors, or to learn where they originated. It seemed to raise morale so they were allowed to take their own course. I wanted to believe them. I was upset with myself because I hadn't tried for the hills earlier in the afternoon. This rumor relieved my guilt problem. I wanted to think that the American army was near and would cut us off before the Japanese got us out of the islands. I wanted to get out now, but when I looked at that line of guards along the fence, with all that combat gear, that idea wasn't so appealing.

Sometime during the night, we were given a small ration of rice. It had been cooked by the Japanese and sent out to be distributed to our people. This was our first food in a long time. I wasn't hungry until I had eaten the small ration; then I felt pangs of hunger. I was soon fast asleep.

Early in the morning of the second day, I was awakened by the noises of rice being brought into our area. The Japanese were again feeding us. This rice had some vegetables in it.

I still had my gear I started with, including a mess kit and spoon. When the rice was rationed I was able to get my full ration. I was more fortunate than some. They had lost everything. I saw many of them eating with their hands, or taking the rice on large leaves or anything they could find. Everyone got something to eat. There were a number of water spigots near the tennis courts and there hadn't been any restrictions.

For the better part, the Japanese had withdrawn from our area. The guards along the fence were still there, but those around the buildings had moved inside and no longer hassled us. As long as the prisoners kept their distance from the guards along the fence, they were not bothered. In general all was quiet.

Most of the prisoners took advantage of this lull from the harassment and got some much needed sleep and rest. After that ordeal on the ship, the quiet afforded me the opportunity to wipe from my mind that seventy-two hours without food and water and the memory of those men who lay in death near the wood buckets. My God! What a nightmare! I wished that it was only a dream.

Chapter 29

In the afternoon, sometime around three o'clock, the Japanese alerted us that we would be moving out immediately. We had no warning at all. It was fortunate that we had been fed during the day, and there had been adequate water. I made sure my water bottle was filled each time I walked to the spigot.

I noticed a lot of activity around the barracks, even before the word was passed that we were to be moved. I had felt it was some sort of drill. I sensed a sense of urgency. The guards scurried about, yelling and screaming at each other.

Among the prisoners, the officers instructed their people to rush their preparation. Most didn't have much to get ready, but others had salvaged some of their things. These men put their gear in order.

The first group moved out within minutes after receiving the word. My bunch had been designated one of the last in the march, and I had an opportunity to observe the men as they passed. The cliques that were in evidence back at Cabanatuan were not in evidence here. The men were acting as one, each bound to the other by a common bond. Without saying it openly, our officers showed this bond by moving among their groups, doing everything they could to ensure each man had water if he had a canteen. This spirit of concern was welcome. The events of the past two weeks seemed to have made a great impact on all of us. Each of us knew we had survived. We had gone through the horrors of those seventy-two hours on that ship and had survived.

During the past two days, there hadn't been any rain, and my pack had dried, making my load lighter. Joe's mattress had dried to some extent. Joe insisted on taking it, so I resolved that I would no longer try to persuade him otherwise. I watched him closely as he walked along with that mattress neatly tied into a bundle and hanging from his shoulder.

Our groups had been assigned an alphabetical designation. We were in four groups, and I was in "D" group. We were strung out for quite a distance. I couldn't see the head of the column, but the jungle growth was very dense and the road was narrow.

We were going directly toward the high mountain away from the sea coast. I was somewhat surprised at this. I had assumed the Japs would put us on another ship as soon as they could get one into the harbor, yet here we were moving away from the port and back into Bataan. Before twenty minutes had passed, we were slowly climbing the mountain. The climb, along with the load on my shoulders, started to tell. I remembered the things I packed away, and wished I had thrown some of it away. There were the notes I had kept, those I couldn't toss, but there were some pieces of paper that I should have—two bundles of Chinese immigration paper. They didn't weigh much and I didn't know why I kept them, but even the least amount of weight would be a problem before the trip was over. I could have rid myself of some of the smaller pieces of clothing I had in the pack. Some of the people had lost everything. I even envied them at this point; they were walking unencumbered up the steep slope toward the mountain. I looked again at Joe. He had that awful load and was saying nothing. This made my small pack seem lighter.

As the afternoon dragged on the mountain loomed high into the sky. I recalled another march through these mountains. Also, I saw some signs of the times when the United States fought the Japanese here. 1942. It seemed like an eternity since that time. On each side of the road were pieces of military hardware, such as steel helmets and rusted and broken rifles. Sometimes I saw pieces of web belts partially covered with the ends sticking from the ground. Along the roadside were markers referring to kilometers. Those things were known to us as "kilometer posts" and when we returned from patrol during the war, we would watch for them as a way of knowing how much farther we would have to go before feeling safe behind our lines. Occasionally there were mess kits, some broken, others usable. I hoped those men who lost everything had the foresight to pick up things they would need later. For sure they needed water bottles.

High on the mountain trail we trudged along. I saw markers that indicated burial spots. Sometimes it was a Filipino or an American soldier. Some signs indicated the spot where a Japanese soldier had been buried and his comrades had marked the spot with some distinguishing item or military trapping. These were somber reminders of a battle fought long ago—at least it seemed long ago. As I remembered that struggle and wondered at what had transpired since, I felt that in all probability it was only a short paragraph in some student's history book—a paragraph that would be read by yet another generation, who would read the reference and go on. Only a few would take the time to read closely enough to understand the personal impact it had had on some of us. I wondered how many would take the time to research the information deeply enough to understand the sacrifices made by Filipino peoples as well as this small group of American soldiers on this spot. For most of the time it would be only a small bit of mandatory reading for a passing grade in their goal toward higher education. Hell! The Japanese soldiers in charge of our group of prisoners didn't give these signs even a second glance. They had been free and had been so occupied with their endeavors in the war, they had forgotten—or did they know it in the first place?

The march continued until near midnight, but there was no indication of stopping. Then, without warning, we were ordered off the road. Either they feared the natives in this area, who were somewhat unpredictable, or someone convinced them we couldn't make it much farther without food and rest. In this part of Luzon were two tribes of natives that little was known about. First they were very small people that survived by their wits in the jungle. Second, they knew every inch of this part of the mountain and could hide until ready to attack. The Americans knew this, and I would suppose the Japs had been informed about them as well. Having such a small force guarding us, they became fearful of these people attacking them and decided they should get us into the smaller area where they could watch us more closely.

Off the road, we were shoved and pushed into a small area and within a short time the guards were surrounding us. Everywhere I looked, one of them was standing. It appeared that they were aware that some of the prisoners who started this trip escaped during the sinking and they were determined there would be no more who got away. In this spot, there was a small clearing of jungle, but only a few feet in back of the guards it was dense. They placed themselves at the edge of this thick jungle where they could easily watch over the entire group.

When we were settled in for the night, having given up on the possibility of getting food, I was surprised when a truck entered the area. We were told there would be a rice ball issued to each of us. This rice ball had become a familiar way of feeding the prisoners on the move. I took the rice when it was given and found a secluded spot near the edge of the group. When I had eaten, I slept for the night.

We were awakened early, before light, and fed another rice ball. I had not heard it, but a truck had pulled into the area with water for us. Word was passed to fill our canteens and drink what we wanted—an indication they would be pushing us hard that day. As we each took our turn at the water truck, I noted that few men didn't have water bottles. I recalled yesterday when I saw the gear strewn along the trail. They got the bottles.

The prisoners were given a few minutes to eat and drink, then were told to move out. Nobody knew our destination.

We were on the road before sunrise, trudging up the side of the mountain. I was grateful we had been issued the water. This had the earmarks of being a very long day, and I knew this part of the island very well. Water would be hard to come by. That morning all of us were walking quite briskly, having had a good night's rest and food, but by nine o'clock the pace slowed. Most men were looking at their feet, trying to avoid the larger stones in the trail. We were strung out now into two lines on each side of the road. This trudging reminded me of another march in this region some two years ago. The prospects of yet another march through these jungles was depressing. Still I trudged forward, one foot in front of the other, as I had done so many times since being captured. I heard noises behind me and saw men getting off the road, allowing a truck to pass. Vehicles in this area were a rare sight, yet one was climbing up the hill passing us. Behind this one were others climbing the grade. Behind the wheels were either Japanese or Filipino drivers. I was unable to tell at this time. All had passed and were out of sight, but the guards hadn't ordered us to start walking again. Blair moved in near me and the two of us sat down while we waited for the Japanese to start screaming. Nothing happened and soon other prisoners were dropping their gear and sitting where they were.

Some more time elapsed. Then there was word from the forward element of the marchers that they were being loaded onto the trucks. I became apprehensive. We were so far back, the trucks would fill and this group would have to continue the march. As I waited, I searched through the contents of my pack and found the Chinese immigration paper and a pencil. I felt very depressed and needed to write something. I started writing. I saw one of the guards watching me. I kept writing: "I am Dick Bilyeu, United States Army. Anyone finding this, forward to Mr. and Mrs. Jesse Bilyeu, Walnut Shade, Missouri. I am somewhere in the northern part of Bataan, en route to God knows where. If this letter should reach you I want you to know that I am still alive at this time, though not as well as I would like. I have received some mail from you as well as a letter from Blanch Harris, who has spent much effort trying to get letters through to me. I was glad to hear of Stanley and Kenneth, but hope you will tell Bob to stay with his present job. I made out an allotment of pay before the surrender but never heard if it went through. If you should get this let me know through the same channels used before about allotments. Please try not to worry; I'll be all right and I'll see all of you sometime. Say hello to all and let them know that I am alive at the time of this writing. As you can guess it is difficult writing from where I am, so I will stop for now. Love always, your son, Dick." I stopped and looked for the guard. He wasn't watching as I had thought he was earlier. I folded the paper and placed it inside my shirt, now knowing for certain what I would do with it. My plan was to drop it alongside the road if we started walking again, and if I was lucky enough to get on a truck, I would throw it out when I caught the guard not looking.

When I had the paper securely inside my shirt, I saw the troops starting to move forward. One of our officers got us back on our feet and onto the road. The marchers started moving, slowly at first, and we dragged along until we were in a spot in the road where I could see the trucks being loaded. The trucks weren't filled yet and that was a relief. It appeared all the prisoners would be able to get aboard the trucks. The loading was very slow now, and we were standing most of the time waiting to be loaded.

At last! I was climbing aboard. I had made it. Very shortly all were aboard and the lead vehicle was on the move. There was excitement among the prisoners as the last of the trucks rolled up the steep grade. We were still on the west side of the mountain and climbing toward the pass. I didn't understand why the Japs would allow us to ride in trucks, unless they knew something we didn't. Maybe they were rushing us because the United States army was on this island. Everything pointed to just that. It wasn't like them to spend anything on making life easier for us. My feet were blistered and sore from the march and with the pack on my back, just to be able to ride wherever they were taking us was enough for the moment.

Before I realized it, the convoy had stopped and I was looking down the other side of the mountain. Looking down the eastern slope of the mountain, the terrain was much the same as on the western side. I could see far into the valley below.

The old trucks were really moving, and soon we were back into the thick jungle again and moving out onto the more level country. The roads were not as crooked as before. Also, they were much better than when we were up on the side of the mountain.

The sun was now behind the mountain and with the trucks moving, there was a cool breeze blowing. We breezed along and before it was totally dark, I saw the lead vehicles pulling off the road into a rice paddy. When we entered the parking area, I noticed the place was cleared of vegetation but there were ridges of soil around the edges of the area like it had been piled there to hold in water during the rainy season. Now it was dry and hard. When we descended from the trucks, it looked more like the place had been drained and the ground had dried as hard as cement. The trucks stirred up much dust as they left the area.

When all the trucks cleared the area, the senior Japanese officer signaled Fitzsimmons to join him across the main road. He and two of the junior officers crossed and a conference was held between the Japanese officer and our own. When the conference broke up and our officers returned, word was passed that we were to move overland to a seaport somewhere on the north coast of Luzon.

It was totally dark and Joe had gone off to sleep. I remembered the letter I wrote. The guards were off somewhere talking to each other and not paying any attention to the men in my area. Taking the piece of paper, I tossed it over the ridge of dirt into the tall grasses on the outside of the paddy. I hoped someone would find it and do something with it. Perhaps keep it and sometime in the distant future they might try contacting my parents. Right now it was important that someone know I was alive. (Nearly one year later, that letter was received by my mother. It was mailed through Washington, D.C., without any explanation as to how they came by it.)

The night was a good one for me. I slept soundly but was awakened early the following morning by the roaring of the truck engines and the screaming of the guards. They were hustling men onto the trucks as fast as they could. No sooner was a truck loaded when it was directed onto the road and it sped away without waiting for the other trucks.

As we passed the exit point, the Jap there handed us rice balls and then pointed to the truck. Again I was grateful they thought that much about us. As I passed him, I took the rice, then felt the canteen on my belt. It was nearly full. I was pleased with myself for having that much water for the day. I heard one officer tell the men to conserve water. I didn't need to be told. I had been down this trail before.

As I climbed into the truck, I saw only one face. Joe had stayed close to

206

me or perhaps it was the other way around. He was the only person in the group that I knew I could trust and depend upon. He still had the great load on his back, but again, I knew it was useless to talk to him about tossing the thing. The Japanese in this group seem to have accepted this as another crazy American carrying more than he could stand up under. That mattress had become a sort of beacon for me. I could follow Joe's progress by watching for the bundle always well above the other prisoners. I knew that large bundle also attracted the Japanese, and they might single Joe out for special treatment. I sure hoped not. He had become so attached to that damn thing, I didn't know what would happen if they made him discard it. He acted as if his life depended upon keeping it, and considering how he used it as a flotation device when he went over the side of the ship, perhaps his life did depend upon keeping it.

It was a little past sunrise when we were out on the road and moving along at a very fast clip. The roads were much better now that we were out of the mountains, but as we moved ever northward, I saw another range. I was not looking forward to going over any more passes with the Japanese drivers. They didn't show much skill as drivers, and thought of us as "cargo." I didn't feel too much at ease.

The truck moved ever north until mid-afternoon. I was tired and hungry. I had stopped watching where we were going. The bastards wouldn't even stop and let us use the bathroom. If we must urinate, it must be done while the truck was moving. I held on, hoping the driver would have to stop soon. Still he kept going. He wasn't stopping for anything.

It was late in the evening after the sun had gone behind the mountain when the truck pulled over and stopped. We had been riding for twelve hours or more without food or extra water. The Jap guard allowed us off the truck and as I moved away to relieve myself, I shook my canteen. It had only a few drops left. I emptied it, hoping there would be more water when we finally stopped for the night.

I was so concerned with relieving myself when we stopped, I didn't see the buildings some two hundred yards to the front. There were dim lights showing from some of them, and at times I saw people moving about in the vicinity of those buildings. It would appear that we were at the edge of a small barrio, but I was unable to see if the people were natives or Japanese soldiers. Perhaps they were natives and we could get some water and food from them. Damn it, I hoped so. The hunger pangs were killing me.

There wasn't much time for speculation. Our guard was herding us along the road on foot as the trucks drove away. Soon I saw this was a small town and we had been unloaded at the outskirts. As the trucks disappeared into the darkness through the village we in turn were being herded inside a barbed wire enclosure where there was another bunch of guards waiting. It was as if they had been expecting us and were just awaiting our arrival.

With all the rumors that had been circulating the past few days about an invasion, I halfway expected to see some signs of combat, but there were none. All of us were praying and hoping that something would occur at the last minute, preventing the Japanese from taking us out of the islands.

Outside the barbed wire some Filipino natives were trying to smuggle food through the wire. When the guards came near them, they melted back into the darkness; when the guards were gone, they returned with rice and some sugar cakes. Some of us were fortunate to get some things from these wonderful people. Joe managed to get a large cake of candy.

Before daylight, the guards were screaming and beating the prisoners. They seemed to be in a frenzy to get us up. The prisoners nearest the gate were the ones taking the beatings. The people back inside where there were no lights were not being bothered yet. There was one light at the gate and that shone brightly.

As I got to my feet, I heard one of the Jap guards yelling over all the others. I remembered that scream. It was "Donald Duck." That son-of-a-bitch had survived the sinking of the other ship and was waiting to take us the rest of the way—wherever that might be. God! I had hoped that one had drowned or had been killed by a bomb.

The guards started moving the prisoners through the opening in the barbed wire and the "Duck" had stationed himself at the point where each of us must pass near him as we left the compound. There was no avoiding him. I'd have to go right by him. I moved away as far as I could as we neared the gate, but everyone was trying the same tactic. That bastard saw what we were doing and stepped into the center of the line, where he could hit us at random. Each time he hit someone he squawked and screamed. He sounded more like the Walt Disney character that morning than at any other time. When I saw there was no avoiding the bastard, I walked right at him. Hell, I didn't give a damn if I walked over him. He was bent on beating the hell out of anyone in his reach anyway. I was no more than two feet from him when he stepped to one side just a bit and hit me squarely in the mouth with his fist. I stumbled under the blow but moved forward. Then again I felt his fist crash against the side of my face. He had seen the arrogance in my face. This time I went forward and he caught the back of my shoulders, but I managed somehow to stay on my feet. I was now outside the gate and he had found another target. I had escaped further abuse from the bastard for the moment. My ears were ringing and my mouth bleeding. As I walked away I heard him yelling and the slaps against the men behind me.

The only thing I could do was walk and try to keep up with the others. Everyone was doing everything they could to get away from the guards at the gate, believing it couldn't be any worse with the ones out here. We had walked for about fifteen minutes when the bay came into view. We were being taken in the direction of the port. I didn't have any idea where we were.

When we entered the port area of the little village, guards were everywhere. They were not ordinary run-of-the-mill soldiers. They were combat soldiers brought in for the purpose of handling this bunch of prisoners. Damn! They were an ominous bunch of bastards in full gear except for steel helmets. They were wearing small caps.

208

There were times I had to trot in order to keep up. I didn't want to leave any space between myself and the people in front of me, lest the guards with the bayonets think I was lagging on purpose.

Soon we were moving out onto a wood pier. The permanent pier was on my right; it had been blown to hell and never rebuilt. Farther down the harbor, I saw other structures running out into the bay. This one had been built recently.

The column slowed and I was able to keep up with the others. I didn't look back. To hell with it. I had all I could do to keep myself clear of the guards. I didn't give a damn what was going on behind me. The movement had stopped. I saw where men were being loaded into small boats. As one filled, it pulled away out into the harbor. I now saw a larger ship far out in the bay. The small boats were heading in that direction. As I awaited my turn to be loaded into the small craft, I saw the first boat pulling alongside that larger ship, but it was too far out for me to make out what was taking place.

The Japs weren't wasting time. The men were being shoved onto the decks of the crafts as soon as they could be made ready. No sooner were the prisoners loaded when the craft moved away from the pier and another was pulled in for loading.

Once again, the rosters that had been worked up previously were useless. All the Japs were interested in was getting the total count of men onto the mother ship. To hell with who you were. There wasn't any leadership at all now. We were just a menagerie of human beings, numbers only, and to hell with what we wanted or needed.

My sector of men was now being loaded onto the small craft for the trip to the mother ship. There was much shoving and yelling along with an occasional hit in the face with whatever the guard had handy.

Within twenty minutes we were coming alongside the large ship. As our small craft approached, one was pulling away. I saw men climbing the gangway that ran down from the ship from forward to aft. There was a small floating landing at the bottom of the gangway and our boat was being tied to the landing by Japanese soldiers.

This completed, the guard on our boat just motioned and we started unloading and climbing that gangway.

Loss of dignity, loss of pride and loss of life

Chapter 30

Once again I found myself aboard ship, trudging up a gangway toward the main deck of an old rusty tub, to be transported away from the islands. Where? I didn't have the slightest idea.

I had become very conscious of detail now. Particularly about the ships we were required to ride. Coming up near the top I noted the ship had two major cargo hatches, one directly in front of me and another forward where other prisoners were being brought aboard. This ship was much shorter than the last. There was a superstructure near the center of the ship and the passageway toward the bow had been closed off.

Stepping from the gangway onto the steel deck, I found myself with about fifty other prisoners. They were awaiting orders from the guards, who seemed to be somewhat confused at the moment.

Along the rails boxes were hanging over the side. I had seen these as I climbed the gangway and noticed there was one board missing on the bottom of each. My best guess was that they were toilets. The boxes were about forty inches square and forty inches deep. I couldn't think of any other use for them.

A number of small boats circled and waited their turn to unload prisoners onto the ship. There was room for only one boat at each gangway. When one boat was unloaded another tied up and rid itself of its human cargo.

Forward, near the bulkhead that divided us from those in the forward compartment, was a large steam hoist, with cables and lines running everywhere. Overhead were tall booms with rope and cable running from pulleys at the top end. Back on the fantail were steps to a raised deck some eight feet above the main deck. This area was occupied by some Japanese guards. They could watch us from this elevated portion.

The air was fresh here on the deck. There was an odor from somewhere, but I was unable to figure out where it was coming from.

The deck was filling with other prisoners. Also, more guards were coming aboard. Our guards had been quiet, but now with this new bunch, the yelling started. The first thing I heard was "Donald Duck." We had that son-of-a-bitch with us. With him yelling and squawking, you couldn't hear the others. He stationed himself near the door that led to the cargo hold. The door had been opened and he was shoving the prisoners through the door as fast as he possibly could.

The "Duck" was slapping and hitting everyone in his reach. He even had a glove on his hitting hand. The bastard had beaten people until his hand was sore. My face and head still hurt from his beating that morning, and here I was again, having to face the bastard. The line got closer to him, and I saw there was no way to avoid him. I had to go by like everyone else and if he slapped the hell out of me, so be it. We kept moving ever closer. He was only four or five feet away now. I would wait until he swung and then leap forward inside the door. Perhaps he would get only one lick. Damn! I hoped he wouldn't recognize me. I could delay no longer. I stepped forward and he swung at me, hitting me on the side of the face. Before he could hit me again, I was inside the door. Then there was a thump between my shoulders. He got me with something, but I hardly felt it. I was at the top of some steps leading straight down into darkness. I couldn't see a damn thing. With one foot I tried to find the steps and at that moment, I was either hit and knocked down into the hold or my feet slipped. I landed hard on my right shoulder and a sharp pain ran the full length of my body. I didn't know if I had broken my shoulder or just jolted the hell out of it. When I tried to get up, there were spots in front of my eyes flying in every direction. I couldn't grasp what had happened or where I was for a minute. Then someone was tugging at the back of my shirt and I was dragged away from the bottom of the stairs so others could get down into the hold. I was pulled to one side, then dropped without a word. Whoever it was was back at the bottom of the stairs assisting the others off the steps.

My head cleared, and the stars stopped floating in front of my eyes. I was becoming used to the lighting down here. Raising to a sitting position, I felt the pain in my right shoulder. There was also pain where my canteen had jammed up into my back. When I tried standing, I found it impossible. I had to remain sitting.

That smell I had noticed coming down was worse now and as I tried moving again, I felt something on the floor of the hold. It was somewhat soft and when I picked some up and smelled it, I realized it was horse manure. This ship was used to ship horses into the islands. They hadn't bothered to clean it before loading us. The odor was from the manure and urine.

I recalled the problem with air on the other ship so I began looking for the air vents overhead. When I looked up I could see there wasn't any cover over the hatch, only timbers. There were cracks in the timbers in places as much as an inch wide and several feet long. The timbers were turned toward the length of the ship, so when we started moving there would be plenty of air.

Some officers along with a few enlisted sergeants were directing people into different areas so they wouldn't trample each other.

I heard the son-of-a-bitch still screaming topside. Men were falling over each other trying to get down inside and away from him. There were two men at the bottom of the steps, one on each side. As a man fell, he was grabbed and dragged to one side by one of these men so that the next man wouldn't fall on him if he were knocked down the steps.

211

This continued until all the men were down inside and away from the guards. With the horse manure and god-awful odor, I doubted if we would be bothered by the guards.

I found my spot and intended to stay there. People were milling around trying to find space where they could get off their feet and also were trying to make sense out of what had happened to them.

Fitzsimmons had been placed in this hold. When I first saw him, he was at the bottom of the stairs as he had stood all those hours on the other ship. He was one of the last to enter the ship and was now telling the others how to organize themselves so we could move about. We had the experience of the last ship to go by, so most of the men were already breaking up into small groups, leaving walkways between groups.

It wasn't long until the compartment was divided into four groups; between each quarter was a walkway. At the center of the group near the steps another space was left open for moving along to that area. There were about three hundred men, and the compartment wasn't any larger than the first one I was in, so the conditions were very crowded.

I guessed there was an equal number of men in the forward hold. We didn't need to worry about them; they had been sealed off in that section as we had.

I saw Blair only a few feet from where I was. He had his mattress laid out. He was under the hatch where the air would come down into the hold. I made my way to where he was. I was simply amazed at how he had managed to keep that mattress through all this. Hell, I was starting to believe he could take care of himself better than I could.

From topside I heard one of the guards yelling down through the door for someone to come to the top of the stairs. Someone went up and was handed buckets; they were passed down into the hold. The buckets were kegs that had been cut off at the top and there were bails on them. At first I thought water was being sent down; instead, I heard one of them tell the man at the top, "Binjo," meaning toilet. After twenty or more of these had been sent down, they were scattered around the compartment. Later they would be placed in a central spot. Fitzsimmons asked us not to move about, but to remain in place until an accounting could be made. That seemed to be the only thing he had been able to do since leaving Manila.

My shoulder and back ached badly. I was unable to do anything but sit and watch. Blair was stretched out on the mattress, while the rest of us were moving the horse manure around to where we could get comfortable. People near us were watching Joe as he stretched out and I could read the envy in their eyes. The mattress sure as hell didn't look nearly as foolish from down here as it did when I first saw him lugging it on his back. Even now, when it was filthy as hell, it was clean compared to what we had to sleep in.

By moving the horse manure around over the deck I had a soft area where I, too, could stretch out. Since I was going to have to live with this damn stuff for awhile, I might as well make the most of it. I sure as hell couldn't get rid of it, so I'd make a bed of it.

212

The longer I was down there the less bothersome the smell was and after those beatings and the fall onto the steel deck, I was so tired and beat up, I didn't care about the smell of the manure. All I wanted was rest. I found a spot where I could put my head on the corner of the mattress. Then, reaching back, I shook my canteen and was relieved to find I had nearly a full canteen. I was not real thirsty, so I closed my eyes and listened to the noises around me. The men were talking and off somewhere an argument was in progress. The Japanese on the main deck were hustling around at their assigned duties.

Someone came by and asked us to move in order to make the walk-way wider. This done, I saw the rope Joe had his bedding tied with. With me having a problem getting up and down, I asked if I could tie it from the beams, letting it hang down over us so I could use it to pull myself up. Joe agreed.

We were at the outer edge of the group, with the walkway that ran across the ship at one side. About fifteen feet toward the center was the walkway that ran lengthwise with the ship's hold. Joe and I were better off than most. We could come and go much more freely than those in the center. Each person had a space about twenty inches wide and the length of their bodies, but when everyone was sitting you could move about some. When we were trying to get some rest, we were sometimes walked on.

During the first night, I couldn't get any sleep because of the fighting. Also, I wanted to keep watch on the people around me, lest they decide to try taking something away from us. I had water and that was enough to get a person killed.

All night long, I listened for the crew to lift anchor. Nothing. We stayed at anchor. Although we were farther north than I had been before, and the nights were cooler, it was hot in this hold. The horse manure seemed to give off heat, but the heat wasn't as bad as when we first got into that hold back in Manila.

Taking my canteen from the cover I saw there were only a few drops left, so I finished that. Joe had also finished his water. Around noon people were becoming very ill and were in a state of shock. They realized there was no chance to escape from the hold, much less an opportunity to escape from the hands of our captors. We were in a cell within a prison, without hope. There was plenty of air, but the smell of the horse manure added to the body odor of the men had started to get in my mouth. I seemed to taste that awful smell. This, coupled with the knowledge that the Japs were taking us somewhere out of the path of the American forces, and not knowing where, was getting to all of us.

By nightfall, there still hadn't been any water and I was completely helpless. I could feel a sort of panic come over me. I recalled that I had that opportunity of possibly getting into the mountains back at Alangapo, but decided against it, waiting for a better opportunity. God! How I wished now I would have tried. The chances of making it through this was zero. Survival in the hills sure as hell looked good.

213

On the third day, the ship got underway and within an hour we were allowed on deck, a rather unusual gesture. When I came out on deck, I saw land in back of us some twenty or so miles. Luzon, I thought, still in view. There was no need to jump.

Three more ships were on our right and traveling in the same direction. Also, there was smoke visible over the horizion, indicating other ships. I assumed we were in a convoy of some sort, but it wasn't possible to tell how many ships were involved.

Men were using those small boxes hanging over the side of the ship, but when a Japanese sailor started bringing water from a door near the main bulkhead, they jumped out of the lines and in no time at all were in a line formed on deck for water. We were issued about one-half canteen cup of boiling hot water. I supposed this water had been boiled for themselves and we got what was left. All prisoners got their small amounts, and before being ordered back into the hold, there was a ration of rice balls. Everyone was thirsty and hungry, grateful for anything.

Late that evening we were alerted that there was to be more water. Each of us expected a good ration and were standing at the foot of the steps with canteen cups waiting. Instead of getting anything near what was needed, the ration was much the same as that morning, only a few spoonfuls. When we became fully aware of this, we were more angry than at any time since coming aboard. Fitzsimmons was aware of the potential trouble and knew what would happen to us physically if we started dehydrating. He located one of the medical officers aboard and the two of them were at the water kegs. As we drew the small ration of hot water, he made us drink the entire ration before leaving the keg. The medical doctor reasoned that we should drink all the liquid at once, so none would evaporate.

By the morning of the fourth day, water was a major problem. The ration that morning was the same—not even enough to sustain life for any length of time, much less abate thirst. Always the eyes of the desperate men on top of the steps, hoping and praying for additional water. When none was brought, this added to the agony. All through the day there was just the small ration of water in the morning and one small rice ball. Rice wasn't the problem. Hell, we could go without food. With the burning and craving inside me for any kind of liquid, it was doubtful I could eat even if the Japs decided to ration more rice.

There was another ration of water, the same as the morning. Time was getting away from me. The following morning, I had no idea if it had been one night or one week. The only thing I recalled clearly was the last ration of water. There had been a number of deaths. This was evidenced by the bodies at the front of the hold. Also, there had been some suicides. I didn't try to separate them. The Japs wouldn't let us take the dead topside, and the bodies were piling up as we hauled them out of our group areas and laid them near the front of the hold. Again, we designated an area for them near the buckets used for latrines. Each time I had to go I looked at these men and knew that in all probability this was where I would wind up. Each man realized this. Everywhere I looked I saw panic in the faces of the living. It had virtually taken over. Everyone was afraid to sleep for fear he would be killed by the other prisoners. Sanity was only a word and meaningless here. The fears were not without foundation. The one thing I had learned the past year was that the human animal would not die from thirst alone or the lack of water. The madness connected with thirst would cause him to get water or liquid in any form or die in his efforts. It was "dog eat dog" and the only person I trusted was Joe. We watched out for each other.

I had been thirsty but never had I been in this stage of dehydration. I was burning from within. It seemed as if my blood was boiling hot and as it touched my brain, I felt scalded on the outside of my head. The feeling drove me mad, to the point I couldn't think of the people around me as people. They represented a threat to any chance I had to get liquid.

It was as if time had stopped. The only thing I remembered that made sense was not to exert any more energy than was absolutely necessary. With this running through my mind, I watched as Joe closed his eyes. He, in turn, watched as I rested.

Only a few feet away, there was an older fellow in his fifties. There was another fellow with him who was much younger. They were like father and son. I noticed them from the time I came into the hold. They consoled each other throughout this madness. I envied the two. They were as Joe and I had been to each other, only in their case, the father-son relationship had been even closer.

The madness grew as the guards continued to hold back on the liquid for us. I expected at any minute that we would charge the steps.

There was some commotion where the older man and the young officer were. The young officer was losing control of his senses and the older man was hanging onto him, trying his best to get him to sit down. The younger man would have nothing to do with this. He struggled with his older partner. There was no doubt he had lost his mind. The bond between them had lost its power. I had seen these things before, so it was their problem. I ignored the fight as did all the others. Throughout the hold, other men were having problems. My attention was drawn away from those two near me. I had no way of knowing the time of day. I couldn't remember when the last water was brought down. There was a strange sound near me and again I looked at the older man and the young officer. There were sobs coming from one of them, but because of the dim lighting, I couldn't see who was making that odd sound. Their image was plainer as I strained to see what was happening. For just a moment their faces touched. The older man had his back toward me, and was standing, hands limp at his side, while the younger man had his face buried near the other's neck. The older man started sliding toward the deck and the other hung on. In the process the two of them turned and I could see the face of the older man and heard a gurgling sound. There was blood falling from his neck and the young man was drinking it as fast as he could. He had cut the man's throat for his blood. There was a look of surprise on the face of the older man, but at the same time an absence of anger or

215

resistance. It was as if he fully understood the reason but not why he had to die. If the younger man had done this to another person in the hold, the older man would have defended his action. As the older man slid to the floor in death, the younger man hung on, drinking as hard as he could until the two of them were flat on the deck. Was it my imagination or did I still hear the gurgling sound? The last look I had of the older man seemed to say, "It is all over for me, but only starting for you."

For the next several minutes all was quiet. The young man allowed his body to assimilate the liquid as he lay alongside the older man. I watched, more out of curiosity than for any other reason. There seemed to be a sudden realization of what he had done and he fell on the deck sobbing like a child. When I saw this I knew the man would not survive this trip and there was nothing to be gained by chastising him for his action. The man was doomed, a living corpse. I turned my head, looking away. When I looked back, he had disappeared from my view. I never saw him again. Some other men in that area dragged the limp body toward the latrine area.

The incident was closed. No one looked closely enough to see that his throat had been slashed nor did they see his blood-soaked clothing. There were no questions asked. This soldier, who only a few minutes ago was alive and doing everything possible to convince the young man that he could survive, had lost his own life. He, like so many others, was "lost in action" somewhere in the middle of the China Sea.

Blair and I were both on the mattress now, a thing that had become so much a part of the two of us, guarding each other and watching for any sign that water would be issued. Our water had long since been drunk. I took the lids off both canteens, letting everyone know there was nothing in them.

There was another ration like the last. I was now resolved to the fact this was all I would get so I drank what I was given, and then sat in one position on the mattress, not daring to burn off any more than I must.

The hot water that we got earlier seemed to heat my blood instead of cooling my insides down. It was running boiling hot inside me. How long had I been here? My nights started to run into my days. The bottom of my feet burned all the time, and there were muscle cramps in all my leg muscles, especially when I tried sleeping. I felt as if I wanted to scream. Perhaps I had been screaming. At that thought I looked at Blair, and saw he was quiet.

I noticed the man sleeping next to me had died. There were no indications that he was ill. He just closed his eyes and died. No one around noticed. I pulled his cap down over his face. When I got the opportunity, I told Joe the man was dead and that nobody knew about it but the two of us. We decided not to tell anyone, but instead, got his canteen cup and mess gear handy so that when water was served again, we could draw his for our own use.

Our group was near the bottom of the steps where the water was rationed, and we had been passing our cups getting our ration. Being near the doctor and the colonel who would oversee those being served, the two of us thought we might get away with it.

The next time water and rice were brought down, we did exactly that. I handed the cup to the colonel and he asked who it was for. I pointed to the lifeless form on the deck. He nodded and rationed the water. The water and rice were set alongside the dead man's face until Joe and I could take it without being caught. This worked once or twice but was not to last.

When the next ration came down, I drew his water as usual, then pointed to the man it was for. Someone said, "Hey, you son-of-a-bitch, that man is dead." Reaching over I lifted the cap and stated matter of factly, "So he is," as if I had just learned of his death. Then I gave the canteen cup back to the colonel and he poured the water back into the container for reissue.

The dead man left his canteen cup and his mess gear and no one had picked it up, so I took the stuff and put it with mine. Glancing around, I noticed nothing else that I could use. The men on the other side moved toward me and I toward them. Soon, the space was taken. It was as if he never existed.

I closed my eyes. I felt the madness come over me. The heat inside my head was driving me wild. I felt something cold on my back and a shiver ran the length of my body. There must be some cold air coming down between the cracks in the timber. I felt it again; it felt like water. I wondered if I was losing it. That sure as hell felt like water running down my neck. The noise in the hold had stopped. It was quiet as a morgue, and I felt the water or whatever it is running across my shoulders. Then I saw it. By God! Rain! It was raining out there.

Everyone realized this was rain at the same moment. They were standing on their feet under the hatch cover, looking up.

There were some drops coming through now and everywhere I looked, people had their cups or mess kits out, holding them where they could catch every single drop that fell near them.

Blair and I were hanging onto the rope that dangled from the girders over our heads. Water was coming through at several points. Blair was having trouble seeing the drops so I took his cup and held it along with my own. I watched for any water that dripped through. In that knot I had tied around the girder, there was a loose end of the cotton rope and it had been soaked with water until there were drops coming down the end. Pushing one of the canteen cups under this, I took Joe's hand and when he heard the first drop he was able to hold the cup and catch what fell. In just a short time, there was a small stream coming from the loose end. Apparently the rope that ran over the top of the wood beam and around the girder was catching water as it ran along the top of the hatch cover. It was the loudest noise I had ever heard when that water hit the inside of the cup. I knew everyone in the hold heard it.

I took another look at Joe's face. He was holding that cup just above his head, not much more than a foot from his ear, and there was a smile on his face that told it all. It was almost comical. There he stood, his waist so small I could span it with my two hands, his emaciated body stretched out holding that cup and the other hand holding onto the rope. The expression on his face told the entire story of this whole goddamned mess. It was all wrapped in this one scene. God! Let the rains continue. As the rains kept falling and that cup continued to fill, I knew we are being spared for some reason. Just when I had given up and was ready to take the guards if water didn't come, the rains fell.

While Joe was getting water in the cup from that stream, I was catching as much as I could in my canteen cup and I also had an extra cup that I was able to get some drops into. Even the mess kit I got from the man who was dead was being used for water. Just the knowledge of having something liquid seemed to have eased the burning inside me.

The two of us managed to wait until the shower was over before drinking anything and we found we had as much as three-quarters of a canteen cup in the one Joe had been filling and I had some in the two cups and the mess kit. When we were sure the rain was over, we waited longer. The water was divided and we drank every drop, saving nothing. Then both of us searched for additional drops. I saw some of the prisoners sucking on their clothing and so I was doing the same. Then we sat on the mattress, conserving our energy. We knew this might be the last.

The hold was filled with muffled voices now. It would appear that everyone had benefited from this God-sent rain, and for the moment there were no moans. I wondered how many days now. I had lost all track of time.

The smell of dead bodies was far worse than the horse manure. I wondered how many there were. I didn't bother looking when I was back that way. The only thing that worked now was to ignore everything as much as possible.

Later in the afternoon after the rain, I slept. I was awakened by yells from topside. Japs were scrambling about as if excited about something. Then I heard an explosion. It could be one of the anti-aircraft guns limbering up on the main deck. But when I heard it, I was on my feet immediately. I remembered the last ship. Blair was also on his feet. He heard the explosion also. We waited. Everyone in the hold was deathly quiet now, waiting. There were more explosions. It was definitely the guns aboard ship. But what the hell were they shooting at? One, two, three short rounds in succession, then a great explosion, and I heard aircraft engines. They had bombed this tub. Then all hell broke loose. There were explosions all around. That erased any doubt about what this was. Planes were bombing this ship.

The guards were running all over the deck, yelling at each other. The "Duck" charged across the timbers overhead, and I heard him yelling at someone but couldn't understand the bastard. I hoped they hit the son-of-a-bitch. With that thought, I had to smile at myself. I was not able to understand all the Japs were saying, but I did understand the phrase, "air raid," and I felt the ship shudder as another explosion boomed right near this part of the ship. The sound was like a large wave breaking over the deck of the ship. We seemed to move sideways. I heard the propellers spin out of the water, and as they did, there was a great shudder back in the hold. Someone

218

was taking the steps as fast as he could climb and was peeking out the door. I heard him call out, "The Japs are gone. They have left the area." It was Fitzsimmons.

He yelled at the top of his lungs, "Get ready to leave the ship. It is going to sink!"

Everyone grabbed his gear at the same time. I grabbed my pack and the belt with the canteen in the pouches and had them on before the sound of his voice had died.

The ship seemed to lunge forward and to the right at the same time as another explosion ripped away the timbers overhead, leaving a wide opening. Two or three of the large timbers came loose at one end and fell into the hold. This tub was on the way to the bottom and unless I wanted to go down with it, I must get the hell out and fast. Grabbing the end of the rope, I swung up and over the steel girder, then to the edge of the cargo hatch. When I was clear, I heard Blair yell from below. Looking down, I saw he was pushing the mattress at me. By now I knew the futility of telling him to leave it, so I dragged the damn thing up and onto the deck. By the time I had it over the edge of the hatch, Joe was climbing out. He was out of the hold. As he grabbed the mattress and moved away, the ship was in a high list on the left side and timbers were crashing everywhere.

Not looking at anything, I charged the small steps leading up to where the Japs had their guard post. There was a cotton life jacket the Japs had left behind, so I grabbed the thing and tied it over the top of my pack.

Down on deck, prisoners were everywhere. I looked down inside the hatch. There wasn't any movement down inside. The ship was lying very heavy on the left side and the engines were still turning. I could hear the slapping of the propellers. Forward there was black smoke rolling from the superstructure and fire fighters in that area were spraying water, trying to get the fire under control. Soon the smoke was replaced by flame; the entire midsection was on fire, and some of the forward part of the ship had been blown away. This aft portion was moving in a circle from right to left.

There wasn't time for speculation. I looked forward. There was a rain squall about four miles away. I couldn't see anything but ocean; the evening sun was shining at my back. I looked for Blair. He wasn't anywhere in sight. He had gone over the side or was behind something. I made my way to the rails and when I was near the side I saw some of the Japanese getting ready to go over the side. One of them was my old nemesis, "Donald Duck." He looked scared as hell but was making his way for the rail the same as I. I knew the minute I saw him what I intended to do, and I had no intentions of losing sight of him in the confusion.

I knew exactly what I wanted—revenge. I was well aware of where I was. There was little chance of being rescued and that son-of-a-bitch would in all probability go down, but all I could think of was revenge. I wanted to kill that bastard and I wanted him to know who killed him.

Over the side he went and I went right after him. The ship was so far on its side that I was able to run down the side for several feet before having

219

to jump. He was swimming as fast as he could, but in this water, no one could do much. If I didn't hate him so much, I doubt that I could have done this. We were getting farther away from the ship and it looked like he was gaining the lead, but I kept striving ever forward. I saw I was not alone. There were others bent on the same thing. One was well over to the right and closing in on him. He sensed we weren't there to give him a helping hand and he tried to put some distance between himself and the fellow ahead and to his right. When he did, I started closing in from behind. Then I saw three or four more men around us. I also saw the "Duck" didn't have a life jacket. I smiled at the thought that I had his. Without one he could maneuver better than I. Still I was closing in on him.

I had had a lot of experience swimming in salt water over the past two or three years. I knew that all I had to do to stay afloat was not knock myself out fighting the rough water and not panic. I'd catch the bastard soon. With this knowledge, and the revenge that I had in mind, I didn't think about what would happen to me out here. I just kept stroking. Slowly but as surely as hell, that son-of-a-bitch was going to die and if I had anything to say about it, it wouldn't be by drowning.

At last we had the little fellow. There were three of us; we were dragging him down, then letting him come up. Just enough to scare the hell out of him. I could see by the fear in the bastard's face, he was about to panic.

I removed the canteen with the bottom cut out and all those jagged edges around the bottom. Running my thumb through the chain on the lid, I got a good grip around the top and waited. I now had my weapon. As one of the men grabbed his feet, I swung down on him with the sharp edges of the canteen. I felt the sharp edges dig into his flesh. He raised a hand to fight back and the others dragged him under. When he was so weak, he couldn't fight back, I struck his face and head and the others kept pulling down until he began hollering, almost begging. God! How I wanted to hear that. The louder he screamed, the harder I hit until at last "Donald Duck" was no more.

I felt better than I should, considering my own situation. The others were gone. I didn't know who they were nor do I know what happened to them. It seemed they just faded away after their job was finished.

The sea was quiet now and darkness was falling. There were some ground swells but no choppy water. I didn't try swimming anymore. I floated on the cotton life preserver and once in a while kicked my feet, hoping all the time the tides were taking me in the direction of land. I had almost passed out. I couldn't think. The moon was out. When I came up at the top of the ground swells, I saw light shimmering on the salt water. I was nearly unconscious, just floating, all alone in what seemed to me to be the middle of the China Sea.

Coming up on the slope of a ground swell, I saw small pieces of debris floating about, but none was large enough to do me any good, so I didn't bother with the stuff. What a lonely place. I felt panic creeping in. I must stay in control. I rolled over onto my back for a time, and when I came up the slope of another ground swell, there was something not far away, going the same direction as I. Whatever it was, it was several feet away and I hoped it might be someone off the ship, so I hollered when I saw it again. I tried to move in that direction and soon, when the object came by, it was only a few feet away and I saw it was one of the large timbers off the ship. At least it was nearly the same length of those over the hatches. I was almost afraid to believe what I was seeing and, what was worse, I didn't know how I would be able to catch it. I watched closely as it passed me going real fast up the slope of the swell. If I got too close, I might get hit when it came down. It was coming right at me. I had no choice. I must grab it as it came by me. The timber and I were now moving in the same direction, down the back slope of the ground swell. Reaching out, I got hold and hung on with every bit of strength I had left. At the bottom, I managed to get atop of the timber and sprawl myself out with my arms on each side hanging down into the water, completely exhausted. All I could do now was lie face down on the large piece of timber and let the tides do what they must. At the moment, the Queen Mary would not have been more welcome.

Thirst had become a problem once again, but I was grateful for the liquid we got that morning. Also, the fact that I had drank everything we had caught at once gave me the strength to last as long as I had. But I wished I knew how far it was from land. We might be out in the middle of the China Sea. Floating along barely conscious of where I was, clutching at the sides of this timber when it got in a cross wave, I knew if I lost this, I was a goner. My only hope was to ride it out until my fate was decided.

If I didn't drift into land, the timber would only prolong my death. That sent panic through me and I gripped the timber harder. I must keep these thoughts from my mind. I was alive and on this large timber. Hell, anything could happen. There might be rescue people on the way at this very moment. Surely the Japanese would try rescuing their own people and they might see me and pick me up. I must remain calm. I closed my eyes and dozed off or lapsed into unconsciousness. A large wave splashed over me and I awoke. I was cold and scared. Letting my arms hang down into the cold water held me aboard the timber, but I was afraid to sleep for fear of falling off the timber.

Remembering Blair and his mattress, I wondered if he could make it in this water. That thing must be soaked with salt water. It seemed like a long time since the bombing. It had been dark for a long, long time. If Joe was able to get off and then was able to hang onto that mattress it would be so water-soaked it might take him down. I felt totally exhausted.

I was jarred awake by something. It was still night, though I must have slept some. It was dark! That moon was gone. I wondered if I had drifted out to sea and if I was totally alone. Suddenly, I was aware of waves breaking. There were sounds of waves cresting or something. I kept peering into the darkness. A dark cloud was up forward. Perhaps there would be another rain like yesterday. Lifting myself up to straddle the timber, my feet touched something and I instinctively jerked them up. Then I saw it! That cloud.

Hell! That was the skyline above a land mass that I was approaching. It wasn't a quarter of a mile away. Looking closer, I couldn't believe my eyes. By God, that was land. I had drifted into land, and at this moment I didn't care where it was. It was the most beautiful sight I had ever seen. Rolling off the board, I was again surprised. The water was only two feet deep. Hell, I could wade ashore. I had no intention of letting the tide catch me and take me out again. Wading and swimming, I made my way ashore and within seconds was on the beach crawling on my hands and knees toward that hill I had seen when I first awoke.

When I was fifty or so feet onto the beach, I removed the water-soaked life preserver, leaving it where I took it off. Now with only the canvas pack, which was almost empty, I moved quickly into the brush at the edge of the sand.

Without even giving it a second thought I moved very fast toward that hill. I didn't care where I was. I never wanted to see salt water again. As far as I could see there wasn't anything but sand and the hill covered with some kind of brush and small bushes. As soon as I was in the brush, I found a place where I was hidden from view of anyone passing this way and out of the wind. Here I made my bed for the night.

I was so happy at being on land I had forgotten my thirst. Now that I was lying in this quiet spot on the grass that I had pulled down for my bed, gnawing thirst showed its ugly head. I knew I couldn't search for water, so I got some green sticks and chewed on them until I fell asleep.

Early in the morning I awoke from the thirst. I was burning inside as I had over the past several days. I must have liquid of any sort.

The little hill didn't look so high, but was rugged. There must be potholes that would catch water when the rains came, and since there was rain yesterday, there might be some rainwater caught in the potholes. With this in mind I started moving about.

Not far from where I slept, there appeared to be a trail leading toward the hilltop. So I made my way up the side, watching as I went for any signs of water. In this semitropical area, I noticed several types of vegetation that grow in the Philippines. I ate without fear of poisoning. Now I needed water. There was dew on the grasses and the farther I got up the hill the damper the grass was underfoot. This trail was well used and that raised my hopes of finding water. I continued to climb.

When I topped the hill, I was taken aback. Right in front of me about one mile away was another bay, and there were ships everywhere. Stepping back out of sight, I crawled back where I could observe without being seen.

To the south, I saw two hills forming an entrance to the port. Scanning across the bay I saw ships anchored in and near the shoreline. Directly in front were a number of piers extending out from the shoreline and ships were tied alongside some of these. Farther around to the northern end was a drawbridge. The mouth of a river that ran from north to south could be seen. A high mountain loomed in back of that.

Sitting, taking this all in, I pulled some vegetation around me and started licking the dew from them as I watched the activity going on over on the docks. I wondered what those monkeys would do if they knew I was watching.

After some time, I moved farther north in search of water. I didn't have to go far. Soon I was almost right in the yard of someone's home. The house was so low I didn't see it until I was almost right on it. I had to duck back into the brush out of sight until I knew what was in that house.

From the crest of the hill, I could peer through the brush and watch. Soon a little fellow came around the lower side of the house with a hoe on his shoulder. He was coming in my direction, totally unaware of my presence. He turned on a spigot, letting water run into a small ditch to irrigate his garden. When I saw the running water, I couldn't wait any longer. I stepped from behind the brush, with both hands in the air, so he wouldn't hit me with his hoe. He stopped as I approached the water spigot. Using sign language I made him understand that all I wanted was water. He stepped back and motioned for me to go ahead. Removing my canteen cup, I drank as much as I could hold down, then filled the water bottle before turning to him.

I thanked him and explained that I was an American prisoner of war, that I had been sunk on a ship yesterday. This little fellow seemed to understand.

He motioned that I should follow him toward the house, and when there, explained that if the Japanese should see him, he would get into trouble. Then he pointed toward the piers across the bay and told me there were many, many Japanese soldiers and sailors and that we must remain behind the house.

Sitting next to the outer wall was an empty bucket and I asked if I could have it along with some matches. He went inside the house and when he returned he had some matches. Then he gave me the bucket. I explained I wanted to cook some of the things I had seen growing on the other side of the hill, but would be sure I was far enough away from his house that the Japanese would not see me.

When I started away, he went inside and came back with a bundle of small onions and some peanuts, still on the root of the vine.

Walking back up the hill by the spigot, which was still running, I filled my new pot with fresh water and then sneaked back over the top of the hill.

The sun was well up now and drying off the dew. I found the plants I saw as I came up the hill. I filled the bucket and then got down into a deep gulch where it was warm. Then, after locating some pieces of wood for my cooking fire, I filled the bucket with wild parsley and some of the onion tops.

As I waited, I lay back against the bank, removed my canteen, and drank long and deep. I had enough water to last all day, but even if I should run out, I knew where there was more.

Down in the deep gully, the sun was warm and I didn't care what was going on anywhere. I had no intention of moving.

Several times during the day, I was awakened by noises across the bay and a number of times I crawled to the top and watched. Before the day was over I saw that the Japanese were gathering survivors from the ship. Small boats were bringing men in and depositing them on one of the piers nearest me. I didn't want to cause the natives any trouble. The farmer was kind to me and cared no more for the Japanese than I.

As I was watching across the bay, I saw the man outside his home again and because it was near dark, I moved through the cover of some low bushes and came down to where he was working his garden. He was nervous, and kept glancing toward the bay. He brought me some cabbage and it was plain that he wanted me to leave. Without hesitation, I took the cabbage and left. That night I had boiled cabbage and onions, topped off with the green peanuts. Later that night I heard someone approaching my area. The fire was all but out, so I listened as the footsteps got closer. I heard someone call out but I couldn't understand what he was saying. It was the man from the house. We talked by sign language and the bit of Japanese we knew. I told him I had been in the Philippines when the Japanese invaded and when my command surrendered. He told me of how they had occupied his country well before the war started, that he cared little for their soldiers. Somehow I believed him. He told me before leaving that evening that I would have to go down very soon, for he had seen the Japs combing the area for survivors, and he was sure they would be in this area soon. This could present serious problems for him and his family. I thanked him for his warning and he was gone. I knew I could not stay long.

The following morning, I was at the crest of the hill watching the people across the bay start working. The man again brought me some of the vegetables from his garden, some onions, another head of cabbage, and a small handful of rice in a paper bag. I asked his permission to get some water and he nodded, but at the same time he looked across the bay. I understood. He was afraid someone would see me. Sometime during the morning, I crawled to the spigot and refilled my canteen as well as the bucket.

It was late in the evening when I finished my rice. I had cooked the vegetables, then added them to the rice, cooking everything together.

Everything in my pack had been drying. The waterproof bag with the notebook and the Bible were nearly dry and could be repacked. Near midnight I gathered these things and left the safety of the gully. When daylight came, I would go over to the pier where the others were assembling.

I remembered the draw bridge and headed in that direction. Before going to sleep, I wondered if I had concealed my other camp well enough. I was so grateful to the man for what he had done for me.

When the sun came up, I could see through the brush all the way to the end of the pier where the prisoners were gathering. They were out in the open, near the end that extended into the bay. Back toward shore, uniformed men were everywhere. I had no choice. I thought about trying the mountains that I saw fifteen miles away, but remembered stories about fierce headhunters on the island. Not knowing if the stories were true, I could not

224

take the chance. At least if I got through the guards on the pier, I'd be back with some Americans.

Walking ten minutes I was out of sight of the bridge and pier. I relied on my sense to get me where I wanted to go. I wanted to avoid the natives. I didn't want the Japs to know where I had been for the past couple of days. I kept low and off a small road and in back of the few houses in the area. I was near the end of the bridge and would have to come out of the brush and into the open. I paused, catching my breath, taking some water as I waited. I wanted to make sure that there was no one on the bridge before coming out into the open. I moved out and stepped very lively until I was across. I moved very quickly toward the port. Within minutes I was at the land side of the pier. Japanese were everywhere. The bunch I encountered were Japanese marines, and it took only a glance to tell these bastards were an angry bunch. One came out from the group, yelling, with his hand drawn back ready to knock the hell out of me.

"What are you doing out here?" he asked.

"I was on the ship that was sunk and have been over on the hill," I replied.

He yelled again, "Where have you been?" This time I said nothing. He was so angry, he wouldn't listen anyway. He charged me, hitting me in the face and knocking me to the ground. I remained on the ground and the solider continued yelling. He stepped back and discussed my fate with the other soldiers, and I was taken and delivered to the holding area for the surviving prisoners from the ship.

They were sitting around waiting for whatever the Japs intended to do with them. Our number had been reduced considerably. I would guess about four hundred were left. I hoped many had escaped somewhere.

I began searching for someone I knew. I hardly believed Joe had survived, but there he was, mattress and all. The mattress had once again saved Blair's life. He would never let it go after this.

I told him what happened to me and as the sun warmed us, he gently turned the mattress, letting it dry. There were large oil spots on it, and the dirt had mixed in with the grease until the thing shone in the sun.

I felt safe talking to Joe. I related what happened to the "Duck," letting Blair know that the son-of-a-bitch sure as hell wouldn't be around for the rest of the trip. I heard others inquiring about the "Duck," but when asked I would only say that I knew he would not be with us.

The rice was good here, prepared in the Japanese kitchen. Vegetables were cooked with the rice, and the ration was far larger than what we normally got. There was adequate water. I didn't mind being on the pier. No work. All we did was rest, wait, eat rice, and drink fresh water.

I knew this was temporary. We were just being held until there was another ship.

Down from the mountain.
Last leg of the journey

Chapter 31

Early in the morning of the second day after coming down from the hill, we were awakened by the military guards and ordered to get ready for movement off the pier. I didn't see any ships alongside the pier, so I knew we were being taken back away from the area. But where? There wasn't time for speculation. The guards were running in and out of the groups, screaming and raising hell. It was impossible to talk.

By now there wasn't any problem with any of us getting ready for movement. We had lost everything except the few things we could attach to our person.

The column was moving out. Up near the end of the pier, I saw men marching back toward the village and out of sight. As I reached the end of the pier, the marchers turned back to my right down a narrow street running parallel to the port area. The street wound in and out of the houses and finally made a sharp turn back toward the dock area. Once again we were on another pier moving toward a large ship.

Our people began to board. Nearing the gangway, I saw the entire length of this ship. There was another loading gangway farther down but there wasn't anyone boarding. We were the only persons going aboard and this time all of us were being loaded toward the forward section.

As I stepped onto the deck of the ship, the guard sent me in the direction of the doorway leading down into the cargo hold. This was much the same as the other ships.

I was far back in the line of march and arrived late, but as I entered the hold, I could see there wasn't any problem finding space. We had been divided in half and there was ample room for all.

The guards were different than most Japanese military men. There was no anger. It appeared that they didn't have any axes to grind with the Americans and were making every effort to assist us in getting settled aboard.

When we and our personal gear were in place, one guard came below and asked for two men to work in the ship's galley preparing rice for the prisoners. Word was passed and in short order, two cooks were on their way to the galley. Things were happening fast.

Throughout the hold men were talking and milling about, looking for a familiar face. Their voices were muffled, but they were talking. Either we had become used to being placed in cargo hatches or had accepted this as much better than the last ship.

Fitzsimmons had survived and was once again trying to organize the group. Over the last few weeks this officer had earned the respect of all. Always he had kept the welfare of the men uppermost in his mind, at times at the risk of his own safety.

The personnel were all seasoned in the art of survival. There were no fights now. The men had learned that in order to survive we would have to endure each other, no matter how we felt.

Fitzsimmons started the same procedure as before, making a list and dividing personnel into four groups, making sure that there were walkways between each group.

The latrine facilities were topside. The Japs allowed us to use them even while on the pier. Prisoners were allowed up from the hold so long as we kept out of the way of the crew. Since coming aboard, not one man had been beaten. I had no idea where we were. Was this Formosa? I had heard people referring to it as that.

Word was passed that we were all to go down inside the ship for an hour. Fitzsimmons wanted a head count, and by now most of us had enough confidence in him that there was no question when he asked us to do something.

The accounting finished, some of us got ready to go topside for fresh air. Then we heard that water was coming and we should refill our canteens and get as much as we wanted to drink for now.

I didn't trust anybody as far as water was concerned. I wouldn't think of leaving my canteen lying around. When I left the hold my canteen was on my belt. Now that I had water and two of our people in the galley, I felt things were going to get better.

There was a chill in the air. I didn't have clothing for weather other than the warm tropics and when the wind blew I felt a shiver running over me. I gladly returned to the hold.

By four o'clock our cooks brought our first ration of rice. It was in large containers and was taken below decks and set up where the rationing could be supervised.

The ship remained tied at the pier for two days. It was late afternoon on the second day when the crew started hustling about, getting ready for something. I became aware that we would be getting underway. Once again, we would be at sea away from the safety of the landlocked port. Since boarding the ship life had taken on more meaning. I found more reasons to want to survive, more than at any time since leaving Manila. Especially now that I knew the guards who were on the other ship were not going to be with us.

I heard the surging of ship engines and the rumbling of the anchor being pulled up. Within minutes the ship was backing away from the pier. No one told us we had to stay below deck, and we watched the crew as they maneuvered the ship out into the channel.

Slowly the ship was moving. Then! There was the sound of the anchor. They were going to anchor out in the channel. Ahead about a mile was a large barge directly in the middle of the channel between the hills. The channel was blocked for the present.

We had fallen into a regular routine now. The food had been served regularly and there was plenty. There had been no indication of a shortage of water. We were allowed to drink when the water was served and also had been allowed to fill our water bottles. I didn't know how long it had been since I felt this secure. I didn't even feel hungry.

Sometime during the early morning hours I heard the noise of the anchor being lifted, then the surging of the ship's engines. Within a short time we were moving. As the old tub shuddered at the tugging from the engines, I felt her start picking up speed. Slowly at first, then I felt her move from side to side. I didn't move, but waited, making sure. Ten minutes passed, then fifteen, and I felt a roll from the waves. We were closer to that narrow channel and out into the China Sea once more, swinging east. I asked one of the officers if that was indeed Formosa, and I was told yes.

Before ten o'clock, the weather changed and we were in the rain. The wind was as cold as ice. Off on the right some two miles away a water spout closed in on us quickly. Even though I needed a shower, the windchill was too much at this time, so I went down into the hold.

I hadn't been down but a short time when Fitzsimmons ordered everyone out onto deck by groups, stating that this was the best time for us to wash before we got into colder weather. After I removed my shirt, I was back on deck scrubbing as hard as I could. When I was back below I realized just how beneficial this had been.

All day long the showers came and all day long we kept going up and washing. By the middle of the afternoon, everything smelled fresh. The deck of the ship was washed clean of debris. When rice was served the morale was high. Later that evening some Japanese military people came below and asked for volunteers to bring canvas down for the steel decks. Most of us were beside ourselves. This was unbelievable.

The next morning when I stepped on deck, there was no shoreline, nothing but ocean everywhere I looked.

There had been deaths in the hold behind the one I was in. Until now, I had been occupied with my own little spot and paid little attention to what was back there. I saw some sort of ceremony going on and Fitzsimmons was having a burial detail near the hatch cover. The Japs had allowed him to bury his dead at sea.

Guards were posted near the bow of the ship, but none of them paid any attention to us. It was as if we didn't exist. They stayed in their area and we stayed in ours.

The weather had turned extremely cold and we couldn't stay on deck for long, unless we had heavy clothing. Most of us were down to shorts or cut-off trousers and were barefoot. If the Japanese expected us to survive they would have to get us clothing soon.

Several days had passed since boarding this vessel and there had been nothing from the officers I saw on board. They were probably officers who had been ordered back home and waited until the last minute to board. Later that day Fitzsimmons told us they were medical people.

228

At last Fitzsimmons announced that the Japanese had been building a shower up on deck and that when it was finished, we would be allowed to use it. Even though this was cold salt water, it was better than nothing. Fitzsimmons again spoke to us explaining that the Japanese doctors were here to make sure that we carried no contagion that would prevent us from entering Japan. This was the first time I learned where we were going. Most of us suspected that was our destination, but nothing had been said before as to where we were going. Fitzsimmons also said, "Their doctors are going to be entering the hold checking on our sick, and I want all of you to be on your best behavior."

I wondered why they had waited so damn long. Those men who died after coming aboard might have been helped if the bastards really cared. If something barred us from entering Japan, where would they take us then? Hell, no one had been able to figure the bastards out anyway.

At this point in my imprisonment with the Japs, I had learned not to question why something wasn't being done or say something being done was wrong. The best thing was to take the good and be grateful.

With the new shower, morale was better. In spite of the cold when we used it, there was a return of sanity for most of us—something that most assuredly was lost in the past. The return to sanity was first obvious by the fact our people were making efforts to help each other. They wanted to help people next to them. If a person couldn't get topside, he was assisted, making sure that everyone got fresh air sometime during the day. There was trust in each other now. This was a complete turnaround from only a few days before.

I refused, however, to tear myself down for the actions I had taken. I had seen too many things done that I knew shouldn't be done and didn't make any effort at stopping it. Things that could have been done differently with better results were not done. I couldn't degrade myself further. Some of these events and actions would remain in my mind forever, but they were unavoidable and would have occurred regardless of what I or anyone else might have done or said. There was no room for remorse or guilt. So I would chalk it all up to experience and go on from there.

For the next twenty days the ship moved ever closer to Japan. Our rice and water ration continued to be adequate to sustain life and with the added shower facility, our health had much improved.

Our ship scurried in and out of island ports, none of which I could identify. Almost daily some small land mass could be seen. On occasion our ship would pull in near the shore and drop anchor for short periods. Seldom did the Japanese take on any new cargo, nor did they unload anything. At times a small boat came alongside and one or two of their people would be allowed to go ashore, but only for short periods. Then they were back and the ship lifted anchor and pulled off once more. We got the feeling the United States navy was operating in this area, forcing the ships into these small ports. During all these maneuvers, I hadn't seen one American airplane, nor had there been any sign of submarine activities.

We had not been run down below decks at any time since leaving Formosa, and could come and go as we wished. Either the crew wasn't worried, or they were sure this ship would not come under attack.

Late one evening, when we were closing in on a small island, a number of us were on deck in spite of the ever-increasing cold. We were watching an active volcano. This was the first time I had ever seen anything like this, and I stood in the evening cold and watched the red hot lava as it ran in rivers down the side of the island and into the sea, some five miles from us. I saw the stuff boil from the top of the island molten red. At the bottom where it poured into the bay, hot steam rose into the air, forming a low cloud in that area. Before the fire glow lost its red color, there was another large fire flow starting at the top. At times there were as many as three waves of different colors coming down the side of the mountain, and always at the bottom, that rolling of steam. I became so fascinated with this phenomenon that I spent most of the night on deck watching.

When the ship once again lifted anchor and we were out at sea, the Japanese doctors prepared to do what they were aboard ship to do. They had brought on deck a number of enlisted personnel. On one of my trips on deck, I watched them work around the roped off area. The weather was bitter cold and the showers were not being used because of the cold. Most of us showered while the ship was at anchor and where there wasn't nearly so much wind. I didn't stay topside very long because of the cold. As I ducked below, I saw several men working around that area, and I knew something was going on.

Down below I sat shivering, trying to get the chill off me. I told Blair what was going on.

Somehow, I knew we were near the end of this trip. Good God! It had been nearly three months since leaving the Philippines. Most of that time had been spent either waiting for a ship or sitting in some small port. At the thought of how long it had been, I turned to Joe and asked if he had any idea what the date was. "Hell, I don't have any idea," he replied.

"Me either, but I know it is near Christmas, or a little after."

We talked about this and someone who overheard said he thought it was December 28, 1944. Christ, I had gone right through Christmas and didn't realize it. We must be nearing Japan. That was why the weather was getting so cold.

We had received our rice and water ration and were waiting until the doctors were ready. At present they were examining the prisoners in the hold in back of us.

The word was received for our hold to start. Since it was in the middle of the afternoon I knew that the longer I waited the colder it would get and so I grabbed Joe by the hand and the two of us started for the steps.

Down where the place was set up were two members of the team. Each of them had a large pair of hair clippers. In front of Joe and I were twenty or thirty men who had been passing through the line. As they passed, the two men with clippers started clipping hair and long beards. Beards were just hit

230

with the clippers but heads were clipped to the scalp. After the clipping clothing was stripped and tossed where we could get it after we were finished. Some of the men hadn't shaved in many months or had a haircut for two or more years, and I had become used to seeing them in this fashion. It looked natural to me. When they moved away from the clippers, their heads looked smaller. Their eyes were sunken in their heads and the bones in their faces could be plainly seen. Now they had stripped and stood bare on the ice cold deck, shivering and confused. Ahead of me one minute was a bearded caveman, then a man skinny as a rail, his head looking like a white bowling ball, face caved in from starvation, knees great large knots pitched out forming a bow-like stance, hugging himself and shivering from the cold, waiting his turn under the ice cold salt water shower. There wasn't any color in their faces except around their eyes where the sun had beaten them over the years. Of course, I couldn't see myself so their appearance was terrible and comic at the same time. It was the other guy that looked like hell.

Inside the roped off area was another Jap with something in a spray gun that smelled like creosote. He had a large tank hanging on his back and in his hand was a hose with a nozzle. As we passed by, he sprayed us from top to bottom. The clippers had cut me several times on my head and face and when the spray hit that area the stinging and burning were torturous. I put both hands over my eyes and a guard shoved me forward and under that cold shower. The water hose had been fixed in such a manner that it would wash us and our hair would float toward a drain along the edge of the ship. The doctors had seen to it that we were given some soap for this special examination. I took the soap but was shaking so hard, I barely knew what I had. I scrubbed as hard and fast as I could, then stepped out and into the waiting line naked. The wind was blowing across the deck. This was the coldest any of us had been in a long time.

The next station was where the doctors were. Someone had drawn small circles on the deck of the ship with white chalk. I watched the man in front of me, seeing what he did, then followed him. The man was ordered to stand with each foot in the circles on the deck; then the doctor told him to bend over and catch his ankles. I stood looking at that bare ass shining at me. If it weren't so cold it would be laughable. I knew I would stand there next. Still, this picture was something. The doctor was holding a glass tube in his hand. My turn in the circles. Hell, I couldn't relax if my life depended upon it. He hit me and as far as I could tell there wasn't any lubricant at all. I was drawn so goddamn tight, it felt like I had been hit with a crowbar. This was the last station. I was finished. Making one great leap and grabbing the little clothing I had as I ran, in seconds I was through the door and taking the steps three at a time. I was back below, trying to get my clothes back on before I froze. It was warm down here and right now I didn't ever intend to leave. Everyone was shivering and getting under anything they could to get warm again.

Blair and I sat and talked. Blair was sitting with his head on his knees, blood running from a large ulcer that had been torn open by the clippers. It had been covered by his hair and I had not seen it before. Those clippers had torn a big hole in his head. Christ! That creosote must have been hell when it hit that open sore. It would just have to bleed for now. It was much too cold to go topside and wash the wound. Later that evening some salt water was brought down and he was able to clean the ulcer and at the same time remove some of the blood that ran over his face.

Two more days passed and there hadn't been any word from the Japanese doctors whether we would be let into Japan, or rejected and sent elsewhere. I sure had been giving much thought to that. This trip had taken so long, the boat was more like another prison camp than a ship. But the thought of being rejected entry and the Japs not knowing where to put me bothered the hell out of me. If anyone had a problem, they would be eliminated.

The cuts on my head from the clipper were much better now, and we had been allowed to go on deck, but because of the cold, I stayed below as much as I could. I went up for short periods and on one of these trips topside, I noticed a large land mass some distance away. This land mass was much larger than any of the islands we had seen on our way here. We were in Japanese waters near their homeland. Each time I was on deck, I saw several members of the crew as well as some uninformed personnel standing on deck, particularly in the area of the superstructure. They all seemed joyous at the sight of land.

Our ship slowed until it was barely moving, but was inching its way ever closer to land. Soon I could make out a large city off in the distance. It appeared that we were entering some kind of channel between two land masses and there were port facilties on both sides. If not for the width of the channel, one would take it for the mouth of a large river. Looking forward over the bow, it looked like this channel parted two major land masses with large populations on each side.

Down in the hold our numbers had been reduced to a mere handful, only 131 men. I had no idea how many were in the other hold. Most of the deaths since leaving Formosa had been in that compartment. I refused to take part in any of this. I had seen our dead being taken out of this hold, but refused to acknowledge the numbers. That is, until I heard someone tell a Jap on topside, "There are 131 of us here."

When I heard that I turned and walked away. There had been 1,619 men in this shipment. Hell, I knew there were more than that here but the only thing I could think of was 131. I refused to accept this; some of the men got away on Formosa and in the mountains of the Philippines. It just had to be. I remembered Alangapo, where I saw the bodies floating in the water only a few hundred yards from shore. I wondered how many of them were not dead and had gotten into the hills. Pondering this question, I waited as the ship inched closer and closer to land and that city on the right.

Then came the order, "Everyone below decks." Japanese military men were running around the deck, screaming for us to hurry. Within minutes the deck was cleared and I was in this nice warm cargo hold. None of us had been segregated out as not acceptable for entry.

I felt the ship stop. We were at the pier. I heard men hollering at each other and the anchor being lowered. That steam-powered anchor chain was grinding as we stopped and I felt a gentle touching of the ship against the pier.

Fitzsimmons climbed the steps and found the door had been secured. We were locked below deck. Someone yelled and the colonel silenced him with uplifted hand. "It's all right. If we have to we can bust this door down." The man stopped yelling and the hold was once again silent. We waited. Soon, the door opened and the two men we had in ship's galley were pushed through the door and the door closed behind them. We waited.

Mid-afternoon I heard sirens from near the ship and out in the channel. There were whistles of a number of ships. These sirens continued blowing. It sounded like an alarm for something. At that thought I felt some panic at being locked down here. Up on deck, the guards were running around and I heard one yell, "Air raid!" Then I really got frightened. How hard it had been surviving this trip, only to be killed in an air raid in the harbor. Across the bay, I heard anti-aircraft guns pumping away, round after round, short, sharp sounds, boom, boom, boom, so close together it was difficult to tell how many explosions. I thought I heard other guns in the city also. They appeared to be on the hill overlooking the port. I noticed the hill as it rose almost straight up toward the sky, just a short distance from the port. The gun sounds were from that direction. Then there were explosions, some across the channel, then some close by it, but from the sound they were inside the city. The port was under attack from someone, most likely the United States. Up on deck, the crew was running around and yelling at each other. I heard them when they crossed over the covered hatch.

Instinctively, I started pulling my pack over my shoulders and Blair rolled his bedding into a small roll. I knew everyone was thinking about the last bombing. The difference was that we were in port. Unless we took a direct hit, we could get off easily. Looking around the hold, I saw that everyone was getting their gear and also trying to understand what was being said up on deck. It was difficult to fathom what was going on in the minds of the men. I had had an opportunity to observe them under some very difficult times, watched them when they looked death right in the eye. It was different here. While there were some signs of fear, it didn't appear to be from the bombs. It was more a fear of what the Japanese might do when we got out of here. I had that feeling. I recalled how well these last crew members treated us, and I wondered if they would feel the same when we came up from the hold and their port was under attack. I feared they would take their anger out on us.

Goddamn, the place was getting the hell pounded out of it. Some bombs were very close by and I heard some fire equipment coming into the area. There must be a fire nearby. We were locked down here. Then there was an explosion near the bow of the ship and I felt her roll just slightly. Then from back aft, there was a great boom. The ship had been hit. Then the door opened from above and a Jap yelled for us to get out. There was a mad scramble for the steps. I remained behind for some time, remembering that I was scared of what they might do to us. I wanted to know what their attitude was before going up. I listened closely. Nothing. Then Blair and I started up the steps and onto the deck. There was smoke all over, and the fire equipment was working back aft from us. The ship had taken a bomb in that area. Down on the pier, toward the land end, there were more emergency vehicles. Another bomb had hit that area and there was fire between us and the city.

We were ushered off by armed guards so quickly, it was difficult to tell what damage the ship had taken. Looking around the bay, it appeared a number of ships had been hit. Also, over in the city across the channel, there were several fires. The area was the prime target for this attack.

The Japanese army guards rushed us down the gangway and out on the pier where there were many Japanese dock workers. We were in trouble if they didn't give us protection. Farther back on the pier, there were several emergency vehicles with red lights flashing. The guards would have to take us off the pier through the mob. Extra guards were being brought in now and we were partially surrounded, with the people glaring at us. Some of them had things in their hands they had picked up from the bombed out area. When they caught the guards looking the other way, they threw the stuff at us. We got through the first group and were now in the midst of the gathering at the end of the pier. These were not all dock workers. Some were small children and their mothers who had come down to look. As far as they were concerned, they had the source of the destruction right in their hands and had no intention of letting us get away. Some of them wanted to kill us. Then seeing our condition, some of them backed away in disbelief. Hell, most of us weighed less than one hundred pounds and some were crippled. They knew we were Americans and that Americans had bombed them. But this bunch? This slowed them a bit, allowing the guards to get us off the pier and out of the unruly mob.

If not for the fear of getting killed by this mob, I would have felt damn good about this. I had survived this trip when all odds were against it. To be killed by an angry mob scared the hell out of me. But the knowledge that the United States had at last knocked the hell out of Japan sent a feeling of pride through me.

The guards would do their best to protect us, but if the mob became real unruly there was little they could do. Some of the guards might want us dead. If that was true, when we got away from the commanders, the bastards might decide to give us to that mob.

We were clear of the pier and had turned toward the mountain directly in back of the city. The guards were screaming their lungs out, trying to get out of the port area. This time, I didn't mind the screaming. Somehow, I associated that loud screaming with their desire to hurry us away from the would-be mob.

I couldn't walk very fast. This was the first time I had walked more than a few yards in some time and my legs were like limp objects under me. The guards were shoving and the men were falling in their attempts to move

234

faster. This was a new experience for me. I was a prisoner of war inside a nation that was getting the hell beat out of it. The natives were up in arms with us, because it was our government beating them. They wanted revenge, and their military wanted us for slave labor. At this moment, it was a toss-up who would win, but whoever it was, we, the prisoners, were going to be the losers.

Along the route I saw many small children. They spit on us and threw small objects as we passed. After about fifteen minutes we were ushered into a large compound enclosed by a wire fence. This wire wasn't like the wire fences I had been behind in the islands. It was more of the type used on farms—three strands of barbed wire. There was a wide entrance with a wire gate. Inside the gate, it was unpaved. There were mounds of dirt or debris that had been removed from the buildings situated inside the compound.

My feet and legs felt numb from the cold. The ground was frozen and there were sharp pieces of rocks and frozen sharp edges sticking up from the ground. These cut into my feet, but because of the cold, there was little feeling. Still I could feel the cutting. Only when I stepped on something with the arch of my feet did I feel the pain. It was some two hundred yards from the gate to the entrance of one of the large buildings where we were going. By the time we entered, both my feet were cut and bleeding.

Inside, I felt the warm air and forgot my bleeding feet for the time being. Hell! We had survived the ship, and the guards had managed to get us through that mob on the pier as well as through the city, where the people had been throwing rocks and sticks at us. We were out of the cold so the pain from our feet didn't seem so great a thing at the moment. Without waiting to be ordered to sit, I found a place where the warm air seemed the best and with Blair right on my heels, staked out a place to sit. This trip was finished. I had survived once again. But for what?

Chapter 32

Things had quieted down. Everyone had found a satisfactory place to sleep. Our guards had left the area. We were left on our own to shuffle for ourselves.

This large building, I soon learned, had been used for housing horses. Those mounds out in front must have been piles of manure. Near the end of the building opposite the main entrance were mangers which ran the full width of the building and stalls where the animals could be controlled while being fed. On the dirt floor in that area hay was scattered about, while back here the ground was comparatively clean. Along this area of the wall were steam heaters. When I came in I was so cold this was the area I wanted. Soon everyone was trying to gather the hay and bring it to their area for bedding. I needed this badly but Joe, with his mattress, was once again reveling in the fact that he had his bedding and as usual, I found myself jealous of him for having a warm mattress under him. At the same time, I was fully aware of how difficult it had been for him to have kept this bedding through what we had been subjected to. My jealousy became respect.

I was completely warm now, and the pain returned to my feet. There wasn't anything that could be done. I hoped that the Japs didn't require more walking before they had some time to heal.

There was no indication on the part of the Japanese that we would be fed, but someone had located a number of water spigots and had filled their water bottles as well as drank their fill of water.

Near sundown, the guards returned. When they opened the door that cold air swept inside, but they brought rice and soon I was in the line, ignoring the cold, being issued rice along with a loaf of some type of bread. This was something I hadn't seen since my capture. Each loaf was about six inches long and four inches wide. As I moved up in the line, it was the most beautiful thing I had ever seen—brown in color and more food in one chunk than I had seen in months. What a sight! I moved closer to the serving area and the rice was ladled into my hand. The goddamn bread felt like lead. What the hell could it be made from to be this heavy? When I had my ration and was returning to my sleeping area, I noticed many of the men ignoring the rice and starting in with this loaf of bread. As they sampled this strange ration, I heard them talking about their good fortune. By the time I was back to my area, I could hardly wait to sample this strange food. I later learned this bread was made from soybeans, a source of protein in Japan. I finished my rice and about half the loaf of bread when my hunger was gone. Carefully, I placed the rest of this loaf inside my pack to be eaten later.

The door had been closed once again and the place was warm inside. The Japanese hadn't placed any restrictions on the water. We drank as much as we wanted and all evening we stood and drank this fresh water. My God! This was the freshest water I had ever drank in my life. The thought of the water on those ships, served from the barrels with that god-awful smell, passed through my mind and I drank more of this fresh and very cold liquid. I could hear the voices of those men in the hold, begging for just enough water to cool their lips as they were dying. I drank deeply at this memory. There was no way I could blot out the sound of those men begging for death, killing one another for liquid. I drank once more from this bottle, then refilled it from the spigot. What a tremendous day. I had been given a loaf of bread, something I hadn't seen in two and one-half years and was standing here drinking the best water I had ever had in my entire life.

Returning to my sleep area, I pulled the hay around me. It was chilly without cover for sleeping. Somehow, I knew things were going to be better here in Japan than at any place I had been since my capture.

I slept the entire night and was awakened by my fellow prisoners near sunup. It was cold as hell, and every bone in my body ached. I had trouble getting to my feet. When I did, I saw Blair on his mattress sleeping like he was back home and again I was envious of him. How in hell had he managed to hang on to that filthy damn thing?

The Japanese entered the building early with rice. All they wanted this morning was someone to serve the rice to us. This took only a minute and the line was formed. Once again we were going to be fed. Standing in line and seeing the steam from the rice kettles, again I thought, "Things are going to get better." I wondered what that bombing had to do with this treatment? Probably nothing. The question went unanswered. Somehow I couldn't see them changing this quickly. In addition to rice we were served hot tea. I ate the other half of my loaf of bread. Again, I would be filled for the day.

Before I finished, I saw some of our men leaving the building through a side door. Some Japanese guards directed them. I couldn't understand what was being said, but soon the word was passed that they were being given an opportunity to take a shower. Something had been set up in one of the buildings down that way.

When time came for the men in my area to shower, I assisted Blair to his feet, and the two of us were directed out the side door and then along the outside of the building toward an open door in yet another building. There were four or five showers operating with hot water and steam was everywhere. The stalls were blocked from my view, but from inside, I heard the men laughing and the sound of the water as it hit them. As men were called for their turn, they were given soap by a Japanese fellow standing near the shower area. Again, something unheard of. It was my turn. Stepping under the hot water, I had never experienced anything that came close to this. And the soap was more than I could take. When the realization that this was actually happening sunk in, I saw the men were being given towels as they finished and being directed into yet another room. I was curious as to what was in there, but let the hot water pour down onto my bald head and rubbed with the soap as long as I possibly could. I was scared the guard would let me get the soap all over, then make me leave without having a chance to get it off. I washed faster at this thought, but the temptation was great just to stand there until someone dragged me away.

The guard yelled to hurry, and we were rushed into that room where the others had been going. A towel was given me as I entered. While drying off, I saw the men at the head of the room were being issued clothing. When I was finished, I walked in that direction. I was given one pair of green-colored trousers and a jacket of the same color. Holding these things under one arm and my other clothes under the other, I went toward the door where the men were leaving and there, another guard issued each of us a pair of black tennis shoes. God! What was happening? The guards were human. I couldn't even imagine having shoes on my feet. It had been more than a year since I had any. Yet here I was holding shoes. A moment ago when I reached for them, I halfway expected him to pull them back and laugh at me, but no! He gave them to me and directed me back inside the building where I slept last night. I was so dumbfounded at this, I hadn't even noticed the cold. My feet were aching now as I sat on the edge of Joe's mattress looking at what I had just been issued. Soon the warmth returned to my feet, and I was able to stand and dress.

Many men around me were finished dressing. I pulled on the shoes. For most of us, this was the best thing that had happened since being captured. The jacket was far too large for me but this made no difference at all. The more material, the warmer I would get when sleeping.

All that could be heard were muffled voices around the group. They were totally in disbelief at this turn of events.

Chapter 33

I was startled from my sleep by noises outside the building. Japanese personnel were yelling and there was the sound of trucks being driven near the main entrance. The Jap detailed inside with us was moving among the sleeping men and waking them with the toe of his shoe. Before he was near enough to kick, I was wide awake and on my feet. It was still dark out, but there were some dim lights, enough for me to know that there were preparations being made to move the prisoners from the city.

Fitzsimmons had accounted for the prisoners. At least he had the numbers, and had given this information to the ranking Jap officer. Then he instructed us to gather our belongings and be ready to leave when ordered.

As we finished packing our gear, we were moved near the wall and formed into lines. A Japanese guard, along with an officer, separated the men into groups. Men who could walk without assistance were placed in one group, while those less fortunate, blind and crippled in some way, were in another group. We were being split up to go to separate details.

Before we finished, the guard on the outside of the building opened that great door and the cold wind roared in. As the wind hit me I drew the oversized coat close around me and was grateful for its size. I shivered from the cold but was thankful for the clothing. If the Japs had not issued us the shoes and these other things, most of us would have died very quickly. I was warmer with the coat pulled close around me, but why in hell didn't the son-of-a-bitch close the door until we were ready to leave?

For the next several minutes we were shuffled from one group to another. The Japanese officer was making sure that he had everyone in the right group. Finally, he seemed satisfied with the way we were grouped. In this movement back and forth, I suddenly realized that Blair and I had been separated. I assumed that the guard felt he should be placed with the people less able to work. We had been together since Bilibid. I knew he could take care of himself better than most, but I needed his friendship and trust far more than he needed me. I continued looking for him among the other groups.

The guard told us we could sit while we waited and when the group next to me sat, there was Joe, standing with his mattress neatly rolled and on his shoulder. He was turning his head as if looking for something. I knew he was almost totally blind and wondered what he would be trying to see. For the past year or more, the two of us had been almost as one, watching over each other, protecting our belongings from being stolen, and sharing water and food. This separation would be hard on both of us. He was in the group next to mine and seemed very confused and disoriented. I asked the guard in charge of my group if I might be permitted to talk to him before we were taken out of here. Permission was granted, and I walked into his group, and touched him on his shoulder. When he turned, I could see his expression change. That look of dispair vanished from his face. Not wanting to give him false hope, I told him that we were being separated, that I was on the detail in the group next to him. When he heard this he walked from the center of the group, took the bedroll from his shoulder, and rolled it out on the dirt floor. At the same time he took a small knife from his gear and began cutting at the mattress. There were tears running down his face as he slashed away at the filthy mattress. He refused to look my way, just kept cutting with that small knife.

"What the hell are you doing?" I asked.

"I want you to have half of this bed. It will be better than nothing. Besides it is starting to get heavy," he said.

"Joe, I don't want any part of the mattress. Keep it. Do anything you want with it, but I don't want it."

"No, I want you to take half of it. It is as much yours as mine."

He continued cutting and slashing with the small knife as I stood aside, helpless to do anything.

This item had become a part of him and I supposed a part of me as well. The significance of this act of cutting away at his mattress, that had now become so thin it wasn't much more than a heavy blanket, cannot be overlooked. It was as if he were giving part of himself because he couldn't go with me. I didn't know what I could do at that moment. I stood there watching this, unable to stop him and unwilling to take the goddamned thing. The harder he cut the more the tears ran down his face. When I couldn't stand it any longer, I just turned and walked away, knowing he would not be able to see where I had gone. He was saying something, but I couldn't understand and I refused to look back. I walked by the guard, who watched this and was grinning at me as I passed, those goddamned gold teeth glaring at me. I had never wanted to belt anyone as badly in my life. Over my shoulder, Joe was hollering, but I wouldn't look in his direction. There was no way I could watch any longer. Somehow, I didn't think I would ever see Blair again.

Fitzsimmons came and stood near me for sometime. He was aware of our friendship over the past weeks and understood. He just stood, saying nothing. Finally, I asked if there were any way I could get with that group.

"He has been assigned to that group because of his blindness. You have been picked in this bunch because the Japs think you can work. It isn't possible for me to get you in that detail," he replied. I sat down on the ground out of sight so I wouldn't have to watch Joe. I glanced in his direction. He was still cutting away at that cotton-filled bedding with his small knife. I never looked again.

My group was alerted. We were to move out. I refused to look back. I just wanted to be out of there, anywhere.

As I passed through the door, I was angry. Mad as hell at Joe, mad at the Japs, but mostly, mad at myself for allowing myself to get entangled with another human being to a point where it had become a tragedy, a loss. I had sworn I would never let this happen, yet here it was. For the first time in a long time, I felt alone. This had never bothered me before, because I refused to let people get close enough so that their death or departure would mean anything. Somehow I felt a great sense of loss as I walked away. Especially I felt that inner anger at how fate was dealing the cards. It seemed that I had found something again that I held dear; then without even a warning, it was taken away. With all the other things coming down on me, I sure as hell did not need this.

I was shoved onto a truck, and that little grinning guard was standing there with his rifle, bayonet fixed, watching my every move. It had been so long since I had thought about fighting back that even he didn't generate that needed adrenalin to lift my spirits. The only thing I could think of now was to get the hell away from there and away from that damn mattress. My God, how I wanted to run!

It was much too late now. There wasn't any place to run. That should have been done months ago. The truck was moving now. I had been so pre-occupied with my loss that I hadn't seen who came along with me or how many. I looked around and saw the truck was loaded with about twenty men. Two other trucks were forward and some were following. Thank Christ, that grinning guard didn't board this truck. At least I didn't have to look at that son-of-a-bitch. But I made a strong resolution to never again, as long as I was a prisoner of war, become close to another human being.

Yet another train

Chapter 34

The Japs were losing no time in getting us away. Unlike the day we landed, there were not many locals watching. It was early, and for the most part, only the workers going toward the port area of the city were out on the streets.

We were on the trucks about twenty minutes when we pulled to a stop in front of a railroad station. There were rails running in every direction and some switch engines moving about the yards. We were taken from the trucks and run through the station as fast as the guards could make us run. When we were through the main part of the station, we were loaded on a waiting train. The guards were not the same ones I had seen back at the old stables. Either we had gotten new guards here at the station or new ones came on the scene that morning before leaving the barn. There were five guards, and they were shoving us around trying to impress the people in the station and those who were waiting to board. We were assigned to the last car, far away from the other commuters, and it appeared that the guards were attempting to keep us away from anyone who might want to harm us. At any rate, we were inside a rather large coach, totally isolated from the civilians. The guards stationed themselves near the front door of the coach, and one of them was posted at the exit door.

We were barely seated when the train started to move. In no time at all we were out in the countryside. I was more surprised at the cleanliness of the train than anything else. It was spotless and the windows were so clean we could see the passing countryside. Also, we were not told where to sit and could move about on the car as we wished.

After fifteen minutes, there was a signal from up front and the guard allowed someone to enter the car. He was dressed in all white clothing and was pushing a cart in front of him. Soon he was coming along the aisle, issuing rice to each of us along with some kind of pickle. Once again, we were issued a loaf of that soybean bread. This rice ration was better than any since getting here. This along with the bread and the pickle made a rather substantial meal. Anything with taste was a treat, but especially the bread. I could almost feel the energy from it as we ate.

Inside the train, there was little noise. The trains back in the States were always noisy, but this one was quiet except for the sound of the wheels as the car swayed from side to side. I asked someone about this and learned that this train was an electric train. I had seen things like this back in San Francisco, but hell, this was a large train with several coaches. It was beyond me

242

to believe this could be all electric, but that is what it was. The Japanese had electric power lines running about the trains, and I saw them when the train went around a bend.

We were traveling in a northeasterly direction, away from the sea. I took time out from eating the bread and rice to gaze out the window. With this much food, I wanted to enjoy it, but at the same time, the countryside was beautiful, so between bites I watched as the countryside slipped by the fast-moving train. Things were going to be better. After two and one-half years as a prisoner of war, I was going to be treated like a human being. At least, this was my dream and my hope. I had been mistreated for so long by these people I did not trust them. Still there was reason for hope.

The train moved along at a very fast pace, and I dropped off to sleep in one of the seats. I felt us slowing down. As we drew to a stop, I looked out the window. A small village sprawled back from the station. I didn't see any workers on the platform nor was anyone getting off or on at the moment. I waited. Finally I broke off a piece of the soybean bread and started eating, wondering what was in store for us.

Then, the rear door opened and entering were three or four Japanese soldiers armed with rifles as well as sabres hanging from their belts. This bunch started screaming as soon as they were given custody of us. They wanted us off the train and onto the station platform. They lined us up, then counted off. One of the guards started down the platform and the others started slapping us. So much for the humane treatment. We were away from the station and on a dirt road. There was still some snow in patches alongside the road. I was thankful for the shoes, remembering the walk from the ship to the stable and how my feet were cut on the ice. This was the first time I had walked with the new shoes. They felt odd, especially the way they were made with a separate place for my big toe. I had seen these on the Jap soldiers before.

It had been so long since I had walked; the muscles in my legs were very weak. Within only a short distance I started tiring and was unable to keep up with the marchers. The guards were slapping the hell out of anyone who was lagging behind. If I didn't want to be beaten, I must keep abreast of the others. I made every effort, but still couldn't keep up. One of the guards was right on my back, pushing me between my shoulders with his sabre and shoving as hard as he dared. At last I told him my legs were weak from the lack of exercise. By this time most of the others were slowing because of the same problem. He let up some, and now there were others around me as the column slowed and all were together. If the bastards decided they wanted to eliminate any of us, they would have to eliminate all of us. The guards seemed to understand and they slowed the pace. If they were to get any work out of us, they would have to build us up by giving us proper food for a period of time. I had not realized how badly out of shape I was until now.

It was mid-afternoon. The sun was out, but it was very cold. There were places where the ice had melted and it was wet and muddy. Soon my tennis shoes were soaked through. This was worse than when I was totally barefoot as far as being cold. I could feel the pain shooting up from my feet. I didn't know if it was from the cold or from the marching. I sure hoped we got where we were going soon. I had come down with a cold and this sure didn't help.

Ten minutes later we were alongside a high wooden fence, right in the center of a village. On my left were a number of buildings with little narrow streets running between them and some children. We walked some one hundred yards farther and were halted in front of a large gate where we were told to wait.

At the right side of the gate was a smaller door. One of their people stuck his head out and then opened the larger gate, allowing us to enter. Inside, people were milling around, and it was plain they were not Japanese. This was a prison camp, but as yet I had no inkling what nationality the people were. At the right side of the gate was a guardhouse with ten or twelve guards watching as we were herded into the compound. The guards were in khaki uniforms with wrapped leggings, but they didn't have rifles. They were armed with wooden sabres. They were not military personnel, but people of the village who had been given the assignment of caring for the camp and whatever this detail was going to be. The soldiers didn't seem to have much respect for them. They didn't even acknowledge their presence. One of the Japs entered another building at the left side of the gate and when he returned, he was with a Japanese officer. They talked for some time. Then the guards who brought us in left the compound, and we were taken over by the garrison people. In an effortless attempt to get us inside out of the cold, the officer talked with these people for quite awhile. It was as if they could care less if we froze. For the next twenty minutes we stood shivering in the cold. Now there wasn't any feeling in my feet at all.

Inside the camp were a number of buildings much like those in the village, except these were two-story. Directly at the ends of the barrack-type buildings were smaller buildings. Once in a while someone emerged from the larger barracks and entered the smaller buildings. These were probably latrines. I heard them talking now and understood them. They were speaking English. There were Americans or British here. At any rate, we weren't being put into a new camp. This one had been in existence for some time. The grounds were clean. From outside the barracks looked good. But the way my feet were hurting, anything would look good. I wished to hell these people would rush whatever they were doing. The soaked tennis shoes were starting to freeze my feet.

From somewhere in back of the formation, I heard a Jap yell, and all the guards in front of us snapped to rigid attention. At the same time one of our officers called us to attention.

Another officer of higher rank stepped in front of the formation and muttered something to the guards I couldn't understand. Then without even looking in our direction, he spun around and left the area for the building at the left side of the main gate. Our guards waited until he was gone, then ordered us to move back farther into the compound.

244

About four hundred feet inside this new camp, we were met by four officers, two British and two American. One Englishman seemed to outrank the others and was the overall camp commander as far as the prisoners were concerned.

He was neatly dressed in a military uniform that appeared to have been recently cleaned, while our officers were in khaki clothing—some American khaki and some green clothing like that issued to us. I did notice, however, that all of these officers were wearing their insignia of rank. The ranking American was a captain. I thought he looked silly as hell standing out there with captain's bars on his shoulders, and one of those dumb-looking caps I had seen the Japanese guards wearing. We were released to these officers by the Japs and as they were leaving, I heard the major talking. When I realized he was addressing us, I stopped looking and listened as he talked.

"We will take you inside your barracks as soon as your numbers are verified."

One of the American officers was counting us as the major spoke. When the number had been recorded by both the English officer and the ranking American captain, we were directed toward the north side of the camp where a number of long, two-story barracks were located. I overheard one of our officers say, "Who the hell does that Limey bastard think he is? These are Americans and our responsibility."

Inside the barracks, there was no heat, but the place was out of the wind and considerably warmer than outside. The walls were of bamboo and the floor was a cement walk along the front of a number of doors leading into some rooms. About two feet off the floor a landing ran the full length of the building and the doors to the rooms slid on a runner. The room had some kind of matted straw for flooring and was somewhat soft. When you put your weight on it, you could feel it give. We marched along the length of the barracks and when we faced the rooms, we were placed four in one room, each of which was about eight feet wide and ten feet in depth. The officer whom I had overheard grumbling about the Englishman told us we should sit on the landing and remove our shoes before going into the rooms as the floor was our sleeping area. "There are no beds," he cautioned. "You will sleep on that matted floor."

"I have sent word for some men to bring enough quilts so that each of you will be given one. It will be up to you how these quilts are used. You can buddy up with someone or use the quilt alone."

My feet felt as if they would drop off at any minute, so I sat on the edge of the landing and removed my wet shoes and then started rubbing both feet as fast as I could, getting the circulation started. Looking down the line, I saw a number of the others doing the same. Within a few minutes several people entered the building with loads of quilts over their shoulders. When I was given mine, I saw it was almost an inch thick. It was cotton lined with a shiny type of material quilted on each side. All in all, a very warm garment. The officers left and the Japanese didn't bother coming inside, so we were left sitting until someone returned and let us know what was expected of us.

245

I had no idea how long I would have to wait, so I wrapped my feet with the warm quilt and pulled the other end over my shoulders. In seconds, it seemed, I felt the warmth run through me. The walls kept the wind out and even with no heat inside, I was warm.

I was so preoccupied with the warm quilt, I didn't notice someone had started assigning men to the rooms. When I saw them entering the rooms I didn't even get up, but turned around and crawled across the rice straw mat where I could push the door farther open and then crawl inside. I found a corner nearest the doorway. As soon as I was inside, I removed my pack and let it lie where it fell. I once again wrapped my shoulders and back with the quilt and looked my roommates over. I hadn't made any attempts at acquainting myself with any of the men who left with me that morning. The feeling of being alone when Blair was assigned to another detail was still fresh in my mind, and the anger was still there. It just didn't seem to make a damn one way or the other if I knew who the men were. If I got close to somebody the Japs would either kill them or they would be taken to some other place. The less I knew about this bunch the better. However, I looked at the faces around me and found them much the same as I, taking care of their own gear and getting themselves settled in this environment. With four of us in a small room, our body heat caused the place to warm up nicely. To hell with it, I didn't give a damn about these men. There would be time tomorrow to learn who they were. Some of them I had seen before, some I hadn't.

This building was quite different from most of the buildings I had been housed in. While we still had to sleep on the floor, this floor was made of rice straw woven quite thick. There was some kind of insulation under the mats that kept the cold wind from blowing under the buildings, and the floor made a rather comfortable place to sleep—much softer than dirt or the bamboo I had become accustomed to. The rooms were clean. The walls were constructed of straw, but were clean and sturdy. There were windows that let the light through. While I couldn't see out, there was ample light. Closer examination showed this to be rice paper. It was thin enough to let the light through, yet heavy enough to block out the cold. I heard the wind blowing against the wall and saw the panel shudder from it, yet there didn't seem to be any wind getting through at all.

Over the many months that I had been in prison, I had slept in some odd and filthy places. This was by far the cleanest.

Outside the wind was blowing hard, and the outside wall shook again. Damn, I sure hoped none of us fell against those paper windows. That paper looked so tight that with a touch of a fingernail it would split.

It was growing dark, and we hadn't eaten anything since morning. I still had some soybean bread left, so without talking or anything else, I got the bread and started eating. At the sound of me eating, some of the others glanced at me. I remembered the time on the ship when I would have been killed for this. I was sure the same thoughts were running through the minds of these men. They left me alone, but at the thought of what could have been, I finished as quickly as I could.

Outside was a commotion. The noise was from the front of the camp. Soon, I heard people moving around inside the camp and heard people talking. Some of the talk was by Americans. Unable to sit and try to figure out what was happening, I left the warm quilt and crawled to the front and put on my cold tennis shoes. I went to the end of the barracks where most of the noise was coming from. Out near the guard shack was a large electric light. I saw men coming in the camp. Others were milling around inside the compound. When the men passed, I saw their faces were black and their clothing was covered with black dust. Only around their mouth and their eyes could I see that they were not Japanese. These men had been mining coal, and their entire bodies were covered with coal dust. As I watched them scurry about when they had been released, I knew that they were American and British prisoners of war. My bunch had been brought here to work in the coal mines. I wondered why those officers who met us did not tell us what kind of detail this was. Probably they saw we were in such bad condition that we didn't need another shock.

I noticed that the British prisoners were all going toward the south side of the camp, while the Americans were in this area.

As I watched the activity near the front gate, I saw that the men had been on a hard detail. When they were released from formation, their voices could be heard as they talked to each other and in some instances, there was laughter. This was somewhat strange to me. Over the last few months, there had been nothing in my life that I could laugh about and certainly few people I would want to talk to.

All the activity had stopped at the front of the camp. The gate had been closed and the guards were inside. The camp was quiet now, but I could see back between the barracks. Men were scurrying about near where the officers met us when we entered the camp.

Reentering the barracks I saw my bunch was still inside their rooms, not interested in what was going on. I moved toward the other end of the building. I would like to learn as much as possible about this place and what type of working conditions were here.

Many of those who came in from detail with coal dust all over them were entering another building near the kitchen. Some of them had towels around their necks, and it was plain they were entering the bathhouse. By the time I reached this spot, some of them had finished and as they passed the men entering, I could see the contrast. Those entering were black while the ones coming out were generally clean. Even here, some distance away, standing in the dark, I could see this as they walked under the light over the door of that building. Inside, people were yelling and talking, and when the door was opened, steam came out. They seemed to have ample hot water. The thought of getting another bath brought a nice feeling over me. I recalled the shower we got back at the port city when we came in and the feeling I had of being so clean—and those new clothes. I reached down and pulled the oversized jacket closer around me. The night was cold. Still, I couldn't go back inside until I had seen everything going on.

247

Things had quieted now. It seemed everyone who was out on detail was finished with their baths.

Back inside my room, I once again wrapped up in the new quilt and huddled in my corner waiting for word that we would be fed. I felt the warmth from the quilt as it seemed to warm me from the inside out. I wished I would have saved some bread. Taking my water bottle I drank deeply. Then pulling my pack into a pillow, I lay back and waited, listening to the camp noises and wondering what was in store for me here.

Nothing happened. There was no rice, but with the food from the train and the adequate water, I slept well.

Before daybreak, I heard people all over the camp. They were yelling, mostly in English, but occasionally the voice of a Jap could be heard over the clamor. I heard someone giving commands in English. Plainly these commands were British and as these commands rang out, I heard some of them repeated in an American accent. There was a morning formation and both British and American prisoners were required to take a head count for the Japanese. I wondered why my bunch had been spared this formation.

I had been listening to those commands and letting my mind run wild at the things there. Then! I heard that familiar scream coming from inside our barracks. We hadn't been spared from the formation. We had been held back for the Japanese to give us our first taste of the camp.

As the bastard walked along the walkway in front of each room, he was yelling as loudly as he could. By the time he was in front of my room I was dressed. He rattled the door. One of the men in the room was in front of me and as he stepped out in front of the guard, he was knocked to the floor. He had made the bad mistake of stepping in front of the son-of-a-bitch while he was about his duties. What a hell of a way to start a day in this new land! I saw the man around the door, so I waited, putting my canteen on my belt and hoping the bastard had passed when I crawled through for my shoes. He was farther down the walkway screaming. I slipped my tennis shoes on and tied them as quickly as possible. Then I followed the others out the door toward the guard shack. Just outside, another guard was standing directly in front of us as we emerged from the door. He had his wood sabre off his belt, and as I came through, he swung at me, hitting a glancing blow across one shoulder. Before he had time for a second swing, I was halfway to where the group was being formed.

The group I was being formed up with was headed by an American officer and was some distance away from the other formations. As I fell in alongside the others, he took my name, then verified it from a roster in his hand. When all were in formation, the wild one who woke us up came out stating that this was all. The list was given to another Jap, who was in charge of this group.

I learned that this formation was to assign us a prison number. As it happened I was never known in the camp as anything other than this number.

There were two groups of British prisoners and several groups of Americans. Parts of the formation were still in mining clothing and as black as those

248

were last night. It would seem that this type of accounting was an everyday occurrence. The shift coming off was held until all the others in camp had been lined up and a full accounting was made of the camp prisoners.

The prisoners who had been in the mines wore little black hats with a piece of metal up front where a light could be attached. Some of the Japanese who were with them still had their lights on the hats.

In addition to those who had come in from the mine, I noticed another group near the gate with mining clothing as well, only they were cleaner. I assumed that this was the mining detail for the day and when this formation was over they would be taken out the gate.

All this was taking place while our officer got our numbers squared away. Near the gate I heard a Japanese guard scream and our people started counting off in Japanese. The thing that amused me was that they were very proficient at counting in Japanese. When the sound of them counting first reached me, I couldn't tell the difference between the Japanese counting and that of the British and Americans. I soon was to learn why they were so good. If they didn't count off correctly, they got the hell beat out of them. This was a very effective method of teaching the language.

Over in this formation we were being left alone. The guards were busy getting the shift changes made and those miners in charge were very impatient with this group of guards. Because of their impatience, our men were getting slapped around by the bastards.

Our group had been turned around and we were now facing the guard shack and the detail that was being made ready for the day. The Japs were slapping the hell out of them, especially the Americans. The British prisoners were seemingly not being bothered. Watching this I felt the anger returning that I felt last evening. It wasn't that I wanted the British prisoners beaten; I just didn't understand why they would be left alone while the Americans were being slapped around.

The hopes I had yesterday had been shattered. I was once again witnessing the same old treatment. There didn't seem to be any indication that there would be any killing, at least not yet.

The detail that was being made ready for the day shift left camp and those who came off the night shift were released and were making their way toward the bathhouse.

The Japanese were now free to do whatever they intended doing with us. There were other Americans in this group, some that came in two or three days earlier but hadn't been assigned to detail yet. My bunch was being meshed with them, and they were being assigned numbers. The numbers were assigned alphabetically, without regard to rank. The Americans had the larger numbers, indicating that the British had been in this camp for many months. I had noticed last evening when the officers met us that there were numbers pinned onto the front of their clothing. The number one was on the chest of that British major, while the American officers had much larger numbers. The numbers assigned to us were in the 300s. Thinking about this, I came to the conclusion that the reason the British weren't being harassed was because they had been in this camp so long that the Japs knew them. That thought made me more angry. I started thinking how they had become friends with the bastards and could cause me problems later. I had seen these things happen back at Cabanatuan, when our own people got so well acquainted with the Japs that they were left alone, while others who didn't know them would get the hell beat out of them. I still couldn't understand why I was so angry at the British. I didn't even know their status here. I just didn't like what I saw with the officers when I first arrived. There was an enlisted sergeant major standing out in front of the entire assemblage, sounding off like he had complete control of us—not just his bunch but all the Americans as well.

When all the details were going about their routine and we had been numbered, we were told to go back to our barracks. We would be called for rice soon.

Shortly the word was passed for us to come to the mess building. This would be the first food I had in this camp. The people who were on the night shift had finished; the newcomers along with the personnel in camp would take their turn. Picking up what little gear I had left to eat with, I proceeded toward the mess building.

Standing in line, not looking at anyone, I was still mad as hell. All I cared about at the moment was how much rice I was going to get and how often.

The line continued moving slowly but steadily. I was closing the distance and was near the serving line. As I approached, I noted that two British soldiers were serving the rice. When I was directly in front of them I glared at the two of them, hoping I would see them cheating in favor of their own people. Each ration was measured carefully by using a large ladle with straight sides. When the rice was dipped, it was then tapped into the ladle and a paddle was used to scrape off the top. I was already judgmental about the Englishmen. What I saw when I came into camp caused me to be suspicious and the one thing I didn't intend taking was ill treatment from another foreigner. That is exactly how I felt about them at this point. Taking my rice and moving along to where the other fellow was, I watched for anything that I could raise hell about but found nothing. Then I heard him say, "I say there, old boy, you look beat. Could you use a spot of tea?" I was so damned surprised, I nearly declined his offer just to be nasty. Then, having second thoughts, I accepted the tea gratefully.

We were given about half an hour in which to finish eating and get our gear put away, then were ordered out in front of the guardhouse where we were to exercise. From what I saw coming into this camp, it was sorely needed. I recalled almost falling when I had walked only a short distance. But after seeing the men who came back in from detail last night, and those when the roll call was taken, I felt that this physical exercise was not just for the sake of our health, but to get us in good enough condition to mine the coal. Whatever the reason, I was aware that without it there was no hope for most of us. So for the next several hours, we continued walking and jogging, then

250

standing in place and doing exercises with our arms and legs until at last we were so worn out, the Japs let us stop and go into the barracks.

By noon, we were told there would be another ration of rice. This ration was small, but more than I expected. I didn't have that gnawing feeling in my stomach that was usually there after only short periods of exertion.

During the afternoon we were taken to parts of the camp where the Japs issued gear for us to use in the mines. At our first stop we were given black caps like the ones on the heads of the miners. Then we were given a small wooden box about two inches deep and four inches wide and six inches in length. This box had a lid that slid into a slot. I learned these were to be used as lunch boxes. The guard who issued them kept telling us, "Binto, Binto," and pointing at the box as he handed them out. I had no idea what that meant, but what the hell, I took it anyhow and went along with the others. Next we were issued more clothing. This time they gave me two pairs of mining pants and two shirts. The shirts had a hard surface outside but inside they felt like flannel. The trousers were green and, like the shirts, had a very hard surface. On the inside there wasn't any flannel, only rough material. These garments looked like they would repel water. We did not receive any more shoes. The split-toed tennis shoes would have to do. What the hell, they were the only footwear I had had since Corregidor, and it was better than going barefoot.

Two people whom I had known before were on this detail drawing equipment: Private Roberts and another man I knew from one of the camps in the islands. The two of them came into camp ahead of me from another ship. The others were just faces. Some I had seen before, some I hadn't. I had heard the names of some, but only for identification, nothing more.

That evening we started searching out men whom we had known before, and started moving about, switching from room to room. I now was in the room with Roberts and Lewiston, while the men in that room had switched with others. This had been a very agreeable swap. The fourth man in our room was on detail on the night shift, but I was assured by Roberts and Lewiston that he was all right. I would be in this room and Roberts and I would buddy up doing whatever was necessary to keep warm with the gear we had. Lewiston told me that he and the other man were trying to get on opposite shifts so they would be able to use each other's gear while the other worked. This seemed like an excellent idea, so Roberts and I agreed to make the same effort.

Once more during the afternoon we were assembled for some exercise and for the next four or five days this jogging and exercising continued. I learned that Lewiston had come on the same ship that I did, but when his group was unloaded from the hatch in back of where I was, they had come directly here. Roberts was on yet another ship that docked the day before us. It seemed the Japanese were in a state of confusion as far as American prisoners were concerned. Other prisoners had been brought into this camp from somewhere in Manchuria. The word brought in by them was that the Russians had moved some of their forces into that part of the world, so they

251

had to be moved away from there. With all the moving around by us and the issue of clothing, which was unlike anything I had seen, I agreed with the general opinion that this war was closing on the Japanese mainland very fast. Hearing these opinions and rumor was sure a morale-builder for me. I had been beaten and tortured by the bastards for such a long time now, I sometimes felt doomed to be their slave for all time.

With all these new clothes, I should be able to keep something clean at all times, especially if we got any days off from the labor detail. I had worn that shirt with the guidon sewn in the back without washing it until I was afraid the Japanese would start wondering about it. This new clothing would give me a break in that respect. I had become obsessed with getting this guidon home.

Thinking about this, I opened my pack and revealed to Roberts that I still had the flag. He had known about it back on Corregidor, but this was the first time Lewsiton had seen it. Roberts was overcome at seeing the flag and Lewiston couldn't believe that anyone would hang onto something like that for this long, especially knowing that they would have been killed if the Japs knew about it.

Over the next few days, I learned there were 160 British troops, including their officers, plus a few Dutch and Australians. They had been here since the camp was first opened in 1942. These men were captured on Singapore when that command surrendered and were brought into this area shortly afterwards. The American prisoners did not start coming here until late 1944, and from what I gathered, those who were here didn't have much to say about how the camp was being run. The British allowed the American officers to command their troops, but when it came to administering the camp, that was reserved for the British. I must admit, the British had kept the camp clean, and over the years had managed to get plenty of water — water for both washing and keeping ourselves clean, but more importantly, water for drinking.

Our period of regaining our health was over. We were told that we were being assigned to mining details. We would work fourteen days, then be given one day off. It took more than fourteen hours from the time the shift left the camp until it was back inside the camp, and from what the men told me, when down inside the mine there was no way of telling time anyway. From that viewpoint, I didn't care which shift I was on.

I had never been underground before, so I gleaned as much as I could from the people in camp. The only people I could talk to had worked underground some time ago and now had jobs above ground. The active miners slept while in camp and would knock the hell out of a person if woken up. However, I got some information like how far we were from the mine and how we must take a car down into the mine and then must walk for long distances before getting where the coal was, and that the miners got extra rice. That was good news. In addition, it was rumored that there had been orders from somewhere that the mine must increase its coal quota and anyone who wasn't real sick would have to help. I didn't feel very able-bodied, but the thought of going underground intrigued me.

Chapter 35

All through the day there hadn't been any Japs around, nor had any of our officers told me or Roberts anything. We were allowed to stay in our room or walk around the camp as we wanted. The only activity had been the rice ration and tea. Then sometime around three in the afternoon word was passed for the night shift to start getting things ready to go into the mine. Someone told us we should get in our new clothing. The guard would be around later checking us to be sure we were dressed for the night shift. All the men who came in when I did would be on this shift, as well as the others in this barracks. A new mining foreman had been assigned to train us to mine coal.

We were rousted out into the front area near the guard shack. A new man checked all our clothing. He seemed to want to assure himself we had all been issued new clothing and that we had the proper hat. This Jap was a very small man. His hair was clipped right down to his skull. Around his neck was a white scarf and in his hand he had a hammer with a long handle. On one end of this hammer was a pick and on the other an ordinary hammer. As this little man walked along the line, he used this thing like I had seen people use a riding crop.

He finished looking us over, and we were marched through the mess building, where we were fed a regular ration of rice. The Limey cook filled that little wooden box. He tapped the rice down tight and I saw there was very little chance of him shorting anyone. The box would hold just so much with this method of rationing.

By four thirty we were finished and the Japs wouldn't allow us back in the barracks. As soon as the last rice was gone we lined up, counted off (in Japanese), the same as I had seen when I first came into camp. During the training period and while we took the exercise program, we had been counting off in Japanese and I didn't have any problem. Some of the men were not so fortunate and were slapped around for not knowing how to count.

The counting was finished and I noted that one of the Japanese guards from camp escorted us through the gate, while the mining supervisor left camp alone. As we marched toward the north from the main gate our guard yelled and screamed as loudly as he could. I was sure he was doing this to impress the civilian population in the building. Hell, I could care less about his yelling and screaming. Over the months I had been a prisoner of war, I had become accustomed to this. If he was quiet, that might be cause for alarm. It had become a foregone conclusion that when we were out of camp on detail, there would be slapping and beatings along with yelling. This camp was no different than the others.

Soon we were in the center of much activity. There were buildings all over the area. I saw piles of coal at different places off the trail we marched through. There were many pieces of equipment, most of which were not familiar to me. There were women, children, old men, and young men. All were busy with the operation. Some were pushing hand carts, some were working with little cars on narrow-gauge rails. For the most part, the people looked as if they were charged with the operation of the movement of coal from the mine. A few were topside miners. I couldn't see anything that looked like a mine, except for the mountains of coal and that long endless belt running from the side of a hill and seemingly up into the sky. At its end I saw coal falling on the top of one of the mountains of coal. I wondered where the coal was coming from. The guard stopped, and I had an opportunity to look about. I followed with my eyes the direction the belt was coming from. That damn thing looked a quarter-mile long. The rear of it disappeared behind a small hill in back of us. The guard moved toward a small building and as we approached a door was opened and that supervisor who inspected us in camp came out and released the guard who brought us here. We were now under new supervision.

He motioned us inside the shack, where there were benches that ran lengthwise with the building along its walls. Also, down the center were two more rows of benches. When we entered, he ordered us all to sit. After he received additional instructions from a small office, the little fellow motioned us on our feet and we were on our way. The supervisor didn't yell or slap at anyone. He took the lead and somehow each of us knew we were to follow. There were no questions about ranks and nobody was placed in charge. We just followed the leader.

At the top of the hill was another small building and here the new boss stopped. We were issued our lamps and the battery-powered box carried on our clothing. Coming out from the top of this battery power pack were a cord and a light. As we took this contraption, he showed each man the switch, letting each man turn his light on and off. When these had been buckled on and the lamp was placed in the catch on the hat, he told us to turn the switch and then look at the others. I saw how the light would work when we were in the mine. At this point, he picked up one for himself. He then said, "Honsho," and pointed at the red box. I learned this meant "supervisor" and that different ranks were indicated by different bars on the light.

We moved farther around the small hill toward where the conveyor belt disappeared. Soon we were on top of a small grade looking into the mouth of a great hole gaping down into the bowels of the earth. Behind that hole was the hill where that endless belt had disappeared. It seemed as though the hill had been cut away, allowing the belt to cross and come into the opening at the mouth of that gaping hole. From inside another belt was bringing coal from down inside, and it was being dumped into the other one that took the coal away from the mine entrance. Here, where the honsho stopped us, we

254

were standing on a small platform alongside a narrow rail. The rails leveled off up here. When I looked down toward the entrance, the rail line disappeared into the earth. In the center of the rail line were two cables, one running toward the top and the other running down into the mine entrance. Looking this over, this sure wasn't what I had expected. Somehow I thought of entering a mine from a cage or something and being lowered down into the earth, but it looked like I would be riding down in a car. I noted that the rail ran down very quickly on a very steep angle from where we stood. Down from this platform was yet another structure. It looked like overhead electrical wiring that also went down into the mine. This was well over our heads, perhaps ten or twelve feet above the rail line. My first thoughts were that this was a power source like the trolley cars in San Francisco. That thought amused me. I was sure there wouldn't be any Market Street at the bottom of that pit.

The cables turned only a few yards past the platform and the conveyor belt that I watched all the way up here ended at the mouth of the great gaping hole. The other belt coming up from the bowels of the earth ended as well at the entrance about one hundred feet away. The coal never stopped coming out. There was a constant stream falling from one belt onto the other that carried it away through the air toward the sky to be dumped on the mountain of coal some quarter- to a half-mile away. All in all, I saw this was a big operation. There must be a lot of people down inside this mine to keep that stuff streaming out all the time.

I waited and listened but that little fellow wasn't offering any information. He stood off to one side, aloof as hell, and listening for something and watching the entrance. I waited. Then, there was a noise coming from somewhere inside the mine, some sort of rumble, and I felt the platform shaking. Suddenly! A small car burst from the great hole. I was looking into the darkness and almost as if from nowhere it burst out into the light. The sun was almost down but was shining brightly and this made the car seem to burst into the light. Before I had time to speculate it stopped right in front of me. I looked down and saw the cables had stopped. This vehicle was attached to the cables and controlled in such a way that it stopped when it was in front of this platform. I didn't get any time to figure out how the thing worked. That supervisor was directing us aboard. He was already aboard and ordered us to sit in the small seats. That took some of the fear out of it. Still, I could feel the fear well up inside as I climbed aboard. I just didn't care for the idea of going down inside the earth. Hell, I recalled going down into some small caves in the Ozark mountains when I was young and experiencing the fear of things caving in on me. This hole was more like going into a carved-out mountain. He gave the signal for us to hurry and when all the seats were filled, the others were told to wait here until he returned for them. This little car had seating for about twenty-five men and I had made the first bunch. I was near the rear of the car. Still fearful of what was to come, I started looking for something that I could hold onto. Directly in front of me across the seat back was a bar welded into the frame of the seat for that purpose and at the bottom of the seat was another bar where I could place both feet. Before the car moved, I hung onto this bar and at the same time pushed myself back against the back of my seat with my feet. Damn! I wished it were darker. I must look stupid hanging on like this. I turned my head and the man next to me was hanging on much the same as I. I glanced around the car and saw hands gripping that bar. This made me feel less stupid. Nobody knew what to expect. Then the car moved toward that great hole in the earth. As it moved slowly, I saw the front end drop over the edge as we started down. Then it was as if we were standing on the nose of the car. The grade was much sharper than I had thought. In what seemed like only a second, the car entered that dungeon. I closed my eyes as we entered and then it was like the bottom fell out and we were falling in mid-air and couldn't see anything. In the darkness, I managed to turn my head and saw the end of the tunnel as a pinhole of light. Then nothing. Turning back, I saw nothing, not even the men in the car. All I was conscious of was the roar of the little car as it dropped into the depths of the great hole. Hanging on as tightly as possible and watching as we dropped, I saw a dim light every two or three hundred feet and the conveyor belt running alongside the rail. Deeper and deeper we went and the thing didn't even slow down, much less act as if it would soon stop. I was getting more scared by the second. I felt I was being transported to hell with no way of getting off. There was warm air hitting me in the face now, adding to that last thought. Almost straight down I saw lights and we were coming to them very fast. The car started leveling off and slowing at the same time. Then it stopped and lights were in front of me. As I looked to my right, I saw rail lines running off at an angle and a row of lights running down the center of a long tunnel of stone.

When I tried getting off I found my hands still holding on to that bar. I wanted off this contraption as quickly as possible. I had had the hell scared out of me.

Then I saw the others. They had all turned on their headlamps so I fumbled around hunting for the switch, not wanting the others to know how damned scared I really was. When all the lamps were turned on and we stood on the side away from the rail, the little fellow signaled us he was going back for the others and for us to wait. Wait here? What the hell did he think I would do? I wouldn't go any farther into this pit without someone who knew where to go than I would want to ride that goddamned monster again. In seconds he was out of sight and there was only the sound of the car leaving this pit and us standing murmuring at one another. What an experience!

After we regained our self-control, I moved about some. It was warm down here and it sure didn't seem like I was underground. If not for the memory of that trip down here, I sure wouldn't have believed how deep we were. I stumbled around on the large pieces of stone and felt the level ground underfoot. Then again, I looked down that narrow-gauge rail line, and noticed yet another line running out from the end of the line where we got off. Apparently this was just another landing. The car could have gone even deeper, or could have gone farther in that direction. We would be working down the line to our right. I also noted that there was another conveyor belt that disappeared into the darkness.

As I stood around waiting for the rest of the crew to get down, I walked about the rocky floorbed. I was surprised that there was running water alongside the rails, the same as it would appear on the surface. The lights on each of our caps were peculiar, but aside from that, I had gotten used to this light and could see as plainly here as anywhere else.

The car with the others burst out of that dark tunnel, and the supervisor had everyone line up to march to the work area. The tunnel was wide, with ample room for a column of marchers. This was a well walked tunnel. The rocks had been pushed off to the sides and where we marched the floor was quite level. Overhead were large steel beams arched over the ceiling of the tunnel. The ends of these arches were set in concrete at the sides. At spots were pieces of timber wedged between the steel beams and the surface, presumably for holding the stone in place or preventing the loose stuff from falling on the people who passed on their way to and from work.

The farther we went inside the tunnel, the more scared I became. What kind of hell had I gotten myself into this time? As we walked, nobody was talking. They were stunned at what they saw. As far as I could tell, none of us had ever been inside a mine. The enormity of this one had me dumbfounded. The thought of being down under the ground and finding everything the same as it was on top of the ground left me speechless.

I heard voices ahead and they sounded like they were speaking English. The lights were somewhat dimmer here than back at the landing where we left the little car. I saw little specks of light jumping as they came toward us. This was one of the day shift crews leaving the mine. As we approached each other, the English crew stepped out of our way, allowing us by. These men were laughing and joking with one another, paying little or no attention as we passed. Their faces were black from the coal dust and only their eyes showed clearly in this tunnel. I supposed we would be replacing them, wherever they did their mining. We passed into the tunnel, ever deeper and farther away from that exit. That opening in the earth, the only way out of here, seemed like a long way away. Still, we kept going. Following the British crew were some Japanese workers, and I noted the red bars across the lights. Our supervisor came near one with a half-moon bar on his light and he stopped and bowed. When he had passed, he turned and told us that this was one of the big bosses of the mine, that we should always watch for that light and let him know if it should be in our area. I gathered he was some kind of VIP.

About a mile farther into the bowels of the earth, there were new signs of life around. Some people were pushing small cars along the rail lines and back into the smaller tunnels where spur lines led off the main rail. Also, the ground was black where coal had spilled from the cars. I had a feeling we were nearing the coal fields. Still, the main tunnel was very big, some sixty feet wide and at least thirty feet high. We moved alongside the rail and still had ample room for loaded cars to roll along.

257

The supervisor stopped and had us wait until he talked with someone inside a small office. As we waited, I saw a tunnel running off the main line toward the left and a rail spur going inside this draft. Just inside was the back end of a car sitting on the rail. The supervisor returned and we passed through the entrance of the smaller tunnel. There were several cars farther in. Some had timbers piled high while others were nothing more than a box on wheels. This tunnel was small compared to the main line—about fifteen feet wide and ten to twelve feet high. The floor of it was covered with coal. Also, it was even warmer than the main tunnel. The rail line was directly in the center of the tunnel and we walked single file alongside the cars.

Finally, we were told to stop. The Jap uncoupled the cars with the timber and directed us to push the cars along. When we were ordered to stop again, he told us to pair off in twos. Each pair was to bring one timber with them as we went farther into the mine. The man nearest me touched my arm and the two of us picked out a small timber. The lighting wasn't as good as in other areas, and we stumbled along with the log until at last we were at the end.

The little bastard turned off the rail line and seemingly walked into the wall of the mine. I was right on his heels with my end of the timber. I didn't have any idea what I was supposed to do with this piece of green timber, so I stayed close to him. There were some short pieces of timber like the one I was lugging standing as posts alongside the tunnel. There were other pieces overhead. I guessed we would carry the timber into the mine to use when digging the coal.

The Jap turned into a small recess at the side of the drift. He was some fifteen feet in from the rail line. A spur off this line led into the recess. At the center of the recess, a chute extended out and down the wall of coal. When he was sure everyone was near, he had us put down the timber as he tried explaining what was expected of us.

We would split into three sections. One section would go with him; one would stay at the chute, and one would be responsible for pushing and switching the coal cars. Those at the head of the column would be with him. I still didn't see where we were going to dig any coal.

He motioned us to follow him. Where? There was a hole no more than thirty inches high and about the same width. He motioned us to follow him. He bent down and crawled into that little hole in the wall of coal. Damn, I had seen bombs fall and ships blasted from under me, but I didn't think I could crawl into that hole lugging this timber. But he turned before disappearing inside like a rat and signaled I should follow. My partner was ready, so, even though I was scared as hell, I pulled the log in after me. The hole ran almost straight up. My feet sank into the coal as I climbed the steep incline. If it were not so steep, one would have problems getting through the hole. The tunnel swung to my left and we were out of that rat hole and inside another tunnel. The first thing I saw was the chute. It was directly in front of me when I came out of the hole. I saw now what had been done here. We had crawled around the tunnel where the coal chute was built. This was the

258

source of the coal that we were told would be loaded into the cars below. I was completely exhausted from the climb. I saw the foreman was still climbing and I had no intention of letting him get out of my sight. So I stayed right on his tail, still climbing. At last he stopped. I was right on him so he had to push me back. He picked up something with a short handle and a wide blade on it and started dragging coal over the edge of the coal chute. After raking several times with the hoe, he indicated that was what we would be doing. As he talked, I saw the coal speed down that trough and heard it hit the bottom. The other men were now in this part of the mine and observed what he was doing. He then moved farther up into the darkness and signaled us to bring all the pieces of timber near him and pile it along one side of the tunnel. He pointed where he wanted the timber laid and all of us repiled the stuff and got away so the rest could add their load. I was standing with both feet immersed in coal, which could be seen everywhere. There was a very strange feeling here. My very life depended on someone outside who was responsible for keeping the air flowing. Hell, there wasn't even any electricity inside. The only light we had was the combined lighting from our headlamps, yet I was able to see quite well, now that I had become accustomed to the environment. It was only when I thought about how far it was back to the entrance to this mine that I felt strange about being down here. If I kept my mind on the coal and the work area, I didn't feel the fear.

When I thought about the fact that the very air I breathed had to come from somewhere on top of the ground, I felt a shiver run from my head to my feet. The timbers we had brought along were supposed to keep the coal and rock from falling in on us. I heard the moans from the timber and each time I looked for something to fall. The foreman didn't even turn his head when this occurred, but it scared the hell out of me. I waited and looked. Nothing. Only the moans and groans from the pressure against those pieces of timber holding back the falling stones.

At last! I couldn't stand it anymore. I must move about to try and see what I was going to do. Anything that would get this creepy place off my mind. Walking forward and up, I saw the glistening on the coal from the light from my headlamp. In the light of the lamp, there seemed to be little bright specks throughout the entire face of coal. Having never seen coal in its natural state, I was fascinated by the sparkles in the light.

Looking back down the steep grade, I saw another tunnel that ran across this one, near where we came out of that small hole. I had been so scared when we came out of that small area I had not noticed it. Also running out of the drift was a large steel pipe. It had an elbow near the point where it came into the tunnel and turned in this direction. It very nearly was buried in the loose coal. As I let my eyes follow along where it was running, I saw it emerge from the loose coal up near the face of the mine. Fresh air was being pumped to us through that pipe.

Over the months I had lived through such horrifying times. I must be very watchful when going into things like this. I looked in every corner, trying to isolate the danger areas. Seeing that tunnel running across this one, I made

259

a mental note that if something went wrong, it would be rather easy to get onto that level with the tunnel being as steep it was. That thought took some of the fear out of me, but there were many things we had no control of here. Still, that Jap foreman wasn't bothered. This was like any other working area for him. He was talking. "Up here on the face where I work, there will be six of you. [He counted on his hands where all could see and pointed to us.] Then two of you will scrape the coal into the chute. [Again, he used sign language.] The rest, I want you down farther making sure the coal gets out from here and into the area down below, at the hopper. I will break the coal loose, you will make sure it is raked away from me."

This fellow was issuing orders everywhere, all in his native language. For the most part, we understood his signs. Most of it was clear.

After he instructed us about this part of the mining operation, he signaled us to follow him as he went back down the shaft. All you had to do was relax and you would scoot down the steep incline. Once again he entered that rat hole and disappeared from sight. There was very little we could do but follow him. So into the hole once more. I sure as hell hoped I hadn't got into a situation where it would be my job to carry the timber up through this place. I heard of people having claustrophobia and this was my problem. The small hole certainly scared me.

When I crawled out from the hole, he was gathering all the others around him and started talking.

"Take all the timber cars back into that tunnel [he pointed farther back into the darkness], then bring the coal cars up behind them. When this is done, the last car will be brought in here on this spur and butted against the chute."

He waited until this had been accomplished, then he took three or four men and stepped back along the cars. Soon they returned with several large bamboo tools that resembled a wide scoop without a handle. There were little ear handles on each side near the back of the scoop. The tools were about eighteen inches wide and twenty inches in length. Also, they had brought with them a number of hoes like the ones I had seen up on the face of the mine. The Jap handed out the baskets to a number of the men, then began showing how we would use this equipment. I remembered that constant stream of coal I had seen coming out of here and looked at this equipment. There had to be an awfully large number of people down there if this was how these people loaded coal.

He took one of the basket-type scoops, laid it on the surface, then placed his foot in back. Then with the hoe, he scraped coal from the floor until the scoop was full. Then picking it up, he dumped it in the car that had been pushed in against the chute. After several demonstrations, he asked one of us to try. The scoop was passed around, each man taking a turn. When the place had been scraped clean, he stated that is the way he wanted this area all the time. When the coal started falling through that chute, coal would get all over the place. That was when the basket scoops would be necessary.

Next we were introduced to how the cars would be handled. When one was filled, it would be taken out into the main shaft and lined up on the rail until there were sufficient numbers to be taken out of the main shaft and lined up on the rail to be hauled away. For the next hour, the foreman instructed us and there hadn't been any coal loaded. During this period, he took some men up on the face as he had us and each time they were required to take timber up through the rat hole (as I had already named the damned thing). During this time, I remained at this level, awaiting his decision as to whether I would work. I had seen enough to know that no matter where on worked in this place, it would be extremely hard work. When that basket was filled with coal, it would weight at least twenty pounds and there was no easy way of picking it up.

The instructions were over. He grabbed his men from the face and was in that hole and gone, leaving us to do what we must. It would be up to us to split up into the crews necessary to fill the coal cars and get them out onto the main line.

We were standing around the chute waiting, no one having the slightest notion of what would happen. When I felt a rush of air from the chute area and from somewhere up in the shaft there was the sound of rushing coal, I knew the work had begun.

From up inside the coal hit the timber on the hopper and there was a blast of dust coming out through the pieces of timber. I reached over and with the help of the other men, we pulled the plank out that was blocking the flow of coal. This was barely done when the coal flowed inside the little car so quickly it was filled before I knew it. I tried getting the planking back into the slot to block the coal. It wouldn't go in and the coal was filling the car and running over the floor of the mine. I yelled for someone to help. It wasn't until after the place was a foot deep in coal that we stopped it. Some of the men were clearing the rails so we could get the car out and the rest of us were standing and looking dumbfounded. I wanted to laugh but was scared someone would not appreciate my sense of humor. Ten minutes later we were loading the next car by hand, using those little hand scoops and the hoe. I heard more coal falling up in the hopper and knowing the size of that place, I told the men we should hurry before the place filled and that son-of-a-bitch came down and found out what had happened. With that each of us were scooping with hoes and the baskets as fast as possible. Then we pushed the car out and brought another in. This time we were more cautious with the plank that held the coal back. I learned two lessons very quickly during this episode: one, take care with that plank, making sure I didn't get it so far out of its slot that it would be hard to replace, and the other, don't overfill those basket scoops. Just in that short time, I felt like I had broken my back with them.

The noise of the coal rushing down the chute stopped and we were given time to fill several of the coal cars and get them out onto the main rail as well as bring the cars down near the spur where it would take only a minute to take out the full car and bring in an empty one.

For the next several hours we continued this process, bringing one car in off the main rail, then, when it was filled, pushing it out of the drift onto the main line. At the chute, we rotated the job of opening the gate and letting the coal out. When this change came I had an opportunity to take a car out of the drift onto the line. There other prisoners picked up the loaded cars and transported them by the rail line away from the area. My first trip out, I saw cars coming from deeper in the mine. Also, about one hundred feet from where the drift entered the mining area, there was another drift going in the opposite direction. Once when I was required to push a car in that direction, I saw fifteen or twenty cars emerge from that area. Combined with the cars from our area and the ones coming from deeper, there were several thousand tons of coal moving along the main line at all times—a very large operation.

Back inside the drift, we were told it was time for rice and a breather. The men from up on the face were brought down by the foreman and all of us gathered around talking and eating a ration of rice neatly packed inside a little box. It was mid-shift, or at least it seemed that way. There were no clocks. Only the supervisor had the time. Daylight meant nothing. Neither did darkness. It was always the same here. Our only light was one small light bulb about fifty feet from where we were out toward the entrance of the drift, plus the lights from our lamps. As all of us sat, I looked at the prisoners. All of us were black as could be from the coal dust, even though when I looked about, there was no dust in sight. I supposed it was because of the poor lighting. It was there, just not visible in this light.

I noticed pain in one of my feet. Pulling my shoe off I saw that the entire inside part of my foot had been rubbed raw from the basket scoop. My tennis shoe didn't have enough material to protect against that bamboo basket. Something would have to be done about that. For the rest of the day, I didn't hold the basket with my foot. I held it with one hand and scraped the coal in with the other. A much slower method, and there was not as much coal in each load, but at the same time, my foot was protected from further damage. The last hours dragged by very slowly, but the foreman didn't bother us. He was up on the face of the coal and only occasionally did any coal come down the chute. We had the area clean. All the coal that had been spilled had been cleaned up and was in a car on its way to the top. The slow period offered me an opportunity to explore the area, especially back through that shaft where the extra cars were held. I was curious about how far it ran in that direction. Telling the men next to me that I needed to use the restroom, I walked back alongside the cars for about one hundred yards. There I saw some boards blocking the tunnel and a sign in Japanese. I knew that sign was a warning for me to go no farther, yet the tracks ran along the floor under the boards and into that forbidden area. I stuck my head through the boards, letting the lamp shine down farther inside. The rails ran farther than the light would shine. Coming from inside was the foulest odor I had smelled since the ships. That odor was enough to keep me ₁rom investigating further. Still, I was curious about that as a means of escape if something should go wrong. As I returned, I had an ominous feeling about that end of the tunnel. It sure as hell wasn't a spot I wanted to explore.

At last! The shift came to an end. The Japanese honsho who had been with us all night brought the crew from up on the face down where we were. He walked around inspecting the area, especially to see how well we had scraped the spilled coal from the loading area. Seeing some still on the floor, he told us to scrape more and put it in the last car. When the car was filled and was pushed out onto the line, he made us scrape around the area and pile the extra coal dust and small pieces under the chute area out of the way of the next car. Additionally, we had to check the rail line all the way out to the main drift, making sure there were no objects on the rails that could cause a car to jump the track. This completed, we stacked the bamboo scoops and the hoes in the designated area for the oncoming crew, gathered our own equipment, and on the way out pushed the last car onto the line.

I had finished my first day as a coal miner and was on my way topside to fresh air. This had been one hell of an experience, and I would be glad to be out and onto the surface of the earth once more.

The honsho set a fast pace out and that raw place on the inside of my foot was extremely painful, but I must keep pace with the others. I was still not able to move about without being with someone. I sure as hell didn't want to be left behind. Trodding alongside the rails and the cable moving about a foot from where I was walking, I was afraid I would accidentally step on it and fall, so I moved outside the track and when I did, I heard something in back of me. Stepping farther away I saw a bunch of loaded cars coming up on our rear. The Jap heard it and was outside the tracks. I warned the others and the cars started by. As they did, the honsho got aboard the small train and we did the same. The cars moved along rather fast, but not so fast that I couldn't see everything. I recognized the heavy arches over my head, the ones I had seen as we came on shift. I watched closely and recognized when we were near the spot where the car stopped. As I rode, I looked back over the last several hours. This had been the hardest work I had done. Either that, or my physical condition was so bad the extreme hard labor had nearly killed me. In any case, I was grateful for this ride.

The main tunnel had been blasted out from solid stone and was at least one mile in length from the conveyor belt to the coal area. When I thought about the size of this and the size of the tunnel where I worked all night, it didn't take much vision to see this was quite an operation. I wondered how long the mine had been in use. It must be years. I noticed some moss had grown in places on some of the stones.

Near the wall, the stream was running in the same direction as we. The thought crossed my mind, "How does the water get out of here?" Hell, they had to do something with it. The cars crawled along and frequently there were streamlets of water coming from the ceiling or running from the walls. Sometimes we went through several of them and it was like rain soaking our clothing. This sight fascinated me, being down under the surface of the earth and there being running water and also the little streamlets squirting from the side as we passed. It was like observing a source of water from a well that hadn't been dug yet.

263

We were at the end of the line. The train stopped and everyone got off as the Jap lined us up for counting off. My foot was burning so badly that I had problems getting in line with the others. I was far back in the line when he finished. Satisfied that all were present, the first in line were loaded onto the car along with the supervisor and within seconds they disappeared into the darkness up that sharp slope toward the top. We waited. Most of the men turned their lights off, depending upon the light over near the large piece of equipment at the end of the conveyor belt. I had become so used to the light, it took very little to see what was going on around me. I barely heard the sound of the car as it zipped up through the darkness, but I heard the swishing noise from the steel cable that propelled it ever upward. It stopped now. It was very quiet in the area, just that squeaking of the conveyor. Then the cable was once again moving and it was only a short time until the car burst out of the darkness. It was back for the rest of us.

It had been very warm in the mine, but up here the air was cold and there was frost everywhere. There wasn't a cloud in the sky. This was the brightest morning I had ever seen. Looking around me, I saw only black faces and bright eyes, some of which had been watering and had streaks under them. They looked silly as hell. I was glad I couldn't see myself.

We were lined up, then marched to the toolshed where we turned in the lamps along with the power packs. We then went down the hill to the building where we first came to the area.

While we waited for all the other crew members from other areas to arrive, our honsho brought some cigarettes out of the office and passed them around. We each were allowed one from the pack. Then we were directed to an electric lighter. It had been months since I had smoked. As I drew the smoke deep into my lungs, I knew this was the best thing that had happened to me in such a long time I couldn't remember. The smoke seemed to clear the coal dust from my lungs and throat. At the moment, it was almost worth the thirteen hours of work just to have this pleasure.

The shack started filling with other men from the mine, but we had to wait until everyone on the shift was finished before we marched back to camp.

The Japs kept a good fire going in the building. But as the place filled up, I saw steam forming on the windows of the mine shack. I knew it must be very cold out there, so I enjoyed the warmth of the building as much as I could, knowing it was two miles back. We would have to march through the frost with only our tennis shoes. With my sore feet, this wasn't going to be any picnic.

The cigarette was finished, and I sat enjoying the warm building while the other crews arrived. During this period, the mining personnel who had been in charge of the prisoners all night left the building and were replaced by those goons from camp. The day shift had been going in the mine since before I came in and were all gone. Only we, with the coal dust all over us, were waiting for the camp guards to take us back to the prison camp.

The order was given and everyone was on their feet and moving toward the exit. We were no longer kept in crews, but were ordered to line up as we departed the building. The bastard held us out in the cold for some time, then ordered us, "Count off!" Again I heard the counting start at the front of the formation, lined up in four ranks. I was in the last row. The counting stopped and someone had the hell slapped out of him. Once again I heard them start counting. This went on for some time before the guard was satisfied that all were accounted for. We waited some more while the Japs verified our numbers. Then the command was given for the group to make a right face and then another command that I had learned very quickly, "Mia simay" [forward, march]. We were off for camp a mile or so away. I had stood so long my foot was aching from the raw place on the inside. This, along with the cold, slowed me some, but I had been with these people long enough to know that I must keep pace no matter what. The column was being led by one of the British crews and they were stepping quite lively. I didn't know if they were doing this purposely, or if the Japs had them in front knowing they were in much better physical condition than those who had just arrived. They could at least slow down enough to make it easier on the less fortunate.

I had learned by now that a lot of my survival had been the result of anger. By being angry at the guards and the British, I didn't feel the pain, nor did the cold bother me. I plodded that much harder and soon felt perspiration inside my jacket. Within minutes, we were at the gate. The high wall blocked the cold wind and again I felt warm although angry as hell at everyone.

Our guard lined us up and again we counted off. The figure was verified by the ranking man on their guard squad. When he was satisfied we were all present, he called out the name of one of the British and the entire deal was turned over to him. I halfway expected this fellow to take more time with us, but instead he called the name of one of the Americans who took charge of us. Then we were dismissed for baths, food, and hopefully sleep.

I went directly to my barracks and got a towel, then made my way to that mysterious building where I heard there was hot water for bathing. Since coming here, the Japanese had kept us away from that area, telling us the baths in that building were for the workers. So the only bath we had had was from the spigots or a hose. On my way to the building I felt a certain apprehension about getting under a hot shower.

When I opened the door, I was taken aback. The room was filled with steam. I couldn't even see where the place was where we bathed. Stepping inside and closing the door behind me, all I could see was naked bodies. Some were drying themselves while others were waiting their turn to get in the water. Then the steam cleared and I could see a large tank made of cement. It stood about four feet above the floor with steps on both sides as well as at the center closest me. Men were climbing up and getting into the steaming water. The line closed in near the tub and I saw several men taking baths together. There were at least fifteen men inside the large vat, splashing about like children. When they finished washing, they stepped out on the side

265

where the steps were so one of us in line could get in the water. I awaited my turn, listening to the hollering and laughter. Suddenly it became very serious in the vat. Someone got his rear end too close to another's face. I heard a hard slap, then the fight. They were splashing about, trying to get each other under the water, as the others tried separating them. At last, the ruckus was over. The two adversaries were separated, one on each side of the large vat. Someone had gotten out and I took my turn in the community bath. Inside along the wall of the tub, I felt a step-like place running around the outer edge of the tub and I sat rubbing the dust off me. There wasn't any soap as yet, but by watching the others, seeing where they had missed the dust, then washing that part, I was able to get the worst off me. The main thing was the hot water. As I sank deep within this thing, I didn't care about anything. Even the brutal fight earlier was forgotten. The warm water on my foot relieved some of the pain and the sore muscles from the hard work were in need of this heat. I sat. I wished I would have gotten back on the back side where the people who were waiting wouldn't know how long I had been in here. I wanted to stay here as long as I could. I rubbed and scrubbed as hard as I could until at last I felt self-conscious about staying longer. I felt I was depriving someone else of bathing, so with some reluctance, I pulled myself out of this hot water and found my towel and other things where I left them. When dried off, I made my way through the crowd toward my barracks. There, I found clean clothing and sat with my quilt wrapped around me for some time. I was trying to get warm after my walk back from the bathhouse.

At last I got my mess gear and headed for the serving area for the morning ration of rice. Everyone had gone through the line when I arrived and the Englishman with the rice pot didn't want to feed me and stated the line was closed. I tried explaining that I was on the night shift and that this was my first day.

"Look, Yank, if you are going to eat, you will have to get here the same as the others," he said.

"I intend eating and I wasn't here with the others. Either put the goddamn rice in the mess kit or I'll come over the counter and get it and at the same time I'll tear your goddamned head off," I yelled.

He turned his head and when he did, I was over the counter slapping him in the face with the mess kit. The other Englishman jumped in and as he did, two or three Americans got into the ruckus. Then it was over. I had my rice and there were officers from both sides on camp in the mess hall trying to hold us apart. As I walked away, I heard him say, "The next time you come in late there will be nothing." I had been in concentration camps for so long that I knew this was the worst thing that you could do—threaten. Threats never worked with prisoners of war. If one intended doing anything it was best he do it without warning. This had been an unspoken rule, as far as I was concerned, for a very long time. I turned and started for him once more but an American officer had me by the arm saying, "It isn't your job to take care of this man, soldier."

266

"It is not my job, but if that Limey son-of-a-bitch ever threatens me again, in any way, I'll make it my job, and neither you or anyone else can stop me."

The officer looked at me as if he could strangle me. Still we looked at each other for a moment and I finished my rice. When I left the mess building and went to my barracks, I resolved that I would not be intimidated by this officer or the Englishman. Somehow I had built up a resentment toward these British prisoners of war and for the life of me I didn't know why.

Wrapping myself in my quilt, angry as hell, I was soon warm and fast asleep.

Late in the afternoon I was awakened by screaming and yelling outside. A Jap was yelling that it was time for the night shift to get up and get ready for work.

Reluctantly, I dressed for work. I remembered how the clean clothing felt that morning, so I pulled the clothing on that I wore last night. As I pulled my pants on, I felt the coal dust grinding against my skin, but to hell with it. I would be covered with the damn stuff five minutes after I got in the mine. When ready, I left the building and seeing everyone going toward the mess building, I took my gear, hoping I'd find that Englishman again and there would be nobody around. But he had been taken off the rice line and all the officers in camp were standing inside the mess hall.

I went through the line, getting my ration, and then having my binto box filled as well. I watched both the men on the line. If one of them acted as if he was shorting me, I fully intended to tear the place apart. They took careful measures to assure I had been given my share. I had established myself as an enemy of the British prisoners.

We once again lined up in front of the guardhouse. The foreman wasn't present and we were accounted for by the camp guards only, but other than that, it was the same. Some other crews lined up with us. After one day with that foreman, we were supposed to be miners.

Weeks passed without major problems or incidents, except for minor run-ins with the British. Things were rather good. They told the story about the cook and me so many times, it had grown out of proportion. I knew it was only a matter of time until one of them would try to get me.

My major physical problem was my foot and leg. That injury the first day in the mine spread up toward my knee. I had had problems with the leg since the gunshot wound in the islands and the injury with the basket started the old problems again. I knew there was little use in asking for medical attention. In the first place, there wasn't very much that could be done. Second, the Japanese sure as hell wouldn't let me off work because of a lame leg. So I hobbled along, each day doing the best I could to keep up with the others.

Each afternoon, I dressed in the mining clothing I wore the day before, washing it only every two weeks on our day off. After three or four days, the coal dust was so heavy in the material, I could feel the rasping sensation when pulling the thing on. When we got off our shift, I was so exhausted there was

267

no way I could rinse the stuff out. I was always glad when we were underground. There, everyone looked the same.

The British had been here since the war started and were in much better physical condition. They had accumulated extra clothing over the years and could keep themselves much cleaner than we could. They also had made friends with some of the Japanese and were able to get soap, something I hadn't seen much of in a long time, especially soap for washing clothing. This developed into a problem with the camp population. Some of the English had been heard making remarks about us and our officers, who didn't leave the camp. They were putting pressure on us to wash our clothing after work. I took the attitude that it was the British who were causing the problem, and I, along with a few of the others, didn't feel it was any of their damn business. We made it a point to let them know they were treading on dangerous ground. This was not a threat. We knew that didn't work well. As a matter of fact, we wanted one of them to be close enough when they made a remark that we could bust the hell out of them. There were some fights and many arguments during this period.

I had had the opportunity to observe the Japanese knocking the hell out of the American prisoners while at the same time allowing the British and the Dutch to get away with the same offense. I couldn't figure out why I was so angry at these people for not getting beat up by the Japs.

Each day started the same. We lined up near the guardhouse and the guard slapped the hell out of us for a time as we counted off. The British were in their groups, the Dutch in theirs, and the largest group, the Americans, were in theirs. During the lineups you could see the preferred treatment given the British. I saw them getting away with things that got hell beat out of us and the Dutch. At times I wanted to charge their ranks and knock hell out of one of them just to let them know how it felt. The slapping was over and the gate at the front was opened. The English were the first out. They were in better physical condition and set a very fast pace. The rest of us followed, and when we couldn't keep up, the guards punched us with those damn wood sabres or hit us with their hands. I knew if there was any rush, they would have started earlier. All they were doing was demonstrating their power over us the only way they knew how.

It was only when I was down inside the mine that I felt free of the pressures of the other nationalities. Down there in that dark hole, deep inside the bowels of the earth, I was not bothered by anyone other than the Japanese foreman and my own people. The foreman was my enemy. I expected him to raise hell. That son-of-a-bitch was supposed to dislike me. I could take that. It was those bastards who were supposed to be on my side that were causing me so many problems.

I found many places where I could be alone with my thoughts and think about where I was and what was happening around me. That tunnel I explored the first day was one of the many places I went. It was only a few yards from where I worked and there was little danger of anyone finding me there. I had been inside a number of times and found there was little to fear except for the large rats that lived back there. If I ignored them, I could get my mind off the English and the Japs, even if only for a short period. On the days when I had been beaten or slapped around, I came here in the darkness with just me and the rats and thought. And in my thoughts I tried to make sense out of what was happening. When I remembered that they beat us the worst when the war was going bad for them, it eased the anger inside me. It meant the war was coming to an end; that my time in this place was coming to an end.

On the second level of the mining area I located yet another abandoned mine tunnel, and like the one down below, there was an awful odor. But because I wanted to have as many places as I could find to hide myself, I entered this one. There was no sign at the front of this one. Inside were some of the largest rats I had ever seen. These things were more than a foot long and when my headlamp shone in their eyes, they seemed even larger. The air was stale and the heat was worse than in the one down below. Still I went inside. This place had been designated as the latrine for the crews that worked this level. This explained the rat population and their size. I sure as hell wouldn't spend much time in this one.

This, I learned, was the system. The Japanese abandoned a shaft when there was no more coal and the area would be used as the latrine until the smell became so bad it must be caved in or it caved in on its own.

My fears I had when I first came down into the mine were gone. I could run through that rat hole and up to the next level as if it were normal. The fear of riding that car in and out of here was no more. I even looked forward to riding it. I felt like a full-fledged miner now.

I had been on the same shift since the first day, and learned which Japs were mean and which ones were easier to get along with. Our foreman turned out to be a rather nice fellow. He seldom hit any of us. Sometime he yelled like hell and tried to scare us into harder work, but for the better part, he was much better than those guards at camp.

Back in the abandoned shafts, the rats were increasing in numbers. At times, I saw them out where we worked, running about the timbers. The foreman told us that they were to be left unharmed. The rats would know in advance any impending disaster and would leave an area if something was going to occur. I had heard this theory before.

As time passed and the food was cut, it was inevitable that someone would try killing one of the rats and sneaking it back to camp where it could be cooked. I was working with a marine who decided that was exactly what he was going to do and to hell with the foreman's warnings. He expressed his thoughts with me along these lines, but I couldn't bring myself around to even thinking about eating one of those damned things. We talked for several days about them. "Hell," he said, "they look like a squirrel, and for that matter, they are bigger than some I have eaten back home."

"What about the fact the Japs are superstitious about killing them?" I asked.

"I will take that chance. If I am caught, then to hell with it," he replied.

Then one day he started taking one of these things out of the mine in his binto box. He would pick out one that he could wad inside and still get the lid back on, and for the next several weeks he carried one out each day. It was only a short time until this marine looked more healthy than at any time since we started working down here. I was envious of him for being able to eat the things. Each morning, as I passed his room, I smelled him cooking that damn thing in his quan pot. Somehow, he managed to find a way to boil water inside his room and cook his "Japanese squirrel." I noted the change in the color of this man's face within only a few days. His cheeks became ruddy and the hollow places began filling out and his attitude was better.

The need for meat was great. Most of us had had nothing but rice for so long that our weight was down at least one-third from normal. The loss of weight and the long hours of work in the mine were taking their toll on us and anything that had protein was sorely needed by all. Once a week, the Japanese served a ration of soybeans, but this was not sufficient protein for the type of hard labor we were performing. Still, I couldn't bring myself around to killing the rats.

I had been in the coal mine district of Japan for well over a month and I had come to know the British prisoners better. I reconciled myself to the fact that they had been here so long, they knew the Japanese by their first names, and for that matter, they even knew the names of their families. As a result, they had more or less become a part of the Japanese community and were not treated so harshly as the rest of us. I started to realize that the British weren't my enemy. They were surviving just as I had been doing for the past three years. There were some that remembered the trouble I had with the cook and they would be a problem, but for the most part I was accepted.

On one occasion when I had received my ration of rice, I was surprised to find some small pieces of meat cooked in with it. The best I had had for some time. We talked about how good the rice was and of course speculated where the meat came from. Nobody heard of the Japanese bringing in meat. I heard one of the Englishmen on the kitchen detail had set up a butcher shop on the back side of the kitchen. During this particular day off, I heard dogs howling and went to see what was going on. There was this fellow killing and butchering dogs and this was the source of meat. I had been eating dog meat for several days and liking it. I had seen people eat dog meat back in the islands, especially at Camp O'Donnel, but this was the first time I had seen our people butchering dogs like beef. At first I was disturbed. I felt a knot inside my stomach at the thought of this and at the same time I remembered how good the rice tasted. I recalled the time the captain at Cabanatuan killed the cat and ate it, and the starved look that he had on his face. I wondered if I looked the same. What the hell, dog meat was better than cat meat and far better than the rats that were being smuggled out of the mine.

In the weeks that passed, I was to be served some soup made with dog meat and by now there was very little resistance to eating it. Much to my surprise, I found it extremely good, even though this soup was nothing more than water with meat boiled it. I found it took only a small piece of dog meat to season a very large amount of water. The broth could be drunk separately or poured over rice. During the spring of 1945, this became a very important part of our ration and was the reason for my survival while in the mine.

When I first came here, they had fish or sometimes meat. Now they had rice with that pickled radish, and seldom did they have fish or vegetables. It appeared the war was taking a heavy toll on the people of Japan.

In this area of Japan they had developed methods of growing vegetables year round and I wondered, with all the gardens, why there weren't more vegetables for us as well as for themselves. But one of the guards hinted that all the stuff grown had to go to the fighting men of the Japanese military and what was left was divided among their people. I gathered from this that the war wasn't going as well as they would like.

Outside the camp every inch of space was being worked for gardens, and everyone who didn't work in the coal mines must do his share by working the gardens. I had become so starved, when I saw these gardens growing, I started scheming how I could steal some of the stuff. The gardens were almost sacred to the people. If an American was caught even looking at them, he was liable to be beaten. To consider taking something from one of them, hell, they might execute you. Just the same, I watched them as we passed going to and coming from the mine. I knew if the opportunity presented itself, I would attempt to steal something.

*Warmer weather and
hotter war in Japan*

Chapter 36

The weather was warmer now. The snow had melted and only the frosty mornings were troublesome. When we came up from the coal mines, the sharp cold greeted us as it had since coming here, but there were clear skies and on the way in, we could see the signs of spring everywhere.

There was an added dimension now, something that lifted the morale but at the same time scared hell out of us. There were American planes in the air. As yet, they hadn't been directly over us and we generally believed that they were not interested in this place as a target. But they were out there, far to the east of us, and this caused the Japs to become nervous as well as irritable at us. They had been mean enough as it was. Now they beat hell out of anyone close to them. They gave us hell each time the engines were heard in this part of Japan.

The camp commander ordered trenches dug inside the camp. Each day before we could sleep we were required to work for an hour or so, digging in the areas designated as the bomb shelter areas. Additionally, the men on details inside the camp were required to dig all the time when not on other details that must be done. The trenches were eight feet deep. Some of that mining timber was brought in to be placed over the trenches so dirt could be piled over them, making a cover for the shelter.

When one dug coal and pushed those cars around for twelve hours, then walked a mile inside the mine, and then was shoved and beaten around coming back to camp, just to be told he must dig some more in wet and soggy soil—well it sure as hell made for a long day, especially when all you had eaten was rice and sometimes a bit of soybeans. Even the dog meat had become short. They had all been butchered.

There was no way to explain to the bastards that the shelter was nothing more than a death trap. The Americans who were on Bataan and Corregidor, who went through the bombing there at the start of the war, knew it was much safer to have an open trench than pile a lot of stuff overhead. If hit, it would cave in. Still, we dug and prepared these things as the Japs had been trained to do.

When we finished the shelters, they were some three and one-half feet wide and at most places deeper than six feet. Also there was much extra dirt after the timbers had been covered. The dirt was spread back at an angle, forming an entrance away from the trench. At each end were steps leading down into the shelter and when the trenches were long, as they were farther back toward the south end of the camp, there were entrances dug at intervals. These were for the use of the Japanese guards and civilians. The Americans were told they would use the trenches nearest the guards. Down inside this death trap, there were no lights at all and after one was fifteen feet back from the entrance it was dark as hell. You couldn't even see the man next to you. There had been rain, and the water had soaked into the trench and the mud was ankle-deep.

When the planes were in the area, we were awakened and forced into the trenches, crowded like sardines where we stood, ankle-deep in mud or water, leaning against the wet wall trying to get sleep so we wouldn't be dead on our feet when the next shift was called out. It didn't matter how far away the planes were, the Japs forced us down here, where we stood and waited for the all clear. I wouldn't have cared if the damn guards had to come down also. They shoved us down this muddy trench while they stood guard and joked. They forced us in here so they could control us in the event something happened or because they were angry at how the war was going for them and this was the only way they had of getting even.

The quality of life deteriorated daily. The stress of the long hours in the mine and the Japs keeping us on our feet when our shift was over was taking its toll. When I got in camp I was so dead tired, I was asleep on my feet. I couldn't remember anything. I walked through the rice line like a zombie, then got wrapped in my quilt only to have some son-of-a-bitch burst through the door without warning and without giving me time to dress. He shoved me in the back with whatever he was holding, forcing me down into that damn mud hole. I was forced to remain there as long as they wanted to hold me. Then, when I was slow getting to my feet when time to go on duty, they beat hell out of me. It wasn't a case of when I would be beaten anymore, it was how badly I would get knocked around. The people who did the beating were careful not to break legs or arms. This would keep us out of the mine. I didn't even avoid their slaps. When they hit me in the mouth or bloodied my nose, I let them get it over with and go on to the next man. I wiped the blood and said a silent prayer that when this war was over, I would be granted an opportunity to get my hands on him and slowly torture him until he was no more.

During one of the air raids I came in as one of the last people and there were some prisoners assisting one of our people down the steps. Both legs had been amputated just below his knees. The men sat him down along the wall in the water and mud. He found a piece of timber that was partially covered and was making himself comfortable and at the same time rubbing away at the stubs. He heard me swearing at the cold and generally raising hell about my cold feet.

He said, "Sergeant, last winter when it was really cold and snow was on the ground, I got caught bringing a rat in from the mine. The honsho followed me into camp and demanded that I be punished for killing the damn thing. The camp commander forced me to stand out in the rain and freezing weather and when they thought I wasn't cold enough, they poured water over me until I was nearly frozen to death. When I was finally brought in, my legs had to be taken off. Personally, I don't think this is so bad, especially when I think about why they have me in here. Hell, as long as I know our planes are bombing hell out of these bastards, I can sit down here no matter how much mud there is, nor how cold it is."

I wanted to say something, but couldn't. When he started talking I thought he was putting me down because I was griping about being cold. Then I realized he was trying to encourage the rest of us who thought we should not have to stand here in the mud. I kept my mouth closed. I was speechless and when the all clear was sounded I scurried from the bomb shelter and back inside the room. I wrapped myself in the warm quilt, and as I rubbed the circulation back into my cold feet, I thought about that man who had no feet he could rub and I knew I was more fortunate than some.

All day long, the Japs kept waking us and taking us into the shelter. I couldn't hear the planes but they must be near. We would barely get to sleep when the alarm would sound again and back in the trenches we went, until it was time for rice and to get ready for our shift. Tonight, if the foreman turned his head, I intended to find a place where I could sleep and where it would be warm.

With the war brought to Japan, the government stepped up production at the mine. We now were given quotas on the amount of coal we were expected to produce each day. The foreman was using all the skill he had for making us get the amounts he was supposed to mine. One thing he started, and I suppose it applied to all the miners, was that when we had finished we were allowed to leave our areas without waiting for the other crews and to go topside where that cigarette was waiting. If we got there first for three days in a row, we would be given an extra cigarette.

The weather was much nicer now. Even the mornings were warm and the air was fresh. With this incentive plus the extra cigarette, the competition became fierce. One cigarette, if you didn't want to smoke it, was worth almost anything, especially food. Hell, a person could trade a cigarette for rice. And even though the British officers stated that trading was not allowed, our people didn't pay any attention to them.

The crews were never in a position where we could see one another. We had no idea what conditions existed with the rest of the miners where they dug their coal. If my crew was fortunate enough to get a good free fall of coal, we were always first out of the mine. By the same token, if the coal was scarce, it was torture making the quota set by the overall supervisor. We had all been starved for so long we couldn't think rationally.

The work continued and the competition got more intense. One English crew was becoming a problem. They were beating us or they were right on our tail as we started for the ginshaw and sometimes they tried passing us on their way out. When this happened, our honsho stepped in and after he argued with their honsho, they decided who would be first on the ginshaw. The only thing about being first was that extra cigarette. When I thought about how important this had become, I questioned my own sanity. The

274

British were determined to be first, so now, I asked, do I do this because I want that cigarette, or is it that I want to outdo the British?

The British crew made some reference to the fight I had with one of their men in the kitchen. They didn't want to admit they were sore because of being beat out. They had the privilege of moving their men around from one crew to another as they saw fit. So long as they kept the right number of men working, the Japs didn't question how their men were assigned. We hadn't been here long enough to have such privileges. One of their men, who had the reputation of being a professional fighter, had been assigned to their crew. I didn't know how much truth there was to the reputation, but he had the British convinced how mean he was and was left alone by them. It didn't take long for him to make himself known in the mine. He hadn't been assigned just to mine coal. The men on the English crew wanted him to do some enforcing, and with all the talk about the fight in the kitchen and their obvious anger toward us, I knew who would be his victim. Word was passed that he intended going out on the first car, whether he was first out of the mining area or not.

On the mornings when we were close and arrived at the ginshaw about the same time, there were times when both crews mixed in with each other. For the most part, the group that came up last would wait until the winning crew was out before getting aboard. It was sort of an honor system and we knew who should take the first turn out. The so-called fighter, who I was convinced was brought down just to make trouble, made his move. When the car stopped, he was watching and when one of us who was weak and unable to defend himself tried getting a seat, he pulled him off, making him wait, and it wasn't long until things started jelling as to who would be the victim. The British wanted their revenge and I was the target. For the next few mornings my crew had beaten them and when I started into the car, he grabbed me by the collar of my jacket and jerked me out, taking my seat. I knew it wasn't just the seat he was after. Hell, the cars ran every five minutes. I knew there was little to gain in turning him in to the British officers. They might be in on the act, and sure as hell, I didn't aim to tell the Japs. I'd wait, see what developed. Perhaps the crap would stop. My chance would come. At this time, my weight was down to around one hundred pounds and if it was true about this fellow being a professional boxer, I certainly couldn't match him in any fight. But at the same time, I had no intention of allowing him to continue.

I decided to confide in my roommate, Lewiston. I had watched him for some time and saw how he was able to survive some tough situations. I also knew he would understand why this had to be kept between him and me, especially if the damn thing should develop into something where I had to plow the son-of-a-bitch under.

While down inside the mine, Lewiston had been assigned to pushing the cars away from the chute while I was on the loading detail. I arranged to change places with his helper, and when the two of us were out of earshot of the others, I explained what the fellow had been doing. When I finished he stated matter-of-factly, "When you are on the way out of here, put a boulder inside your jacket, and when he pulls you back, bash his damned face in."

"I have thought about that. It would be easy, but when he falls the others will see him and with their connections with the Japanese they could get me into problems with them," I said.

"Then I'll help you. I'll stand near you and when you bust him, I'll help you throw him over that rail and onto the conveyor belt, and send him up through the crusher," said Lewiston.

At the time, this seemed like a very harsh way of handling the problem and I ignored it.

Just the same, the seed had been planted and as the night passed, this kept running through my mind. Again, I left the mine as I had for the last few days and the same thing happened. I no more than started for the car when I felt that big hand gripping my collar, and I was jerked back toward the belt and he took my seat. All day when I was awake, I remembered what he did. I had trouble sleeping and what Lewiston suggested kept running through my mind.

That evening when we were busting our tails getting our quota and that Jap kept harping on what a great favor the Japanese government was doing for us by giving us the cigarettes for doing so well, the anger kept building until at last, I once again talked with Lewiston about what I was going to do. During this talk, he said that for today we would make a sort of dry run, look the area over real closely so it could be done with no one knowing what had been done.

"I will go out with you in the morning and stay right next to you at the car. It is dark there, and I haven't seen him do this as yet, so don't do anything today. We'll just watch his every move," he said.

As had been the case for the past few days, my crew was ahead of the British, waiting for the car, and as in the past, I was toward the rear of the Americans as the British came on the scene. I couldn't see him but I was aware that Lewiston was right beside me. There was some light, but it was very dim. The car burst out of the dark tunnel and stopped in front of us. I stepped forward and started inside the car when I felt his hand grabbing my collar. I was jerked back toward the belt and he had my seat before anyone could see what had happened, and the car was on the way out of the mine leaving me and Lewiston. When I regained my balance I turned and in the dim light I saw Lewiston's face. He had seen it all.

While I waited for the car to return, I took the time to look the place over. I had been going in and out of here for a long time, but had never noticed many things. That conveyor belt was speeding by much faster than I realized. I saw what Lewiston meant about it being no problem getting the son-of-a-bitch over the rail and onto the belt. With the two of us we would be rid of him in seconds, and in this darkness and men scrambling for seats, we wouldn't be seen. I saw the crusher under another single light some two hundred yards up into the tunnel. The more I looked, the more appealing it became. The memory of how I was pulled from that seat was fresh in my mind. I had the bastard now, it wouldn't be any problem at all putting him over that rail.

The car was down and within seconds I was on the way out of here, but I now had a good picture of what was down there at the bottom of the rail. As the car sped toward the top, I sat in the darkness, contemplating.

After dropping off my headlamp and the power pack, I entered the mining shack and there stood the bastard talking with one of the guards and smoking his cigarette. As I walked by, he turned and looked me in the eye with that smirk on his face. I felt the hair on the back of my neck tingle, and as I passed he said, "I beat you out again." If there were ever any doubts about what I planned to do, they vanished at that moment.

After my bath and meal, I went to my room. Lewiston was there alone. Roberts and the other men were out.

"Lewiston, it is on. If you will help me, that is great. If not, I intend to stop this crap tomorrow morning, no matter what," I stated.

"Hell, I'll help. I saw what the son-of-a-bitch did and also saw him in the shack when we came in. If he gets away with this kind of stuff, no telling where it will wind up," he replied.

Someone was at the door and we stopped talking. It was Roberts and I sure didn't want anyone else in on what was coming down.

During the day, I had trouble sleeping. Between the air raid warnings and having to get up and get in the shelter and the things going through my mind with the Englishman, I got very little rest.

When we were eating the rice and getting ready for the night shift, I saw him in a crowd of his fellow countrymen. He was waving his hands around in a boisterous manner. He forced the people around him to listen to him whether they wanted to or not. When someone tried to ignore him, he became loud and threatening. The anger rose within me, and I was unable to stay near the son-of-a-bitch.

The night went as usual. The coal fell well and we met our quota in good time. I worked the entire shift with Lewiston, planning every detail as closely as the two of us were able. I was nervous, and I hoped in a way the English beat us out, but again, I knew I would not change my mind. It had gone too far. Before he had gone more than halfway out, I knew we were the first to be finished. This was it. Lewiston was right beside me and we were the only ones in on this operation. I trusted him completely.

I found the right weapon, a large rock that I could hold in one hand. It was heavy enough and had sharp edges that would do the trick. As I slipped it inside my jacket, I gripped it hard, getting the feel of which side was the best. As I walked, I tested and rested my hold on it. It was all right. There was no turning back now. Lewiston sensed my tensions. He touched my shoulder, and when I turned I saw all was in readiness as far as he was concerned. We walked side by side until we were standing at the loading area. Standing near each other, I heard the English crew as they came on the scene. Some were making remarks about the Yank crew beating them again. I waited. The car burst from the tunnel and there was screeching from the rail as well as from the speeding belt. The son-of-a-bitch was near me. I sensed it more than saw or felt him. Staring in the dark, I made out Lewiston standing at my right. The Americans were getting ready to board as the car stopped. There was a moment of silence and then everyone was talking and crowding in against the car. I had my right hand inside my jacket and a good grip on the stone, its jagged edges cutting into my hand. Then! That large hand that I had become so familiar with took hold of my collar and as he started to jerk, I swung around and at the same time I smashed him directly in the face with all the force I could. I could feel his flesh give way as the stone sank into his face. I knew I had him solid. He was sinking before I could drop the rock. Lewiston had his shoulders and I picked up his feet and within seconds we rolled him over the railing and onto the conveyor belt. Everything was over quickly; his body was being transported away from the loading area. Without a word, I climbed inside the car, and it was on its way out of here. On the right the belt was constantly moving the coal along the same route, but I wouldn't look in that direction, afraid I would see that great hulk as we passed.

At the top, I was afraid to look at Lewiston, afraid of giving our secret away. We were in the shack and a Jap was passing out the cigarettes while another one was issuing this crew the extra smoke. This was the day for the extra bonus. It was almost as if I were being rewarded for my crime.

Ten minutes passed. Then the English crew entered the shack. They were excited as hell about something. One of them was telling the guard that the Englishman was on the loading area when they arrived from the work area and that none of them had seen him returning into the mine. As they talked one or two of them were scanning us, trying to find their lost comrade.

The other miners were now up from the mine, but the guards wouldn't let us go because of one missing man. The Jap in charge of my crew was raising hell because he couldn't go home. The overall honsho said everyone must stay until everyone had been accounted for. I had to smile at that statement. They would have a difficult time accounting for that bastard. If we had to stay here until then we would be here awhile. I had taken the extra cigarette and was smoking it. I might as well relax until the Japs were satisfied they had lost one of their prisoners. We waited. An hour passed. Then in came the Englishman. He was being helped inside by one of the day-shift honshos. He knew who bashed his face in, and I worried about what would happen next. His face was a bloody pulp and he couldn't talk, his mouth was split up so badly. Both eyes were almost closed. Apparently he wasn't completely unconscious and managed to get off the belt before he was run through the crusher. He kept trying to say something to the Japs, and they were unable to understand. Some of the British had been pushed around by this man, and only a few of them paid him any attention. Finally, someone got a stretcher and the crew picked him up and he was on his way out. Back at camp he was placed in the dispensary until he was able to talk. He identified me as his attacker, but on that morning I had witnesses that I was in another part of the mine when this unfortunate accident occurred. In a few weeks, the incident was forgotten, but from that day forward, I had absolutely no problems with him or any of them.

The cave-in

Chapter 37

It was early spring and the gardens were in full bloom. Each day, as we went to and from the mine, I watched the Japanese women and children fussing with the victory gardens. The vegetables seemed to double in size overnight. It was that, or I was so hungry for fresh vegetables I imagined they did. I knew when they were ready I would make an effort to steal something out of them.

I was still working the night shift and things were so routine now I didn't fear those small holes I had to crawl in and out of all the time. I was like the rats. If there was an opening and I needed to go in, I got on hands and knees and crawled, without even a second thought.

Pressure was being put on the honsho to increase production, and as a result the supervisor had sacrificed safety to some extent, especially with the timbers. There had been some minor cave-ins, but nothing serious. The only thing that meant anything at all was making sure the quota was met or beaten. The top honshos were the ones establishing the quota.

We were nearly three hundred yards higher into the coal field than when we first came. It was difficult to estimate how much coal had been mined from this single shaft, but we were through the main field, and where we had entered there were slabs of stone with the coal wedged between. Because of this, we followed the vein of coal, which was very thin most of the time. The digging was fast, so fast we had to bring in an extra length of the chute as well as an extra length of pipe for air every evening. This caused us to make another trip down from the face to bring in more timber.

Since my problem with the English, I had moved away from the cars and was working up in the face of the coal. On one of the days when I was right on the face assisting with the timbering, we came to the stone over the top. It was as if the stone had been broken and the other part taken away. The honsho didn't seem surprised at this, but not having done any mining before coming here, this was a strange phenomenon for me. I watched him as he pecked away at the coal along the edge of the stone, digging back about a foot, then moving across to the other side of the face and repeating the same action. He worked carefully along the edge of the roof stone, inspecting every centimeter of the face. For more than an hour he worked, sending down small bunches of coal. Then he came off the face and directed us to attach the extra piece of steel onto the chute. We also put the other piece of air pipe on and placed the screen across the end that kept the falling coal from entering the air pipe. The honsho inspected our work, then returned to the face and once again started picking away at the coal. Our people were scattered along the chute, scraping coal from the floor, getting it into the chute, sending it on its way down the long dark shaft toward the coal hopper. Then! I saw the stuff falling. It was crashing down from the face. I yelled to the men below that the coal was falling. They had been through this before, and immediately were alert for the onrush of coal. This was the first free fall for several days. The goddamned stuff rolled like a raging river down the shaft. It was falling so fast, the chute wasn't even needed. It crashed down the shaft and I saw it backing up below. The men were fighting to keep from being buried and had to make their way up the shaft because of the depth. Within only a few minutes the tunnel was filled down below and the honsho moved to the wind piping, scraping with all he had to keep it open. Still the coal continued to fall. Looking up toward where the face was, there was nothing but darkness—a great gaping hole so vast that the lights from my headlamp didn't show back. The honsho stepped back against the timbering. He could do nothing. Whatever was loose up there would fall. All we could do was hope it had a place to go.

Turning my eyes down the shaft, I watched the coal continue filling the tunnel below me as that great cavern above grew ever bigger. I was somewhere in between and as the coal slowed from up above I saw we were trapped. The entire shaft was filled solid with coal. It was more than 300 yards to the bottom level where the rest of the American crews were, and at least 250 yards to where that second-level tunnel crossed the only other escape route. In all probability, the way the coal went crashing down the chute, it took the new air pipe out in passing and most likely caved that tunnel in as well.

The coal stopped. Only trickles were coming down over that slick stone. Even the trickles sounded loud and ominous. I listened.

I could hear the air coming through the pipes. That was a relief. At least we wouldn't suffocate. No one was saying anything. Down below, some of the men were trying to extricate themselves from the coal. They were waist-deep in the stuff. I looked down and saw more than a foot of the loose stuff around me. The one thing I knew was that we were at the mercy of the people who ran the air station. There was plenty of room. It was more than fifty yards down to where the coal had closed off the tunnel. This was a very large pocket that we were trapped in and with the fresh air there wouldn't be a problem unless something else happened below us.

We left our rice and canteens at the second level, so there would be no food or water while here. That thought scared the hell out of me. It was quiet. Everyone was trying to figure out what had occurred.

I heard the supervisor yelling for us to come up where he was and suddenly everyone was talking and climbing in that direction. During the time we had been in the mine, nothing we had learned had prepared us for this, and we gathered around; each of us was waiting for guidance.

When I was near the supervisor, I could see he was rather calm, but I could read the fear in his face. Still he was the best chance we had at getting out so I listened to his every word.

He said, "I have no way of knowing how long we will be trapped here, but I want you to turn off your lamps. We may need the light later. There will be only one headlamp left on while we wait."

This made sense to me, and all the lights were switched off and put in one place. Only the light from the honsho's lamp was left on and it was placed near the timbered edge where it would shine in our direction. After some time, my eyes adjusted to this one lamp and I saw that all of the men along with the honsho were in one huddle.

When all of us were as calm as could be expected, he said he wanted to look back into the large cavern to see if by chance there might be a stream of water. I had not seen any running water in the fields before and doubted if there was any, but I respected this little fellow for daring to think there might be. He was gone for only a few minutes and returned with the word—no.

Someone said in a low tone, "We are going to die right here." Then whoever it was hushed. It was quiet once more. Each time any coal broke loose from back in the great hole and cascaded down the slick rock, I saw every head turn in that direction. There was no need for them to say anything. Each of us knew what was going through our minds. We sure as hell didn't need any more coal.

During the hours that passed, the fear of being left underground got harder to take. The honsho seemed to understand the feeling and when he heard mumbling he started talking about anything.

"All we can do is wait. If we try digging we don't have any place to get rid of the coal." The little group grew quiet at this and we waited.

The hours dragged by and there was nothing. Then! There was noise from somewhere. Everyone was deathly still. There it was again. Someone was pounding on the steel air pipe. All of us seemed to recognize where it was coming from at the same time and we were on our feet. The honsho was standing by the air pipe, and when the pounding stopped, he beat it with his pick. Again we heard the pounding. It came in very slow licks, then there was a pause and the honsho started hitting again. In a few minutes he established some sort of communication with the rescuers. When he turned facing us, he told us we were going to be found. They knew we were alive and were on the way to us.

In a mine such as this, when one is trapped in the face of the mine, there is very little he can do, because the coal that is mined has to have a gravity flow. Because of this the miner is always above the escape tunnels. By the same token, anyone rescuing a trapped miner can come in under him and with very little effort dig a rescue hole.

We were underground for nearly twelve hours before we heard the signal and then within eight hours we were found.

During this time the honsho would beat on the pipe at intervals and get their return signal. This would keep us in good spirits.

Twenty hours after the cave-in, I saw them break through. They were several yards below us and coming up through the drift along the chute as

282

they came near us. The coal was cascading down the chute and I saw the workers long before they realized they had opened the shaft.

We were free from the grave and except for the horrors of being buried alive, trapped under the earth, we were none the worse for the experience. But from that time forward, I never went below the ground that I didn't remember the day I was buried alive. Also, I noticed, the honsho took more care when he was working with the timber.

Chapter 38

Since my arrival, the only thing I had seen was along the road to and from the mine and down underground. In one way this was good. The winter was cold and inside the mine the temperature was constant. This was especially good in the afternoon when we came on shift. I was freezing when we arrived, and it was a good feeling knowing that down in the mine it would be warm. But when I had to come out in the early morning, that bitter cold would cut deep inside my lungs until I had difficulty breathing. It was because of this sudden exposure as I was making my way to the mine shack, that a sharp pain hit me in the left side of my chest. When it hit, I knew it was my bad lung, but I passed out immediately and collapsed on the spot. When I came around, I was on a stretcher being carried back to camp and to the dispensary. In camp there was no X-ray equipment and only the barest of other equipment, like a stethoscope. The doctor examined me and after my explaining that the lung had been collapsed back on Bataan, he deduced my problem was pneumonia and that I would have to remain in camp for some time. When I was considered ready to be released, I was placed on a detail on top of the ground. Fortunately, the worst of the cold was over, and there were only the spring showers. For the better part the weather was good and I had an opportunity to see what the area around camp was like. Also, there was the possibility of stealing some vegetables from one of the many gardens.

Here on top, the guards were different. For the most part they were mean as hell, and the entire detail took on a different meaning with this bunch. Out on the work detail, the guards took on a quasi-military stature. I knew they didn't belong to any military organization, yet they wore Japanese uniforms from the army. They were not allowed to carry arms. Each one of the guards had a wood sabre, and some were so much like the real thing, you couldn't tell the difference. It was very impressive to watch these people compete with one another to see how authentic they could make the sabres appear. Some went to the extent of wrapping the hilt of the weapons with special colored silk with ornaments, which made them look like the great samurai swords. Each of the guards took great pride in their handiwork.

The primary use for the wood sabres, aside from an ego trip, was for beating prisoners—especially the Americans. The guards carried these where they could be taken off easily and quickly, but they took great care not to damage their work on the hilt-end of the instruments. That is where all their prized work was and to damange that would be unheard of. Sure as hell, when one of us failed to get out the proper quota of work or if they thought we were not doing as we should, the sabre was unhooked from the belt and the victim was beaten. There were times when the honsho had done so much work on his sabre that he ordered one of his subordinates to do the dirty work with his weapon. On other occasions he would hold the sabre out of the way and use his fist. When this happened the victims learned to try and fall in such a way as to tear the goddamned thing loose from his belt, just out of spite. Anything to make the son-of-a-bitch feel embarrassed, or cause him to have to redo all his handiwork.

I had been informed that on this detail we were to build some sort of building. We were to dig the dirt back out of the side of the hill so a foundation could be poured later.

This part of Japan is very rainy during the winter and spring months and because of this we had to dig out the side of the hill far enough back that erosion wouldn't be a problem later on. This site was at the lower end of a small valley; the hill was very steep at the eastern side of the valley. We had to dig back into the hill, forming a level site for the pouring of the cement.

For the next several days a crew of forty Americans and some British prepared the site for construction. The method of earth movement was the wheelbarrow. The American crew did the digging and the British were two hundred yards down the valley spreading the dirt and making the road bed into the building area. Our guards were scattered along the route of movement, always watching for something they could slap us for or pound us with those wood sabres.

The dirt had been removed and the next thing was pouring the slab for the foundation. The Japanese had a small building erected for storing the cement that had begun arriving. At the site we built places where the cement could be mixed and poured. I knew there would be much hard labor doing it with only shovels and wheelbarrows, but that is the way we were told the work would be done.

Each day we finished small sections of the foundation, and each day we had hell slapped out of us because we hadn't done as much as the guards thought we should.

The war was closing in on Japan. The guards had been ordered to save everything, even the string from the bags. They had to be counted at the end of each working day. The bags were piled in one place and one of the guards counted them. Then the strings were counted. Twine was a good trading item in camp and at times someone would try holding out a piece of twine to mend their clothing. But now, the way the bastards were watching, it had become very dangerous to try this. There were two pieces of twine for each cement bag, so the paper sacks were watched just as closely as the string.

I kept thinking how stupid it was for this country to engage in war with the United States and all her industrial capabilities. Yet they acted as if they would lose the war if they didn't account for each and every piece of this stuff.

The days dragged on. Each day our planes could be heard in the distance. Their drone could be heard as they proceeded north. The drone of the engines caused the guards to become fidgety. They were nervous and each day this nervousness took on a different aspect. Some days we were taken to a bomb shelter and the guards would be subdued, and at other times they became angry and beat hell out of us.

The British had been formed into a detail, the Dutch into another, and the Americans into yet another group. I was sure this was no accident, but rather, by design. They wanted to demonstrate how they could force the great American military people to slave on the dirtiest details and how they could degrade and beat the people who were pounding hell out of their homeland. And by showing preferential treatment to the British, they kept the Americans and the British at one another's throats all the time—until we got back to camp and had the opportunity to talk with our British counterparts and hear how they were treated when they were on a detail. With this new knowledge, I had become more tolerant of the British and they of me.

It was sometime in the latter part of June 1945, on one of the days when the shift was storing the wheelbarrows and shovels and getting ready to go back to camp. The last piece of equipment had been stored. The honsho emerged from the shack and announced that there was one piece of string missing. He had the string in his hand, swinging his arms over his head and screaming. One of the other honshos came on the scene and had him recount the bags and then the string. One piece was missing.

The Americans were lined up in two files and then the supervisors asked, "Will the person who took the string step forward?"

No one moved. Hell, I thought. The damned thing could be anywhere. Why didn't he ask the same question of his own personnel?

Again. "Who has the string?"

No one would admit having it, or that they knew anything about the lost twine.

The son-of-a-bitch screamed and walked up and down in front of us, yelling, "It is our responsibility to keep track of the material. The other prisoners couldn't have it. They worked elsewhere."

Still, no one stepped forward. Then one of the guards started down the line. As he stepped in front of each man, he asked for the string. When there was no response, he slapped the prisoner, then moved along to the next. Soon other guards took their turn beating us until their hands were bruised and sore to the point that they couldn't bear hitting us anymore. Then! It was the wood sabres. I had been in prison camps for a long time but this was getting worse than any of the beatings we had had to endure. If a person was knocked off his feet he was made to get up and was beaten some more. Still nobody would admit to taking the twine. The guards huddled, then decided to try yet another method. I had seen this before, and as soon as we were made to separate into two groups and face one another, I knew what was in store. We would have to beat each other. The man directly in front of you would be ordered to hit you, and it was up to the guards what rank would get the first swing. After he had made his lick, the other man would then get his lick back, providing of course he was conscious. But you only got one swing. Their goddamned hands were swollen and black from beating on us and still nobody admitted taking the string. In the past the bastards got their kicks out of watching the Americans fight among themselves, and it was easy to see they were going to enjoy this. Many of us in this group had gone through this before and we had made pacts with each other. If this should happen, whoever got the first shot would hit as hard as possible, knocking the other out with the first shot. In this way, the punishment was short-lived. The only problem was we had been beaten so badly by them we were too weak to knock out our man. However, each of us did as well as we could. Whatever we did, the only thing accomplished was we were battered and beaten to the ground and nobody had come up with the missing string. When I realized where I was, I was being carried back to camp by two British soldiers who had been forced to stand by and watch this brutality take place. I was knocked out early, and when I woke I could hear the two British soldiers cursing the Japanese for what they had done. At that moment I became closer to them than at any other time. Also, I became fully aware of how the minds of the guards were working regarding the Americans and British. I recalled how I had treated some of them and I vowed this would not happen again.

I had no way of knowing how many of us had to be carried out. When I was taken to the dispensary, I was washed up and given a quick examination and told there were no broken bones, just some loose teeth and loss of blood. At the barracks I was able to get out of my bloody clothing and get into the community bath tub where I was allowed to remain as long as desired.

Beatings had become so commonplace that nobody asked how you got a black eye or swollen face. They knew the answer. They had had theirs, and they were wrapped up in their own anger at the Japs.

I couldn't eat the ration of rice that night because of my aching head and loose teeth. All I could do was stay in my little room with a pail of cold water, hoping I could get the swelling to go down. I had time to think of the day's events. That little piece of string, no more than eighteen inches long, couldn't be that damned important. Also our officers, when told of the beatings and the reason given, didn't act as though they believed we were beaten this badly over a little piece of twine. That morning I had heard what sounded like explosions. Not like bombs. They rolled across the countryside and continued for several minutes. Bombing would be one great bunch of explosions. These sounds rolled out toward us from the coastline to the east and seemed to last longer. The way the Japs had been acting caused me to think these explosions were shells from the U.S. navy. Good God! Our forces were close enough to shell Japan. That was why the bastards were so worked up. The thought caused me to smile in spite of the aches. Hell, I could take their beatings if that was the reason. When I went to refill my pail with fresh cold water, the aching in my head wasn't nearly so bad. The Japs had also taken a beating this day. Not these bastards, but somewhere they had had their tails blown off. These would get theirs soon. My day was coming. All I must do was stay alive and wait.

287

*The price of stealing
from a victory garden*

Chapter 39

It was near mid–July now, and I had been relieved from the building detail. I suppose because of the beatings I had taken from that crew. Someone saw fit to get me away from those people and under someone I hadn't worked for before.

I was once again back underground. I didn't know for sure if this change was deliberate or if it was just a toss of the coin. Hell, I could care less. Actually, it was better. I was on the day shift and it was during the day that the air raid alarms were generally sounded. Being down in the mine during the day we could get a full night's sleep while off. We were seldom rousted out at night.

Another advantage was that I had spotted some gardens near the entrance to the mine, and they had the largest cabbages I had ever seen. The only problem was that we were underground as much as thirteen hours. The honshos had increased the quota of coal. As was to be expected, we had brought it on ourselves, trying to get out of the mine early for the damned cigarettes. In effect we had gotten to be too good and they just increased the quota. We now had to stay down longer.

Each evening I went right by the garden as we returned to the mine shack. I had seen this place when it was first planted in spring and I knew even then that I would try to steal some of the vegetables when the time came.

When we got off the ginshaw, we walked up a light grade before going down a steep grade to the shack. The garden was off on the right hand side some thirty-five yards off the trail. It was partially hidden from view by small trees. There was never anyone working the ground late in the evening, so I assumed the garden was tended during the day or in the early morning before it got too hot. Also, most of the time the honsho took the lead when we got off the car and was halfway down the hill before the last man in the crew passed the garden. My plan was taking shape. All I had to do was get on the car last, then take my time getting off, giving him a chance to get out of sight down the hill. Then I would drop behind the brush and pull the cabbage. All I could do was steal it and eat as much as I could, then hide the rest for the following day or when I could manage to get back to it. I was fully aware of the consequences of being caught. Christ! It was almost as bad as killing one of them to steal from the victory garden. By now the rations had been reduced still more. The only thing we had to eat for weeks was rice with an occasional spattering of curry powder. My weight was now below one hundred and I was starved all the time. The fear of getting caught stealing vegetables was less and less important. I waited. Two days passed, then I knew this was the day I was going to get something extra, and nobody knew of my plan. This was mine and mine alone.

We were the first crew to be taken up topside, and I knew it would be some time until the miners would leave the camp. When we got off the ginshaw the Jap waited. The son-of-a-bitch. He usually went in front. Hell! I must wait. When we arrived in the shack it was as usual. The cigarette was given for our day's work. I could almost taste that raw cabbage. I waited and smoked my cigarette. Still none of the other crews came from below, so it would be some time before we left the camp. Then, the back door opened and one of the British crews started filing inside and picking up their smokes as they passed their honsho. The Japs were busy. I slipped out the back and up the steep bank. In less than a minute I was at the edge of the victory garden, and I had my cabbage spotted. I would have to expose myself to get it, so I scanned the area. No one was watching. My first thoughts were that the next crew could come out of that mine at any moment, and I sure as hell didn't want to be caught by them. It was all clear, and I grabbed that large cabbage and scampered back under the brush, stopping just long enough to get my breath. Then I started pulling the outer leaves away. Then I was down to the white cabbage and cramming it in my mouth as fast as possible. I soon slowed down and ate at a slower pace. I enjoyed that cabbage more than anything I had eaten in many, many months. I kept pulling the tender leaves off and stuffing them in my mouth. Then it happened! From somewhere out of the blue a damn Jap was standing over me with his wood sabre, and he screamed and at the same time brought the sabre down on my head. It was as if my head had been split wide open, and I heard his screams over all this. Down the hill other Japs came on the run. The son-of-a-bitch couldn't hit me fast enough. He had gone completely crazy. At that moment I was sure he was going to kill me right on the spot. I rolled from under his blows and down the side of the hill toward those coming on the run toward me. He was right behind me, swinging as fast as he could, and I was evading his blows by keeping some of the small brush between us. At the same time I was rolling toward the others. They also had their wood sabres off their belts. There was a brief break in the swinging and when I looked back up the hill I saw he had picked up the remaining part of the cabbage and was holding it above his head and screaming as loudly as he could. The others now knew what the problem was and were ready for me. I ducked the first one, then broke inside the shack, with all of them on my tail swinging and cursing. Inside were several prisoners and they also knew about the problem. The guard had the cabbage and was waving it around and screaming. The son-of-a-bitch was hysterical and everyone knew what was in store for me. For just a moment I got a break from the beating. All of them were gathered in a circle around me, talking so fast I couldn't understand anything.

The guard who caught me acted as if he should be rewarded while the others were afraid they wouldn't be recognized. But all were huddled, deciding what justice could be meted out that would be commensurate with the degree of the crime.

The camp guards lined the other men up and got ready to march them back to camp. It must have been longer than I thought since they caught me. I looked around the shack and saw it was empty. Everyone was gone except the man who caught me and the other Japanese people who worked the mine. There were four of them left.

For hours, I was beaten with wood sabres, beaten in the face with their fists, and slapped when their hands were sore. My entire body felt like a bleeding pulp. They soon realized there was little more they could do to me. They marched me back to camp.

I was aware of the distance back to camp. Also, I knew how weak I was. I wondered if I could make the trip. I was glad to have had the extra food. It had given me strength and I knew I would need everything I could muster if I was to make it back inside. My vision was hampered by the swelling. Still I trudged forward with the little bastard on my back yelling and hitting me across the calf with his sabre. I was getting tired. There was blood running down into my tennis shoes. At last, the gate was opened and I was inside. I could walk no farther, and as I slipped to the ground he turned away. It was as if I were on my own, and no longer his responsibility. I was left alone.

Minutes that seemed like hours passed, and no one came near me. Even the Japanese on the porch refused to help me. The other prisoners were too scared to come to my aid for fear they would be killed. I seemed to be regarded somewhat less than a dead dog. Darkness had fallen around me and still there was no indication that they intended to help me. I made myself get to my feet and started dragging my weary body toward the dispensary. When I stumbled through the doorway, there were two Americans, one officer and one enlisted medic, and the two of them helped me inside. They had been watching me all along but were unable to help.

They moved me inside the section of the building where people were taken when they were not expected to survive. A pan of water was brought in and the medics started washing my face with wet cloths. I felt one of them cutting at the legs of my trousers, and one of them said my legs were so swollen the clothing wouldn't come off any other way. My blood-soaked shoes were removed and I was wrapped in a quilt.

During the night, the enlisted medic came around often, washing the blood from my face and rinsing my mouth, which was still bleeding. I couldn't tell if it was from loose teeth or if there was bleeding from internal injuries.

When my mouth filled with blood, the medic forced me to rinse my mouth, then told me to swallow some of the cold water. I slipped in and out of consciousness and the only thing I knew was I was still alive. I remembered the cabbage and thought what a price for a small amount of food.

When I awoke it was daylight outside and the same medic was standing at the foot of the bed looking at me with more water. Both my legs felt

290

paralyzed and when I asked the medic to check them he said he had wrapped both legs to try to stop the bleeding. He loosened them shortly and that eased the pain.

Later that morning an American officer and one of the British commanders entered the dispensary. The two officers came in front of the bay where I was lying and looked me over for some time but said nothing. It appeared to me they were just confirming the fact that I had been beaten but was still alive. Not one word was spoken to me or to the medic.

When they had gone the American doctor examined me. He made some notes, then gave me some medicine and said that this would ease the pain. Then he was gone. It looked like the Japs had scared hell out of all of them. They were afraid they would become victims as I had. That was the last visit I had from a doctor. The enlisted medic continued coming around the bay but now the Japs ordered it locked. I was in jail inside the building and the one medic was the only person with a key.

By the end of the second day, they sent a guard around about once an hour to check on me. On the third day, they came in groups of two or three with one man in charge of the detail. He brought them in front of the cell and then they talked in Japanese about their prisoner. Some peered through at this caged animal. Some muttered about me stealing from the emperor's vegetable garden, shaking their heads as though that was the worst crime that one could be accused of. I felt like some sort of freak, and like they were just waiting until I was out so they could do the job all over again. I believed if I were given any treatment for my wounds those treating me would be punished. My God, I hoped that was what had happened. I sure as hell didn't want to believe my own people had deserted me.

For the next ten days, I was kept in the cell. I was not allowed any visitors, only the medic who brought my rice to me. Periodically, I was made to sit up and show myself to the Japanese who were being brought in.

Each day, I heard the sirens sounding the air raid signal, and I heard the prisoners as they scurried around getting down into the shelters. The Japs screamed and yelled, and off in the distance I heard that now familiar drone of the great engines of the American aircraft as they flew northward to their targets. When the sound died out in the far distance, at times I heard the low sounds of explosions; I sat and smiled. Even with the soreness in my body, I wanted to throw my head back and laugh. I knew some heathen bastard would be sent to hell on this day and for my part I could only wish it was right here in this compound. I wished one of the bombs would fall off and blow this entire compound to hell.

The swelling was gone from my eyes, but the bruised spots remained. There was a large cut under my chin that wouldn't heal, and with the beard and no water for cleaning up, it continued to bleed. My teeth once again became tight and only the soreness of a broken jaw bothered me at the time.

The one thing that pleased me was I was left alone. Only two or three Japs came around. They had stopped bringing the observers to stare at me. The others prisoners still couldn't visit.

The rice rations had been reduced to almost nothing and only once a day. My ration was brought inside the building and given to the one American medic who was allowed to see me. He brought it to the locked bamboo door and pushed the stuff under the door in a tin pan along with my drinking water, all the time being guarded. He didn't dare ask me anything or try to talk to me. If I must have something, I told him and he then got permission from the Japs before it could be delivered.

Sometime during the last part of July 1945, I was taken from the isolation cell and allowed to return to the barracks. I didn't know if the punishment was finished or if there was yet more.

There were still problems with my chest. I apparently had some broken ribs, but nothing could be done with that. The pain around my collarbone was bad. I felt it every time I turned my head.

The biggest problem was walking. The back of my legs where the son-of-a-bitch beat them with his sabre was swollen and on the left leg was a large area red from infection. I had difficulty getting trousers over it. My pants were so tight, I finally had to cut the legs off. Goddamn! If they required me to go back in the mine, I wouldn't make the march to the shack. I knew I couldn't keep pace with the British.

Sitting here all alone in the room waiting, with no one to talk to, was the lowest time since my capture. I knew the United States was closing in on Japan, and I should be in better spirits, yet the thought I might be killed at this late date depressed the hell out of me. I was at my lowest weight ever. I had been rationed rice well below normal. Everyone had had their rations reduced and anyone not able to do heavy labor got even less. I was dying of starvation alone even if I didn't have the injuries to deal with.

I made one more attempt to see the doctor. I had to try to make him see that to allow me to go underground was to send me to sure death. He might just as well tell the Japs to finish me off. He examined me closely and when finished, he informed the Japs that I should be kept inside camp, that it was physically impossible for me to do anything until my legs healed. He was able to get this point across and I was grateful. No limits were set as long as I stayed in camp. The following day I was informed that a Jap doctor insisted I be brought in front of him for examination. Only he and he alone could approve my being exempt from the mining detail. I was ushered into his office. By now the swelling had gone down somewhat. I was scared this would cause him to disagree with the recommendations of the American doctor. Still, I went in and stood in front of him.

He asked me to turn my back to him and place my leg in a chair he pushed out from the desk. Holding on to the back of the chair, I laid my leg across the seat. I saw large red areas from the knee almost down to my ankle, but the swelling was slight. He pinched the muscle and I flinched with the pain. He sneered. I wanted to knock his damn head off. I knew he was playing a game. All of a sudden and without warning, he smashed down with his fist on the sore area, and I screamed and fell to the floor unconscious.

When I came around, the pain was killing me and I couldn't stand.

Someone had picked me up and placed me in one of the bays and that same medic was working over me.

The hate inside me was eating my insides out. I was swinging away, and the face of "Donald Duck" loomed in front of me. The same desire to kill had returned. As the medic hung on, I kept screaming and seeing that face. I heard him call for help and then someone else grabbed my arms, holding me down on the floor. I knew if that doctor was here I would kill or be killed in the attempt. To hell with it. As the two men held me on the ground I heard the Japs yelling and the men scrambling to get in the shelters. Off in the distance the low drone of aircraft engines could be heard. I became quiet and listened. Listened for the sound of bombs. My God, please let one fall.

Later that afternoon I was allowed to leave the dispensary and return to my barracks. I knew one thing for certain. If this leg got worse, I would endure the pain. Never again would I allow that doctor to look at me.

I had been taken off the roster and wouldn't be required to go underground again until later. Somebody convinced the Japs I would be of no value to them as a miner. Some other type of work would have to be made available.

Moving again and the bomb—
hysteria and revenge

Chapter 40

The day shift had left camp and the night shift had bedded down for the day. Outside the barracks some Japanese guards were screaming and yelling for some prisoners to hurry. Then I heard one outside my area. He was beating on the sliding door with something. Pulling myself free from the corner where I was resting my sore legs, I asked what he wanted. Sliding the door open, he was motioning me to get my gear and report out to the guardhouse to be moved from camp.

Some time had passed since the Jap doctor hammered the back of my legs and while I could move about, there was still much pain when I walked. I had done this so many times before, I just gathered my gear, stuffed it into the canvas bag, put my arms through the straps, and was ready to leave.

Outside, I saw several other prisoners lined up, and recognized them as being injured or extremely ill. These were men who couldn't mine the coal and were of no use to the Japanese. I had been through so much over the past two weeks, I wondered if I was being moved to a prison where I would finish my sentence for that awful crime I committed by stealing one of their heads of cabbage. I didn't recognize anyone in this group that had had problems such as mine with the guards.

I looked about the compound for some of the officer personnel. There was no one out here. Then I wondered if the guards had informed the officers about us being taken from camp. From all appearances this could be some sort of special work detail. I got the feeling since we had our belongings on our backs, that this was not a labor detail but a transfer from this camp to somewhere for a specific purpose.

Outside the gate a truck was being brought up. I heard more vehicles out there. Nobody was saying anything, just looking toward the gate or searching for some indication that our officers would come and let us know what was in store for us. Nothing. The camp was quiet, and, of course, these guards weren't saying anything. No one was told anything about where we were going, or what we could expect.

I now could get a better view of this detail. Some of them had been beaten; their faces were swollen and they had cuts and bruises. Two had canes and crutches.

Then the gate opened and the men were moved in the direction of some strange guards standing near the tailgate of the trucks. As the men got to the trucks they were prodded aboard. There were three trucks for the prisoners.

When all these were loaded, a guard got in the cab and after some exchange of instructions, the trucks started moving through the small village. At the northern edge we joined another small vehicle and then we were off toward the north on what seemed like a secondary road.

When we had cleared the village, the drivers didn't waste any time. They picked up speed on the road, which was partly blacktop and in other places dirt. It was early August, and the heat had dried out the countryside and the much-used roads were dusty as hell. The drivers were moving fast enough that they were not giving the dust time to blow in their faces.

It was near noon when the trucks crossed through the pass at the summit of a mountain range. It was very high and I could see for miles into a bay, some forty miles away. We started down and were moving quickly again. Soon we were out of the pass and moving alongside a rail line. It was clear now. There was a bay far below and across the stretch of water I saw a large city. There was much industrial smoke at different places in that area, but the city could be seen rather clearly.

Our convoy continued down the mountain in the direction of the city. Before we were halfway down, the lead truck turned off the main road and we stopped in front of another compound. We waited and soon a guard came from a small gate. He was greeted by one of the other guards and he walked along the trucks and looked at us as he passed.

The new guard hollered through the gate at someone and the large gate was opened. We were ordered off the trucks and inside the new camp. Inside we were lined up for inspection and as this fellow moved along the front of us, all he could do was mutter and shake his head. I knew what he must be thinking, especially if he was expecting prisoners who would do hard labor. This bunch was not able to care for themselves, much less do any labor.

We were taken farther inside the camp and were met by other American prisoners as well as some more British. It appeared that this was a camp where prisoners were brought that were unable to work in the mines or steel mills or other details the Japs had in this part of Japan.

After we were assigned to a sleeping area, I spent half the night exchanging rumors with the men. From what I could learn, this camp was a subcamp for all other prison camps in southern Japan, a place they brought prisoners when they were unable to perform the details inside their camp. This was some sort of marshaling yard where coal from the mining camps was brought in, then transferred onto coal cars and shipped throughout Japan.

Someone here had learned from a Japanese newspaper that the Philippines had been retaken. Also, the men had information of other islands near Japan that were either under attack or had been taken by our forces. I was much interested in the Philippines, so by searching around and inquiring, I learned the Americans were in there sometime around the last of 1944 or the first of 1945. This was the first solid evidence of the war in that area since I left there in October. I was sure the United States was near when I left. That was what made me feel so depressed when standing on the pier at Manila and watching the long line of Americans boarding that ship. I just knew if

295

I could have remained behind a few days, I would have been liberated. Damn! What a thought to remember! I kept searching. I wanted all the information I could get. It seemed we had a man who could translate Japanese into English and some of our people were stealing newspapers from the Japs and smuggling and circulating them about camp. If we were on detail outside the wall and saw a newspaper, we were to steal it. Anything that was printed would be smuggled inside.

The following morning, I heard about places I had never heard before. Places like Okinawa, and an island named Iwo Jima. The Japanese papers had been filled about a great victory by the Japanese army on that island. From a map that had been smuggled inside, we saw that it was a little dot in the middle of the ocean only a short distance from where we were. When I saw how close it was by comparing the distance from there to the Philippines and the distance to the island of Kyushu, the southernmost main island, it could be seen that the United States was right in Japan's front yard.

In the newspapers, I found it very interesting how they reported how many ships they had sunk or how many American airplanes they had shot down in a certain area, but each place, as I found it on our map, was closer to the Japanese mainland. Hell, I didn't give a damn about their claims about U.S. losses. As long as the place where they were reporting about was closer to Japan, I could care less. But it didn't take much imagination for me to figure out that this news was for the benefit of the hometown folk. The bastards were losing the war. Liberation was getting closer and closer. I only prayed that I would survive long enough to watch these people go down.

The one thing that bothered me about the situation was how the war was coming so near the end and yet the bastards were becoming meaner as the days passed. Hell, the way I was beaten at the mine, one would think the war was going on forever. Then again, I recalled their fanaticism on Bataan, how they would charge right into our machine guns to sure death. I assumed that their government had been able to do the same to the people here. They were prepared to fight to their death when the Americans finally did attempt to land on their homeland. I tried thinking how I would react when it became apparent the United States was on the mainland of Japan. "Where will I go? How can I hide from these people long enough for our forces to get inside the camp?" I wondered how the Americans made out in the Philippines when they were retaken. Nobody seemed to have any information on the prisoners there. There must have been some prisoners left. The Japanese couldn't have gotten everyone out before the takeover. Then again, they could have gone into the hills. Here there was no place to hide. I didn't trust the civilians any more than I trusted the military. If anything happened, I was on my own. With all this running through my mind, I had very little confidence that any of us would survive when that invasion started. But, God, what a sight it would be! I imagined being able to see our fighting men come aboard this place, taking the people prisoners. When they resist, they will be killed on the spot. If there was only some way I could survive to see this—see the looks on their damn faces when they realized they had lost.

It was quiet. Not even the sounds of the Japanese guards could be heard. I curled up on the floor with my thoughts. I recalled those stories about that officer in command of the camp. God, how I hated that son-of-a-bitch. The way he accounted for the men when they died or were killed. It was always the same. "Died of pneumonia." It made no difference if one was trampled to death by the guards or died from injuries, it was always the same. I wanted more than anything to watch that Jap when the Americans swept down into the camp and took him prisoner. I would like to get ahead of them and when they opened the gate, I would like to report that he had "died of pneumonia" as so many of the prisoners had. Why was I moved out of that camp so suddenly? I couldn't get the memory of that camp from my mind. The normal thing would have been to let me die or have me killed. That would have me out of the picture. I wouldn't have been able to tell anyone what had happened to me. That was what I believed they were going to do with me as I was loaded on that truck and brought here. Still I was alive. There wasn't any indication that I was to be punished further. The last thoughts on my mind before dropping off to sleep were how it would be when the big gate swung open and the United States army swept through.

I slept well that night, but was awakened early by the loud screams of the guards. They were running through the buildings much like they had done since my arrival in Japan. Everyone was hustled outside and made to form up in groups as the guards counted off the ranks. When all were accounted for we were dismissed, then told to draw our morning ration of rice before being assigned to work detail.

A large number of prisoners were taken out the main gate to a detail. I had come to believe that this was nothing more than an extension of the mining operation. The men were in the shipping end of the coal that was being mined by other prisoners throughout this part of Japan.

Everywhere I looked I saw rail cars. Down on the northern side of the camp was a very high fence. We were so high in the mountain I could see down toward the waterway. There was an opening in the trees below the camp and some rail cars were in that area. Some were being moved in the marshaling yard in that direction. On the eastern side, there was much smoke and at times the sounds of train whistles. The detail left in that direction. North and east a half-mile away I saw mountains of loose coal, and there were some cranes sticking into the air above the fence.

When the men had been taken outside, I was left under the control of one of the guards. I was told I would be required to work in the camp digging the bomb shelters deeper. I was down in one of the shelters digging when the siren went off. Within minutes everyone in camp was swarming down into these death traps. The work had stopped. All we could do was sit and wait. There wasn't any mud and it was actually cooler than up on the surface. I listened for the sound of engines, but nothing. The all clear siren sounded and we were allowed up on the surface.

I went back to digging detail. In the afternoon the sirens again sounded a warning and back into the pits we went. This time I heard the engines and

297

after we had been below for a few minutes I heard that low roll of explosions. I knew that somewhere the Japs were being blown to hell.

I was once again on the surface and was able to see. There was much smoke off to the northeast of camp. It was rising high over the mountain but I was not able to tell if the fire was from the bombs.

The following morning, it was much the same, except this time after the outside detail had left, I was singled out by one of the camp guards and told that he wanted me to be the camp barber. The man who was on this detail had been taken back to his main camp, and there were some Japanese guards who needed haircuts. I had no experience at this, but the Japs didn't need barbers. If one could shear a sheep, he could be the camp barber as far as they were concerned. You just got them in the chair and started cutting and when there was no more hair you were finished.

It was sometime in the latter part of July or early August 1945. I had lost track of dates. But each day as I clipped away at someone, they told me how they had shot down our bombers and that it wouldn't be long now until we wouldn't have enough planes to bomb them. But I had come to understand this mentality very well. I got the feeling there were many face-saving stories in their conversations. Still, the more they talked about the war the more I was convinced that if there was an invasion there was little or no chance at all any of us would be rescued. They were so angered by the Americans bombing their homeland, I didn't see how they would ever let us go.

During the day I stood around the barber chair and listened for anything that sounded like bombs or shells exploding. When there was more than one Jap at the barber chair, I listened for anything they might say that I could understand. If I got anything I relayed it to our news people and they put this with what they gleaned from all their other sources. We got more information than at any other camp I had been at.

Their radios were going all the time, and when there was an interruption in the regular programs everyone stopped what they were doing and listened. I now had an opportunity and I listened, trying to understand what was being said by their government. I couldn't get much, but there were times when I understood. They were telling how their brave soldiers were fighting off the enemy and how each and every Japanese should be willing to sacrifice everything in defense of the homeland. It was after one of these pep talks that I dreaded seeing them coming toward me. Hell, I could read their faces now, and I knew that unless I was very fortunate, there would be another slapping.

All the swelling had gone from the beating taken back at the main camp. I hadn't been beaten here around my face, just slapped alongside the head or beaten across the back. Even that large cut under my chin had healed. My broken jaw still hurt as well as those places on my legs, but for the most part, I looked much better than when I came. I dragged one leg behind me when I walked, otherwise I was improving. There were still some large red spots on my left leg and when I touched them they burned like fire and sharp pains ran up into my body at the slightest touch to these areas. But I'd be damned

298

if I'd see another of those sadistic doctors. They could all go to hell. There wasn't any hard work details for me at the moment. All I did was cut hair, and I could stand on my right leg and do that.

On the morning of August 6, 1945, I had finished my rice and had gone to the end of the barracks where the barber chair was located. I waited for the guards to come for their haircuts. There was a rather large tree here and the chair had been set up under this some thirty feet away from the east end of the barracks. My first customer sat down and I clipped some of his hair. Just before he sat down there had been a large number of heavy aircraft going by far off to the east. We could hear them but couldn't see them. We knew there were many of them and they had passed in that direction for quite some time before this bastard had sat down. Over toward that large city across the waterway some forty miles away, the sun was shining but there were some spotty clouds. East of us toward where the planes had gone, there was a rain squall, but other than that, everything was normal. The synchronized sounds of the bombers had died out in the distance. I knew they had to be American bombers by that familiar sound. They were on their way north toward Tokyo, I was hoping. I wondered why with all those planes in the air we had not been ordered into the bomb shelters. Always before in the main camp, if a plane got within hearing distance, we had to get into the shelter. Also, since I had been here, we had been in them even when there were no sounds. I finished cutting his hair and we stood, watching the high clouds and that rain squall off in the distance. Another Jap arrived and the two of them talked as I cleaned the tools and waited for him to get in the chair. As I was doing this, there was the sound of a lone aircraft somewhere, but it was so high I couldn't seem to locate exactly where it was. The two Japs were craning their necks trying to locate it. It sounded as if it was east of us but was closing toward that city across the waterway. The engine noise was barely audible now and the guard sat down for his haircut. It was as if they dismissed this aircraft as one of their own. I had become familiar with that drone, and knew that was one of the United States bombers. Still, I didn't understand why it would be flying alone. If there were any other planes, they were so high or so far away, I couldn't see or hear them. This one was a loner. The guard started talking now. He was kidding me.

"The Japanese gunners have shot down all those planes that went over earlier. That was all that is left."

I said, "Yes, I suppose you are right."

Goddamn this bastard. I'd like to slit his damn throat.

"Very soon now, America won't have any planes left. Then the Japanese Imperial army will win the war," he gloated.

As the anger ran through me, I had to control myself to keep from gouging him in the head with the clippers.

Several minutes passed. Then I heard the bomber again. His engines were roaring. There was something wrong. I had heard more than enough of the aircraft engines now and I knew that wasn't normal. He seemed to be pulling away from something. I scanned the sky for fighter planes. There weren't any that I could see. The plane sounded like it was breaking up. I glanced at the two Japs and they were looking for the plane. I couldn't see anything, so I looked back toward the city across the waterway some forty miles away and there it was! The plane had dropped its load on that city. Looking back in that direction where I had last heard the plane, there was nothing. Either he had passed from my hearing range or had gone into the ground. When I returned my eyes to the city where I saw the puff of smoke, what I had originally identified as the point of impact was gone. That smoke had scattered out in all directions and there were many red streaks running through the smoke. From here it appeared as fire, yet the colors were not as bright as fire. There were red, orange, and a tinge of blue as the smoke rose from the center of the area. From here one could see the entire city and that bomb was blasting hell out of things. I had seen bombs falling in places far away before and even though I had no idea how far that was from here, I knew this was one of the biggest explosions I had ever seen. The smoke-like stuff kept spreading out at ground level and at the same time there was something in the center that started rising higher and higher. I had become so entranced with the way the fire and smoke were merging and riffling out toward me that I couldn't take my eyes off it. That Jap I had been talking with was now looking in that direction. I watched him and the riffling effects of the smoke. I saw he had his mouth wide open and his face was white as hell. He and I both realized this was no ordinary explosion. But what? As the smoke got higher, it partially blacked out from sight the riffling effect and the orange and red streaks were high in the air and seemed like lightning crashing through the black smoke. Down on the water I saw something like the heat devils I had seen on the great American deserts. They were dancing where the sun was glistening on the water surface. The smoke was now higher than the mountain and spiraling off east from us. The fire was near the ground and still crashing through the smoke cloud at lower levels. The smoke, high in the clouds, was swirling about but I couldn't see any of that fire, only a mixture of extremely black smoke and a white or steam-like portion. Still it swirled about as if there was much wind in it. I once again stared at the heat devils coming our way. I knew that not more than a few seconds had passed. I couldn't understand how one plane could do this. That heat wave was now coming directly at me, and I noticed the Jap guard nearest me was seeing the same thing and was scared. His face was ashen. The open area in front of us had a queer-looking tinge to it. The three of us fell face downward onto the ground as this unknown phenomenon seemed determined to absorb us. I waited for what seemed like an eternity. Then there were hot winds blowing over me. I heard something that sounded like a swishing sound in the tree over me, but I was afraid to raise my head for fear of what might be going on. I remembered the bomb shelter and wished I was in it. For the first time in a very long time I wished I had something over my head. In the past, when I was underground in the bomb shelters, I wanted out. I could feel the roofs caving in on me. But this fear was strange. I would like to be under something. The swishing noises were gone. It was very quiet. When I raised my head, I had problems getting oxygen. There was adequate air but it didn't seem like I could get enough inside my lungs. I tried getting up but couldn't. Then I felt more heat and fell back with my face in the dirt. I knew I had never been in anything such as this. When I was once again on my feet and looked across the waterway, I saw the entire city in flames and smoke everywhere I looked. As it settled down into the valley below, the city was barely visible. Looking about for the guards, I found they were nowhere to be seen. All the guards were outside and looking in the direction of that city. They were chattering like magpies and from what I saw, they didn't have the slightest idea what had occurred over there. They were as scared as I was. This time it was plain they had no knowledge of the true meaning of that explosion.

That smoke was so high now one had difficulty seeing the top. That white, grayish-black smoke mushroomed at three different levels and was drifting away from camp and into the interior of the land mass north and east of the city. If that aircraft went down, I couldn't see any smoke in that direction. When I looked at the city and thought about that one aircraft I couldn't help but wonder how one lonely plane could carry enough bombs to cause that kind of destruction. They must have hit an ammunition factory. That was the only thing I could think of that would blow up an entire city. Whatever it was, it sure had the Japs screwed up. None of them were near us. They were all down below the guard shack. Some of them had binoculars and were focused on the city. Perhaps this would keep them quiet for a while.

Across the valley where the city was, there was nothing but smoke. Any fire was blacked out by the smoke that had drifted in this direction. Not only was it out over the water but the hills in back of the city were covered and could barely be seen. Here in this area, there was something. I couldn't tell if it was smoke or clouds but the sun had been blacked out as well.

I couldn't think of anything I'd rather see than that city being burned to hell. I remembered back there when the ships were being bombed how good it felt to see the American bombers and hear those explosions from our shells. Since I had been captured back in 1942, the only thing I had seen was the Japanese war machine steamrolling over everything in front of it. Now I was witnessing them getting their asses blown off. The bastards were now losing the war, and I was getting the opportunity to watch it happen. God-damn! This was something. Whatever happened over there was the hardest blow I had ever seen. My eyes were glued to that spot where the fire was.

Some of the prisoners in camp had gathered around the chair and were taking in the scene. As they did, they also speculated as to what it all meant, what the damn thing was that had blown up over there. None of us could have guessed at that time that we had witnessed an event that would change forever the course of history and mankind. This was the bombing of Hiroshima, and none of us had the slightest idea what it was. Some of the men were babbling about the earth shaking during the bombing, but because the city was so far away, we all agreed the earth shaking was probably an earthquake that just happened at the same time as the explosion. "Hell!" I heard someone say, "I didn't even hear an explosion." This sure as hell was a weird time for most of us.

Looking back through the barracks area there were some things that could be attributed to the explosion, or the shaking of the earth, but then again, I had been here only a short time and those things could have been here all along and I wouldn't have noticed. At the present I was looking for signs of damage. I really wanted to see something that had happened that I could say for sure was caused by that bomber. One thing was certain. The Jap guards sure as hell were shook up. They were the quietest I had ever seen any of them since the start of the war. Every one of them were below the guardhouse, looking at that city. The main gate opened and someone drove a vehicle through. An officer from the Jap army dismounted and entered the commander's quarters. He stayed in there for some time and then all the guards were called into a group where they were addressed by this officer. I couldn't understand what was being said, but all the time he talked, the guards stood and shook their heads.

By the middle of the afternoon the details had all been brought into camp. A strange thing to happen to any work detail. As they were released inside the camp, they were told there would be no more work details until further notice, that we must remain in camp until orders were received from higher authority. I had a strange feeling that there would be no more details. I couldn't explain it, nor did I understand why I felt this way. The guards were much subdued as well as very confused. I knew something very big was going on. As for me since the bombings had increased, and the news of the war efforts south of here, all I had on my mind was, how in hell could I get away from here and back with the invasion force before someone killed me when it happened. I knew damn well it wasn't going to be long.

From outside the fence, I heard radios blasting away and the natives scurrying about from house to house, but still I couldn't make out what was going on.

The evening rice was ready for rationing and there wasn't a Jap anywhere. Since I had been here, there was always at least one of them in the kitchen area. They were all in their building and at the moment out of sight.

As night fell around us, we saw the fire from the city across the way. Nobody was able to sleep. Instead, we gathered into small groups and talked and speculated. In the darkness the fire showed up that area much more clearly than daylight. I heard someone saying, "Hell, with a fire like that, I would bet that most of their fire equipment was destroyed during the explosion and anything they had left couldn't handle that big a blaze. I once worked for a city fire department and I know that is one hot son-of-a-bitch."

At last I was overcome by the day's events and went to sleep. I left the group where I had sat for hours and my last thoughts were about that red glow in the north.

It was quiet as I tossed about and outside the walls I still heard people

302

scurrying about from place to place, with radios blazing loudly. They also were having problems sleeping.

Morning came and there were no guards yelling for us to get up. We were left alone.

I picked up my mess kit and headed for the kitchen for rice. When I left the barracks, I turned toward the city. The fire was still going strong, and the smoke from that area made the city almost invisible from this vantage point. When I breathed, there was so much smoke, it was choking me. I saw the water way down below. There were no fishing boats. That part of the water was clear. All there was over that way was smoke.

When I arrived at the mess building, everyone was wondering why they had not been alerted for the work detail. When I finished my ration of rice, I walked about the camp, which had been left in our hands as far as I could tell. There were Japs but they were keeping to themselves. Walking near the guardhouse, I saw some of them and that look on their faces said something. I had never seen anyone as subdued as these people were. Yesterday morning they were the most arrogant bunch of people I had ever known, and now they looked like whipped dogs. I was afraid to hope that this time it was the real thing, that the war was fast coming to a close. The one thing I didn't think I could stand was another letdown.

The guard that was in the chair when the bomb dropped walked from the guardhouse. Before he went inside the other building I stopped him and asked, "What has happened over there? It isn't like the other alerts."

"The Americans are using big bombs that not only explode, but they contain poison gas," he replied.

"You are crazy as hell. The United States wouldn't use gas. They don't need to. They will knock the cities out without that," I said.

"Just the same, they have dropped gas on Hiroshima, and it has killed everything within ten miles."

I became real scared now. I knew the United States hadn't used poison gas, but I also knew the Japanese, and I believed they were sure the invasion was at hand, and they were preparing the people for that eventuality. They wanted to create the impression that the enemy would use anything, that their lives would be lost if they allowed the enemy on their homeland. I was sure of this. I also knew that we, as prisoners, were as good as dead when the invasion came. It was just a matter of time.

The man was glaring at me in such a way that I wanted to get away from him. I turned and quickly got away from this part of the camp.

When I was out of sight, I found one of the British officers and related what the guard had just told me. Also, I let him know what I felt was the reasoning behind spreading this kind of rumor.

All I could think of was I hadn't survived all that hell for these months just to die in this spot. Damn! I wished I was back in the main camp. Had it not been for that head of cabbage I wouldn't be here with no place to go if the Americans invaded Japan. I had made plans where I could go back there. Here I hadn't had long enough to plan anything. I couldn't figure out anything I could do. I was at the mercy of the guards, at least for the time being.

All day long I avoided the guards as I would the plague. When I saw one step outside the building, I slipped out of sight. One could almost feel the tension among the prisoners as the day dragged on.

By nightfall, I got the feeling the guards would as soon break out of here also. They didn't seem to want anything to do with us and continued to keep in their own area. I took advantage of this and as soon as the sun was down I moved along the back fence trying the boards. I wanted to find one that I could open just in case one the bastards went crazy and wanted to kill someone.

At last, I was exhausted from the pressures of the day, and when I entered my sleeping area, I no more than lay my head down than I was asleep. I slept the entire night without waking.

Near mid-morning on August 8, 1945, I heard several trucks outside camp. Within an hour we were loaded. This camp was empty. I looked back through the main gate and there wasn't anything. Even the Japs were gone.

Only a few Japanese were out here, and they were receiving instructions from an officer. Soon the trucks were being moved out, not all at the same time nor were they going to the same place. It would appear we had been loaded according to the camp we came in from and were being sent back to that camp.

There was only one guard with each bunch of prisoners and he was in the lead vehicle. We hadn't been gone more than fifteen minutes when I started seeing familiar spots that I saw on the way in. This was it. We were being taken back to our respective camps. No one was talking in the back of the truck. I was the most confused. Nothing I had been thinking was taking place. I knew the war was over, but still I was under Japanese control and didn't have the slightest idea what was happening.

It was near noon when we stopped at the front gate of the main camp and were unloaded. Inside people were moving about, excited as hell over the events of the past three days. They had heard about Hiroshima and there were stories about the city of Nagasaki somewhere down south being blown up. They heard that other cities were going to be hit with these big bombs.

Here in the main camp, the officers had the place much more organized than the subcamp. These officers seemed to know that something was going to happen and were making every effort possible to be ready when it did.

After I was told where I would sleep, I started trying to find out what information these people had gleaned out of the Japanese that we hadn't heard.

The fence along the northern side of camp was very high. The homes of the people had been constructed within five feet of that fence, so by getting onto the second floor of the barracks, we could observe some of their activities and overhear some of their conversations.

My room was next to this fence and for the next several hours I listened.

304

Damn! They were excited about things. Their radios were blasting away everywhere, but I couldn't make out what the stations were telling the people, only that there were bulletins coming in all the time.

With the knowledge I had about Hiroshima plus this new news about that city down south, I was able to understand enough of what was coming over those radios to know there had been many Japanese killed in those two cities. It had had an impact on each and every one of the people out there. And with the threat of more cities being hit, the people were more frightened than I had ever seen them. The rumor about gas had many of the prisoners frightened. Like me, they felt that the Japanese government was preparing their people for the invasion. It didn't matter how much we tried to convince them that the United States would not drop chemicals. They continued spreading this story.

Sometime near the middle of August 1945, I was listening to the people outside the fence. Their radios were still loud. Each time something special came over the airways, the civilians ran about telling everyone in earshot what they heard. They didn't try keeping the noise down. It was as if they didn't care if we heard what was being said or not. On this day, I heard something that I was afraid to believe, but they kept repeating it all along the line of building. "The war is over and there will be no invasion." Over and over this same message was relayed from house to house and to everyone in the street. I took the steps at the end of the barracks two at a time, getting up where I could see them and hear better. I refused to believe my ears and wanted to be sure of what I was hearing. Again. "The war is over and there will be no invasion." This time I heard them mention the emperor. They were telling their neighbors that the emperor had announced that the war was over and there would be no invasion. This message had become somewhat hysterical as it was being relayed. Someone near the fence hollered at no one in particular that the war was over. Then I heard it across the way behind the buildings. At the same time there were hundreds of radios going inside those homes.

I couldn't bring myself around to tell anyone what I believed I had overheard, and for the next half-hour I sat and listened. That message never stopped. I heard it passed along out through the village until it was barely audible. In some of the voices I detected dismay, in others joy. There seemed to be much joy in the voices of the women, while the group of quasi-military personnel were much less happy about this information.

The ranking American officer in the camp slept on the second floor at the opposite end of the barracks. All the fuss out there and my not knowing what to make of it was getting to me. I couldn't wait any longer. I had to speak with someone about this. I started toward this officer's room, armed with all I had heard over the last half-hour.

Entering his room, I saw he was also listening to those voices over the wall.

"Captain, what do you hear over there?" I asked.

"I think they are passing the word that the war is over," he replied.

"I heard the same thing but I couldn't believe what I was hearing," I said.

"Believe it. It is over," he exclaimed.

He continued to look over the wall and listen. I didn't want to disturb his thoughts, so I stood beside him saying nothing. Then, almost under his breath, I heard him repeat, "Finally it is over." This officer seemed very much occupied with his thoughts and this turn of events, but he didn't seem at all surprised. I could hardly hold myself together. I had been mistreated by these people for such a long time and now to hear that the war was over and that there would be no invasion caused a shiver over my entire body. Yet this officer repeated exactly that. I had been built up in this way before only to have my hopes shattered. I just couldn't allow myself to believe that this was it.

"Captain, what do you make of that rumor about the United States using gas on these people?" I asked.

"You and I both know better than that," he said.

"Do you know what that bomb was in the city across the mountain?"

"I don't know what it was, but it sure as hell wasn't a chemical bomb."

"It was different from anything I have ever seen," I explained.

"My guess would be, the United States has split the atom," said the captain.

"What the hell is splitting the atom?" I asked.

"Before the war started, there was some speculation in limited circles about efforts to split the atom and create a bomb of sorts," he said.

"I don't see how anything could cause that much fire at one time," I exclaimed.

"I can't explain what it means. I don't have enough information about it myself. I only remember talk of the efforts being considered," he said.

I assumed this officer knew what he was talking about and because of his background education, he certainly would know more than I what had happened. I accepted his explanation about atomic explosions as fact and certainly more plausible than chemical warfare. There was something about this explanation that relieved my fears about the rumor.

When I left the captain's room, I still had problems with his statement about splitting something called an atom and, in doing so, creating a bomb. The only thing I remembered about an atom was that it is the smallest object known to man. How in hell could anyone make a bomb out of something that small? It was more than I could comprehend. I was more confused now than when I entered his room. At least he had heard the same thing I believed I heard. The greatest thing I had going for me at the moment was that if the Japanese surrendered before the Americans invaded, there was an excellent chance of being liberated and not being killed by the people who lived around this camp.

It was totally dark now. The time had gone by without my realizing it. I kept thinking about what I had heard.

I recalled, back in the islands, how this kind of rumor would bring on fantasizing about how it would be when the Americans came through the gate, what I would do when I was sure I was free. I didn't feel this now. I would rather get some sleep. Wait until tomorrow, see what that brought. Sleep, however, was impossible. The people over the fence kept yelling at each other as they had all afternoon, and I kept trying to understand what they were saying. I found myself attempting to separate their conversations from my thoughts. All I heard was the same phrase, "The war is over and no invasion." That was mixed with the other things they were telling each other but I could only make out that single phrase. I wanted this thing to be over so much, I supposed that was all I wanted to understand and at the same time was afraid to believe. Goddamn, I remembered the rumors back in 1942, even before the surrender of Bataan, about there being hundreds of airplanes and thousands of troops on the way and then that god-awful feeling when they didn't arrive. Could this be another of those? I couldn't allow another disappointment such as that in my life. There were rumors in the prison camps in the Philippines about how the United States had landed in some of the islands down south and that the army would be there any day, and we would be free. Nothing happened. Then there would be the depressions and that feeling of being deserted by my government. I remembered that solemn promise by General MacArthur, "I shall return," which never materialized. How in hell could I believe this? Especially when this great revelation had been revealed in such a matter-of-fact way. Had there been gunfire or some military persons entering the camp bringing the news it would be different. This way, Hell, I couldn't believe it.

I closed my eyes once more and tried to get to sleep. Outside the building some British personnel were talking. They had heard the Japanese talking over the wall. They were confused. Hell, they had less information than I had. At least I saw the city over the mountain burning. These people for the most part, didn't even have that much. I listened and detected the doubts in their voices. One of them was saying, "Recall another time when we had freedom in our grasp and had it snatched away. There is no way I can believe the war is over." I could sure understand that.

Try as I might, I couldn't sleep, so I gave up and once again made my way back to the captain's room. As I looked through the open door it was as if he hadn't moved from the open window. I was reluctant to bother him in his deep thoughts, but he sensed my presence and bade me enter. I told him I wasn't able to sleep because of his explanation about the bomb and that yelling over in the village. He nodded in understanding.

"Sergeant, I assure you this war is over. It is only a matter of time until all of us will be out of these prisons."

"I understand what you are trying to tell me, but I sure have a problem with it," I said.

"I understand, but since you have been gone, I have had time to sort things out myself and I would like to ask you not to tell the others in the camp what I have said, at least not now. I keep thinking those Japanese out there have the guns and should our people think the war is over and take things

307

into their own hands, some of them could get killed very easily. With this war being over and all of them so near liberation, it would be a shame for someone to be killed now. Also, it isn't beyond them to make a suicide run on us with them not knowing what has happened. We, who have survived thus far, are well advised to use caution at this stage of the game. There will be ample time for raising hell when this mess is cleared up and all of us know exactly what is going on," he explained.

"I understand what you mean, and I won't talk of this with anyone," I assured him.

"I keep thinking that the Japanese have been in a very long war with the United States and have been made to believe that they would win. It is going to be difficult for them to accept this. I don't give a damn about them and that problem, but I do care what happens to the men in this camp." He continued talking as if I wasn't in the room. "I know that you have been aware that your chances of being killed by these people if the United States had to invade their homeland was almost sure. With this thing being as it is, that has changed. I think if we will be extremely careful, there is a good chance of getting out of here alive. On the other hand, if word gets around that the war is over with these guards still having their weapons, someone could go off half-crazy and get themselves killed as well as get a lot of others murdered."

I started to understand his thinking and as I left the room. I once again assured him that I would keep quiet. His parting words were: "There is every good reason for us to believe the war is over but there are many people out there over that wall who will not believe they have lost and are completely committed to fight the enemies of their country till death."

During the night, word leaked. About three in the morning, it seemed as if the entire prison camp population was out in the compound. Even the British were yelling and throwing things at the buildings. Some were screaming insults at the Japanese guards. In this building, I heard things being thrown through the walls. The straw windows didn't even slow the stuff down. I opened my window and saw bedding all over the yard outside. I remembered the winter when I worried about tearing holes in that thin stuff and now these men were throwing everything they had through the walls and out the thin windows. I knew there wasn't anything that anyone could do. The situation was out of control. I closed the window and went back to my quilt remembering the warning from the captain earlier. I refused to be drawn into this mess. I had been lost inside the prison system for so long, I was afraid to do anything. I wouldn't know what to do if a guard wasn't looking down my neck all the time, so with the warning I got from the senior officer in the camp, I was scared for these men.

The rampage continued for what seemed like hours and I was not able to sleep the entire night. There were times when I thought I heard Japanese voices yelling at the men in the mob, but had not heard anything that sounded like rifle fire. The yelling and crashing kept up until daylight. I hoped the captain didn't think I had anything to do with this. I never said a thing about

308

what he told me, but the riot started long after I left the room. For a minute or so I worried about that, then there was more crashing near me. Someone had thrown something through the wall near me. I waited and listened. It was quiet now and I saw the sun shining through the window in my room. They were still intact.

When I could stand it no longer, I got out from under the quilt and ventured outside my room and down the walkway toward the door nearest the guard shack. Standing back inside the barracks and looking out into the compound, I saw a few prisoners down that way. They were bunched into a small group but there were no Japanese guards to be seen. They were either gone or had locked themselves inside their building. I waited for a full minute before venturing outside. It was comparatively quiet now. Back toward the mess building was a large number of prisoners, both American and British. They also were in small groups laughing and talking among themselves. I had expected to see some guards with bayonets but there were none anywhere. Back toward the Japanese officers' building and office was one of the junior American officers with several American prisoners. He was mad as hell and determined to raise hell with the Japs. I again remembered what the captain said last evening and went in that direction thinking, perhaps there had been a change as to what was going to happen. I walked through bedding and clothing that had been strewn all over the place until I was within hearing range of what was going on. This officer was telling the men with him, "I don't give a damn what they said, I am going in there and get that son-of-a-bitch and if necessary kill him. Is there anyone here who will go with me?"

I could see this officer was not going to stand around and let this opportunity slip by, so when he asked if I would join him and help him talk to the Japanese commandant, I said yes. This younger officer knew that I had some ability to talk to the Japanese and he didn't want our regular interpreters with him because he thought they were on the side of the more conservative officers in camp. At this time being conservative wasn't on this officer's mind. Revenge was more to his liking.

When he asked, I assured him that I would do anything he felt needed to be done. I, at the moment, believed that with an American officer with me, telling me what I should do, made everything I decided to do more official. Also there was a degree of safety being under his command. Even though I was convinced the senior officer was right in his judgment, I was in a rush to let the Japanese know that we knew the war was over and that they had lost and would soon be the prisoners and we the captors. So with this conflicting thought running through my mind, I took the route most appealing to me at the moment. That route was to kill the bastards if they so much as looked the wrong way. I would like to kill this one more than anything I could think of, even if it meant taking chances. I had been humiliated by them for so long, I would do anything at the moment for revenge.

With all these thoughts I joined this officer and several other prisoners.

We were at the bottom of the steps leading into the quarters of the Japanese commandant. Just as I reached for the door it opened, and there he stood. It was as if he was waiting for us. In back of us I heard more crashing against the walls of the buildings and that son-of-a-bitch was staring in that direction. For a moment a strange fear rushed over me. I had no idea what he would do. I had been subservient to these people so long, just the sight of him standing there with that sabre on his belt scared the hell out of me. I couldn't stop. It was in motion now and if I was to be killed, so be it. I stepped into the entranceway and felt the officer in charge of us at my side. Damn! I had dreamed of this moment, what it would mean to me. Now it was at hand. I felt myself shaking from head to foot. What if I should awake and find this a dream? What had I done in my sleep? That son-of-a-bitch sure as hell wasn't a dream. There he was standing right in front of me.

The captain stepped in front of him with an air of confidence. This helped some of my fear subside. That short distance closed between them and they were now face to face. The Jap backed inside the building and the two of them were standing under a very bright light.

The commandant asked, "What do you want and where is your senior officer?"

"I don't know where he is nor do I give a damn," he answered.

"Captain, your men are tearing the place apart and you stand here looking at me. What do you want?"

"You know what has happened. You know the war is over and neither you nor any of your people have let us know anything," said the captain.

I saw the face of the American captain as it started turning red with anger. He was nearly hysterical. Both he and the commandant were screaming at each other and neither could understand the other. I also noticed the little bastard was scared at this sudden change of events. I didn't speak enough Japanese to translate all that was being said, making the situation even more dangerous. After this shouting match had slowed, the captain turned and told me to tell him once more that the war was over. I did as told, speaking slowly and making sure he understood exactly what the captain was saying. As I spoke this time the Jap commander's face turned white, then again there was that angry look. Our captain saw this and said, "Tell him he is to remain inside the building. I don't want to see him or his guards again."

By the time I got this message across, he had regained some of his composure. He said, "I have heard the rumor about the war being over, but as yet I have no official information from my superiors."

I relayed this information and then it was the captain's turn for anger. He pointed his finger in the Jap's face and shouted, "I don't give a damn about official notice. This war is over. You know it and the sooner you understand the full meaning of that the better off all of us will be and that includes you."

The conversation was over and without another word the captain spun away and as one the entire group moved away from the office.

The little group moved back toward the mess building. The men had worn themselves out and were sitting around staring at the mess. Some were crying, totally unashamed. There was clothing and bedding all over the place and in some cases the doors had been torn loose from the buildings and were on the ground. For the most part, the men were sprawled on the ground, resting. They were exhausted.

As we neared the mess building, we were met by another bunch of officer personnel. Captain O'Conner and several British officers were in a group waiting to see us. There was a difference in opinion between McMurray and these officers. As soon as they met, I made myself scarce. As they were leaving us, one of them could be heard saying to no one in particular, "Keep calm, men, don't arouse the Japanese any more than they already are." I looked back toward the building where the Japanese were normally housed. There wasn't anyone in sight. That commandant hadn't wasted any time getting them out of here.

The men who were with me during the confrontation with the commander were gone, and the officers had disappeared into one of the buildings on the British side of camp. Exhausted men were lying everywhere. I felt my anger returning. I wondered why these people got something started, then stopped, leaving the entire thing hanging. Couldn't they understand? Some of these men had been out of their minds and were in need of guidance, something stable, some kind of authority figure to calm them or explain what was expected. At this moment, my mind was racing in every direction. I had been beaten by the Japanese for so long, I couldn't survive any unexpected movement by them. I would be too scared. Yet I had already been involved with the Jap officer. I ran from the area and into the barracks. I wanted to be out of sight. When inside, I peered out through the holes in the walls and saw others as they made their way back inside. The camp was slowly becoming quiet after a night of madness.

Inside the room, I crawled back into the corner and once again, I asked the question, the thing that had been running wild through my mind. Is this thing over? Would I be liberated by the United States soon? Was it realistic for me to believe that this war could end without an invasion of Japan? That hadn't been considered by any of us as a possibility. What happened over there in that city that would cause the Japanese to surrender? Up until now, the only thing I had in mind was how the hell I could get outside this wall and into the mountains where I could wait for the invading forces to find me. Now this turn of events. I had been wrapped up in what had been happening so much I had forgotten about my legs. Pulling my trouser legs up, I saw large red places running up the back of my legs. If the Japs decided to do anything, I would have trouble even moving, much less making an escape. At last, I lay back, stretched out and let the million questions run through my mind, without one single answer. My last thought was that in all probability, the guards would try killing all of us, if for no other reason than to cover up for their criminal acts over the past year. As I fell asleep, I remembered the statement about keeping our heads at this critical time.

The following morning, there was activity everywhere. Prisoners were yelling at each other, but not like they were during that rampage. That was different. Everyone was hollering without any restrictions. When I opened the sliding window, I saw the sun high in the sky. I had been allowed to sleep as long as I wanted. Extra rations had been brought into camp and that was what everyone was yelling about. By the time I was at the mess building, some of the men had finished and were lined up for more. In this line I was given as much rice as I wanted and before I was through the line a British officer was waving his hands and telling us that there would be all the rice we wanted. In addition, we would be rationed fresh fish before the day was over. He stated, "The Japanese have promised we will have all the fresh fish we want." There would be no further work details. This was the first sign for me that it was true. The war was over.

I tried to keep as calm as possible but things were happening so fast it almost overwhelmed me. At the moment there was food. There was more rice than I had seen since coming to Japan, so I intended to eat as much as I could get before the bastards decided the war wasn't over and cut us back to that starvation diet again. That promise of fish was just that, a promise. With that thought I once again started through the line. I knew many of the men in the line felt the same as I. Get all you can while it is available. The past record with the Japs had been such that I didn't trust them with anything they said or promised. Hell, I'd probably be down in the mine before the day was finished.

When I had eaten as much rice as I could, I decided to find out something, anything. Everything was so damn confusing. There wasn't a Jap anywhere. All the guards had disappeared. The Americans and British officers seemed to be in control.

During the afternoon the truck with the promised fresh fish entered the camp. The prisoners were yelling at each other and gathered around the vehicle and were checking this new supply of food. For this group of people who had lived on only rice for such a long period, this was a very special event. I found it very difficult to believe this was really happening, yet there it was, as big as life. That truck had a load of fresh fish, which was being unloaded and carried into our mess building. In the past when fish came into the camp, it was always taken to the Japanese mess. In addition to the fish, they brought in some cooking oil in which to cook them. Back in the islands when we did get fish, we had nothing in which to cook them and had to boil anything we got. This was certainly a treat. I waited eagerly for this meal and when it was ready to be served, I was one of the first in line.

With a full stomach, I slept well. Early the following morning, when rice had been served, I noted the Japanese were conspicuously absent inside the camp, and as had been the case for the past few days, no one was being sent out on a work detail. I was starting to believe the war really was over. There were many men in this camp who wanted revenge and were on the prowl for Japanese guards who had mistreated them at some time or other. As I moved about the compound, I found many in the mood for anything. I wanted that

312

Jap doctor who hurt me and also refused to treat my leg. Others wanted different guards, while Americans wanted to get hold of some of the British whom they believed had betrayed them. For the most part, these men were out for blood—anybody's blood. We, the revenge seekers, banded together into small groups searching the village for our marks. In some cases we were becoming very dangerous, not just to the guards, but also to ourselves. Some found liquor and were drunk, adding to this already dangerous situation.

By mid-afternoon, the American soldier who had lost his legs had joined my group. He was after the camp commander who he believed allowed the guards to cause his injury. He wanted him or anyone else who might be remotely connected with that act. All this anger, plus the added stimulus of alcohol, had made all of us very crazy and of course very careless. By now, I didn't give a damn about the officers, what they wanted or what they might be thinking. The only thing I could think of was revenge. I wanted that Jap doctor who hit my leg. As we drank and searched, the anger became worse and caution was thrown to the wind. Revenge, revenge! That was what I wanted and to hell with anything else!

Our group of marauders searched and pillaged the village looking for anything or anybody while getting drunker all the time. The guards had all fled. Only the women and children were left behind, and they were huddling in the back rooms of the homes. No punishment was meted out to them. They had not been allowed near us, and had never done us any harm. It was the men who worked the mines and who guarded us. When we entered their houses and found the men gone, the only thing taken was their liquor and any food that might be convenient.

By nightfall, we were joined by Captain McMurray. He was the one officer I felt I could trust. He had been degraded by the Japanese as much as anyone in this group. He wanted revenge as much as we. His presence gave this marauding group a feeling of being official, thus making our acts less criminal. We were being held together by McMurray, but were unable to find our targets. That doctor had disappeared from the area, and there wasn't a sign of the camp commander. He also had left the camp and gone into hiding. Those we had caught up with earlier we treated so badly, word got around, and all of them went into hiding. We had the camp to ourselves. The only people we had to deal with were the civil authorities, and at the moment they were so fearful of us they didn't do anything without asking first.

Word was passed around that we wanted the commander and that anyone who protected him would be treated as he was to be treated. This paid off and soon we heard he was hiding in an attic of one of the mine buildings. The building was surrounded by the angry men and he was found huddling in a room near the top of the building. The man with the legs off was carried up the steps and placed inside with his intended victim. Then when all were inside, the commander was placed in the center of the room while all of us sat around the wall. There was one small light in the center of the room but this gave enough light so that everyone could be seen.

Soon the trial began. It was explained to the commander that he would not be leaving this room, that this night he would die. But before he did he would be told by each and every one of us why he was to die. The men in the room wished to refresh his memory as to some of the things he was guilty of before he was killed.

The principal of this group was the fellow with his legs off. He was sitting directly in front of the Japanese officer, where the stubs of both legs could be seen. The room became silent. Not even the night noises were heard. At last the legless man began to speak.

"You see these stumps? [He pointed to the scarred ends of his legs.] Back in Kentucky my father owns a small farm. A farm where we make our living with horses. We don't have tractors that I can ride. When this war was over, it was my intention to return to that farm and take over the work from my father who is old and unable to make the farm pay off. I wanted to take over that responsibility. With these legs missing, that will never be. Back in those hills I ran like the animals and was able to hunt like other people do in my part of the country. Because of you, I can never do this again. Instead of being an asset to that farm, I will now become a burden."

As he talked the tears welled up in his eyes and it was plain these things had been on his mind for some time.

"This night, major, it is my intention to repay you in a small degree for the things you have deprived me of."

I watched the face of this Jap officer. The son-of-a-bitch couldn't look him in the eyes. As tears ran down the soldier's face, the Jap turned away. I waited for some sign he would start begging for his life. There was nothing. He only hung his damned head as this man talked, saying nothing. After some time of refreshing his memory of that event and the others taking turns telling him of their grievances, his head was very low. Still he said nothing. He seemed resigned to die. Then, without saying another word, the man with his legs off started smashing the side of the commander's face with his fist. After he was hit, he would sit back up and would be hit by someone else. Within minutes he was beaten into unconsciousness. I watched this torture for several minutes, then, when I could watch no longer, I arose from my position and went down the steps and outside to await the finish. I knew that if there ever was anyone who deserved this punishment, this man would head the list. Still, there was something about this that bothered me. Somehow, I just knew this scene would be in my mind for years after this war was over.

At last all the men came from the building. There wasn't nearly as much glee among them as before. We were all subdued to some extent. Without anyone saying anything, we returned to camp. That night when I did finally lie down I spent a restless night. I kept seeing the tears running down that man's cheeks and then the battered face and head of that Jap. I knew there would be nightmares of the man from Japan and the man from Kentucky for years to come and somehow I wouldn't be able to separate myself from this act.

Try as I might, I couldn't erase this thing from my mind. I tossed and turned, remembering that torture room in every detail. I rationalized the great loss of the American farm boy against the killing that I had taken part in and wondered if revenge was worth it. That young man had survived all the prison camps in the Philippines. He had survived the hell ships out of that area only to lose his legs here in Japan, only a few months before the war was over. This loss could surely be laid at the feet of that bastard. The suffering this man withstood out there in that subzero weather and them pouring that ice water over him. I sure as hell didn't blame him for what he did. I felt as if I had committed something equally as bad without asking anyone or waiting for normal processes to take form. I wondered who was the worst. Before this night there was only one barbarian. Now I felt as though there were at least two: the Jap who was dead and I who took part in this act.

When daylight finally came I dressed and left the building for the mess hall by the way of the back door. I saw the door of the Jap commander's office. Someone printed a sign in both English and Japanese and hung it on the door. It read: "Died of pneumonia." The door had been nailed shut.

Sometime during the day the mayor of the village entered the camp wanting to see the commandant. He was shown the sign on his door and then warned that he should be thinking more about his own health, that he also might come down with a severe case of pneumonia as the major had, that it would be well advised to let things remain as they were. He left without saying more.

The activities outside the camp continued, but since that night there had been less violence. For the most part all anyone wanted now was to see the countryside. During one of these ventures, three or four of us took a truck. I had been telling these men about that great explosion on the other side of the mountain range. On August 15, 1945, my little group left camp early and headed for the mountain range and that city.

By noon we were at the outskirts of the place. We had been meeting people walking toward the hills for the last hour. Some of these people seemed to be in a daze, walking aimlessly along, not even seeing us as we approached. They weren't even talking to each other. Some had large sores on their bodies and their arms and hands; others looked as if they had been burned by something. As we entered the southern end of the town, I saw buildings blown down as they would be in a hard windstorm. Also, there was an awful odor coming from somewhere. The farther we went inside the city the worse it became. People were still passing us. The way it smelled, who could blame them for wanting to be away from here?

From here it wasn't possible to see more than a few yards. The roads were filled with torn-up buildings and we skirted them as we came closer. The road was clogged with large timbers and other debris. We got off the truck and took another round from the liquor we brought with us. Here in this hot sun and with that awful smell the liquor only made the place more sultry. There was a sort of ominous feeling about this place. After two or three drinks, we started toward the pile of lumber and debris blocking the

315

way. As I climbed toward the top, I glanced back and saw the others close behind me climbing toward the top. When I got to the top of this heap, what I saw caused me to shrink back for just a moment. After I regained my composure, I looked once more over this totally demolished area. What had been a thriving city was as barren as could be. In every direction in front of me were charred structures that had been blown down and burned. In most instances there was nothing but the foundation or small parts of the walls still standing. I recalled seeing that explosion from the mountain a few days ago, but from that distance I could never have guessed the extent what had happened. I looked for craters. There were none. How in hell could this place have been so completely destroyed without there being any craters? All the bombings I had seen left large holes in the ground. Here, there were none. The buildings had been blown into large heaps out on the edges of the blast area and as far as I could see nothing had escaped this blast. From up here I couldn't even see how widespread this destruction had been. Nearly a mile away, right in the center of the blast area, was a lone structure. It looked out of place. Off to my right some eight hundred yards, some buildings had been blown into a stream and were still intact as they lay, half-covered with water, while on the bank of the stream the earth was bare. It had been swept clean from the blast. Far out to my left I saw some buildings standing. From this distance I could not tell what damage had been done to that area. I watched for people moving about. In this area there were none, but some five hundred yards from my vantage point toward the eastern side of the destruction, some people were moving and there were a few trucks in that sector of the blast area. I heard someone in back of me say he was getting back to the truck and as he spoke I saw him slowly climb down from this heap of lumber and other materials that had been swept into a large pile from the blast. Another man passed the bottle around, and I drank deeply of its contents. I couldn't leave this place. Whatever had happened here, I wanted to see more. I must. There was more out there in that area than met the eye. I got an urge to go down into the blasted out area for a closer look. I wanted to drive the truck but there was no way of getting through that debris. If I was to see any more I had to go on foot. One of the men next to me turned and told the fellow down near the truck that he was going farther into the area, and for him to watch the truck until he came back. I followed this man down the other side and into the area of mass destruction. When I reached the bottom of the heap, I noticed there were two other men with us and together we walked farther into this blasted out area, keeping away from the people I had seen working some five hundred yards east of us. The deeper we went the cleaner the area. Whatever this blast was, it had cleaned out everything. For the next hour, I moved about, not quite knowing where I was, or for that matter what I was looking for. Walls of buildings still stood but the tops had been blown away and at some of these partial walls, there were bodies of people who had been swept against them and as yet hadn't been hauled away. The heat was intense and the smell was smothering me until I had difficulty breathing. Everywhere I looked were great swarms of flies. There were a number of water spigots and once I tried to turn these on. There was no running water. In some cases the buildings were completely gone and water pipes were standing alone. It was as if there had been a project started here and then suddenly stopped. That blast cleared everything in its path. I wondered if there were people in this building when the thing went off, and if so, what happened to their bodies. Could those bodies I saw back there against the wall have been these people?

I had been here for more than an hour, moving around, kicking through the odd-looking stones about the place. But with the limited knowledge I had, I couldn't for the life of me figure out what had happened. This place had been completely destroyed and from all I knew it was from a single bomb or explosion and at this moment it appeared there was nothing being done about the people who were killed. The only activity anywhere were those people some distance from here and I couldn't tell what they were doing. I would not go closer to them, especially now that I had heard the rumors about the United States using chemicals. With these things in mind, I started retracing my footsteps and soon was almost running toward the truck. Suddenly I wanted to be out of here and back in those mountains. I looked over my shoulder and saw the other men following me. They also had seen enough. By the time I was down the truck was running and we were on our way out of this place that reminded me of a man-made hell. The bottle was again being passed. With what I had seen in the past few hours, I needed something to block out things. I drank deeply as the truck pulled away. Soon our little group of sightseers was climbing the side of the mountain and there was more drinking now than when we came down the hill that morning.

It was late when we returned to the main camp. We returned the truck to where we had stolen it, then sneaked back inside the wall.

It was nearly eleven o'clock when we reentered camp. Some prisoners had been wondering what had happened to that roaming bunch who failed to get back inside before dark. When I heard this talk, I was determined that I wouldn't let anyone know where I had been. Our officers were angry as hell because we disappeared from sight without letting anyone know our whereabouts. I decided that if I let anyone know where we went there could be problems. Besides, we were all so drunk we didn't make sense anyway, so we just went to our barracks and kept our mouths shut.

As I attempted to sleep, the piles of Japanese bodies in that blown-out city ran across my mind, but were soon blocked out by the memory of that odor. The fact is, the revenge I had in mind for the bastards was coming true. The people in that city sure as hell paid for anything they had done.

In my blurred mind, I finally went to sleep and I actually felt more at ease than at any other time since the rumor of the war being over started.

The following morning, the ranking officer in camp issued an order that each man would check in and out with the ranking enlisted men when they had reason to leave the camp. I knew he had done this because of us leaving the mining area without letting anyone know. Most of the men thought he was trying to assert his authority over the prisoners and resisted more than a little. We said, "To hell with it," and went on doing what we wanted, but this last order slowed down outside activities to some extent.

Some two or three days after our trip over the mountain, I was outside the camp looking for that doctor. I still wanted to get hold of that man, so together with a few more rebels, I was searching the area once more for him. We split up and agreed we would meet at the old mine shack before we returned to camp. A time was set and off we went on our separate missions.

I came upon a strange fellow. He was not Japanese or English or American. He wore strange clothing and was armed with a sidearm. He was about five feet, ten inches tall, in his late twenties, and the clothing he was wearing could pass for some kind of uniform, although very dirty. He had no hat and was obviously very intoxicated. He was friendly and doing everything he could to talk to me. I couldn't understand a word he was saying. After a time, we found some shade and sat. He passed his bottle with an indication to have a drink with him. The two of us communicated with sign language. I understood him to be Russian, that he had jumped in here by parachute for reasons that I couldn't understand. As we sat, I noted he had another small weapon concealed inside his jacket in addition to the one he carried on the outside.

The two of us talked for more than an hour and all I got from him was that he was gathering information to be taken back to his command. I informed him there was plenty of space and food inside the camp, and that he could go there with me. He declined, saying he could not get mixed up with the American or English prisoners, that he had found a Japanese woman and was living with her until his mission was finished. The one thing that amused me was his cautioning me not to tell any of our officers of his being here. His reason was that he was on a classified mission for Russia, an American ally, and as such, felt his mission should be kept secret. With that, I promised him that his mission as well as his presence was safe with me. By now the two of us had become close friends, with the booze and the feeling of freedom I was experiencing. This area was off-limits to the prisoners, and that was what had drawn me into coming here in the first place.

Soon it became very hot. With the sun bearing down, the heat began taking its toll on the two of us and we started looking for some place out of the sun. After going around for a time we heard voices coming from one of the larger buildings and through one of the unlocked doors. Before trying to learn who was inside, we found a large office area where it was very cool. Sitting and drinking from the saki bottle we listened. For some time it was quiet and we made no noise either. Then we heard talking again. The Russian sobered very quickly and was alert for anything as we moved in the direction of the voices. Together we slipped along the hallways and soon were very near the voices. They were coming from the next room and without warning, the Russian was through the door with me right on his heels. Inside this room were three Japanese men. They were dressed in mining gear. I recognized all three. They were supervisors in the mine as well as topside supervisors. One of them was the shift supervisor when I was beaten because of the stolen cabbage. Although he didn't actually take part in my beating, he sure as hell allowed it to continue until I was nearly dead. The little son-of-a-bitch stood and watched as I was being beaten. As far as I was concerned he was guilty as hell.

The three Japs stopped talking. They stared at us. I got the feeling they had seen this Russian before. The Russian broke the silence and began to speak to them in their native tongue. This suprised me. We had been talking for the past hour or so and I didn't recall either of us talking Japanese. We were under the influence of the saki and could have been communicating in any language and I might not recognize it. Had I known he spoke Japanese so well, it would have been less hard work understanding each other. He was giving them hell about something and as he talked they were bowing and scraping. I had no idea what was expected of me, but watching the bastards bowing and almost prostrating themselves in front of him sure as hell pleased me. The only time I ever saw them bowing like this was when they were in the presence of high-ranking Japanese officers. For the last two hours this man had been my best buddy and now these former supervisors were bowing and scraping. Goddamn! This was something else.

One of them raised from a deep bow. We were very close. He was the supervisor when I was beaten for stealing that head of cabbage. I read the recognition in his face, and I was sure he was aware that I remembered him. He must see the anger in my eyes. All the pain and humiliation I went through because of him on that evening returned at this moment, and I wanted to knock his damned head from his shoulders and with the liquor in me, I had little control of myself. We stood face to face for a moment.

The Russian said, "Do you know this man?"

"Yes, he was a supervisor in the mine," I told him in Japanese.

The fellow turned ashen as he listened. I knew he was terrified at my answer. Then the Russian told all of them to leave the building through a side door. The two of us followed them. Outside we were under a shed where there were several pieces of horsedrawn equipment. They were under the shed parked alongside the wall of the building. On the wall were pieces of harness. Farther out from the building was a barn, but the animals were gone. Only their droppings were around to indicate this had been where they were kept. The Russian asked, "Do you like this man?" [he pointed at the man I said I knew.]

"No, I hate the son-of-a-bitch," I replied.

He reached inside his coat and took the concealed weapon from the holster and handed it to me, saying as he did, "Kill him." At this point I knew I was in so deep I couldn't get out. If I didn't kill him, I would seem less a soldier to this Russian and if I did, I would have committed cold-blooded murder. Ten minutes ago I believed that killing the bastard would be a pleasure. Now when given the opportunity it was much different. I knew I couldn't kill him, but what the hell could I do? I knew I must get out of this somehow, but how? Taking the weapon, I looked around. I knew the Jap understood what the Russian said. Now he had drawn his other pistol and, holding it on the three of them, again said, "Kill him." I looked down and there, right in front of the man, was a pile of horse manure. It was rather fresh and as I was searching desperately for a way out of my dilemma, I pointed at the horse manure and almost without thinking said to the Jap, "You eat," and I pointed at the manure. As I repeated my order, I saw the Russian bending over and laughing. He acted as if this was the most amusing thing he had ever seen. Seeing this I became aware that I was off the hook with the killing. Again I told him to "Eat." The Russian was almost on the ground laughing. The Jap was begging me, his mouth wide now and repeating, "No! Please no!" At this moment I hit him with the barrel of the pistol and at the same time screamed for him to do as he was told. He looked at the Russian for a sign that he would help him, and the Russian was splitting with laughter. Before I could bring the weapon down on him again he was on his knees eating the horse manure, stuffing it into his mouth with one hand and gagging, then stuffing more when he saw me with the pistol over his head. By now that Russian was beside himself and I joined him laughing as the three Japs split in a dead run, each of them going in separate directions. The two of us were blinded with laughter and booze. We let them go without even shooting at them to make them run faster, if that were possible. The last I saw of the three of them, they were breaking all records getting away from us.

I handed the gun back, feeling grateful this had turned out as well as it had. Never again did I want to be boxed in with this maniac again.

When I met the others at the mine shack for our return to camp, I never mentioned the incident, nor did I relate the presence of the Russian. He wasn't seen by me after that episode. He seemed to have just vanished into thin air.

I remembered the way I treated that fellow with the horse manure, and I rationalized that had I not made him eat the manure, I would probably have had to kill him and this way I saved his life. But I knew if this war didn't end that man would be after me for sure. My life wouldn't be worth a dime if he decided he wanted revenge.

A rumor spread that the war wasn't over, the Japanese wouldn't surrender. What a mess! Some of us had done enough to warrant being killed by the Japs if they took over again. This thought was sobering, to say the least. I started once again trying to make a plan to get up to that mountain. Our officers were more confident than I was that this was just a rumor, nothing more. Then, being suspicious, I thought they started the rumor just to get better control. Still, it kept me inside the camp.

Then on August 23, a large truck entered the camp and the driver, a Jap, had a load of tuna fish for us. I moved in close and looked the truck over. I couldn't see anyone with weapons. A good sign. Also, I had never seen so many fish. I thought there were a lot when they brought in that other truckload, but this! Hell, there must be five or six hundred pounds, possibly more, and the size of them—some weighed twenty or thirty pounds.

When the evening meal was served, there was no ration. We could have as much as we wanted. I ate until I was sick. That evening, I started itching

320

from eating more protein than I could absorb into my system. Also there were red spots all over me, and my head was splitting. I had no idea what was happening but I knew I was as sick as I had ever been. When I tried getting something for this illness, I found others with the same problems. Half the camp had overdone it, eating fresh tuna. Our people learned one lesson and from then on, the fish was rationed. By the following evening the red spots were gone.

Food from the sky

Chapter 41

On the morning of the 26th of August, the camp had been awake for several hours and there had been no indication that the Japanese were going to return and take revenge for some of our acts. Tensions had receded to some extent, but the rumor persisted that the war wasn't over; the Japanese refused to surrender. By then I had an emergency kit of extra rice and also had my clothing rolled where I could get the hell out of there if I needed.

As I contemplated what I might have to do, I could hear airplane engines. There were big engines and they were very close. The noise got louder and I ran for the door to see what was coming down. It sounded as if the damn thing was crash landing right in the camp. The largest plane I had ever seen was coming down at an angle from the mountain on the south side of camp. The wing span seemed to be as wide as the camp itself. All four engines could be seen; even the propellers could be seen turning it was so low. I could even see the United States insignia on the wings. The craft was ours. I knew it was a bomber. I remembered the times when we had been bombed by our own planes and I wondered why they would be making a bombing run on that place. I managed to fall face downward and waited for the explosion that I knew would come. Nothing. Raising my head just a little I saw his tail as it went out of sight. Someone was yelling behind me and I turned in that direction. They were looking into the sky. When I finally looked up, the air was filled with pamphlets floating down toward us. Some of them were near the ground and men were grabbing desperately for them. Everywhere I looked I saw small pieces of papers floating downward. One of them floated near me and I grabbed it in mid air. I was scared what I would learn. If it was telling me the war was not over, things could have gotten bad very quickly. At that moment there were a million things running through my mind and none of them were positive. I fumbled with the piece of paper. At last the paper was in front of me and I was able to hold it steady. It said:

"TO: Every American who can read this.

"We are writing this en route to Japan where we will attempt to find you fellows and drop these supplies. Before going into a long letter here are a few instructions.

"The other day we were up over a few POW camps and dropped some supplies and the result was tragic. The drums in which the supplies were packed went careening down on the POWs and their barracks. At least two POWs were killed. The chutes failed to open and the POWs had gathered in a group and I think the barrel went right in the middle of the bunch. This time we intend to fly a little higher and give the chutes more time to open. Also, we have been given instructions not to drop supplies right in the camp but near it. So watch the stuff when it comes down, get to it as soon as possible. We don't want the Japs to get the stuff any more than you do. We are sorry as hell about the damage caused by the B-29 to personnel and property. We don't mean that we alone did it all. We hope we didn't hit anyone. We are hoping you are all as well as can be expected and our crew sends you its best wishes.

"Here we are lined up:

1st Lt. E. S. Hollis, First Pilot, Toledo, Ohio

2nd Lt. C. O. Ling, Radio Operator, Fort Wayne, Ind.

2nd Lt. Gumphery, Navigator, Washington, D.C.

2nd Lt. Salmon, Bombardier, Wilmington, Del.

M/Sgt. Wheelloch, Flight Eng., Tulsa, Okla.

S/Sgt. L. Thalberg, (No city listed).

"We are a Siapan based crew. Other islands with B-29 bases are Tinean and Guam. If you get a chance in the near future to write to any of the crew, use the following address: 488 GR, 878 Bomb Sqdrn, Apo 237, San Francisco, Calif. We would love to hear from someone there and find out if we helped any at all.

"It won't be long now before you will see American troops. A few special troops have already landed in Tokyo to prepare for the occupation forces which are coming in the next few days. The Pacific Fleet is in Tokyo Bay, waiting for MacArthur to arrive and lead the boys ashore. Incidentally, if any of you are from the Philippines, General Wainwright was found in a prison camp in Manchuria by the Russians and is right now witnessing the surrender of the Japs to the Chinese. The damn war is over but for the signing of the papers. Hold on a bit longer, fellows, and you will be on your way home. You are top priority on the list to go stateside.

"Good luck and let's hear from some of you;

"Most sincerely, the crew of V-23, our real ship is in repair, V-37."

When I finished, I was crying. Tears were running down my face. My knees buckled under me and I found myself prostrate on the ground. My face and eyes were in the hot dirt. The war must be over.

Getting to my feet I started toward the mess building where I could see others gathering. There were many others crying at the message they had just received and were overcome by the enormity of it. I moved into the shade near the mess building, took the leaflet from my pocket and started reading once more. As I was reading I heard the roar of the engines again. They were coming from the south as the first plane had. My first thought was that it had taken him a long time to turn that thing around and return. Then I saw them. There were three of them and they were heading in the direction of camp, only these were much higher than the one that dropped the pamphlets. Still, they were very low compared to the bombers that I had seen flying over. Then the air was suddenly filled with bright colored parachutes. I had been concentrating so hard on the planes that I didn't see the barrels as they were dumped from the bomb bays. Everywhere I looked there were chutes—red ones, blue ones and orange ones. Also there were a few white chutes that were extremely hard to see in the sky with the sun on them. One after the other the bombers came across the camp and moved out of sight toward the north. We all remembered what was written in that leaflet at the same time. "Get to the stuff as quickly as possible; we don't want the Japs to get it any more than you do." Everyone charged from the camp at the same time. Some of the chutes were falling on the southern side near the front gate. At that moment, there were nearly four hundred men—American and British, along with the few Dutch, scrambling over walls and through the holes we had made for escape during this period of not knowing what was going to happen. The only thing on our mind was, "Get the stuff before the Japs get it." There were holes all along that southern wall and some near the eastern wall. Men were scrambling through these and screaming at each other when they had gotten to one of the chutes. There wasn't any organization at the moment. The officers and enlisted men were all grabbing at the barrels. Some of them hit the ground hard and split, while others were still intact and had to be opened with tools, but the men weren't waiting. They wanted to get this food and other supplies. They were scared there wouldn't be enough to go around and were bound to get their part on the spot. I remembered the warning about the barrels careening down and I had seen something coming down near the center of the village, so I headed in that direction. It was nearly three hundred yards from where I went through the wall but I covered the distance in seconds. When I arrived near the spot, I had very little trouble seeing where it was. The people were outside the buildings, huddled in groups, the mothers protecting their babies and the older ones standing wide eyed as I approached. One woman shouted at me that the thing was in an area near where she was. She pointed and I made my way in that direction. There were two or three other Americans coming on the scene from a different direction. One of them had an ax on his shoulder. I heard someone from inside yell, "It's in here." Then the men with the ax started chopping the wall of the building. Even though there was a door not more than fifteen yards away, he still chopped his way into the building. I stepped through the hole and could hear children crying somewhere down the hallway. Looking up, I saw that the barrel had hit the roof and come through all four floors to the ground level. I remembered what the warning said about the barrels careening down into a group. If any of these people had been in the way, they would have paid the ultimate price. I recalled that the leaflet said two POWs were killed, and thought, "This one has paid for that loss." Nothing slowed the men from what they were there for. The cries of the children went unheeded as the horde of starved and mistreated men continued chopping away at the walls and were bringing the stuff out through the hole. Someone took charge and ordered the stuff taken back into camp. I didn't even know who was ordering us about, but I did gather some of the supplies and headed toward the front gate which is only a short distance from the building. As I entered the gate, there were two officers along with a senior enlisted man from the British side of camp. They were directing people to pile the stuff into designated spots; clothing in one place, cigarettes in another, food somewhere else and medical in yet another. As I placed my load in the correct location, I saw candy bars in large boxes piled high. There were other boxes with a large letter "K" and one of the officers opened one of them to examine the contents. There were canned meat, cereals, vegetables, crackers and even canned butter in it. These were things I had dreamed about for three and one-half years. I wondered if this was one of those dreams. Would I awaken and find I was still a prisoner? I stopped long enough to reassure myself that what I was seeing was true. I hadn't seen this much food in my life and it was still coming in. Also, clothing was being piled all over the place. There seemed to be enough clothing to issue each and every man two or three khaki uniforms. Before I returned to the areas where the supplies were, I took a candy bar from one of the boxes that had been opened. I halfway expected someone to tell me to keep my hand out of the stuff. No one did and I took a handful. It wasn't until I had taken the wrapper off and tasted the candy that I began to believe that this was not a dream. This war was over. As I walked away from the piles of supplies, feeling half guilty about having all the candy bars, I saw others munching on different things they had gotten from the piles or from the barrels. If I live forever, I know I will never again see anything that will match this scene.

Within an hour I amassed several packs of cigarettes and managed to get some of the canned goods. I took the things into my room. I took one of the cigarettes from a pack, lit it, and then I remembered the pamphlets. I wanted to understand what they meant. The small piece of paper had become a personal message for me. The fact that there were thousands of them in the air that morning meant nothing. They had dropped this one for me. I read it again. Were they trying to tell me the Japanese have surrendered? Aside from that statement about the war being over but for signing the papers, the knowledge of General Wainwright being alive was the most important news of all. I had wondered for two years whether he was still living. I doubt if anybody could have thought he had survived.

Replacing the leaflet inside my jacket, I left the security of my small room and made my way toward the mess building where the officers were getting everyone assembled for a briefing on how the supplies would be handled.

Captain O'Conner took charge and assured us that the food would be issued fairly. Before the day was over, I had been issued a shirt and one pair of khaki trousers. I considered myself to be in good shape.

When the evening meal was served, there were several different types of American food including a slice of canned meat. Each man was issued one large slice that had been heated before it was served. As I found a place where I could eat without being bothered, I contemplated the day. I was eating American food and had clean clothing on my back. I felt more human than at any time since being taken prisoner of war. When I finished, I returned to my small room. It had been a most eventful day.

The next morning I couldn't wait to get out of the room and to the mess hall. I stopped by the water spigot and splashed water on my face, then went to the mess building. There I was issued rice along with cereal that was served with canned milk that had been diluted with water. At the end of the chow line there was hot water and soluble coffee, something we hadn't seen since the war started. We ran out of coffee within the first week of the war. I asked where this had come from and was told there was lots of coffee in the supplies in this powdered form. I had never seen powdered coffee but this was the best thing so far. I relished the wonderful taste.

There had been so much happening over the past few days, my mind couldn't keep pace. There were times when I believed we were free, then at other times I was scared. I feared that something would go wrong or that I would awake and find it was all a dream. I couldn't completely give in that the war was really over. One thing was certain: the food was real, so there must be something to that statement in the leaflet. The war was over but for the signing of the paper. I asked myself: "Did I dare accept that as true?"

It is over

Chapter 42

September 2, 1945, was like any other day. We were awake early and by now had become accustomed to having that new kind of coffee. We got cereal along with powdered and condensed milk. The rice was barely touched anymore. Even though there hadn't been any more air drops, we had managed to ration. Adequate foodstuff was being added from outside: extra rice, fresh vegetables, and fish. Still, there had been no concrete information that the war was over.

I left the camp and was out in the village. I noticed some strange activities. The women and children had been told something, but as yet I had not been able to find out what was happening. Finally at about noon, I stopped one of the women who had her children with her. She was scurrying across the village where a crowd was gathering. When I asked what was going on, she said, "The war will be over today, and all of us are being assembled in the community building by the mayor."

"I have heard the war has been over for several days," I said.

"Today they will sign the paper," she replied.

I told her to go on and I followed close behind, not wanting to alarm her or the children any more than they were, but wanting to get as much information as I could.

Arriving at the building, I saw excitement all through the crowd. I was told to stay outside by one of the mayor's people, but I remained near the door. Soon the mayor told them that war had ceased; that the emperor and the officials in Tokyo urged them to remain calm and to stay in their homes; that there was nothing anyone could do, for now. "It is over," was his last statement as he left the building.

Before the people could get to the door, I was on my way back to the compound. Thinking I had big news for everyone, I found there had been someone here telling the officers the same news I had accidently found out in the village. Everyone was excited about this new development, but we had been advised we were to stay here until further word was received from Tokyo.

The rest of the day rumors came from everywhere. The British were spreading the word that some high-ranking British official would be here to pick them up. There was word that the United States would be in camp soon for the American prisoners. My first thoughts were, "I don't give a damn who gets here first. I intend to leave with that group and to hell with orders." Right now I would follow a St. Bernard dog if it would get me out of here.

By nightfall I was convinced the war was really over, but as yet, I couldn't find out anything about where the United States forces were. Our officers seemed to know everything, until asked point blank where the American troops were. All they could do was relate what was in the leaflet. Hell, I had read that damned thing a thousand times. I knew what it said, but that was dropped a week ago and still there hadn't been one word about anything. Now this story about the signing of the surrender. I wondered why, why we couldn't just bundle up what things we had and get the hell out of here and join our command wherever it was. One would have thought the United States would have at least dropped something else letting us know where they were. The longer I thought about this the madder I became. We were here without weapons and if just one of the fanatic bastards should get the idea that he didn't care about that surrender, he had access to weapons and could get inside this camp and slaughter hell out of us. Still they hadn't sent us anything. Surely our officers knew this but if they did, then why weren't they showing some concern? Before going to sleep, I resolved that if I hadn't heard or seen something positive about getting away or getting something to defend myself with, I would get a few men and prowl the village until we had weapons. There was something out there and I hadn't survived this ordeal this far only to be killed by some fanatic son-of-a-bitch who didn't want to surrender.

All day long I waited for further word. I had awakened early hoping the officers had received something from our troops. They just stared and said nothing, or if they did reply, they said there was nothing any of us could do. We must wait. There were ample food and medical supplies. But this wasn't enough as far as I was concerned. When the day ended and there had been no word, I started moving among the prisoners, people that I had known for some time. My story to them was the same. That we were sitting ducks for any fanatic that refused to surrender. We needed guns in case one of their soldiers returned home and decided he wanted to die for the cause. I spread this and at the same time invited anyone who wanted to go with me on a raid for guns.

The following morning I felt the tension building inside me. Several men expressed their desire to get hold of weapons and by ten o'clock we had our squad and were joined by our captain. This officer best represented my own feelings, and now with him, I didn't feel so much like a renegade. Still, he asked what the group had in mind and why. I related that we had no intentions of sitting and doing nothing until some soldier came down out of the hills and didn't give a damn about any surrender. We wanted to be ready if that should happen. He agreed and we slipped through the gate and into the village.

Some distance from camp, we found what we needed, a truck. Soon it was running and we started looking for extra gasoline. When the tank had been filled from gasoline found in the mining area, we drove north. In our village the men had been driven off or had been scared out of town and we reasoned that they would have taken any weapons with them. Our thoughts turned to areas away from the prison camp. Taking one of the secondary roads, we looked where there had been Japanese soldiers or where it was most likely some of them would be traveling.

We had seen a map of the area and believed we could get to a city not many miles from the camp where there would be weapons.

Some of the men brought their saki bottles along and these were passed among us. It didn't take much of this along with being out in the countryside for all of us to loosen up. The booze plus the officer being in on the raid made us all feel freer than we had felt in some time. Our captain gave this raid an official connotation.

Some forty-five minutes later we were on the outskirts of a city. At first I was afraid of what was ahead. I had been held by these people for such a long time that when I saw one of their soldiers something inside told me he was going to kill me. At the same time, I wanted to jump from the truck and start choking the son-of-a-bitch. The truck moved slowly down a side street. Most of us had khaki uniforms on so we looked enough like military men that these people thought we were from the United States forces and were occupying their city. They looked the other way as we approached. These people were as scared of us as we had been of them.

Our truck moved into the city and soon we were at the main train station. People were moving about, coming from the station. The truck stopped and waited and watched. Soldiers and sailors were coming in on trains. Some of them had rifles, while others had sabres. Not the wood type. These were the real thing. The captain told us to take it slow and easy, that he would make the decision when to move. The people turned their heads as they came by, not wanting to offend us if possible.

At the exit door, some of the uniformed men exited. Seeing us, some dropped their gear where they stood and walked away, while others turned and went in the opposite direction. We waited. When the time was right, we all dismounted and moved in. The people who came in on the train were gone and only a few people were on the station platform. As we approached the building we found exactly what we came for. There were a number of weapons along with pouches of ammunition. The captain ordered us to pick the stuff up and return to the truck. When all were on the truck we drove very slowly away from this area and to the outskirts once more. Here he explained we would learn how to use the stuff we had before trying to get anything else. This completed, we now had enough arms so that we could move about in search of more.

Two men were designated as guards for the truck while the rest of us walked back into the city. We hadn't walked far when we spotted a Japanese still in uniform, sitting with head down as if asleep, his rifle leaning against the wall. One of our people moved in near him and grabbed the rifle, thinking he would make an effort at stopping him. We had our rifles at the ready. Instead, he only raised his head and then dropped it once more as we took everything he had, his rifle, his ammunition, one grenade, then jerked his belt loose and took it as well. It was as if he expected we would kill him. He never dreamed we were former prisoners of war. When I saw his dejected look, I remembered when that was me, and the two Japanese soldiers who felt my forehead and then offered me tea from their canteen. My God! That seemed like a million years ago. All day long we gathered weapons in this fashion. We moved about the city at will, taking what we wanted without any resistance. This raid continued until nearly dark, when the captain determined we should return to the prison compound before our luck ran out or something went wrong.

The truck was an arsenal now and we had obtained several more bottles of saki, enough that we would have something to drink for a long time. I did have enough of my wits about me to know that driver wasn't as cautious as he was when we came down the back road earlier.

By the time we were back at camp, all of us were very brave. With all the booze in us we stopped the truck right at the front gate and started unloading the stuff we had acquired. We placed it in the old Japanese guard shack. This would be our small arms supply room. The attitude now was, to hell with the people here, especially those British officers. We now could defend ourselves against any fanatics that might try to get revenge. I was convinced the Japs in this area wouldn't just turn over and play dead. I felt safer now.

I searched and found a lock for the room where the rifles were placed.

When I went to my room and tried to get some sleep, I remembered that Japanese soldier with his head down and how all the fight was gone from him. I thought, "What a strange way for him to act." The others who saw us dropped their rifles on the station platform. Something big had happened. Once again I asked, "Can it be true? Is this war over?"

That night, after the raid, I was having problems sleeping. When I finally gave up and went out in the compound, I heard voices coming from inside one of the buildings where we had the medical dispensary. Entering, I saw a group of men working with material they had cut from the parachutes used in dropping the supplies into camp. These men had cut the material into strips of red, white, and blue, and were in the process of making an American flag. I joined this group and throughout the night we worked, sewing and cutting. Each star was cut from the material and then sewn onto the solid background and by morning the project was completed.

There was something about these men wanting to raise the United States flag over this damn place. I wanted to be away from here more than anything I could think of. By hoisting the flag, it created something of a garrison. Still, the fact that I wanted to leave didn't lower my pride in these men who wanted to see it hang over this camp.

Daylight came around before we emerged with the finished flag. One of the men in the group left and talked to O'Conner, getting his permission to hoist the flag, while the others stood around and waited. When permission had been granted, I stood on the sideline, watching. I saw McMurray near the mess building watching. As I came near him I saw tears streaming down his face at the sight of the flag. Taking me by the shoulder he guided me toward the guard shack where the weapons were stored. Inside he picked out a rifle and loaded it. He handed it to me and said, "Take this for now and if one Jap comes near that flag, kill him." I took the weapon and moved back near the area where the flag was to be hoisted and waited in the shadows.

Our officers saw me. Fifteen minutes later, McMurray came out and I was relieved. He said some of the other officers disagreed with him having a guard out there with the rifle. Another man was armed and inside another building where he could see the flagpole, that he had no intention of dropping the matter. He was angry as hell, but I had no intention of getting mixed up between any faction of officers. As far as I was concerned, as long as he wanted, I would follow his orders.

Within an hour we had our rebel group outside the gate and were leaving the camp once more. McMurray wanted more weapons, so we took the route over the mountain where I was taken out of here on the detail at the marshaling yard.

The first city across the mountain was Omani. We had learned the importance of the uniforms so we all dressed in rather good khakis. In spite of the tennis shoes, we easily passed for occupation troops. Here we found several more pieces along with ammunition. We then proceeded farther on toward another town named Motoyama. Here we found the same situation as at the railroad station. Weapons could be had for the asking or by picking them up from the floor inside the rail depot. Also, we were able to take some sabres from the soldiers coming off the trains. For the most part, there was no resistance. Besides, by this time most of us had become very brave. We asked and if they resisted they got hell knocked out of them. The news of our presence traveled fast, so most of the time when they saw us they dropped their weapons and ran in the other direction. In most instances the civilians had deserted the area. We hadn't been in this town more than an hour when the truck was full of weapons and all the ammunition we could ever need.

To this point we had been very fortunate and McMurray seemed to know we could get in a hell of a mess very easily. So before these people could figure out what had happened to them, we boarded the truck and were on our way out.

Over the past two days we had amassed a very large arsenal. Even those skeptics agreed we could hold off any radicals that might decide the war wasn't over and want to get some revenge against those who had surrendered to the United States.

The others couldn't deny the fact we had the weapons so an understanding was reached between McMurray and his renegades and the others in the camp. Especially, there was harmony among the officer personnel.

Then we waited. Damn how we waited, and nothing happened. We couldn't get word from anyone. Even the Japs clammed up. That rumor about the high-ranking British officer died on the spot. They couldn't get any word about their command either. Tension was building with every hour.

The British were determined they would remain in camp until they were liberated by their people and some of our group would just as soon wait with them. Still others of us were willing to take things into our hands and get the hell out of here. Find our command and join them. Break out of here and raise so much hell that the brass in Tokyo would have to send in someone to take charge of us and take us out. For the most part, our officers were in agreement. They wanted to make their move.

Finally, on September 12, it was decided by our officers that we would go. We would take enough food with us to get us to Tokyo, leaving what was left for the British. We would confiscate a train and force the Japanese authorities to take us north where there were American forces.

The next several hours were spent loading food into a car that had been brought in at the railhead. All the clothing was issued out, reducing the amounts to be hauled but increasing the gear for each of us to carry. Another car was brought in for the food. This was a car used as a kitchen by the railroad. Cooks were assigned to this car and were given responsibility for the supplies. Some of the men were issued a few weapons and others had sabres they had taken from the returning soldiers. In some cases the men brought aboard hand grenades in sacks and these were stored inside the cars. I had two sabres and I fully intended to take them with me. These would go to the United States with me even if I must lop off someone's damned head to do so.

When all was in readiness, the men boarded. I heard more laughter than I had heard in many, many years. Something that had been absent in the lives of these men. I felt some sort of release from inside. I didn't understand fully what it was. It had helped going out into the countryside and into the cities and seeing what had happened to the people here, but there was still much apprehension. I was afraid something would happen to extend the war and my captivity, but the way our officers were reacting gave me cause to be hopeful.

I found a spot at last where I could be alone with my thoughts and where I could contemplate my actions when we first saw American troops. That thought lifted my spirits.

The train moved out. There was hardly a glance at the village as we moved away from this place that had been hell for me for almost a year. I didn't want to remember what the damn place looked like or what the people were like here. All I could think of was at last I was leaving for a new adventure. Just what that adventure would be was out there somewhere.

By mid-afternoon, the train was on the outskirts of Hiroshima. I recognized some of the landmarks I had seen when I was here a week or so ago. From inside the train, I saw the destruction that had befallen this city. The rail lines out away from the city were intact. Right near the rail some buildings were still standing, but in sad shape. All of the buildings were empty and as we passed, I noted the absence of people. From here it was nothing but a barren area for several thousand yards. In the distance it wasn't possible to tell where the destruction stopped. It was even worse than I had thought when I walked in from the other side of the city. That strange odor I had noticed the other day was still present and even inside this car. I still didn't understand how anything could do this much damage. Once again I recalled being told it might have been an atom bomb, and again I was dumbfounded. Out on the northern side of the city, everything was blackened. Blackened like it had been burned real quickly. The train slowed now, barely moving, and the sight became worse. I wished we would get the hell out of here. For about five minutes the train moved very slowly. Then, without ever completely stopping, we started picking up speed and soon we were away from this sight and out into the farming areas. Moving across the car, I looked out across the countryside and as far as I could see there was green. Nothing but farming out here and from all indications there were no signs of bombing. The farmers were out in the fields working as if they knew nothing of what had happened. For the most part, they didn't even glance at the train passing, taking people to their freedom.

Our officers made sure we had plenty of cars on this train, and we had all the room we wanted. I was still thinking in terms of being a prisoner of war, and I recalled other trains, the boxcars that crowded us in like animals. The thirst and hunger on those prior trips. All this was fresh in my memory and I felt a cold shiver run throughout my body. Hell, I had dreamed of cars like this one when I hung by my belt inside that boxcar heading toward Camp O'Donnel. Which, I ask, is the reality of the time? What am I thinking and seeing or what was I thinking then? With that I stretched my arms just to see if I touched anything. There was nothing and nobody cursed at me. Opening my eyes, once again I saw all this space and the countryside racing by me. Getting close to the window, I saw up forward. The train was heading in the general direction of some high mountains. We seemed to be in a rather large valley with farmland on both sides of the rail. The train was speeding now and the villages went by quickly. One barely saw them in passing, as we drew ever nearer to that range of mountains.

Drinking a cup of coffee, I noted nobody was sleeping. We were wide awake and watching. Watching for what? I was interested in what I saw out these windows, but still, the only interest I really had was when I would see a sign that the United States did in fact have troops on this island. Anything that showed me a sign this war was over. So far there was nothing, only there were no Japanese guards standing around glaring or hitting at anyone. That wasn't enough for me. I was still apprehensive. I wanted more proof. I reached and fondled the hilt of one of the sabres. Then I got up from my seat and walked back to where the rifles had been stacked at the end of the car. They were still there.

The train sped northward all night long, stopping briefly at cities during the night. I slept some, but for the most part I only napped for short periods, not taking any chances of being caught off guard.

When I was awake, I wondered if anyone knew what we were doing or where we were headed. Or were they just guessing what was out there? If the latter, where in hell would this group wind up?

333

Some on the train could care less. They were stoned on Japanese liquor and were still drinking the stuff. I envied them in one way, yet was scared to drink, afraid of what might happen. When I watched them drinking and stumbling around, I saw they had no problem with this at all. They either knew they would be back in American hands or if not, they wouldn't know what happened. In any case they were enjoying this trip while I sat and worried about the unknown. I was sweating out every turn in the track, wondering what was just around the next bend.

I looked at the east and saw it was nearing daybreak. I had catnapped all night long, but hadn't gotten any rest. The train slowed as we came into a city. Out the window, I saw parked freight cars on the siding and almost before I realized it, we were stopped. Steam from the engine rolled back alongside the window, blocking out my vision for a moment. To now I hadn't been forward and had no idea how many cars were ahead, but I did know the kitchen was up that way. Getting to my feet I started through the train in that direction. I didn't know what I was looking for.

The first car had the supplies we brought aboard and this stuff was stacked neatly along the sides of the aisle, leaving a clean walkway forward. In the next car, the cooks were preparing breakfast. As I opened the door and entered, I smelled coffee. I asked if I could have some and was told to help myself, that there was plenty. He saw my hesitation and said, "Breakfast will by ready soon. Go ahead." Filling my canteen cup with hot water then adding the powdered stuff, I proceeded through the kitchen and through another car where more prisoners were; then through another door to the engine. As I stepped through the passageway, there was activity everywhere. Especially on the ground level, it appeared the Japanese had been waiting for us and were working frantically to get us ready for movement. From what I could see they wanted us out of here as fast as they could manage it.

Our commander detailed an American sailor to work in the cab. He was supposed to know how to run this type of equipment. As soon as I saw him I could see he was drunk as hell. He was up in that cab, screaming at the Japanese on the ground. I wondered if he was running the engine alone. If so, I thought, we could be in trouble, but we had been traveling for several hours and had made it this far without problems. At least we had kept moving and since I knew nothing at all about this thing, I let my suspicions drop and started back through the cars where food was being prepared.

In the chow line, I saw everyone was wide awake. The men were all talking about our trip and wondering how far we had come since leaving the camp. The cooks wanted to get us fed while the train was parked, so they rushed us through the line. Before I was served the train lurched forward with a giant lunge. People were cursing the engineer and hanging on to anything they could to keep their footing. That engineer wasn't wasting time. We were at full speed very quickly and by the time I was back in my seat eating I could see we were coming close to that range of mountains. East of us the range ran clear out of sight. We had been running through a valley all night, but now we must cross and were pulling into the foothills. Looking from my window, I saw a very high mountain and we seemed to be going directly toward one of the highest points.

After some time the train slowed. As we started our ascent whoever was running that engine was blasting away at the steam whistle. I remembered that sailor and how drunk he seemed. I could just imagine what he was doing. Still the train continued climbing and that mountain got closer and closer. The train was very slow now. Somehow, it had become very important to me to get on the other side of this mountain range. I had a feeling we were getting farther away from danger, and somehow this range of mountains was holding me back. Yesterday it was the reverse. The farther we went the more I thought about running into something. Now things had changed. I wanted to be away from that prison camp and this mountain seemed to be obstructing me from freedom. Yet the damn train was slowing. I wanted it to speed up. I heard that whistle and the mountain was right on the edge of the track. There was a sharp hill running almost out of sight right at my window. The whistle blew again as if trying to warn something. Then! Without warning at all, it was dark as hell. I couldn't see anything. I heard someone yell. We were inside a tunnel. I was so scared I could hardly move. Then I started smelling smoke. That coal smoke was seeping into the car and we were barely moving. Someone at the rear of the car turned on a light of some sort. I had no idea there was electricity on this train, but apparently there was. Another light came on at the other end of the car.

The train slowed more yet and the smoke became very thick. I heard men coughing as the train came to a complete halt. I heard the wheels spinning but the train wasn't moving. We were stuck in this tunnel. Within minutes, the cars were filled with coal smoke. The stuff was getting worse and that silly bastard kept trying to go forward. I heard McMurray yell from somewhere back of me, "Get up there and tell that man to back this train out of the tunnel. We will suffocate fast if he doesn't." I assumed he was yelling at me and without a second's hesitation I was on the run through the kitchen car and the other troop car. When I was on the tender all I could see was light from the firebox and someone shoveling coal inside. There were two or three people in the cab, including the navy chief and one Japanese fellow. I screamed as loudly as I could, trying to make myself heard over the noises in the cab, "Back this damned thing out of here and fast."

Up near the engine, there wasn't nearly as much smoke and the people didn't realize the danger in the cars in back of them. Once again I yelled, "The commander has ordered you to back this thing out of the tunnel. The troops are suffocating back there."

Not one word was said by these fellows, but almost without my knowing it was happening the train began rolling back down this rather steep grade. I hung on for dear life. There was no air at all as we moved back through the dense smoke. Now these people saw how thick the smoke was and were throttling the train in reverse.

When we burst out into the daylight, my eyes were burning and I was gagging from smoke inhalation. The train kept moving away from the tunnel.

When I opened my eyes and was able to see, the smoke was gone and we were speeding down the grade. Soon the crew had the train slowed and we were moving slowly back the way we came.

I learned later that the civilians the chief was yelling at in that town wanted him to wait until another engine could be put on the train. He had refused to wait. That is what caused the problem. On this particular grade it took two engines to pull this many loaded cars.

I was hanging on to a steel rail that girded the tender part of the engine when we were in the rail station and the people were all over the place. It was as if they had been waiting for this to happen.

The engine stopped and I saw McMurray along with two officers standing in the doorway of the front car. The three of them were mad as hell. The Japanese on the platform detected their anger and were scurrying about. They acted as if they would be blamed and were doing everything they could to explain that it was that navy chief who insisted on taking the train out with only one engine.

One of the officials on the platform climbed the ladder and in broken English explained what had happened, that one engine couldn't get us over that pass through the tunnel and that another engine was being brought onto the track. He would assign us a qualified engineer. The navy chief was retired from the engineering business, much to his chagrin.

Time passed slowly for me. I wanted to be out of here as quickly as possible. Still there wasn't any indication of the extra engine anywhere.

Down on the platform, the Japanese were as fearful of us as I was of them. They thought we might want revenge for allowing the train to get inside the tunnel without enough power, and I was scared one of them wanted to restart the war.

Captain O'Conner appointed another man from the group to ride the cab. Soon we had the other engine and were on our way once more. As the train neared the tunnel this time there was little slowing, and we were through the mountain in record time.

I felt the train as we started our descent down the mountain on the other end of the tunnel. We were in another valley, much like the one we were in before, only in this area there were more cities. Or at least it seemed that way for me. This train wasn't slowing.

We once again had only one engine, but we were speeding across Japan faster than I had ever ridden on a rail.

I noted several areas that had been bombed, especially around the train stations, and in some cases the railroad beds had been blown out and there were recent repairs. In some areas, there was only one single track. Down south we always had two rails running side by side. The train was traveling so fast, I was unable to tell if the bombings were recent or if it had been a while since the raids were made. The one thing that impressed me was there were more cities that had been bombed than those that had not, and in some cases, there were complete sections bombed out. Rising in the places where houses once had been were tin buildings or shacks.

By nightfall, everything looked the same. Occasionally there were people working the fields, but for the most part, there was nothing. Some of the rice fields were filled with water and were left that way. For all intents and purposes, this part of Japan had come to a complete stop. They were people without leaders just waiting for whatever was to happen. This was quite different from what I had previously known of the people of Japan.

I stood between the cars watching the countryside as it zoomed past me. The car seemed stationary and the earth was passing in review in front of me. I let my mind drift back over the past months, how the Japanese people I had come in contact with treated me. They should not be permitted to live. Then that bomb dropped and how things changed. Almost overnight they changed from the most arrogant bastards I had ever known into a race of scared people. I asked, "What could have been in that bomb that would change an entire nation as it has?" Back there on that station platform, miles away from the bomb, they acted as though we might eat them alive if we had the slightest notion they were the cause for the train stalling in the tunnel. They even seemed relieved when the captain agreed to take on their man as engineer. Everything was strange.

It had been so long since I had slept I couldn't remember. Still I knew there could be no sleep now. This trip must end before I would be able to sleep. With that thought, I wondered if this trip would ever end. Hell, I couldn't recall how long it had been since we left the prison camp. That camp. It was only a faint memory in the cool of the evening as the train sped along. My stomach was full. There was no thirst and no Jap guards. Good God! This train was all American. There might be a Jap in the cab, but this train belonged to us. Doubt I might, but that was a true fact. Everything I ate was from the United States.

I shivered as darkness fast closed in on me. I couldn't see any of the countryside, only occasional lights in the distance.

Back inside I found an empty seat. As I passed along the aisle, some of the men were snoring, and others were unable to sleep. I had enjoyed the solitude outside. I felt better when alone.

By ten o'clock that evening I saw we were entering a large city. There were lights everywhere. The train had slowed and on each side of the tracks I saw houses. Off in the distance there were moving auto lights. I wished it were not night. Now the train was barely moving and I heard the escaping steam from up forward. The train was stopped. Someone yelled from the forward part of the train, "There is an American Jeep!" And everyone in the car sprang to their feet at once, and stared in the direction of where the man was looking.

Down alongside the train a Jeep was moving toward the front end of the car. There were three men in it, in full battle dress, steel helmets, ammo belts, rifles, and side arms. And around their necks were white scarves. "My God!" I heard myself say, "Those are Americans!" What a sight! I tried for a moment to remember what I had thought this would be like. Nothing in my wildest imagination could compare with what I was seeing. Those men

337

were American soldiers and they were right outside this car. Up front everyone was trying to get out the door at the same time, finding the car blocked. At the other end, some more military personnel entered the car.

From among this bunch a young man emerged. Our lights were on and he looked no older than nineteen. On his shoulders was the rank of captain. He stepped upon one of the seats and held up both hands.

"Gentlemen, we are glad to see you. Welcome back to the United States. Please be seated, relax, you are safe here. At the moment, I don't have word on what we are to do with all of you. That will come soon, I assure you. You are under the control of the United States here and I have food coming. Please be patient with us until I can find you quarters. This is your first stop on your way back to the United States."

I couldn't say anything. I just stood gawking at this kid with the captain's bars on his shoulders. Hell, he couldn't be more than twenty. I never in my life saw a person who looked so healthy. It was difficult to accept, that this was about over. I had never seen so many pieces of equipment. There were trucks, tanks, Jeeps, and other trucks pulling field artillery pieces. Everywhere I looked there were pieces of military equipment on the move and on each of them was the insignia of the United States. I stared through the window. There wasn't a Jap in sight.

Inside the car, our officers gathered around this young captain. They held the same rank as he, but when I looked at the contrast in their appearance one might think this young man was one of their sons.

The other troops with this officer were asking questions of men in their areas, but I was so dumbfounded I could only watch as all this was taking place. I was happy they weren't asking me anything. I couldn't answer them. Everything I had dreamed or fantasized about this day was different. Nothing was like I had thought. Right at the moment I didn't know what else I could have expected, but it sure as hell wasn't this.

I had imagined there would be some high-ranking officer who would come around and announce we would be court-martialed for surrendering to the enemy without being ordered to do so. At that thought I started recalling that day back in 1942 when the Japanese overran my position and how I had gone into the mountains. A flash of fear ran through me. I remembered reading that pamphlet that said that General MacArthur was in Tokyo. Hell, he could have me tried for the act.

I was brought into the present by the entry of another officer. He called the young captain aside and then announced that we would not be taken from the train into the city, but instead would be taken somewhere else. There was a low groan from the prisoners at this announcement and he quickly added that he would be traveling with us; that we should not worry, it was only a short ride.

He was finished with that information and as he turned back with our officers other army personnel entered the car. They were bringing with them large containers of food. They had more food than I had ever seen and as it was opened for serving, I saw it was hot. Another man was passing out large

338

tin platters with spoons and knives and forks. This was something. It had been so long since I had eaten with mess utensils.

In those large covered containers were fried chicken, beefsteaks, mashed potatoes, gravy, steaming vegetables. There was even something like butter. There was steaming hot coffee. This time it was the real thing, and there were cream and sugar, all we wanted. As I took my tin platter in front of the cooks and they served, each asked if I wanted more. Just when I thought I had been served everything I found a large can filled with fruit salad, and I could have as much as I could hold in the tray. My God! What was happening? The entire world was spinning. I had no idea what was going on around me. The voices around me could barely be heard. As I sat down with this meal, I felt the car start moving, and the officer who came on last yelled as he left the front door, "It is only an hour or so when all of you can get off this train." With all this food, and them staying on the train, who in hell cared? Hell, at this point I didn't give a damn if I left this car or not. With that much food I could live here for a long time.

I had been so preoccupied with this hot food, I didn't realize we were going full speed. As I looked through that window, only the lights were visible and they were speeding by as we moved along.

When I finished, I felt sick to my stomach, but refused to tell anyone. When I took the tray back where the cooks were, one of them took it and reached inside a box. He handed me a package of cigarettes with matches. I could hardly thank him. I knew this must be some sort of delusion. Lighting a cigarette, I walked near where the officers were in a huddle. They were talking in hushed tones. Again I had the opportunity of comparing this young captain with Captain O'Conner. I thought no one that young could be a captain. Or was it that our officers looked so old? I stood waiting for something, and then he turned in my direction. He saw something in my face and repeated what he had said several times before. "It will be only a little longer Soldier." Soldier! Good God! How long had it been since I had been referred to as a soldier? Faced with all this evidence, one would think I'd have to believe the war was over. I thanked him and turned away, not understanding why I didn't want to talk. I returned to my seat and waited. Waited for what? Hell, I didn't know. Some of the men were watching through the windows and the train was slowing once again. My mind had been so preoccupied with all the unknowns, I hadn't realized we had arrived at our destination. Someone yelled, "Hey look, there is an American woman!" I fell across the aisle, wanting to see this. Right outside the window was a lady in a military uniform. Good Christ! What the hell was this? Women wearing army uniforms! I knew I was experiencing a nightmare now. I remembered reading a headline in a newspaper that was dropped with that food drop, that read, "Congratulations all you GI Joes and GI Janes, on a job well done." I didn't understand what they meant but supposed they were referring to the American public in general. It never occurred to me they meant there were female soldiers fighting the war. Yet there one stood, big as life, in full uniform watching this train as we came to a dead stop. I was so dumbfounded

I didn't hear the officer telling us, "This is it men. Get your personal gear and prepare to leave the train." I still had my canvas pack, with the shirt and some other things under the seat. There were some notes and my prison badge, along with the guidon in the back of the shirt I had guarded for so long. Men all around me were scrambling for the doors. I marveled at how they could get off so fast. Try as I might, my legs wouldn't allow me to get up. Somehow I just knew there would be a Jap guard out there. Here it was safe and there was still ample food for a while. Everyone was past me now and I was alone. I must move. Strapping the pack on over my shoulder, I made my way toward the open door. For just a moment I hesitated, then there was a gentle hand on my shoulder. Turning, I saw the face of that young captain. He was gently urging me forward and saying, "It's all right." He seemed to understand my apprehension and again said, "It's all right," and that there would be a truck waiting that would take us away from here. Stepping out the door, I saw the men on the platform laughing hysterically and slapping each other on the backs. I was glad they didn't see me and the fears I must be showing. I stepped onto the platform and very quickly joined the mob being ushered onto trucks that had been waiting for our arrival. Being one of the last off the train, I was far back in the line that was already loading onto trucks. I looked for Japs. There were none. Only Americans here.

Moving along the platform toward the trucks, I passed near an American woman standing near the wall of the station. She was dressed in some sort of gray uniform with white trimming. Without warning, without telling anyone what I intended, I stepped from the line and walked in front of her. I gazed into her eyes for just a second, then put my arms around her without saying a word and kissed her. This lady was so shocked and dumbfounded by my action she was unable to say or do anything. She just stood with tears running down her face. As suddenly as I had done this, I released her and walked away. I had just fulfilled a promise I had made to myself long ago, that I intended kissing the first American woman I saw when I got out of the prison camps. At this very moment I almost believed I was free. If not, where did she come from?

My truck was now loaded and we were on our way. I still hadn't allowed my mind to catch up with events but I was aware there was something big happening in my life.

Much of my skepticism must be attributed to the fact I hadn't slept for more than thirty hours plus the fact that things were occurring much faster than my dulled mind could comprehend. As the truck sped through the night, I hung tightly onto my pack, still scared someone would steal it. These men didn't seem to understand. They had in many cases thrown their personal belongings out the truck. All they had was what was on their backs. I sure hoped, for their sake, this thing was over.

We halted and some navy men around the trucks helped the men unload and formed them into a line.

Even in the dark, I could make out the cliff directly in front of me. The damn thing seemed to run right up into the sky and at the top was a building lit up like a large city. We were on some sort of beach. I could feel the sand underfoot. What the hell were we doing here? I couldn't see any boats and there didn't appear to be a pier of any kind in sight.

These sailors weren't losing any time; the line was moving very fast. Forward some thirty yards, I saw a large pile of clothing and other things. They were making us throw our personal gear on this pile. I resolved that I would not do it. No matter what, I would keep the sabres and my personal things. Someone near me said, "Toss it." I said, "You go to hell. I have no intentions of throwing my things away." I heard him call for someone. An officer arrived and took me out of the line.

This officer tried to explain that we must throw everything away. We would get all new clothing when we had gone through the line and been fumigated, and that fumigation included our personal gear. I still refused. Finally I was allowed to take my shirt that I pointed out to him was part of my organization colors from the Philippines, and a plastic package with my notes and a copy of the New Testament and my prison number. First I must let this stuff be fumigated, and I would have to carry it through the tent. Reluctantly, I agreed, but I stripped naked and carried everything through. This stuff, especially the shirt, was as much a part of me as my arm. After I went through this process, I still had these things, although soaked with the fumigation spray. I was issued blue denims along with clean underclothing and an extra T-shirt, then directed toward an open door where an elevator was waiting to take me to the top of a cliff and into a large waiting room where there were hundreds of reporters and newsmen. The navy officers were holding them back, keeping us separated from them. Only a selected few were allowed to talk with these people.

At the extreme end away from the elevator in this room was an open kitchen, and between here and there were many tables. This was some sort of restaurant, I thought.

Someone was telling us the mess line would be open all night, that we could eat as much and as long as we wished.

Looking over this place, all I could see were navy officers in dress uniforms. They were everywhere. Scattered among these were some marine officers and a few from the other branches. All of them were in dress uniform. At the same time and by contrast, all of us were dressed alike, in navy dungarees and T-shirts. I had never felt more out of place than at this moment.

Some of our men were in the chow line, filling their trays as if they hadn't eaten back there in the train. I must go through the line if only to get out of this spotlight that I felt I was in.

When I had gone through the line, I noticed behind me a wide open area with railings some four feet high. There was no roof over it. Some of our people were out there bent over that rail. Finishing my tray I walked in that direction. There I found many of the men who had overeaten vomiting over the edge. This soon became the thing to do. We would go through the line then come out here and rid ourselves of it over the rail.

From out here I could see far out into the bay. There were a number of ships anchored in that area. Some had lights and were easily seen even in the darkness.

It was rather dark and I could see back through the large ballroom. I had never seen such a sight in my life. I could watch this crowd from here without feeling like I was in a fishbowl, so when I was not eating and coming out here to vomit, I stood in the darkness and watched the activities.

I had no idea as to the time, only that it was dark and I was being ushered out of this place and down the elevator. Lights had been set up over a walkway that led off to the right from the bottom of the elevator toward the water's edge. There they had small boats. We were told to board to be taken out to one of the larger ships. The boat rocked in the water and I was extremely seasick. Either that or I was ill from overeating. I could hardly think where I was or where I had been. I looked up from where I was lying sprawled in the bottom of the small craft and saw only the side of a large ship. It seemed like early morning, but I was not sure.

Someone yelled near where I was, "This one is very sick and will require a stretcher." I didn't realize it at the time, but he was talking about me. A stretcher was brought aboard and very quickly, I was being lifted up the side of the ship. I noted it was white, a rather odd color for a ship, I thought, but I was so sick, I could care less.

The people on deck wrapped me in blankets and very soon, I was in a large room, with white sheets everywhere. This is the cleanest place I had ever seen, or was I just dreaming again?

They placed me on a bed with white sheets and I heard music coming from far away. Where in hell could I be now? Was this a dream, or was I dead and this is where I was supposed to go? I didn't have the faintest idea. I was somewhat scared once again. Everywhere was white. White sheets, white pillows, white ceilings in the room, white beds, nurses dressed in white. Nurses! What the hell was I seeing now? Nurses! They were all over the place, all in white. There was one standing right by the bed. She was holding me, talking ever so softly. Good God! I knew I must be in heaven and these nurses were angels, but again, this wasn't what I had been taught. Angels didn't look like these do. She was holding me very close now and whispering, "It's all right, it's all right, you have been sleeping for some time. This is a hospital ship."

There was no way I could believe this. Still she whispered, "It's all right." Then I started crying, but still, this angel held onto me. It was as if she had been assigned to care for me alone.

At last I was able to open my eyes more and look this place over. No one was paying me the least attention because of my breaking down. The nurse seemed to understand. Everywhere the white was still there. I had lost my mind completely. Nothing like this had ever happened before. Yet that soft voice still whispered, "It's all right, it's all right." Then once again I slipped back into unconsciousness, into a deep sleep.

When I opened my eyes again, I was surprised that things were like they

342

were when I went out. The white sheets, the white ceiling, the music, and yes, the nurse, she was still by my bunk. I believed at last. I was free. There would be no more Jap guards. I had been found; all doubts were erased. For three and one-half years I had been lost in action, but at last I had been found. There was no way a dream could repeat itself so exactly. It was over!